The Greatest Matches and Rivalries of the WrestleMania Era

By "The Doc" Chad Matthews

This book is dedicated to my kids. May you always chase your dreams, no matter how trivial others may deem them to be; nothing that you are passionate about is trivial.

"The Doc" Chad Matthews
The Greatest Matches and Rivalries of the WrestleMania Era

ISBN-13: 978-0692086780
ISBN-10: 0692086781

Disclaimer - This book is not an official WWE publication. It is not affiliated, associated, or otherwise endorsed by the WWE. The names of all WWE programming, talent, images, likenesses and logos are the exclusive property of the owner, World Wrestling Entertainment, Inc. This book is analytical and editorial. All information contained in this book has been obtained through resources readily available in the public domain.

Editor: Matthew McIntyre
Front Cover Design: Trey Cox
Back Cover Image: Matt Nelson

Contact

Chad Matthews is very active on social media, posting daily questions to wrestling fans on various topics to stimulate engaging debates. He can be contacted on Twitter @TheDocLOP.

To read "The Doctor's Orders" column by "The Doc" Chad Matthews, please visit:

www.wrestlingheadlines.com / www.lordsofpain.net

To listen to "The Doc Says..." weekly podcast, please visit: www.blogtalkradio.com/lordsofpain

Books by "The Doc" Chad Matthews

The WrestleMania Era: The Book of Sports Entertainment

The Greatest Champions of The WrestleMania Era

Starrcade vs. WrestleMania: The Prelude to the Monday Night Wars (e-book)

The Greatest Matches and Rivalries of the WrestleMania Era

Table of Contents

Introduction

Hello and welcome, ladies and gentlemen, to *The Greatest Matches and Rivalries of the WrestleMania Era.* I am your host, "The Doc" Chad Matthews, and from wherever you may be reading this journey through sports entertainment lore, thank you for making this book a part of your life.

Momentarily, I am going to begin sharing with you a five year labor of professional wrestling love, a long-form discussion regarding the greatest performances in NWA/WCW and WWE history. The origins of this book date back thirty years to a time when a younger version of me first became fascinated by the tales told on the 20'x20' canvas. I knew even then that I emotionally resonated with The Ultimate Challenge in a different way than I did Bret Hart vs. Davey Boy Smith, but as the years passed and my younger self grew into an opinionated commentator on sports entertainment, I began to study the intricacies of the art form, reading the opinions of Dave Meltzer, Wade Keller, and the columnists at Lordsofpain.net (LOP) and trying to piece together the commonalities between them that seemed to define how to critically judge pro wrestling; I dove inside the minds of the wrestlers themselves as well, absorbing their takes on what constituted greatness. Since January 2003 to be specific, I have basically rewatched all of modern wrestling lore over and over again, picking apart the critically-acclaimed from late 1983 to present day in order to develop a logical pattern that differentiates between the near-perfect, the awesome, the very good, the worthwhile, the average, and the avoidable.

For fifteen years, as a reviewer of WWE's major programs for LOP, then as a columnist (Doctor's Orders on LOP) and later a podcaster (The Doc Says on LOP Radio), I have been honing systems, of sorts, to help contextualize history so that I could answer some of the most intriguing questions asked by pro wrestling's most ardent enthusiasts in a manner that satisfied my analytical mind's desire to find objectivity in areas others consider too subjective.

It has never sat particularly well with me the blanket statement that pro wrestling greatness is completely up to each individual, period, end of sentence. In fact, I strongly disagree. I have long posited that professional wrestling is reasonably objectifiable. The greatest wrestler argument, for example, can be dissected by evaluating all the pertinent data points that have shaped the careers of the industry's most successful stars. These statistical categories, in no particular order, are as follows:

A) Biggest draws – The wrestlers who generated more money than their peers through pay-per-view (PPV) buyrates, television ratings, merchandise sales, and digital media influence.

B) Championship glory – The wrestlers who won a greater volume of overt symbols of success than their peers, with priority given to World Championships, and singles titles ranked ahead of tag team honors.

C) Longevity – The wrestlers who stayed relevant in a major promotion for the longest, with emphasis placed on headlining special events/PPVs.

D) Performance – The wrestlers who consistently outshone their peers, putting on matches that created unforgettable memories.

Since professional wrestling is not really about the winners and losers, it is challenging – but not impossible – to find apt comparisons to prove the reasonable objectivity that is the central tenet of my stance; I will provide one example from sport and one from entertainment for clarity's sake.

From the sporting side, let us compare wrestling to modern college football circa the Playoff Era. In America's gridiron pastime, the college game relies on a select few, organized into a committee, to choose the best four teams worthy of competing for the championship each season. Though the decisions are also considered subjective, the Playoff committee rankings are reasonably objective too. It is not as if Alabama is picked because their crimson jerseys are pretty or USC is chosen because the President of the United States has an affinity for Los Angeles. There is basic criterion used to evaluate the resumes of each viable candidate. Breaking down wrestling's greatest is no different; you put the top guys side by side and use the above mentioned statistics to rank and file.

Exhibit A: Steve Austin vs. Shawn Michaels – Austin drew more money, the titles (when weighted for length against number) put them as virtual equals, and Michaels performed for longer at a generally agreed upon higher level. Austin 1, Michaels 2, and a Tie; HBK wins.

From the entertainment arena, Hollywood provides perhaps the most applicable comparison. Actors and actresses are judged on virtually the same things as professional wrestlers: their big screen abilities, box office drawing power, longevity, and critical accolades. Though it may appear purely subjective, it is actually just very dynamic. Jason Statham is quite clearly not a greater actor than Leo DiCaprio; if acting greatness were so subjective, someone could logically argue that he was. Objectively, Leo out acts him, out draws him, has been performing at a higher level for far longer, and has won plenty of critical awards. Put Leo up against Tom Hanks, however, and we have a fascinating situation on our hands, but never should fascinating be confused with infeasible. The same should be said of professional wrestler rankings.

Exhibit B: Chris Jericho vs. Greg Valentine – Obviously not even close; Jericho drew more money, won more titles, wrestled in the big leagues for longer, and had more classic matches. Clean sweep.

Exhibit C: John Cena vs. Hulk Hogan – An amazingly level playing field; Hogan drew more money, Cena's championship success usurped Hogan's, the Hulkster wrestled for much longer (to date), and Cena has performed at a higher level. It is a tie, so the details become important. If you rank them both against their peers, there is not a single category in which Cena falls out of the Top 10, but Hogan's classic match list is comparatively limited. Thus, Cena edges out Hogan.

I wrote an entire book designed to more definitively answer the "who's greatest" question. *The WrestleMania Era: The Book of Sports Entertainment* builds the discussion using essentially four tiers. It begins with the back end of the Top 90 wrestlers (#61-#90), in which the Rick Martels and Yokozunas of the world were given their due. It continues with the mid-range guys (#31-#60), the Booker Ts and Kanes credited for their larger contributions. It progresses to the First Tier (#11-#30) (think Brock Lesnar, Sting, etc.) and peaks with the all-important Top 10, where the most intriguing arguments are formed.

The foundation for my monster of a first book was built on the term "objective subjectivism" - a euphemism that acknowledges pro wrestling as obviously somewhat subjective but petitions for acknowledgment of pro wrestling also being inescapably capable of objectification (like Hollywood and College Football). Objective subjectivism made answering the "greatest wrestler" question fairly simple; statistically analyze the WrestleMania Era using basic criteria and let the results help shape the rankings. Let us back up for a moment, though, to the fourth category listed above: performance.

When fans discuss performance (i.e. quality), it highlights the difficulties in objectifying sports entertainment; there is not a more inherently subjective part of the equation. I have a frequent social media discussion partner who swears to me that Rey Misterio Jr. vs. Eddie Guerrero at *Halloween Havoc '97* is the greatest match of all-time. If we want to compare that work of art to CM Punk vs. John Cena or "The Mega Powers Explode" or the 1992 Royal Rumble Match, we have to tackle the most ambitious proposition in professional wrestling analysis: finding the common elements among all of the greatest performances.

For the WrestleMania Era, I have mined the annals of WWE and NWA/WCW lore to discover the specific traits that define the greatest matches and, having pinpointed these elements, I have spent the last five years separating the truly great from the very good. As the level of detail increased, it became important to me to expand the conversation beyond just matches and further classify the forthcoming Top 100 list to include broader stories that were by-products of multiple matches; in some cases, the multi-match sagas involved the continued competition between a specific set of competitors (i.e. a rivalry) while, in others, the aggregate of several bouts created an epic tale not confined to traditional pro wrestling vernacular (i.e. Bret Hart's crusade against America). Hence, you could quite easily extend the name of this book to *The Greatest Matches, Rivalries, and Stories of the WrestleMania Era*.

Stand-alone, ranking the greatest matches would have made for a captivating project, but to be able to broaden the scope in order to compare the totality of a story like Daniel Bryan vs. The Authority to the overall rivalry between Edge and Undertaker or the iconic Steamboat-Savage match was, to me, a far more rewarding experience that produced a much more interesting list (I hope that you will agree). Take the best from each pairing – from Taker vs. Michaels, Flair vs. Sting, Austin vs. McMahon, etc. - and, be that their best winds up better classified as a story, rivalry, or individual match, pit them against each other to shape the ultimate pro wrestling countdown. To me, there was no more psychologically-engaging a book that could ever be written about wrestling.

Admittedly, answering the question "What are the greatest matches and rivalries?" in a similar manner that I answered the question of the greatest wrestler was a taller task. Specifying the greatest among individual wrestlers is made easier not just by the simplicity of the stats, but by the limited number of wrestlers pertinent to the topic. I chose 90 for *The WrestleMania Era* because the book was inspired by the Bill Simmons masterpiece, *The Book of Basketball*, which selected the roughly 90 greatest ballers ever. The truly greatest wrestler or basketball player discussion, though, probably ends after about 20 tops. Think of all the great pairings of opponents that have shaped the past thirty-five years; it presented a much wider range of possible answers.

To give you another example of the challenge that the "greatest performance" breakdown presents, each February, I spearhead the voting process for the Hall of Fame inductee selection at LOP aka WrestlingHeadlines.com. I ask our readership to, among many categories, nominate two matches and two wrestlers that they deem worthy of Hall of Fame status. It has become a yearly litmus test for popular fan opinion on wrestling's historically extraordinary. Since starting it in 2013, *dozens* of wrestlers have been nominated and *hundreds* of matches have been nominated; paring down the match list is really hard because of the sheer volume of candidates.

Difficult as it may have been, I picked apart every classic match at each high profile event from WrestleMania to Summerslam to In Your House to Raw to Nitro to The Great American Bash to Starrcade, within each gimmick library from the Ladder to the Cage to the Last Man Standing to the Royal Rumble, spanning each level of the hierarchy from the curtain jerker to the upper mid-card to the main-event. Just as in my first book, the statistical analysis did not extend beyond what I refer to as the "WrestleMania Era" - professional wrestling in its modern form beginning with the first Starracade. In my opinion, any attempts to include pre-1983 performances or wrestlers in these discussions proves the previously thought-to-be "so subjective there's no chance for a definitive answer" declaration correct. With all due respect to those marvelous mat men of the distant past and their in-ring achievements, there is too stark a contrast between theirs and the modern era to properly compare them.

The evaluation procedure was separated into two phases. The first was heavily rooted in identifying the candidates and establishing a viable rough list combining the generally thought to be excellent performances (for various reasons) from *Starrcade '83* to the present; there were nearly 200 of them. I started by going year-by-year, event-by-event, and gimmick-by-gimmick, watching and ranking the matches against their categorical peers; the famous Ric Flair-winning Royal Rumble, for instance, was judged initially against the other matches from 1992, the other matches from Royal Rumble (event) lore, and the other Royal Rumble gimmick matches. Comparisons were based on the following criterion, in no particular order:

A) Pure Storytelling – The basics of a pro wrestling match are **selling** (via facial expressions and body language), **psychology** (performing actions and moves for a specific purpose within the framework of the story being told in the ring), and **execution** (the quality of the actions and moves performed).

B) Crowd Response – The cliché states that the pro wrestling industry is all about its fans. In the context of a single pro wrestling match, it is not *all* about the fan reaction, but eliciting a pronounced response from the audience is important.

C) Intangibles – Certain matches have elements working in their favor that are not necessarily just about the wrestlers directly involved. Sometimes it is a manager who had a significant bearing on the story being told, an elaborate special entrance that enhanced the atmosphere, an innovative move or sequence never before seen, commentary that adds an indelible audio soundtrack to the memory created on the 20'X20' canvas, or a gimmick that takes a physical confrontation to another level.

D) Historic – What the match meant to its time / or was it timeless? (i.e. the Ladder match at WrestleMania X popularized the most common gimmick used in pro wrestling's modern lore, while Hogan vs. The Rock set a new standard for the dream match concept).

E) Financial, Event Prestige – What impact did the match have on the economic success of the show on which it took place (the number of people in attendance combined with the number of pay-per-view buys)? More credit was logically given to headlining matches. This category had to be tweaked when the WWE Network replaced the nearly 30-year old PPV business model; today, the primary event-specific comparison point from past to present is the prestige of the event, as though the subscription service has eliminated previous standards of analysis, the pressure still mounts when the weight of the situation peaks, making a 5-star classic on the WrestleMania stage most impressive. Thank Al Snow and, more recently, Bruce Prichard for this part of the criterion; it cannot be ignored.

F) Build – Just as the event magnifies the match, so too does the hype behind it before the event happens. The quality of the storyline drives much of the other aforementioned categories; a great feud amplifies the emotional resonance of the match, which stimulates more financial interest from the fans, more heat from the live crowd, an extra something from the performers involved, etc.

G) Time – As with movies or television shows, the quality of a pro wrestling match is more often than not influenced by the run time allotted for the story to be told. Epically long matches have to be weighed against their more compact peers. Which matches made the most of their time?

H) False Finishes – Call them near falls, hope spots, false finishes, or simply plot twists, these moments in a match when the end seems near, only for them to prove fleeting progressions of the story are vitally important to establishing and/or intensifying drama; they are designed to further engage the audience.

I) Climax – When the end of a match finally comes, how effective is it in concluding the story told?

The end of phase 1 yielded a composite ranking shaped by the year-to-year, event-to-event, and gimmick-to-gimmick comparisons. The second phase involved even more scrupulous detail, as the initial rankings were put under a higher-powered proverbial microscope. Classics, instead of being analyzed against multiple matches, were put head-to-head. Every detail was scrutinized to the nth degree, from briefly inexplicable breaks from storyline psychology to one wrestler inadequately selling a moment or move on down to crowds that lost interest for long stretches. The matches became like my patients in the real world; and I fully intended to find out all that was right and wrong in each case. The Top 100 you are about to read was finalized by factoring in the overall resumes (see HBK-Jericho), and applying a touch of simple logic.

It has indeed been quite the journey. Each of the forthcoming 100 descriptions will explain why each match, rivalry, or story was worthy of its ranking among the greatest, making it a reference guide for fans of all ages. It is not to be mistaken as a list of my favorites (though many listed are favorites of mine). Rather, it is an unapologetic answer to one of the most intriguing questions ever asked about pro wrestling's history and an invitation to any and all to *prove* its conclusions incorrect.

Honorable Mentions

In a moment, the journey will begin. The definitive 100 greatest matches, rivalries, and stories will be revealed. First, though, let us celebrate (in chronological order) the 50 honorable mentions that missed the cut but still deserve to be acknowledged.

Tully Blanchard vs. Ricky Steamboat at Starrcade '84
NWA Television Championship
Top 20 All-Time at Starrcade / Top 5 Match in 1984

Among the themes to be discussed across the forthcoming pages is the evolution of the in-ring product. The game has undoubtedly changed over the years and the differences between past and present have to be weighed against each other for proper historical rankings to be established. Steamboat and Blanchard, for instance, were masters of making the little things count; they could make people care as much about a headlock sequence in 1984 as someone would care about a corkscrew moonsault through a table in 2017. Nevertheless, a four-star match then would not necessarily rate equally today. This gem from the Starrcade franchise also brings into focus for the first time the difference in perception between WWE's grandest stage (WrestleMania) and NWA/WCW's. Critically, the best matches from the early Starrcades quite easily trumped their WrestleMania counterparts, but the scope of greatness goes beyond simply what happens on the 20'X20'canvas.

Magnum TA vs. Nikita Koloff (1986)
Best-of-Seven Series for the NWA United States Championship
Top 10 Match in 1986

If it is possible for a rivalry's profile to be boosted solely by word-of-mouth from the generation who was fortunate enough to witness it, then due to the absence of any archival footage that would allow younger generations to inform themselves about it,

Magnum TA vs. Nikita Koloff may get the chance to prove it. Though grainy YouTube videos still existed when researching *The WrestleMania Era* circa 2011, the digital trail has been eliminated since and rumor has it that no high quality footage of the famous Best-of-Seven Series for the US Title exists anymore. Nevertheless, if following the principle of "the crowd is loud, so the work is good," Magnum vs. Nikita was tremendous; The Russian Nightmare drew the considerable ire of American patriots, who in turn vicariously lived through Magnum's attempt to retain America's championship title.

Barry Windham vs. Ric Flair (1986/1987)
NWA World Heavyweight Championship
Top 5 Match in 1986 / Top 5 Match in 1987

A name you will see featured in ten different entries on the Top 100 countdown is Ric Flair, who several generations of wrestling fans consider to be the greatest of all-time on account of his numerous classic rivalries. Flair was a showman who wrestled marathon matches at an incredible pace, especially in the era which played host to his prime. Each bout called exclusively in the ring with nothing but a result predetermined, his performances between the ropes, in hindsight, do not necessarily flow as well as more modern and heavily scripted peers, but they were some of the most compelling matches of the '80s and early '90s and they have maintained a gritty charm. Look no further than his work with Barry Windham, who Naitch has spoken of in the same breath as Steamboat and Rhodes when recalling his top rivals, for a prime example.

The Road Warriors, Paul Ellering, and The Super
Powers vs. The Four Horsemen
War Games Match at The 1987 Great American Bash
Top 5 All-Time War Games Match / Top 5 Match in 1987

During The Great American Bash Tour in the summer of '87, the brainchild of Dusty Rhodes that would become the signature gimmick in NWA/WCW lore was introduced. Featuring two rings enclosed by a giant steel cage with a roof – a longer, shorter Hell in a Cell for newer fans – War Games pit in its first ever iteration the faction of the '80s, The Four Horsemen, against The American Dream and a quartet of his frequent collaborators in past efforts to tame the galloping grapplers. It was exceptionally violent given the novelty in seeing that many wrestlers bleed simultaneously and it felt completely chaotic, to the point where the action became challenging to follow right up to and through "The Match Beyond: Submission or Surrender," the gimmick's trademark climax. All of the versions from the '80s had an experimental tone, but the original has an endearing quality to it.

The Rock 'n' Roll Express vs. The Midnight Express (1986-1990)

Tag team wrestling holds a special place in the modern history of the business thanks to what proved to be the Herculean-efforts of teams like the Expresses to elevate its status. Their lengthy rivalry, which spanned multiple promotions and multiple decades, was most notably featured in the NWA/WCW. Rock 'n' Roll, Ricky Morton and Robert Gibson, were babyfaces of the highest order and very diverse storytellers, thriving if asked to play either the underdogs or the hot shot heartthrobs. Midnight, "Beautiful" Bobby along with either "Loverboy" Dennis or "Sweet" Stan, were the perfect elitely athletic cowardly heels and have strangely become underrated for their influence on the genre. Aesthetically fluid as they were emotionally engaging, Midnight vs. Rock 'n' Roll matches never failed to generate wild enthusiasm from the audience. Only their lack of a truly great match on a defining stage kept their feud out of the Top 100.

The Ultimate Warrior vs. "Ravishing" Rick Rude (1989) Intercontinental Championship
Top 25 All-Time at Summerslam / Top 10 Match in 1989

WWE gets on the board with the superlative overall efforts of "Ravishing" Rick Rude's in-ring career. Mostly because there was more emotional depth to the stories they told in the payoffs to featured rivalries, the NWA style drew greater critical acclaim than the WWF throughout the '80s with rare exception; WWF was sizzle, NWA was steak. Rude vs. Ultimate Warrior was one such exception. Warrior embodied the spectacle of the WWF's main-event approach, but Rude brought out the best in him, basically taught him how to work, and guided him to the first of the three greatest matches of his career (at *Summerslam '89*). Studying Rude's body of work in the WWF and later WCW, his talents were honestly better-suited for the 15-minutes of character-heavy wrestling that became the calling-card for the early WWF style. He thrived against Warrior, displaying the full-extent of his abilities as both an athlete and a showman.

The 1990 Royal Rumble Match
Top 10 All-Time Royal Rumble Match / Top 20 All-Time at Royal Rumble / Top 5 Match in 1990

The most anticipated wrestling match every year is the Royal Rumble. Its unmistakable connection to WrestleMania, even when a title shot on the grandest stage had yet to be established as the victor's spoils, has always given it an extra-special aura.

Not only was 1990's Rumble stacked – it was like a Hulkamania Era All-Star showcase – it was also the year that the gimmick found its footing, laying a foundational formula for all future versions to follow. Its most memorable moment (Hogan and Warrior's interaction) ignited a wave of momentum for the WrestleMania main-event; many of its other top talents went out in style and there were several spotlight eliminations for wrestlers looking to leave their mark; and it helped establish the role of the Ironman, a relevant headliner (Million Dollar Man in '90) tasked with giving the match a centerpiece to build around. 1990, simply put, was the blueprint.

The Midnight Express vs. The Southern Boys at The 1990 Great American Bash
WCW United States Tag Team Championship Match
Top 5 All-Time Standard Tag Team Match / Top 5 Match in 1990

"Limited" is the best way to describe the historical accounts of World Championship Wrestling produced by WWE since they took ownership of the WCW video library in 2001. A few years back, a pair of excellent podcasters hit the airwaves determined to promote the memory of WCW and provide proper historical context to its pay-per-views. They called it the "WCW Legacy Series" and it is well worth your time to seek it out; their work will often be referenced on the ensuing pages. About this hidden gem, one of the greatest pure tag team matches ever, they said, "It [was] ahead of its time. The pacing [was] fantastic...lots of tight striking, lots of good mat wrestling, good storytelling. They were doing things that nobody else in the business was doing at that time and at a different pace and style. [It] was an elevation of what could be done in the ring."

The Rockers vs. The Orient Express at The 1991 Royal Rumble
Top 5 All-Time Standard Tag Team Match / Top 5 Pay-Per-View Opening Match / Top 20 All-Time at Royal Rumble / Top 5 Match in 1991

A half year later, a tag team well-known in WWE lore for redefining what could be done in the ring offered perhaps its defining effort. The Rockers, Marty Jannetty and Shawn Michaels, found incredible chemistry with another pair of innovation savants in The Orient Express. In a match that thrived on the intricacy of the sequences performed, these four wrestlers re-set the bar for creativity in the tag team genre. The bar has arguably not been raised since, at least not in a traditional, non-gimmick environment. The spots may not have always been executed perfectly, but they were so exciting that it almost did not matter (except by comparison to its peers, in which case it did matter); timing and selling were the difference that allowed the pure tag team match that made the Top 100 to beat this one head-to-head and relegate it to the Honorable Mentions.

Ric Flair, Barry Windham, Sid Vicious, and Larry Zbyszko vs. Sting, Brian Pillman, and The Steiner Brothers
War Games Match at WrestleWar 1991
Top 5 All-Time War Games Match / Top 5 Match in 1991

One of the two most critically acclaimed versions of its gimmick, War Games '91 requires historical contextualization to fully appreciate. Truth be told, it pales in comparison to War Games '92, which can be watched by even a novice fan and have its critical acclaim be immediately understood. War Games '91 features underwhelming performances from all but one member of the heel team (Barry Windham). So, while watching it, pay particular attention to the babyfaces, as they are the ones that make the match worthy of honorable mention. Beforehand, all four had predominantly been personalities judged more so on their craft than their mettle. Since WCW was geared toward a more mature audience, babyfaces needed to show more toughness, and they offered no better environment to showcase fortitude than War Games. Leaving the match battered and beaten, Sting, the Steiners, and especially Pillman gained an edge to their characters.

Sting and Lex Luger vs. The Steiner Brothers at SuperBrawl I
WCW World Tag Team Championships
Top 10 All-Time Standard Tag Team Match / Top 5 Match in 1991

In its standard two-on-two format, tag team wrestling in the late '80s NWA / early '90s WCW was regularly a headlining-caliber attraction not far below the World Heavyweight Championship; and Sting and Lex Luger, two of the biggest stars in WCW as of

1991, joining forces to challenge The Steiner Brothers for the World Tag Team Titles exemplified one of the fundamental differences between WCW's and the WWF's traditional tag team methodology. To the WWF, tag team wrestling at a main-event level was a gimmick for use by major singles stars; to NWA/WCW, it was a destination division capable of producing upper echelon matches fit for the marquee as readily as Ric Flair or Dusty Rhodes. Sting/Luger vs. The Steiners was rightfully treated as a huge match and it stands the test of time as one of the greatest sub-12-minute matches ever and one of the overall greatest matches in WCW history.

Jake "The Snake" Roberts vs. "Macho Man" Randy Savage (1991-1992)

It is not so much the matches that they had that has allowed Macho Man vs. Jake "The Snake" to stand the test of time, but rather their deeply-affecting over-arching narrative, a tale that serves as the first shining example of this book's inclusivity of the distinction brought to the forefront by a great rivalry that left an incredibly strong memory on wrestling fans without the assistance of a signature match. Roberts gifted Savage and Miss Elizabeth a king cobra at their wedding reception; that king cobra later gnawed on Savage's arm to the horror of anyone who watched it; the sadistic Roberts retaliated from his ensuing defeat by knocking out the avengeful Savage and physically striking Elizabeth; these were a few of the memorable moments that defined a classic Snake-Macho feud complimented by short, intense matches, opposite of the typical formula of memorable moments complimenting feature-length matches.

Brian Pillman vs. Jushin Liger at SuperBrawl II
WCW Light Heavyweight Championship
Top 10 Match in 1992

The cruiserweight wrestling genre did not become a viable commodity among either of the two mainstream promotions until 1996, when WCW brought back and re-branded their short-lived Light Heavyweight Championship most prominently held by Brian Pillman during the title's ten month original run from 1991-1992. Though not the foundational showpiece that was its successor, the WCW Light Heavyweight division did offer one truly outstanding performance in Pillman vs. Liger that laid the groundwork for all that followed. Featuring somersault planchas off the top rope to the outside, aerial assaults galore, and simultaneous attempts at dropkicks, spinning wheel kicks, and even a dropkick counter to a top rope missile dropkick, it was basically the first high profile match of its kind to WCW or WWE fans. It is the father of cruiserweight wrestling as we know it and holds up well against its more popular peers from later years.

Shawn Michaels vs. Marty Jannetty (1993)
Intercontinental Championship
Top 5 Match in 1993

From great moments to great matches to far-reaching impact, this rivalry had it all. Michaels emphatically broke free from The Rockers when he superkicked Jannetty and threw his head through *The Barber Shop* window. A year later, they clashed over the Intercontinental Championship, with Marty shocking the world on May 17, 1993 when he made a surprise appearance on Raw and defeated HBK to win the gold in Pro Wrestling Illustrated's Match of the Year. Two months later, they wrestled again on Raw in another Match of the Year candidate. With Michaels going onto an all-time great career and Jannetty floundering beyond his association with HBK, every WWE tag team from then on was pegged with a "Michaels" - a potential breakout singles star – and a "Jannetty" - a wrestler destined to flame out when on his own.

Bret Hart vs. Hakushi (1995)
Top 10 Match in 1995

Bret Hart was to the WWF in the 1990s what Tim Duncan was to the NBA throughout the 2000s; he had a very workman-like way of handling his business that perhaps prevented him from being a huge hit at the box office, even though it proved not to hinder his ability to achieve great success. Many fans most closely associated WWF's New Generation with Bret, but Vince McMahon was trying constantly to find his next mega-star during that period, advertising the era around talents like Diesel. Meanwhile, The Hitman consistently kept producing a steady-stream of excellent matches like his often forgotten pair of gems with Hakushi in the spring and summer of 1995. Hakushi, a heavily-tattooed Japanese wrestler known for his combination of striking and risk-taking, introduced a move-set unique to most WWF fans, offering Bret an opportunity to show what he could do against a more dominant high-flier.

Shawn Michaels vs. Jeff Jarrett at In Your House 2
Intercontinental Championship
Top 5 Match in 1995

Michaels rose to main-event stardom in 1995 after years of climbing up through the mid-card ranks. He joined Bret near the top of the WWF hierarchy by regularly out-performing his peers with standout matches, like this excellent Intercontinental Championship match with Jeff Jarrett. Double J, as a guest on "The Doc Says" podcast in 2015, shared that his match with The Heartbreak Kid was one of the favorites of his career. The two of them meshed quite well, wrestling a smart, athletic, graceful bout with bursts of stimulating pace. Jarrett is underrated, historically, complimentary-speaking kind of a poor man's Ric Flair; about the closest we ever came to seeing Michaels in his prime wrestle his idol, The Nature Boy, in his prime was this match between HBK and Jarrett. It is worth mentioning that Double J was never featured more prominently in the WWF than on this night.

Shawn Michaels vs. Diesel at In Your House: Good
Friends, Better Enemies
WWF Championship

Top 5 Match in 1996

Michaels and Bret Hart had an unforgettable competition over who would be remembered as The New Generation's preeminent figure. In 1996, HBK became "The Man," taking the WWF Championship from The Hitman at *WrestleMania* in the midst of one of the greatest years anyone has ever had in between the ropes. His first title defense proved to be his very best encounter with his real-life good friend, Diesel. The Heartbreak Kid vs. Big Daddy Cool title bout at the prior year's *'Mania* had a higher profile, but their No Holds Barred scrap in April '96 was one of the most rewatchable matches of the decade. Characterful and innovative, it was the kind of work from Michaels that earned him such a glowing reputation for wrestling against giants and it was the caliber of performance from Diesel that showcased just how engaging a personality that he could be from bell-to-bell.

Shawn Michaels vs. The British Bulldog at King of the Ring 1996
WWF Championship
Top 10 Match in 1996

One of the things that made HBK's 1996 so extraordinary was the number of stylistically diverse opponents against whom he wrestled so many great matches. The British Bulldog was unique to anyone else that Michaels faced, a combination of raw power and elite athleticism that made him one of the New Generation's top stars. Davey Boy's finest work may have come against Bret Hart, but HBK tested the upper-limits of his physical abilities and prompted perhaps his best-rounded in-ring performances, a statement exemplified perfectly by this June '96 WWF Title bout at the fifth biggest pay-per-view of the year. HBK vs. Bulldog was a memorable main-event of a terrific show, *King of the Ring*. At over 26-minutes in length, it told a thorough tale of one-upmanship that highlighted HBK's guile and resilience while putting over just how much of a gamer Smith truly was during a historically undervalued period.

Shawn Michaels vs. Mankind at In Your House: Mind Games
WWF Championship
Top 5 Match in 1996

Many will be taken aback to find this gem in the Honorable Mentions. Trust that no match during the evaluation process entered and exited the Top 100 more often, but bear the following in mind: Though it truly remains a joy to watch, stand-alone, and though it was influential in several ways – it established HBK's tough guy credibility, it advertised Mick Foley's importance to the development of the Attitude Era's in-ring modus operandi, and it was one of the defining performances of the 1990s to a future generation of wrestlers who were watching as fans back then – Mankind vs. Michaels never held up well head-to-head against its peers, its innovative bell-to-bell action failing to offset its challenger-of-the-month feud, clunky moments, non-finish, and poor pay-per-view buyrate in a competitive environment that only rewarded its hindsight hype ever so much. Most fun ever? Absolutely; its Top 25 maybe. Greatest ever? Unfortunately no.

Rey Misterio, Jr. vs. Dean Malenko (1996)
WCW Cruiserweight Championship
Top 10 Match in 1996

The WCW Cruiserweight Division was born in 1992, but it was popularized in 1996. WCW Monday Nitro utilized it to help add a unique quality that WWF Monday Night Raw could not equal. Rey Misterio, Jr. was the most famous member to emerge from its ranks and, though another of his Cruiserweight Championship rivalries earned a spot deep into the Top 100, his reputation was built through his work with Dean Malenko. "The Man of 1,000 Holds," Malenko was a technical wrestling marvel on-par with more famous peers Chris Benoit and Kurt Angle who, it must be said, did as good a job as anyone ever did of

24

making Misterio's bursts of high-flying offense emotionally resonate. Too often, Misterio's opponents engaged him in competitions for who could string together the most aesthetically-pleasing spots, but Malenko would work him over for extended periods that made his comebacks cathartic.

Diamond Dallas Page vs. Macho Man Randy Savage (1997)
Top 10 Match in 1997

The most satisfying story of the entire New World Order vs. WCW saga from 1996 to 1998 was DDP's ascent to the upper echelon of the wrestler hierarchy during his 1997 feud with NWO member, Randy Savage. WCW was largely unable to build a new crop of strong-drawing top stars to replace the old guard because the inmates ran the asylum and would not loosen their stranglehold on the main-event, but Savage plucked the hard-working, late-blooming Page from relative obscurity and gave him the platform to succeed; and succeed he did. DDP was unquestionably the most underrated icon of the Monday Night War. His trio of intense, creative marquee matches with Macho Man (at *Spring Stampede*, *Great American Bash*, and *Halloween Havoc*) were incredibly engaging and only the lack of one truly epic performance among them prevented the Savage-Page rivalry from avoiding the final cut list for the Top 100.

Sting vs. The New World Order (1996-1997)

Fans who personally bore witness to the rise of WCW in 1996 on the strength of Hulk Hogan turning heel and forming The New World Order with Scott Hall and Kevin Nash ought to be able to sympathize with the internal struggle that led to Sting's amazing character transformation and his subsequent revolt against The N.W.O. not making the Top 100. The build to Sting vs. Hogan at *Starrcade '97* was every bit as riveting as Stone Cold's rebellion against Mr. McMahon the following year or so, making it deserving of a place in history right alongside the very best ever. However, just like in a match (or a movie), the climax to a story has to deliver in order for the overall product to be considered maximally successful; and, honestly, the manner in which Sting defeated Hogan was one of the dumbest things that has ever happened in the WrestleMania Era. Many fans cite *Starrcade '97* as the night that their fandom for WCW was irrevocably damaged.

Stone Cold Steve Austin vs. Dude Love at Over The Edge 1998
WWF Championship
Top 10 Match in 1998

Among the things that will make this journey through the WrestleMania Era fascinating is the dichotomy between a match that in itself echoes throughout history, a classic rivalry that spans many memorable matches, and an all-time great story that encompasses several rivalries. Mick Foley, as Dude Love, was a key part of the Mr. McMahon vs. Steve Austin saga that stimulated the famed Attitude Era; his solid rivalry with Stone Cold was not, by itself, particularly praise-worthy, but their match in May 1998 deserved at least an honorable mention separate from its involvement in the Austin-McMahon story to be discussed much later. The Attitude Era developed a signature main-event style influenced heavily by Foley's tendency to add hardcore elements to his matches and the neck injury sustained by Austin the year prior that limited his otherwise stellar in-ring game; overbooked to delight, this was a hallmark example of that style.

Goldberg vs. Diamond Dallas Page at Halloween Havoc 1998
WCW World Heavyweight Championship
Top 10 Match in 1998

Though it could be viewed as a case-in-point of caving under the pressure of the WWF's Austin-led comeback, considering that most of it had to be aired for free on Nitro after WCW failed to recognize the limits of their *Halloween Havoc* pay-per-view time,

Goldberg vs. Diamond Dallas Page was just as much exemplary of how the Monday Night War for television ratings between the WWF and WCW in the late '90s brought out the best in both companies. DDP and Goldberg were two of WCW's greatest success stories and their short and action-packed match for the World Championship was a quintessential representation of less is more, featuring the kind of creativity that Page was known for in the ring. Had WCW been able to bottle up the lightning that struck with Goldberg vs. DDP and to subsequently reproduce it in bulk, they could have thrived for years.

The Rock vs. Chris Benoit at Fully Loaded 2000
WWF Championship
Top 10 Match in 2000

In the early 2000s, the WWF employed the most stacked talent roster in its history. The addition of great wrestlers like Benoit lent each show a chance to shine from the opening match to the main-event, stimulating some of the best-ever years of both TV and pay-per-view quality. Benoit deserves vilification for the final moments in his real life, but The Rabid Wolverine's achievements on the 20'x20' canvas will not be ignored on these pages, as to pretend he did not exist would leave gaping holes in the overall discussion at hand. His first taste of WWF headlining, opposite The Rock, made clearer his technical wrestling wizardry and, though we never got the dream match between The People's Champ as we grew to know him and Bret Hart, there were spurts against Benoit that showed how Rock's vastly underrated in-ring style might have meshed with The Hitman's. A blast to watch...

Stone Cold Steve Austin and Triple H vs. Chris Jericho
and Chris Benoit on the May 21, 2001 Raw
WWF Tag Team Championship Match
Top 5 All-Time Standard Tag Team Match / Top 10 All-Time TV Match / Top 15 Match in 2001

The vast majority of the Top 100 and the Honorable Mentions consists of bodies of work that established their rankings through pay-per-view pay-off matches. On super cards, there are no commercials, allowing stories to be presented without interruption. There is also the built-in advantage of being more likely to create memories that stand out given that PPVs are monthly (with roughly 90 total matches combined per year on the modern average), while TV shows are weekly (with several hundred matches in total each year). Occasionally, there are pay-off matches on television that are so good that they can hold up against PPV-quality competition. Benoit and Jericho winning the Tag Team Championships from The Two-Man Power Trip was one such exception. The match was a microcosm of the Attitude Era, with enthralling chaos reigning supreme before the climax saw Triple H famously tear his quad but still finish the match in one of wrestling's gutsiest displays.

Chris Benoit vs. Stone Cold Steve Austin on the May 31, 2001 Smackdown
WWF Championship Match
Top 25 All-Time TV Match / Top 15 Match in 2001

Hall of Fame commentator, Jim Ross, had a signature saying that a wrestler would "dance with what brung him." Austin, with whom JR developed a special bond, had spinal fusion surgery in 1999, keeping him out of action for most of 2000. When he returned from injury, he was once again able to "dance with what brung him," mixing under-appreciated technical wrestling skills with a sort of relentless brawling style, a combination most evident when he was playing the heel role as he did for seven months in 2001. Benoit was in the midst of one of the greatest stretches of TV matches ever that May when, in his hometown, he famously challenged Austin for the WWF Title. Despite eleven straight rolling German suplexes from Benoit, Stone Cold retained on account of his evil associates, concluding a classic match that would have felt strange to have left out of this book completely.

Rob Van Dam vs. Jeff Hardy at InVasion
Hardcore Championship
Top 10 Match in 2001

One of the best things to come from the ill-fated WCW/ECW invasion angle was RVD, who lived up to the hype he created in the extreme world. He was later marginalized but, at thirty years old and in his physical prime, he dazzled throughout the back half of 2001, starting with this gem that ranks among the most spectacular mid-card matches ever. WWE's public service, "Don't Try This At Home" video in the early 2000s featured two Jim Ross quotes from this match, including "How do you learn to fall off a twenty foot ladder?" and "How's he even able to stand? That's what I want to know." In taking the Hardcore Title from Hardy, who had made his name as a daredevil in the TLC Era of tag team wrestling, RVD showcased his mastery of the hardcore grappling arts and proved himself to indeed be "Mr. Pay-Per-View."

Kurt Angle vs. Stone Cold Steve Austin (2001)
WWF Championship
Top 25 All-Time at Summerslam / Top 10 Match in 2001

Stone Cold himself has said on many occasions that his turn to the dark side at *WrestleMania X-Seven* was a mistake, but fans of sports entertainment's artistry might counter that his seven month run as an antagonist was some of the best work of his main-event career, both because he was believable as the psychopath obsessed with the WWF Championship and because he had a lot of very well-regarded matches within that period. Your opinion of it probably hinges on how you feel about his rivalry with Our Olympic Hero, whose prodigious rise from amateur to pro wrestling was completed in the summer of 2001. Their feud stretched from the spring through the winter, peaking with their one-on-one matches over the WWF Title at *Summerslam* and *Unforgiven*, where Angle temporarily took on the role of America's hero in the aftermath of the 9/11 terrorist attacks.

WWF vs. WCW/ECW Alliance
5-on-5 Elimination Tag Team Match at Survivor Series 2002

Top 10 All-Time Survivor Series Elimination Match / Top 5 All-Time at Survivor Series / Top 5 Match in 2001

The Royal Rumble Match aged much better than the classic Survivor Series Elimination gimmick through the decade that followed their respective inventions, partially due to the fact that the Rumble advanced its standing through the creative decision to put a WrestleMania title shot on the line starting in 1993. The conclusion to the WWF vs. WCW/ECW Alliance storyline gave the traditional Survivor Series Match and the pay-per-view itself a much-needed shot in the arm when five of the best from each "company" were pitted against each other with a "Winner Take All" stipulation. Though the match's epic aura was hindered by, at times, less than stellar execution, its theme of substantial consequence began a trend that helped the Survivor Series maintain its status as an event on-par with the other members of the exclusive "Big Four."

The 2002 Royal Rumble Match

Top 10 All-Time Royal Rumble Match / Top 20 All-Time at Royal Rumble / Top 10 Match in 2002

Few Royal Rumbles have ever produced the same caliber of excitement that Triple H's comeback from a career-threatening quadriceps tear sparked in 2002. The Game built a ton of momentum as the returning hero hell-bent on winning the Rumble so that he could regain the World Title. His victory and the cathartic release that it generated from wrestling fans has been historically tarnished by the mundane creative streak that followed, but it should forever be remembered just how over Triple H was in January that year. Supported by memorable performances from Steve Austin and Kurt Angle, a shocking elimination of Undertaker by Tough Enough winner Maven, and an awesome cameo that culminated in a Final Four finish by Mr.

Perfect, Triple H's Rumble quest produced one of the best iterations of WWE's most popular gimmick and, financially, one of the highest grossing Royal Rumble pay-per-views of all-time.

Edge vs. Kurt Angle (2002)
<u>Top 10 Match in 2002</u>

Known best for being the rivalry that gave us the American Bald Angle and popularized (not to be confused with invented) the "You Suck" chants in-tune with Our Olympic Hero's theme music, Edge vs. Kurt has otherwise struggled to establish much of an historic foothold since 2002. While their pair of pay-per-view matches at *Backlash* and *Judgment Day* and their Cage Match on the May 30th *Smackdown* combined to form one of the best in-ring resumes of any mid-card feud in the WrestleMania Era, that they were not propped up by bigger stages (i.e. the WWE Big Four PPV events or more prominent gimmicks than Hair vs. Hair) has handicapped their ability to leave quite the same mark as some of their peers. Nevertheless, they deserve recognition for their incredible pace and high octane action, which put them in a similar class as the highly touted Savage vs. Steamboat classic.

Eddie Guerrero vs. Chris Benoit
US Title Tournament Final at Vengeance 2003
<u>Top 10 Match in 2003</u>

Throughout the WrestleMania Era, there have been transitional periods in between the dominant runs of the biggest stars of all-time. Between Hogan and Austin/Rock, there was the New Generation; between Austin/Rock and Cena, there was what some refer to as "Ruthless Aggression," so named for Vince McMahon's on-screen comments in 2002 but embodied by the hunger of Benoit and Guerrero-types to reach levels of stardom not previously thought possible for them. At a time when the diehard fan was more appreciative than ever before of a top notch in-ring performance, smaller wrestlers with strong but not larger-than-life personalities like Guerrero and Benoit became as popular as they were respected. They were technicians who taught the audience the revised textbook definition of a "wrestling clinic," exemplified by their 20-minute borderline classic that began the lineage of the United States Championship in WWE after the title had been retired during the Invasion.

Kurt Angle vs. John Cena at No Mercy 2003
Top 10 Match in 2003

The Doctor of Thuganomics was exactly the larger-than-life persona that WWE had been looking for since Rock and Stone Cold began distancing themselves from the company. Cena took a chance on himself, bringing a natural penchant for freestyle rapping to Smackdown and thriving in 2003 as the cutting edge, new age master of the verbal insult. His match with Angle flashed his potential as an all-around star capable of stepping up his game when it came time for a payoff match; plus, the dueling chants that became synonymous with Cena were as prevalent against Our Olympic Hero as they had ever been before (though, at that time, he had the support of the adult males). Angle brought out the best in Cena and delivered one of the most underrated matches in his stellar body of work; he deserves historical extra-credit for elevating the biggest icon of the post-Attitude Era.

Eddie Guerrero vs. Kurt Angle (2004)
Top 40 All-Time at WrestleMania / Top 10 Match in 2004

Injury prevented this eye-popping historical pairing from maximizing what it could have achieved, with Angle re-aggravating his chronic neck problem just before *WrestleMania XX* and Guerrero struggling to overcome a bad hamstring strain heading into *Summerslam '04*. It is difficult to reflect back on their series and not wonder, "What if?" Nevertheless, Angle vs. Guerrero at 75% was still better than 99% of the in-ring rivalries of the WrestleMania Era. Anticipation had centered on the tantalizing prospect of them squaring off at their athletic peaks, but what we instead ended up with was a couple of mat-based wrestling matches in the vein of what might have been expected from Guerrero or Angle vs. Chris Benoit, giving Latino Heat two of his highest profile opportunities to show that he was far more than just a risk taker. Of course, Benoit stealing the show from them did not help their cause either.

Randy Orton vs. Chris Benoit at Summerslam 2004
World Heavyweight Championship
Top 20 All-Time at Summerslam / Top 10 Match in 2004

Appraising the entirety of the last thirty-plus years, it goes without saying that the most successful WWE "rookie class" ever was 2002; its headliners – Cena, Randy Orton, Brock Lesnar, and Dave Batista – went onto become four of the Top 20 stars of the WrestleMania Era. Lesnar experienced massive success the fastest, but his departure in 2004 opened the door for the others to rise sharply. Orton, in defeating Benoit in a very intelligently worked main-event at *Summerslam* that has aged quite well, became the youngest World Heavyweight Champion in WWE lore, giving his 4-star caliber effort with Benoit just the intangible nudge it needed as one of the fringe Honorable Mentions. It will be interesting to see how their celebrated performances are received in the forthcoming Top 100, as there have been strong criticisms levied on them by fans that prefer either the style wrestled during Attitude and prior or the more indy-influenced style wrestled in modern times.

Trish Stratus vs. Lita (2004-2006)
WWE Women's Championship

WWE's Women's Revolution a decade later will likely prove to have been a far more influential series of watershed moments for females at the top of the sports entertainment sphere, but there was certainly something to be said for Stratus vs. Lita paving the way for it, especially as it relates to Trish as the quintessential queen-bee of the division's modern history. Personalities create much of the drama that builds to heated pay-offs, and not even Charlotte Flair vs. Sasha Banks could equal the nuclear heat that Stratus was able to garner at her evil peak in 2004. Together, Trish and Lita showed that women had the ability to push beyond perceived boundaries, becoming feature attractions based around more than novelty, celebrity guests, and pin-up spreads; Lita and Trish, especially to those of us who lived the first half of the WrestleMania Era, brought competitiveness and credibility to women's wrestling.

Chris Jericho vs. John Cena at Summerslam 2005
WWE Championship
Top 20 All-Time at Summerslam / Top 10 Match in 2005

Aside from his match with Angle, the early part of Cena's in-ring career was marred by his clumsy athleticism. Though innovative on the microphone, he was a work-in-progress when the bell rang. That did not stop him from becoming WWE's #1 star in 2005, but it put him under a microscope when he was expected to wrestle at a main-event level. After a below average title-winning performance on the grandest stage, Cena's match with Jericho at WWE's 2nd biggest event of the year was an important step in the right direction. His movements were still awkward and there were several issues in communication with Y2J evident to the studious eye, but you could tell that he was increasingly capable of raising his game. This was also the match that most prominently began the trend of vocal males being split from the kids and females in their opinion of Cena.

Triple H vs. Undertaker vs. Jeff Hardy vs. Big Show vs.
Vladimir Kozlov vs. Edge
Elimination Chamber Match at No Way Out 2009
WWE Championship
#2 All-Time Elimination Chamber Match / Top 5 Match in 2009

In 2002, WWE punctuated a decade-long run of top notch gimmick innovation with a match borrowing on concepts like random selection and a reverse battle royal from the Rumble, the elimination format of the Survivor Series, and the visual appeal of the giant cage from Hell in a Cell or War Games: the Elimination Chamber. One of six stipulation matches to earn its own yearly pay-per-view of the same name, the Chamber has generally been a critically well-received concept. Two iterations stand out from the pack, the first from February 2009 featuring Smackdown roster members competing for the WWE Championship. All six participants were at the peak of their character's powers, creating an environment ripe for success. Edge, the defending champion, getting eliminated in the first few minutes has provided the Chamber with one of its defining moments and the final stanza classically previewed the iconic HHH vs. Taker rivalry.

Christian vs. Alberto Del Rio
Ladder Match at Extreme Rules 2011
World Heavyweight Championship
Top 20 All-Time Ladder Match / Top 5 Match in 2011

One of the essential carry-overs from the Attitude Era was the popularity of the Ladder Match, a gimmick that boosted the profiles for a substantial percentage of the Top 100. By 2011, there had been so many iterations of the stipulation (thirty-six standard versions alone) that, when one of them stood out like Del Rio vs. Christian, it was a noteworthy achievement; theirs was not just a collection of spots to temporarily spike crowd enthusiasm, but a dramatic, flowing story with a memorable finish that saw Christian, a Ladder Match pioneer, capture for the first time the World Heavyweight Title. The trope of the long-time veteran finally winning the big one has been another key development in post-Attitude lore and one that in its own way offers additional verve to a match, rivalry, or story in historical discussions such as the one stimulated by this book.

Daniel Bryan vs. Sheamus
Two-Out-Of-Three Falls Match at Extreme Rules 2012
World Heavyweight Championship
Top 10 Match in 2012

Daniel Bryan's saga is one of WWE's greatest stories ever told; it is also a perfect example of how WWE developed during the course of the Reality Era, which was characterized by the company's on-screen reactions to the unique dichotomy of fans generally accepting that wrestling is scripted but demanding greater influence over the script. Bryan was organically chosen by the people and became the most universally beloved protagonist in a decade. The match over a year in the making between Bryan and Sheamus showcased an important step in the Reality Era's progression. In addition to being a fantastic performance well worth the wait after only 18 seconds of action to show for two WrestleMania matches booked between the pair, it was an admission on WWE's part that Bryan was a gamer who had earned, if by crowd reactions alone, the opportunity to be booked like a legitimate competitor.

Brock Lesnar vs. John Cena at Extreme Rules 2012
Top 10 Match in 2012

On the night after *WrestleMania XXVIII*, Brock Lesnar made his shocking return to WWE after an intestinal illness stunted his MMA career. With him coming from the UFC, he brought a renewed sense of legitimacy that not even the NCAA Heavyweight Wrestling Championship won during his youth could equal; and, perhaps more than anything, he brought considerable box office appeal. Brock, like The Rock, left WWE and came back a huge star with mainstream credibility. Seeking to immediately cash-in on Lesnar's name, WWE put him against John Cena. Though the Golden Boy picked up the victory, what transpired prior to the shocking three-count was the first instance of what would become Brock's signature in-ring style – dubbed on "The Doc Says" podcast as "Beast Mode." Lesnar mauled Cena, busted him open the hard way within 30 seconds, and was on the defensive for maybe a minute. It was utterly fascinating to watch.

Bray Wyatt vs. Daniel Bryan at The 2014 Royal Rumble

<u>Top 20 All-Time at Royal Rumble</u> / <u>Top 10 Match in 2014</u>

This instant classic highlights the opportunity that the Royal Rumble affords to wrestlers who perform on its undercard. There are less matches, increasing the chance to make an impression. Bryan and Wyatt had one of the ten best non-Rumble matches in the history of the annual January spectacular, but their spirited encounter has been underrated in its contributions to both of their careers. For Wyatt, it was the breakout performance that deepened the emotional investment of the audience to his character. To that point, he had been all talk and no walk. By match's end, he was a bonafide star. For Bryan, the match and the events leading up to it were invaluable in furthering the Yes! Movement that became the story of 2014. If connected to his overarching story, it characterized for him that the night is always darkest just before the dawn...and that the dawn was coming.

Evolution vs. The Shield (2014)
<u>Top 10 Match in 2014</u>

It is possible that, with the further passage of time and the establishment of greater context, an Honorable Mention from recent years could find itself in the Top 100. In all likelihood, we will soon ruminate about The Hounds of Justice as the greatest faction of the decade. Should that be the case, their matches against the greatest stable of the previous decade will benefit from an added historical boost but, no matter what the future holds, the 2014 clashes are already worth celebrating. WWE, in this decade, has struggled to make new main-eventers, often opting to shun sure-fire star-making opportunities in favor of putting legends over fellow legends. However, Evolution so thoroughly stamped The Shield as major players in consecutive defeats that Ambrose, Reigns, and Rollins all became cornerstones of their generation. Alas, the momentous pair of battles between The Shield and Evolution just narrowly missed the cut.

Seth Rollins vs. Dean Ambrose vs. Dolph Ziggler vs. Kofi Kingston vs. Jack Swagger vs. Rob Van Dam
Money in the Bank Contract Ladder Match 2014
Top 20 All-Time Ladder Match / Top 10 Match in 2014

2014 was one of WWE's peak recent years, when many elements coalesced including the extraordinarily well-handled break-up of The Shield, which led into the second greatest Money in the Bank Ladder Match of all-time. The Ladder Match gimmick can essentially be separated into two primary sub-genres: the stunt-brawl, motivated by innovation in spot-creation, and the story-driven (see Christian-Del Rio), which typically is more cognizant of the rivalry leading to the stipulation's use. One might say, and pay attention to the semantics, that a stunt-brawl features ladders and two or more wrestlers, whereas the story-driven features two or more wrestlers and ladders. Money in the Bank is always a stunt-brawl first and foremost but, thanks to Rollins and Ambrose, the contract-MITB Ladder Match in 2014 had a riveting back-drop that made it the rare version of the stipulation to actually fit into both categories; and that is something worth celebrating.

Randy Orton vs. Seth Rollins at WrestleMania 31
Top 40 All-Time at WrestleMania / Top 10 Match in 2015

One of the most fascinating pro wrestler traits is that he/she often makes the decision to pursue a career in sports entertainment by resonating with a great match or identifying with a future peer. Essentially, then, when someone like Seth Rollins performs, he is trying to top that which he grew up idolizing. The Architect has quickly established for himself a reputation as a "redefiner," so it was not surprising that he maximized the minutes of his first singles match on the grandest stage with a performance sure to become one of the most rewatchable in WrestleMania lore. It was attending *WrestleMania XXVI* to see Shawn Michaels vs. Undertaker that prompted Rollins to chase his WWE dream. Against Orton five years later, he packed nearly as much content as was seen in

Michaels-Taker II into less than half the bell-to-bell time, punctuated by Orton nailing the RKO in classic fashion.

Kevin Owens vs. John Cena (2015)
Top 5 Match in 2015

As the former Shield members ascended, John Cena began to transition into a different phase of his career. To see him drop down the card was a strange sight at first, but it proved a welcome one when he altered his in-ring approach, speeding up the pace and unleashing weekly barrages of very entertaining matches wrestled like pay-per-view main-events with big moves and near falls galore. For a top star who had been admonished by the fans ad nauseum for his "Five Moves of Doom," his run of Open Challenges for the United States Championship showed what he could accomplish when not tasked with being "The Face That Runs The Place." Cena was able to more readily advance the next generation. Kevin Owens was one of the recipients, pinning Cena clean in his debut match. The game of one-upmanship that they played across three PPVs made KO an instant star.

Roman Reigns vs. AJ Styles at Extreme Rules 2016
WWE World Heavyweight Championship
Top 5 Match in 2016

The volume of excellent matches has been on the rise since WWE altered its new talent recruitment strategy in the early 2010s and started stockpiling the best wrestlers in the world from the various independent promotions across the globe, none better than AJ Styles. With more television and pay-per-view time to fill, WWE's deep roster of fantastic performers has been unleashed and a unique challenge has arisen in selecting the cream of the crop; when there are a dozen or less four-star matches all year, picking and choosing the best of the lot is a lot simpler than attempting to sort through twice the highly-regarded pool, especially when someone like Styles has nearly a dozen all his own. In 2016, The Phenomenal One was WWE's

MVP, his matches with the very game Big Dog a perfect example of the very HBK-esque fluidity that set AJ Styles matches apart.

The Usos vs. The New Day (2017)
Smackdown Tag Team Championships
Top 5 Match in 2017

Present day volume of outstanding performances acknowledged, one has to be careful not to get too hasty with its praise of the current generation's best efforts before they get the chance to endure the scrutiny born of multiple years of comparative analysis and replays. The upper limits of The Usos vs. The New Day legacy probably will hinge on how long their reinvigoration of tag team wrestling in WWE proper lasts. However, even in the event that 2017 was a one-year thing, their outstanding series will put them squarely in the discussion with the Smackdown Six era for the division in 2002, which produced the winner of a three-way competition for the Top 100's lone standard tag team match representative; if tag team wrestling experiences another golden era, their rivalry may earn even higher historical praise as arguably the biggest stimulus, further justifying its status here.

Johnny Gargano vs. Tommaso Ciampa (2017/2018)
Top 5 Match in 2018

Ahead of the forthcoming countdown, be advised that despite NXT being under the WWE umbrella, its content from the past four years of its existence since the WWE Network launched was not considered for this project (with the exception of the Women's Revolution). Further establishing a dichotomy between WWE proper and its very popular developmental brand will be an important task as the all-time greatest discussion evolves because there has been some utterly phenomenal work produced by NXT, perhaps none better than Gargano vs. Ciampa. As this book went into its final editing process, they had just completed a 5-star chapter of their emotionally-gripping saga in New Orleans over WrestleMania weekend. When someone whose opinion you respect decrees a performance was "the best in WWE's entire history," then you cannot help but take notice. What does this list look like at the turn of the decade if NXT is included?

#100
Bret Hart vs. Roddy Piper
Intercontinental Championship
WrestleMania VIII
April 5, 1992
Top 40 All-Time at WrestleMania / Top 5 Match in 1992

We begin our journey with a match that emphasizes the importance of atmosphere, both to the presentation of an in-ring performance and to the weight that it carries historically. There are great matches every year on wrestling TV shows and pay-per-views. Creating separation among them is made easier through the memories left by the occasions; and the greater the sense of occasion, the greater the ability a match has to leave its mark.

Bret Hart vs. Roddy Piper is a perfect example. There was barely a storyline in place for their Intercontinental Championship bout in April 1992, but any residual drawback was eliminated by the WrestleMania stage, upon which the future Hall of Famers painted a masterpiece. Take their same brilliant backstage segment with Mean Gene Okerlund and their ensuing match in front of 62,167 people and have it take place instead at Survivor Series and it would not have been the same. Fans can develop preferences for other wrestling shows (Royal Rumble, Starrcade, TLC, or even Raw), but there can be no denying that WrestleMania is pro wrestling's Super Bowl/NBA Finals/World Series and, as such, provides the greatest platform for delivering landmark performances.

Decidedly mid-card matches that take place at 'Mania can, therefore, naturally expect an intangible boost over their mid-card peers from non-'Mania events and can also, as proven by this match, overtake headlining matches from cards as significant as Summerslam.

WrestleMania lore is filled with great mid-card matches, many of them to be featured later. In order to secure the final spot in the Top 100, Hart vs. Piper successfully won head-to-head comparisons to several Honorable Mentions but, given the nature of its excellence, its strongest challenges came from fellow WrestleMania overachievers, Christian vs. Chris Jericho from *WrestleMania XX* and Randy Orton vs. Seth Rollins from *WrestleMania 31*.

Y2J vs. Christian was, in addition to its strong mechanics, noteworthy for its elevation of Captain Charisma to singles heights not previously reached and for being the career turning point for Trish Stratus, whose heel turn during the climax yielded one of the most underrated characters of the 2000s. Orton vs. Rollins was an amazing blend of athleticism and psychology, a how-to guide for the modern era on taking a main-event-level story and packing it into 13-minutes and change; of course, its amazing finishing sequence bears reiteration.

Both matches were indelibly enhanced by "The Grandest Stage of Them All." The difference between Hart vs. Piper and the others was superlative storytelling. "If you watch the match from bell-to-bell," Hall of Fame commentator, Jim Ross, has noted, "[it's] probably one of the best, fundamentally sound, understandable stories that has ever been told."

The story was about the legendary Hot Rod trying to stave off the challenge from the emergent Hitman. He found out quickly that he could not outwrestle him, that something as simple as an armbar was an almost inescapable weapon in the arsenal of The Excellence of Execution. Piper was resigned to a cheap shot out of frustration; in fact, Hart's resolve so exasperated him that he nearly walloped Bret with the ring bell, a move that would have shaken the foundation of a "babyface" match in 1992 had he gone through with it. The Hitman's resilience left a lasting impression, as he overcame a nasty (blade-induced) cut above the eye and countered Piper's Sleeper Hold with a clever reversal to earn the pinfall victory.

Then there was the story behind the scenes, which further stimulates the bout's reputation. "Bret Hart was at a point when he was an emerging superstar," Ross claimed during Piper's documentary, *Born to Controversy*, in a discussion about the match. "His time was near and, probably in Bret's mind at *WrestleMania VIII*, his time was past due." The Hitman was a big victory away from ascending to headlining status in the WWF. Piper, who likes to say that nobody had previously pinned his shoulders to the mat in 17 years, had enough respect for Hart to be the guy to give him that win; he won the Intercontinental Title at *Royal Rumble '92* just so that he could drop it to Bret at *'Mania VIII*.

On camera after the match, Piper strapped the title around Hart's waist. Off camera, Bret told Roddy, "Thanks, I'll never forget what you did for me today." Bret described it in his book as the biggest thing to have ever happened to him to that point. He went onto main-event *Summerslam '92* and, a month later, win the WWF Championship.

In doing the honors for The Hitman, The Hot Rod also got the chance to perform at a higher level than he ever had before. "The knock on Roddy was that he was mostly a mouth and that he didn't have the wrestling to back it up," Mick Foley said in *Born to Controversy*. "So it's nice if you're Roddy Piper to have that type of match to say 'Hey, look what I can do when the pressure was on.'" The pressure Foley spoke of was WrestleMania.

Undertaker, perhaps the most respected man in pro wrestling history, once said that "When you're on the card at WrestleMania, you stand in front of millions of people and you stand before your peers and it lets people know that you mean something." If you have a great match at WrestleMania, it means that much more.

#99
Rey Mysterio vs. Kurt Angle
Summerslam
August 25, 2002

#1 All-Time Sub-Ten-Minute Match / Top 5 All-Time Opening Pay-Per-View Match / Top 20 All-Time Summerslam / Top 10 Match in 2002

Kurt Angle vs. Rey Mysterio earned its place on the list by unconventional means. In the wrestling world, a sub-ten-minute run-time is generally reserved for the matches tasked with helping to make a show better, sort of like a role player in basketball. Rare has it been that such a match excelled to the extent necessary to leave an all-time caliber impression; Angle vs. Mysterio is one of the exceptions.

Rey Mysterio was the last among a group of world-renowned in-ring performers from WCW to debut in WWE. By the summer of 2002, then, WWE had amassed the most athletic, talented roster ever. The wrestling style, particularly on the Smackdown brand, evolved to match the elite athleticism on hand. Matches were executed with incredible pace; they were shorter, but packed with a comparable amount of content to a match double or triple the run-time from another era. Perhaps no match better exemplified that style than Mysterio vs. Angle.

The Olympic Gold Medalist's physical gifts were virtually unequaled at that point of his career; Mysterio was widely regarded as the most innovative wrestler in the world. The combination of their respective skill-sets proved magnificent.

In what was Mysterio's WWE PPV debut, they flew out of the gate with a lightning quick series of intricate sequences that would have made Dean Malenko proud. The aesthetically pleasing early game of cat and mouse ended with Angle taking full control, which he would maintain for much of the match. The Wrestling Machine's counters to Mysterio's high risk offense was often breathtaking, one particularly brilliant example being a Wheelbarrow Bulldog shifted into a perfect German Suplex. Angle gave much more than he took, but when he was selling Mysterio's attacks, he made the newcomer look awesome. Despite a spirited comeback and several moments in which he was inches away from victory, Mysterio took the loss but, most importantly, shined brightly from a star-making performance.

The entire presentation, book-ended by the start and finish of Angle's entrance music, took 11-minutes, 55-seconds (including 9-minutes, 22-seconds of bell-to-bell time). A valuable contributor can become an invaluable cornerstone of a wrestling promotion by maximizing his/her minutes of screen time. Current and future generations can look to this match as a microcosm of that theory. It was the kind of match that helped Mysterio become a future headliner and World Champion and that helped Angle solidify his main-event position en route to a Top 15 all-time career.

Not only is it the greatest match of under ten-minutes in length of the WrestleMania Era, but it is one of the best opening contests in PPV history. As compared to the previous entry, it must be stated that "atmosphere" is certainly not limited to the WrestleMania stage. If WrestleMania is the diamond event for pro wrestling, then Summerslam is the pearl. It is widely thought, in fact, that the show opened by Mysterio vs. Angle – *Summerslam 2002* – is the most legitimate contender to one of the top WrestleManias being the greatest wrestling PPV of all-time. They set such a wonderful tone that the rest of the roster was forced to rise up to or exceed their level.

#98
Seth Rollins vs. Roman Reigns
WWE World Heavyweight Championship
Money in the Bank
June 19, 2016
Top 5 Match in 2016

It could be said that the previous two matches found their way into the Top 100 by so very well standing the test of time. Perhaps another half decade may need to pass before we are able to fully gauge the place that Seth Rollins vs. Roman Reigns will occupy in these historical rankings, but here is what some may consider a bold prediction about it: #98 will be far too low when all is said and done and their initial pay-per-view encounter and any substantial rematches that follow will quite easily pass time's test.

Rollins vs. Reigns has sizeable long-term potential to be regarded as one of the most gripping sagas of its generation. With all due respect to the Ambrose vs. Rollins rivalry that has emerged as the most popular combination when a pair of the former Shield members clash, Reigns and Rollins are just as inexorably linked but in a higher profile manner, their fates destined to intertwine throughout their careers as they struggle to knock each other off the very top of the WWE hierarchy, brass-ring having already been grabbed and lacking any desire to share it.

Since The Architect first blasted The Big Dog in the back with a steel chair in June 2014, they have each spent large portions of the WWE calendars that followed developing claims to the #1 spot in the company at each other's expense. *WrestleMania 31* looked to be a torch-passing moment featuring Reigns, the 2015 Royal Rumble winner, dethroning the dominant champion, Brock Lesnar. Rollins, via greed and guile, became "The Man" that night instead, cashing in his Money in the Bank contract.

Unfortunately, The Architect had to forfeit the WWE Title when his knee buckled in late 2015 under the weight of carrying WWE; Reigns subsequently plowed through the remains of the Triple H and Stephanie McMahon regime and became "The Guy."

Money in the Bank '16 was the culmination of a two-year journey, their fateful collision-course managing to put their budding rivalry in as prominent a spotlight as possible without ever having them fight each other on pay-per-view. It was heralded accordingly in the preceding weeks as a match that could "main-event WrestleMania." Take the same overall presentation (including the post-match Ambrose cash-in) and put it in front of 75,000 fans on the grandest stage and it would look right at home in such a historic position.

Two things currently hold it back from a higher position: the controversy surrounding Reigns and a general lack of consensus for their *Money in the Bank '16* World Title bout's status as a modern classic. The Big Dog has taken up John Cena's mantle as the man "chosen by WWE to dominate all comers," constantly interfering with his perception by the vocal diehard fan contingent even in the absence of complete truth to the sentiment; to many, no matter how many great matches that he has, Reigns casts a shadow over the product itself, and any excellent performance in which he is involved is weakened by it. As to the aforementioned lack of consensus, a popular style has emerged, initially exemplified best by Cena's matches with Kevin Owens in 2015, that emphasizes high spot-heavy content and that derives much of its drama from false finishes. Rollins and Reigns have certainly proven adept at that style, but their modus operandi is a little more old school, thriving on a deliberate pace and a steady progression toward climactic moments; Rollins vs. Reigns was simply not wrestled in the popular style.

Both hindrances are the sorts that ease with the passage of time and the match will presumably go on to age quite gracefully given its strengths are based in the history between generational icons and, most importantly, character potential realized.

Reigns strikingly acted the part of the frustrated Samoan bad-ass reveling at the chance not only to unleash two years of pent-up aggression toward his turncoat former brother-in-arms, but also to prove to Rollins that the "Guy" was the better "Man." Though the scripting of his persona was notoriously inconsistent in his early years as a headliner, on that night against Rollins, he took full ownership of his direction and let loose his natural attitude, viciously talking trash and exuding a supreme confidence that said via his body language, "There is no way that you can beat me, Seth."

Rollins matched Roman's borderline arrogance with incredible resiliency. Seeing as it was his first match back from reconstructive knee surgery, every high risk successfully landed was a triumph inching him closer to the ultimate victory of regaining the title that he never lost; the execution of the sunset flip and the running Turnbuckle Powerbomb – the combination he was attempting when he snapped his knee ligaments – answered the remaining question surrounding his potential physical limitations and allowed him to steer the bout toward the springing of the perfect climactic trap: an amazing Spear-into-Pedigree counter.

Adding in the Ambrose cash-in, it was the complete WWE storytelling package.

Some might suggest that authorial interpretation played the biggest role in Rollins vs. Reigns even making the Top 100 cut, but bear in mind that the above review of the match in question, and others like it still to come on these pages, could not have been described in such flattering terms absent the strength of both character portrayals, which translate to rewatchability on a greater scale than any series of big moves alone.

<u>**#97**</u>
Edge vs. Rey Mysterio vs. Kane vs. Big Show vs. Drew McIntyre vs. Wade Barrett Elimination Chamber
February 20, 2011

<u>#1 All-Time Elimination Chamber Match</u> / <u>Top 5 Match in 2011</u>

While it may lack the gravitas of other multi-man stipulation matches such as TLC or the Rumble, the Elimination Chamber certainly has become a distinct entity since its *Survivor Series 2002* origination. Its stakes have always been high and its quality assurance ratio, if you will, is very impressive. Edge, Mysterio, Barrett, Kane, McIntyre, and Show combined for the preeminent edition at *Elimination Chamber 2011*.

The Elimination Chamber is at its best when, within the confines of its two miles of chain, its combatants are participating in a story underlying the central goal of the gimmick, which is to be the last man standing and win the considerable prize of a championship or a very high profile title shot. It does not always have to be an epic story, like the dissolution of Evolution in 2005 or the continued WrestleMania vision quest of Daniel Bryan in 2014, but even something as simple as the backstage mention that Edge, the defending World Heavyweight Champion, was stacked against the odds of it having been five years since a champion had retained the title in a Chamber Match was a subtle but effective enough plot device to help separate the Smackdown version in 2011 from its peers.

Edge was abruptly forced into retirement seven weeks later, so there is also a historical boost to the Smackdown '11 Chamber for the bout serving as truly the last great performance in The Rated R Superstar's Hall of Fame career and arguably, considering that he was involved from bell-to-bell, the home of the single greatest overall performance in Chamber lore; and it almost goes without saying that the final 8 ½ minutes of Edge and Rey Mysterio having a match within the match comparable to the '07 Rumble's HBK-Taker climax was assuredly the top candidate for the most enthralling finish in the history of the Chamber.

It never seemed to drag in its 31-minute run-time, the first break in action not coming until right at the 20-minute mark, so its fluid, very deliberately escalatory pace makes for an incredibly easy rewatch leading up to the awesome ending.

Inspired nights from all involved were the collective reason for the success of the endeavor, as a pair of both younger stars and veterans brought considerable depth to the fiction. Big Show, a last-minute replacement for the recently "fired" Dolph Ziggler, was right in the middle of the peak four year stretch of his lengthy WWE tenure and contributed as much while standing in his pod, trash-talking and taunting Wade Barrett, as he did before he memorably took a flurry of offense from four other combatants to end his brief but impactful time in the match proper. Barrett, the first eliminated (by Show), acquitted himself quite well and looked every bit the star that he was back then, having come off of a huge debut-six months in 2010. Kane did as he was often prone to do throughout the back half of his storied career and very efficiently added a steadying presence.

Drew McIntyre was perhaps the revelation that elevated this particular Chamber to all-time #1 status within its sub-genre. After the gimmick's inception, it quickly matured as a platform for a star on-the-rise to make a splash. McIntyre, who had joined Smackdown in 2009 to substantial expectations thanks to Vince McMahon introducing him as a "future World Champion," was kind of an odd choice by early 2011 after his momentum had stalled; he seemed to treat the opportunity like a chance at redemption, both when he interrupted Edge in the midst of a pre-match interview and later during the match itself. He embraced the moment and had many pundits discussing, in review of the show, his intensity and breakout potential.

Mysterio and Edge were the anchors, though. Rey was no longer in his physical prime by then, but he still offered the bout's signature spots; Edge, who would later admit to around that WrestleMania Season beginning to feel as though his pro wrestling clock had nearly expired, was his co-MVP of the match. The finale that they put on display, again, was just tremendous; you would struggle to find a more captivating eight-minutes of WWE action. They interestingly, for two wrestlers who had such chemistry, never had a really great singles match; their superior work together was done either as a tag team or in the closing moments of Chamber matches.

For being the pinnacle achievement of its stipulation's history, the Smackdown Elimination Chamber Match in 2011 deserves a spot in the pantheon of all-time in-ring greatness.

#96
Hulk Hogan vs. "Mr. Wonderful" Paul Orndorff
WWF Championship
Saturday Night's Main Event October 4, 1986 to Saturday Night's Main Event January 3, 1987

<u>Top 5 Match in 1987</u>

Though the in-ring action throughout this feud struggles to keep pace with most of the Top 100, the strength of its story – fueled by genuine behind-the-scenes animosity – places Orndorff vs. Hogan on a similar pedestal as other Hulkster rivalries from the 1980s.

Hulk Hogan and Paul Orndorff, each blessed with an indomitable competitive drive, were not exactly chummy with each other when each was reaching his WWF peak in the early years of the WrestleMania Era, a fact that inspired believability when their noteworthy TV alliance ended in treachery. Unfortunately, the amazing rivalry between the two has practically gone unnoticed by fans who started watching WWE in the 1990s or later. In all likelihood, the number of people who consider it Top 100-caliber is similar to the number that remembers that Benedict Arnold, to whom Hogan prominently compared Orndorff, was an infamous turncoat in the American Revolutionary War.

When a Steel Cage Match ended the Hogan vs. Orndorff saga on *Saturday Night's Main Event* in January 1987, WrestleMania was still the only special event regularly offered by the WWF. Payoff matches on television do not carry the same weight with an audience largely brought up to recognize pay-per-view as the standard platform on which great rivalries conclude. If Summerslam had existed in 1986, surely Hogan vs. Orndorff would have main-evented it instead of the virtually unknown Toronto (mega) house show later released on video called *The*

Big Event. Perhaps the Cage Match would have then headlined a hypothetical Royal Rumble in 1987 had the Winter Classic come to be one year earlier, suffice to say that the lack of historical settings has largely left the trio of Hogan-Orndorff matches hidden in the memories of those that were watching back then.

To set the stage for the uninitiated, The Hulkster and Mr. Wonderful prominently battled in 1985 at *WrestleMania* alongside Mr. T and Roddy Piper, respectively. That most fans recall; not as often highlighted is that Orndorff sided with Hogan due to their mutual interest in the demise of The Hot Rod, who had attacked Mr. Wonderful in frustration for their *'Mania* defeat. Hogan and Orndorff teamed up to battle the most heinous heels of the period, but the seeds of jealousy eventually sprouted, prompting the dissolution of their powerful duo at the behest of Mr. Wonderful. If it reads as familiar, it is because the WWF used a comparable storyline to split up The Mega Powers (Hogan and "Macho Man" Randy Savage) just a few years later.

While, admittedly, Hogan vs. Savage is one of the biggest feuds ever in WWE and thus cannot be put on equal footing with such an historic afterthought, that Hogan vs. Orndorff has become an afterthought is an injustice. It is analogous to the 1980s NBA rivalry between the Pistons and Celtics being overshadowed by the league-defining Bird/Celtics vs. Magic/Lakers saga. Hulkster vs. Mr. Wonderful was quite substantial in its own right and the quality of its matches was arguably better than the fairly routine Hogan vs. Macho Man bouts.

Though the rivalry featured great psychological ploys such as the exploitation of corrupt official Danny Davis as a second referee in the Cage Match and Orndorff stealing Hogan's "Real American" theme song (the classic Rick Derringer tune continuously played through both their entrances in all three matches), its x-factor was Mr. Wonderful's association with Bobby "The Brain" Heenan, a perennial thorn in Hulkamania's side. Viewed by the fan from the WrestleMania to WrestleMania perspective, Heenan swaying Andre the Giant to the dark side ahead of *WrestleMania*

III was a dastardly act by the power-hungry manager of Hogan's unsuccessful challenger at *WrestleMania 2*, King Kong Bundy. An important missing ingredient in that incomplete contextualization is that Hogan and Orndorff's Cage Match took place a month before Heenan coerced Andre into turning on Hulk; it was not just that the beloved Giant wanted to fight wrestling's greatest hero that created a monumental surge in momentum for the WWF, it was that Heenan was the one pulling the strings.

Hogan vs. Orndorff should be remembered as the storyline that made Hulkamania, to borrow from Gorilla Monsoon's verbiage, "the irresistible force" that the world so badly wanted to see collide with "the immoveable object" at *WrestleMania III*. Their heated series over the World Heavyweight Championship drew the third highest rating ever for *Saturday Night's Main Event* and attracted 74,000 people into the Toronto Exhibition Stadium. It was, with all due respect to Hogan vs. Piper, the first great championship feud of the WrestleMania Era on the WWF's side.

#95
John Cena vs. Batista
Summerslam 2008 and WrestleMania XXVI
Top 40 All-Time at WrestleMania / Top 5 Match in 2010

John Cena is often credited as the superstar who sparked the completion of WWE's transition out of the Attitude Era, his status as one of the Top 5 draws in modern wrestling lore largely shaping that perspective. However, there once was a competition between Cena and Dave Batista for which wrestler would lead WWE into the late 2000s, a quiet rivalry that spanned their initial forays into the main-event scene that then grew louder as they became firmly entrenched as the new faces of each respective WWE brand in the middle of last decade.

Batista had always been full of potential, but he was arguably the lowest of the four major players on the OVW Class of 2002 totem pole. In the latter part of 2004, however, The Animal got over huge, succeeding where Randy Orton had faltered with an organic revolt against Triple H that led him to win the 2005 Royal Rumble Match and defeat The Game for the World Heavyweight Championship in the main-event at *WrestleMania 21*. Cena was a controversial runner-up in the Rumble that year (after the only overtime in Rumble lore) and won the WWE Title from JBL on the same night that Batista became champion, sparking the competition for the new #1 overall star. Despite WWE's decision to move Cena to Raw and Batista to Smackdown, 2005 ended as Batista's year.

With The Animal sidelined by injury in 2006, Cena aggressively wrestled firm control at the top of the hierarchy away from him. Upon his return, Batista did well to make up for lost time and, by *WrestleMania 23*, was right back in the mix; he was set to defend the World Heavyweight Title against Undertaker in The Deadman's first championship opportunity at 'Mania in a decade, while Cena was tasked with defending the WWE Championship against Shawn Michaels. The main-event at WrestleMania being wrestling's Holy Grail and with Batista and Cena having taken out Triple H in consecutive 'Mania show-closers, it seemed that whichever one of them was given the nod to go on last at *WrestleMania 23* would simultaneously be acknowledged from that point forward as "The Man" in WWE. Sure enough, it was Cena, to the public dismay of Batista.

Cena had a career-year in 2007, rounding fully into WWE's franchise player, but Batista also had a career-year in 2007, highlighted particularly by what many considered his show-stealing effort at *WrestleMania 23* that was fueled by his disgruntlement with the main-event slight. Though Cena never looked back and Batista never caught up, it could certainly be said that The Animal was the second biggest star in the industry between 2005 and 2010. The fact that they had such limited interaction during that time only heightened the interest in seeing them fight each other when they prominently wrestled for the first time at *Summerslam '08* and then again in the spring of 2010, most notably at *WrestleMania XXVI*.

All of the aforementioned behind-the-scenes history between them was cited in the on-screen build-up, giving the matches themselves the aura of era-defining battles. Michael Cole mentioned on *Summerslam '08* commentary a poll on WWE.COM that revealed 73% of the fans thought Cena was the bigger star which, by that point, seemed about right. Batista winning their first bout so decisively – the only clean Cena loss at a major pay-per-view until 2012 – combined with his top rope leg drop-counter into a powerbomb being credited with legitimately putting Cena out of action for three months gave The Animal a big shot in the arm, at least in theory.

An injury-plagued 2009 for Batista segued to an anticipated heel turn that led to some of the best character work of his career and sparked several tremendously authentic interviews when his rematch with Cena was made official for March 2010. Between The Animal's promos and WWE's dominant booking for him, they created a chasm favoring Batista so wide on camera that it helped off-set the giant gap separating Cena from Batista in the true pecking order, but the *WrestleMania XXVI* match saw Cena defeat Batista to win the WWE Championship and confirm on camera what had long since been decided in their real life rivalry.

Cena vs. Batista should be remembered as an engaging story born from the true competition started between them as rookies in Ohio Valley Wrestling which culminated in several very good matches and should be regarded as proof that the dynamic of seeing the two top stars of an era go at it has unmistakable appeal that instantly raises the stakes of a match, rivalry, or story, especially when such titanic clashes are reserved for the WrestleMania and Summerslam stages. Delivering, then, something on the 20'X20' canvas worthy of universal praise yields the reward of "all-time classic" status; Batista vs. Cena did not deliver to that extent, but the fact that it is not a stretch to call their clashes the Hogan vs. Savage equivalents of the original Brand Extension Era gives credence to their rivalry's composite ranking inside the Top 100 and edges it just ahead of Hogan vs. Orndorff.

#94
The 2008 Royal Rumble Match
January 27, 2008

Top 5 All-Time Royal Rumble Match / Top 10 All-Time at Royal Rumble / Top 10 Match in 2008

Recall from the Honorable Mention of the 1990 Royal Rumble the keys to the stipulation's success, the most important on the list being an Ironman, memorable performances from top-tier stars, a finish that sets the tone for the Road to WrestleMania, spotlight eliminations for mid-carders, and what can best be described as "Royal Rumble Moments." The 2008 Royal Rumble Match gets a check mark in each box and also features awesome financial figures (Top 10 all-time Rumble pay-per-view buys, 3rd all-time Rumble attendance) and arguably the best live audience of any of the contenders in Rumble lore thanks to the faithful in Madison Square Garden.

Of course, it was the MSG crowd's reaction to one particular happening that stands out as the '08 Rumble's most famous achievement and one of the January Classic's all-time greatest moments: John Cena's early return from injury as the final entrant. Enthusiasts may have become immune to his real life recuperative powers over the years since there have been so many instances of Cena shattering common rehabilitative timetables but, 2008 being the first example, it remains a spine-tingling, mind-blowing occurrence to watch in replay as the roof nearly blows off of the "World's Most Famous Arena" when the fans finish their customary countdown to #30 and the opening riffs of "My Time Is Now" hit the speakers. Everyone is going bananas, unanimously thrilled to see him if but only for a few fleeting minutes.

"It is difficult to keep shock values intact these days with rumors and the leaking of information circulating on a daily basis, [but] the reaction from the New York City fans confirmed that the element of surprise was very much alive," Sean Coyle wrote for ESPN in 2017.

On the night of, you almost could not help but think, until Cena lifted his head up to reveal that oh-so-recognizable mug, that some newbie heel was playing a trick to get heat (that would have been a great career move for Mr. Kennedy). That Cena would go onto win the Rumble after his shocking return immediately boosted the '08 Rumble historically like the '90 Rumble was so positively influenced by the memory it provided of Hogan and Warrior's initial face-off.

The remainder of the match was certainly not without its moments as well. Undertaker and Shawn Michaels entered at #1 and #2, respectively, starting the '08 Rumble Match where the '07 Rumble Match gloriously finished and further previewing their eventual WrestleMania series with a plethora of engrossing early elimination teases. Batista and Undertaker built off of their 2007-spanning epic. Later on, Triple H and Mick Foley, wearing a Cactus Jack shirt, renewed their rivalry made famous in a Street Fight in MSG at *Royal Rumble 2000*. Two others intertwined in MSG lore, Roddy Piper and Jimmy Snuka, were back-to-back surprise entrants and all of the wrestlers in the ring paid their respects by stopping and watching them add a nostalgic flair to the proceedings; it was, as Jim Ross aptly put it on commentary, "As if time stood still for a few moments." Lest we not forget the impactful final trio of Cena, Trips, and Batista – whose WrestleMania main-event exploits ushered WWE into a new era, post-Attitude – was stronger than most final fours.

The Ironman role was basically split between four different wrestlers who each clocked in between 30 and 37 minutes – Batista, Michaels, Taker, and John Morrison, who turned in a highly entertaining effort that included more near-eliminations than any other superstar involved. Jo Mo, along with CM Punk and Cody Rhodes, were the stars on the rise given the time to showcase themselves in the year's second most important match outside of the WrestleMania main-event. Rhodes was solidly unspectacular in his Rumble debut but had one particularly engaging sequence with Kennedy; and Punk, it could be said, played a role similar to Michaels in 1992, even having a brief scrap with The Heartbreak Kid reminiscent of HBK mixing it up with Flair sixteen years prior. Not to be outdone, Carlito added a visually cool sequence and, despite a strikingly brief appearance, Shelton Benjamin displayed his amazing athleticism both in his leap from the canvas to the top turnbuckle and his back flip over the ropes elimination-of-the-night courtesy of Sweet Chin Music. There was even comedy provided by Santino and Hornswoggle.

Royal Rumble '08 offered a little bit of everything that makes the annual over-the-top rope Battle Royal special, culminating in a thoroughly engaging climactic match-within-the-match between Cena and Triple H that pit two of the Top 10 stars of the WrestleMania Era against each other once more and popularized the trend of pointing to the hanging WrestleMania sign to heighten the importance of the occasion.

The Royal Rumble Match has produced a dynamic body of work in its storied history, with but a few specific iterations universally earning spots among Top 5 fan lists. The 2008 version's reception would never be mistaken for 1992, but in a thorough evaluation of each of the top candidates for the best Rumble match ever, it holds up well enough to make the Top 100 as one of the greatest examples of WWE's preeminent gimmick match.

#93
Eddie Guerrero vs. Brock Lesnar
WWE Championship
No Way Out
February 15, 2004
Top 10 Match in 2004

Eddie Guerrero's victory over Brock Lesnar to win the WWE Championship is a moment that transcends time and rankings, resonating as one of the most powerful title wins of the WrestleMania Era because of how it connected with wrestlers and fans alike. Fellow pros around the globe saw a small Latino star become nearly as popular as anyone from Steve Austin's day and were given tangible proof that anything is possible. Fans and wrestling media members, often accused of not being able to understand the inner workings of the business because most of them were never in it, viewed the Guerrero triumph as a triumph of their own. It was the audience, not the higher-ups of WWE, who recognized the full potential of Eddie's talents and who made Eddie the most over man in the business, much as they had Austin before him, proving again the old adage that one need not have been a horse to be a jockey.

Truth be told, the primary reason for this match to be included in the Top 100 was the gravity of its finishing touches: the Frog Splash, the 1-2-3, and the post-match celebration. The thirty prior minutes leading up to the climax were often very slow moving and were certainly not flawlessly executed. The story of a soon-to-be milestone World Champion leaping his final hurdle was so palpable, however, that much of the presentation that a critic can find lacking about the match was usurped by the emotional weight of Guerrero's achievement.

WWE has been known throughout the last thirty years as "The Land of Giants" and with that moniker has come certain stereotypes that needed to be defeated by pioneers such as Bret

Hart, Shawn Michaels, and Chris Jericho – smaller men without the hulking physiques of the Hogans and Orndorffs or the size and innate presence of the Andres and Undertakers. Yet with each barrier broken, another sprung up to replace it. Guerrero was the first to answer affirmatively the question about Vince McMahon's global sports entertainment empire, "If three smaller, good looking white guys can be the World Champion in WWE, can a small Latino guy without a Hollywood face be the World Champion in WWE?"

Creative deployment of the feud on television gave the inherent saga of the long-time veteran Mexican-American and former Cruiserweight Champion ascending all the way to Heavyweight Champion status a boost as well. "I've been here before...backed into a corner; another huge obstacle...time to make a choice" were the storyline-appropriate words of Eddie Guerrero in the opening montage of *No Way Out '04* and one would be extremely fortunate not to be able to relate to them. Struggle and strife are part of the fabric of a well-rounded individual and the 20'X20' wrestling canvas is as compelling a place for dramas about such themes to be acted out as Broadway or big screen theaters.

For his part, Lesnar played the monster as well as could have been expected; he might very well have tapped into some very real frustration both about being the kind of prototype star to have to step aside in favor of the slighter-statured Latino and about his mounting desire to end the rugged travel schedule typical of a star like him. More than any previous main-event in two years full of headlining matches, Lesnar let loose his emotions while still professionally conducting his brand of physical domination. His raw power against a man as light as Guerrero was on full display, a vertical suplex on one leg perhaps the most impressive representation. Also, Suplex City may have been founded that night. Ten suplexes of a variety of types were employed by the future Mixed Martial Arts Heavyweight Champion. He had been known to use them before, but never to that extent on any prior occasion.

In hindsight, the match was all about Guerrero. The Lesnar vs. Goldberg set-up should remain happily tucked away in the subconscious with similarly awful experiences such as hospital stays and awkward coital exploits. The exhaustive half-hour affair, about as old school as they came in that era, was a prime example of Eddie's in-ring versatility. Though a reasonably innovative athlete capable of high-flying, he was also one of history's most underrated technical wrestlers. It would have logically taken equal parts of both skill-sets to topple a champion of Lesnar's caliber, and Eddie's transitions between the two styles during the bout were accordingly balanced. Aerial assaults, amateur take downs, strength-dependent grapples, and submissions were all utilized with a tinge of desperation that well sold the stakes and made the triumph that much sweeter in the end.

"What a journey for Eddie Guerrero," said Michael Cole at the conclusion of the match.

Indeed.

#92
Harley Race vs. Ric Flair
Steel Cage Match
NWA World Heavyweight Championship
Starrcade
November 24, 1983

Top 10 All-Time at Starrcade / Top 5 Match in 1983

It was the one that started it all.

On Thanksgiving night in 1983, the National Wrestling Alliance, spearheaded by Jim Crockett Promotions, presented professional wrestling's first Super Bowl – *Starrcade '83* – headlined by the World Heavyweight Championship match between reigning titleholder, Harley Race, and the man he beat to win the gold for the 7th time, the soon-to-be incomparable "Nature Boy" Ric Flair. It was the first main-event of the first modern super card; it was the swan song in the NWA for arguably the wrestler of the 1970s; it was the torch-passing moment that basically *made* Flair and unofficially crowned Naitch arguably the wrestler of the 1980s.

The Nature Boy played such an integral role in wrestling during the transitional years from the old traditional territory model to Vince McMahon's monopolistic vision of sports entertainment. As wide as the gap between the WWF and Flair's NWA truly was during the prelude to the Monday Night War from a financial point-of-view, Flair exuded his influence in ways that went beyond the fiscal bottom line. Without him, one must ponder what wrestling today would even look like.

If pro wrestling is about three primary things – the talk, the walk, and the look – then Hulk Hogan taught the post-McMahon takeover world of sports entertainment how a superstar should appear while Ric Flair taught it how a superstar should both act and perform between the ropes. Flair's mastery of the microphone, for example, to this day has few peers; his wrestling style, while remaining grounded in basic principles instilled by the likes of Race, Jack Briscoe, and Lou Thesz, was also more athletic and more entertaining, setting a new in-ring standard. Just look at the number of Top 10 all-time caliber stars who claim Flair as their idol and inspiration and who now serve as the idols and inspirations for the generations that will hope to supplant them; Flair's was a gift that has kept on giving.

Watched while studying all the matches that followed it in the last thirty-plus years, certain aspects of Race vs. Flair's presentation still hold up incredibly well against its peers: the engaging commentary primarily from Gordon Solie, who made clear why the inarguable greatest play-by-play man of the last three decades – Jim Ross – has always spoken so highly of him; the savvy and psychological awareness of Harley Race; and the exuberance, passion, and skill of The Nature Boy. Unfortunately, it watches in replay as fairly slow and mostly dull as compared to matches that took place even two years later. Much of the blame, however, falls not on Race and Flair, but on the flow-killing worst refereeing job of all-time by Gene Kiniski, whose constant grabbing at the wrestlers under the guise of strict adherence to the rules seemed a blatant attempt to gain back the spotlight from his own NWA Championship days.

Nevertheless, it will be a long time before modern matches like #93 can cement a reputation on par with it.

For being authentically historic, Race vs. Flair remains one of the most significant bouts of the WrestleMania Era. As Flair himself has stated, the vote of confidence he received from the NWA and from Harley Race in winning the title for the second of his record-sixteen times at *Starrcade '83* meant the world to him and fueled the most famous stretch of his incomparable career. Flair wanted and needed to carry the company as World Champion to be at his best; him without the gold in the first decade of the WrestleMania Era was like watching Michael Jordan in a Wizards uniform. It was for only 170 days between

Starrcade '83 and *Great American Bash '90* that the NWA Title was around the waist of someone besides Ric Flair. Beating Race unequivocally made him "The Man" and was the catalyst for all that followed: the development of The Four Horsemen and the rivalries with Dusty Rhodes, Lex Luger, Ricky Steamboat, and Terry Funk that largely built his reputation as one of the top two or three wrestlers ever.

#91
CM Punk vs. Chris Jericho
WWE Championship
WrestleMania XXVIII to Extreme Rules 2012
Top 30 All-Time at WrestleMania / Top 5 Match in 2012

While certainly not on the level of Flair vs. Race, "historic" would also be an appropriate description for the rivalry between CM Punk and Chris Jericho in 2012. The WWE Championship feud that peaked at the most purchased wrestling pay-per-view of all-time is quite underrated, its well-rounded story offering two different hooks to capture the imaginations of fans. Though the critical ceiling of the matches at *WrestleMania XXVIII* and *Extreme Rules 2012* has been a source of division in the analytical community, there should be no denial of the quality on display when Punk clashed with Y2J.

All the while, it remains a fringe pick for the Top 100 because of how easily it manages to be overshadowed. Punk and Jericho fought an uphill battle for attention throughout 'Mania season in 2012, competing with Rock vs. Cena and Taker vs. HHH; the reaction from the audience in Miami was muted compared to their more epic peers; in Punk's hometown a month later, they were lost in the shuffle again, on a card that featured the cathartic match between Bryan and Sheamus that many had felt robbed of seeing at consecutive 'Manias, as well as Brock Lesnar's first WWE match in eight years. Then, judged first against Top 50 and later against Top 75-caliber rivalries, Punk vs. Y2J did not hold up particularly well.

Oddly, it may have benefited from a little less depth in its storyline offering. There was a simple concept in place that took the match from idea to reality: CM Punk had begun proclaiming himself "The Best in the World" in 2011 and Jericho, who had referred to himself as "The Best in the World at What I Do" in 2009 and 2010 but who was on hiatus for the third time in his career, came back to reclaim the moniker. Punk was in the midst of his finest two year stretch and really was the best in the game at that time; Jericho really had been the best in the game for about two years himself, so his return had enthusiasts, especially wrestling purists, in a frenzy at the prospect of a match between him and Punk at *'Mania XXVIII*. Their first verbal altercation, highlighted by the outstanding line from Punk "I was here, on top, swimming with sharks while you were dancing with stars," served only to escalate the anticipation.

To add an element of deeply personal animosity, the original plan according to Jericho's third book was to have Y2J legitimately tattoo his initials on Punk's heavily-tattooed body, but the innovative touch that may have vaulted this angle to more legendary reverence was nixed by Vince McMahon in favor of Jericho lambasting Punk's family history of substance abuse, which led to a last-second stipulation addition that changed the complexion of the match's presentation away from a purely catch-as-catch-can classic. Jericho had originally envisioned it a modern day Steamboat vs. Savage, but "Punk loses the title if disqualified" added a timid dynamic to the first quarter of the match.

The storytelling was excellent, with Jericho playing his evil role very well via two superbly delivered audible barbs as well as his physical actions. When it shifted into more of the style that many had expected from it, several of the more intricate sequences were thrilling to witness, most notably the submission-laced finish that ranks far higher than #91 as compared to its contemporaries. However, it could at least be argued that the match would have been better if it had stuck to a crystal clear vision of what it wanted to be from the opening bell and that it was a less is more approach to the back story that drove its in-ring narrative away from being mentioned about two hundred pages from now.

With its exuberant audience and unambiguous intent, the Chicago Street Fight at *Extreme Rules* was considered in some circles a substantial upgrade from *'Mania*. It was a version of its gimmick from the old school, its understated use of furniture and intelligently deployed ring psychology perhaps its greatest hallmarks. Much like its 'Mania predecessor, the Jericho-Punk rematch watches as highly skilled action with a story that, for some, limits the overall effectiveness of the presentation but that, for others, could represent the rivalry's term of endearment.

After much debate, it settles here as a series of matches boosted slightly by its WrestleMania status, greater than other contenders on the fringe but not great enough to move ahead of the 10th percentile of the greatest ever. Punk and Jericho combine for twelve entries in this book and, though this match clearly belongs in the Top 100, the rest of their all-time caliber body of work just as clearly ranks ahead of it.

#90
Bret Hart Becomes King of the Ring
King of the Ring
June 13, 1993
Top 5 Match in 1993

One night stories that span multiple matches are difficult to rank against their historical peers, but they are an awful lot of fun and, in the case of Bret Hart's treble to win the first King of the Ring tournament broadcast on pay-per-view, they can become the source of something truly special. The Hitman's incredible night, defeating three of the Top 50 superstars of the WrestleMania Era in Razor Ramon, Mr. Perfect, and Bam Bam Bigelow, deservedly cracks the countdown on account of his uncanny ability to tell a story on the 20'x20' canvas; nobody in modern pro wrestling lore has ever equaled the achievement of having a trio of matches so distinctly impressive on the same night.

Bret's opening round match was with the incomparable Razor (Scott Hall), against whom he had defended the WWF Championship at that year's *Royal Rumble* in an underrated January Classic gem. It would have been difficult for the tournament to begin on a more exciting note, both in terms of Hart having to overcome the challenge of a fast-rising star in the midst of a breakout rookie campaign who had already taken him to the limit before and in terms of the top notch in-ring quality on display; it was among the finest 10-minute bouts ever wrestled.

One of the amazing things about The Hitman was how seamlessly he developed chemistry with almost every opponent, but the fluidity and especially the creativity that he brought to the ring were often more pronounced against larger wrestlers, especially ones who could move around the ring as swiftly as Ramon or Bigelow. In Razor, Bret found an equally motivated performer prone to maximizing the potential of whatever he was

71

given, and they unequivocally succeeded in providing Hart a highly competitive first chapter in his night-long Ironman story.

As a former WWF Champion who had just main-evented *WrestleMania IX* a couple of months prior, The Excellence of Execution may not have fit the description, to borrow a term from NCAA March Madness, of a "Cinderella," but the injuries that he accumulated from round-to-round – and, most importantly, the manner in which he physically sold them – made him into an underdog. Razor targeted his hand in an attempt to make it more difficult for Hart to apply his go-to Sharpshooter submission (Bret won via pinfall after countering Ramon's superplex). The Hitman's Semi-Final opponent, Mr. Perfect, exploited the hand and added further injury as an insult, catapulting Hart from the ring apron awkwardly, with Bret hurting his knee on the fall.

Recall that Mr. Perfect had been defeated by Bret at Madison Square Garden to win the Intercontinental Championship in 1991; he made mention of the loss in a face-to-face backstage interview just before the King of the Ring Semi-Final, claiming that he "owed him one and he was coming to collect" and setting the tone for their frenetic return match. Mutual respect quickly dissipated as Perfect attempted quite desperately to prove that he could beat The Hitman, mirroring through his character a genuine desire that Curt Hennig had in real life to show Vince McMahon how good he still was after returning from the back injury that prompted his retirement, post-*Summerslam '91*; as masterfully as Bret's underdog story began coalescing during the match, it was Mr. Perfect who offered arguably his career-best performance. Though by that point a respected, very popular veteran wrestler, Perfect slowly devolved throughout the match into his more traditionally antagonistic role, taking short-cuts and showing ample villainous attitude; his exploits added a layer of emotional depth to the entire tournament presentation.

If pro wrestling is a combat-simulating dance, it could be said that Bret Hart had more natural chemistry with Mr. Perfect than he had with any other dance-partner; they were just one of those pairs that connected so well, flowing from sequence to sequence like Steamboat and Flair in the 1980s, Rock and Jericho in the early 2000s, and Ambrose and Rollins more recently. In his autobiography, The Hitman compared his timing with Perfect to that of Ginger Rogers and Fred Astaire.

It was an awesome encounter, one of the best of the 1990s. In the end, Mr. Perfect again came up short (though Curt Hennig damn sure accomplished his real life goal); his roll-up pin-attempt was thwarted in mid-count when Hart managed to get Perfect's shoulders down for the one-two-three. It would be negligent not to mention that Perfect begrudgingly shook Hart's hand afterward, the finishing touch to a wonderfully acted sub-plot on the night.

Bret's Round 1 hand injury had been exacerbated in the Semis, but was overcome by his savvy mat skills; his adrenaline, meanwhile, had been sufficient to overcome the hip and leg contusions he suffered midway through the match against Perfect. As The Excellence of Execution noticeably limped to the ring to face a well-rested Bam Bam in the Finals, it became crystal clear that Bret was in for the fight of his life. Bigelow had lucked out with a bye through the Semis thanks to a double count-out in the Tatanka-Lex Luger match, as if outweighing Hart by well over one hundred pounds, his rough-around-the-edges look and demeanor, and his other-worldly talent were not intimidating enough for a wounded Hitman and the legion of supporters rooting on his, by that point, full-blown Cinderella tale. Luna Vachon, Bigelow's associate, even blasted Hart in the back with a steel chair while the referee was distracted. There was no way that Bret could win...

Bam Bam, one of the most agile super-heavyweights ever, destroyed Bret, pinning him following his patented diving headbutt from off the top rope (and Luna's chair shot). It seemed a depressing end to a valiant effort from The Hitman. However, a ray of hope came in the form of senior official, Earl

Hebner (how ironic), waving the result and restarting the match. A captivating final few minutes saw Bret make a glorious comeback, but he had sold being inches from the jaws of defeat so well that it did not seem believable that he could muster up enough offense to win until his Victory Roll had pinned Bigelow and his theme song was playing. To this day, Bret's win is cathartic to anyone who commits the time to watching the entire story play out.

King of the Ring '93 is Bret Hart's borderline forgotten classic, its status shrouded by the now-defunct tournament's fading memory and The Hitman's other extraordinary contributions to the WrestleMania Era. Yet, wrestling a quintessential hot opener / mid-card show-enhancer, a feature length catch-as-catch-can masterpiece, and a great David vs. Goliath match all in the same night is a feat to be all-time-level celebrated and it would be historically irresponsible not to ensure that such excellence is acknowledged with the highest of praise.

#89
Kane vs. The Undertaker
WrestleMania XIV to Unforgiven: In Your House
Top 10 Match in 1998

One area of sports entertainment yet to be discussed, thus far, has been the supernatural-stylings most prominently associated with The Undertaker. Theatrics took on a new meaning as The Phenom's character evolved in the 1990s, as television production teamed with pyrotechnic expertise to create scenes filled with lightning bolts and flames. The WWF spun those occurrences as "powers" possessed by The Deadman.

Love it or hate it in principle, such over-the-top visuals do indeed have an audience, despite the fine line that they walk in testing the limits of our ability to suspend disbelief for the sake of the show. Undertaker, the greatest gimmick performer of all-time, characterized that fine line; he always so immersed himself in his persona that it made it easier for us to buy into it, even as time went on and the wrestling world got smarter. Kane has been similarly successful since he burst onto the scene as The Big Red Machine after the man behind the mask, Glen Jacobs, had failed to find his footing with two lame-duck previous gimmicks. Their characters have been afforded a rare level of acceptance in the mainstream world due to their 25+ years of commitment and the respect that they have earned.

Back in 1997, Taker was still very much in the early stages of forging his legacy when Kane debuted at the end of the first-ever Hell in a Cell Match between The Deadman and Shawn Michaels. Before he had ever ripped the door off of Satan's Structure, Kane's story arc was one that bordered on the ridiculous – he was Undertaker's presumed-dead brother, disfigured by the same fire that had killed their parents, and Paul Bearer pegged Taker the secret arsonist.

However, it is important to remember that the tale they wove between *In Your House: Badd Blood* and *WrestleMania XIV*, day-time TV-inspired as its back-story may have been, was intricate and thorough; it was just covered in a strong layer of overt theatricality (Taker locked in a casket on fire, the burning effigy of Kane, lightning bolts shooting onto the stage and the announce table, a WWF employee lit on fire in the magical melee, etc.). Kane wanted to fight Taker because of their past, but The Phenom refused because they were brothers; Kane lured Taker into thinking he had put the past behind him, only to betray him, prompting Taker to reluctantly decide to fight. It worked because the three principle personas involved (Taker, Kane, and Bearer) were fantastic in their roles.

Paul Bearer deserves to be singled out for a moment. He was one of WWE's best ever character-actors and he evolved at just the right time from *Are You Afraid Of The Dark*-type creepy in the early 1990s to a few notches below *American Horror Story*-level scary for the Attitude Era. Kane quickly proved himself as Bearer's mute instrument of destruction, crystal clear in his purpose without ever saying a word. His little sideways nods of the head and overall body language were monster-movie good; plus, as he proved in his matches with Taker, he was an incredible athlete who would go onto become one of the Top 5 big men in history. He really was a lot like his storyline-older brother. For The Deadman, the entire situation was the best chance he had been given to that point to show range in his emotions.

Their matches throughout 1998, but particularly at *WrestleMania* and *Unforgiven: In Your House*, were prototypes for modern big man brawls. There will always be an expectation when seeing Godzilla vs. King Kong and, in the WrestleMania Era, there has maybe been no better example than Kane vs. Taker. They slugged it out as two titans would be expected to when clashing, with Kane becoming the first to ever kick out of a Tombstone Piledriver (he actually did it twice in the same match) and The Phenom enduring beatings the likes of which he had never received. The agility on display, however, was incredible for men of their size. Taker's first two dives over the top rope to the outside came during these matches, the first sending him crashing through the announce table and the second highlighted by the image of flames underneath him during the first-ever Inferno Match; it sort of became his special spot that he would only use at 'Mania or other occasions of that magnitude. While their matches alone were certainly not the primary reason for their Top 100 status, they were indeed noteworthy.

A legacy is something that each match, rivalry, or story must leave to be considered among the pantheon; Undertaker vs. Kane qualifies for many reasons. It produced some of the best big man matches of all-time; the extent of its use of theatricality was novel and arguably more memorable to those who watched it than any Batista-Cena or Punk-Jericho match; and perhaps most of all, it was the launching pad for Kane's Hall of Fame career and one of the greatest sagas in the Hall of Fame careers of Taker and Bearer.

#88
Sgt. Slaughter vs. The Iron Sheik
Madison Square Garden Series
April to June 1984
Match of the Year in 1984

Allow your mind figurative use of *Back to the Future's* DeLorean time machine and travel mentally back to 1984. It has been forty years of major conflicts with a near constant threat of nuclear war. The stream of information is still very slow moving, the personal computer seldom purchased and the internet years away from popularization; the things that connect us worldwide are limited and mostly destructive, namely war. Patriotism is reaching its modern peak in the United States of America; Lee Greenwood's "God Bless The USA" hits #7 on the Billboard chart in May, highlighting the number of people so very "proud to be an American."

In the World Wrestling Federation, the foundation for the WrestleMania Era is being laid. Hulk Hogan has just become World Heavyweight Champion at the expense of The Iron Sheik, who had taken the title off of "The All-American Boy" Bob Backlund. With the hostage crisis of 1980 not far from public consciousness, the frustrated and fuming Iranian Sheik curses the United States, only to be interrupted by the Marine Corp hymn and legitimate former USMC drill sergeant, Sgt. Slaughter.

Coming back to present day, it may be hard for you to comprehend why the ensuing rivalry between Sarge and Sheik deserves a spot in the Top 100 without properly contextualizing the era in which it took place. *Pro Wrestling Illustrated* was a big deal back then and it named Sgt. Slaughter the most inspirational wrestler of 1984 ahead of Hogan, Backlund, Dusty Rhodes, and the Von Erichs. Why? Because he stood up for America, damn it, and it was just that simple.

The emotional fervor that Sheik vs. Slaughter created was so different than anything we would see today or in any recent time. Of course, the matches necessary to earn that kind of reaction from fans in 1984 would be considered by many "only pretty good" by today's standards while, to be fair, the truly best in-ring performances of the 1980s that are ranked ahead of this have, in most cases, held up very well to modern standards. Nevertheless, it is difficult to equal what Sheik and Slaughter were able to do; their rivalry remains (and probably always will) the shining example of the role patriotism played during the early part of the WrestleMania Era.

Consider, for a moment, that in the first match of their famous Madison Square Garden series in the spring of 1984, the crowd willingly accepted Slaughter repeatedly spitting on The Sheik, raking the Iranian's back with his finger nails, and taking off his combat boot to use as a weapon (which ultimately got him disqualified) and responded to it with heroic praise. Sheik even prayed to Allah, begging off further punishment from Sarge in the process and, when Slaughter kept on punching his lights out, the crowd roared on. Even though he lost, it was clearly satisfying to the people in NYC that they got to see The Iron Sheik get his butt kicked by a proud American.

It was uncomplicated, unadulterated pride in one's nationality that drove the Sheik-Slaughter feud to the heights that it reached. After the second match in the MSG trilogy, Sarge even led the crowd in a hearty rendition of the Pledge of Allegiance despite a non-finish that again denied him the elusive victory for his country. It is hard to imagine how this match would be received if it took place today; it might be easier to envision a heel doing the Pledge in satirical fashion to massive heat than a red, white, and blue clad grappler reciting it in hopes of resonating with the people, and it is a given that the no-contest decision at the end of a very basically-offensed affair – though it was a master class in selling and building to a (very bloody) babyface comeback – would have been hyper-analyzed by a more critical fanbase.

Certainly, another era-specific trait of the mid-1980s was patience. In a world unaccustomed to the level of instant gratification that we now associate with the expression, stories in wrestling could take far more time to reach a climax. Disqualifications and no-contests were booking patterns for ending matches that finally led to bigger matches during which the score would conclusively be settled. The "Boot Camp" Match that concluded the MSG series between Slaughter and Sheik was one of the most famous payoffs of the decade; you will struggle to name one that further invested its audience, which was 100% locked in to the story and which felt its own sense of victory when Sarge got the cathartic win.

That Hasbro would acknowledge Slaughter's status as an American hero by making him a character who appeared both in their action figure line as well as their animated TV series, *G.I. Joe*, should tell you all that you need to know about what his rivalry with Iron Sheik meant to his perception as a patriot, especially considering that he was out of the WWF before *WrestleMania*.

#87
Edge vs. Mick Foley
Hardcore Match
WrestleMania 22
April 1, 2006

Top 40 All-Time at WrestleMania / Top 5 Match in 2006

"Stealing the show" is a concept to be discussed numerous times throughout this book. It is the phrase in professional wrestling vernacular that describes the phenomenon of a match rising to a level beyond its place on the card.

Our first exploration of show-stealing takes us back to 2006. Edge cashed in the very first Money in the Bank contract in early January, winning the WWE Championship from John Cena. Monday Night Raw ratings went up immediately and consistently over the course of his title reign, suggesting that WWE had found a hot new commodity. However, the powers-that-be could not find reason enough to change their original WrestleMania plans and had Edge drop the strap back to Cena after just three weeks as champion.

Edge was not happy, which brings us to the first of two primary motivations that lead to a match stealing the show: feeling slighted.

"He felt like he should be in the main-event; that he'd earned the right to be in the main-event," Edge's best friend and long-time tag team partner, Christian, has previously noted. "And if he wasn't going to be in the main-event, he was going out there with Mick Foley and he was going to steal the show."

Mick Foley had pretty much done it all by 2006. The only box left to check on his career bucket list was having a defining match at WrestleMania. It seems odd, reflecting back, to think that a superstar of his caliber had never had a classic on the grandest stage. Foley, though, was the type that often put together his 4-5 star work in the months leading up to or immediately following WrestleMania, helping to get someone else ready for their ultimate moment or aiding in the process of confirming someone else's WrestleMania-earned status. So, for the vast majority of his career leading into his semi-retirement, Foley had become a legendary figure and a future Hall of Famer without the requisite "WrestleMania Moment"; Foley, himself, has said, "You can't really be a legend unless you've had [it]."

Foley's opportunity to work *WrestleMania 22* with Edge brings us to the second of the two primary motivations for show-stealing: having something to prove.

When combined, the chip that Edge had on his shoulder from not getting to main-event WrestleMania and the desire that Foley had to finally have a great match on the most important night in wrestling created a situation ripe for something special. It was written all over Edge's face throughout his battle with Foley how much he wanted to say with his performance, "To anyone who thought that I wasn't good enough or a big enough name to be in the marquee match at 'Mania, let me remind you of the lengths that I'll go to prove you wrong." Foley, meanwhile, lived up to his reputation as The Hardcore Legend, while also displaying a touch of cerebral ingenuity (i.e. wrapping himself in barbed wire hidden beneath a flannel shirt so that, when Speared by Edge, it would be The Rated R Superstar who suffered greater damage).

The choice to make Edge vs. Foley a Hardcore match was shrewd. It was an ideal environment for mixing their respective skill sets, which included as great a willingness to put their bodies through hell as anyone in wrestling lore. Characteristic of Foley, the level of violence witnessed in their match has not been repeated at WrestleMania since; they each purposefully bladed, but were also lacerated the hard way by barbed wire and thumb tacks. Even Lita, who played a key role in several important moments, had her mouth cut courtesy of a barbed wire-wrapped Mr. Socko.

It was also a gimmick that afforded them plenty of space for innovation within a sub-15-minute time-frame, a common run-time for non-main-events featuring major players over the last twenty-five years. The clear difference between Edge-Foley and Piper-Hart, Rollins-Orton, or Jericho-Christian was that the former was distinctly Hardcore. The memory of Edge Spearing Foley through a flaming table, for instance, has been burned into the minds of everyone who saw it and could not have happened without the stipulation; that is one of the greatest finishes ever in a wrestling match.

William Regal, a renowned talent evaluator and Top 90 star of the WrestleMania Era, called the match "an absolute masterpiece." Edge would later say, in reference to his message to WWE management about the place he could and perhaps should have occupied at *WrestleMania 22*, "That match in my mind helped prove my point."

Stealing the show has its benefits. It was no surprise when, after *'Mania 22*, Edge was immediately thrust back into the WWE Championship scene, where he would remain for the rest of his career en route to establishing himself as a future first-ballot Hall of Famer. It also got the WrestleMania monkey off of Mick Foley's back. 2006 provided, perhaps expectedly, the final in-ring moments of his WWE career; he had nothing left to prove after all.

#86
Seth Rollins vs. Triple H
Non-Sanctioned Match
WrestleMania 33
April 2, 2017
Top 35 All-Time at WrestleMania / Top 5 Match in 2017

At the heart of this entire process lies a question that digs beneath the surface of the criterion laid forth in the introduction: though it is obviously possible to compare most aspects of a match, rivalry, or story from one generation to another from a different generation, how can you compare a *modern* match, rivalry, or story to a match, rivalry, or story whose legacy is already etched within WWE mythology?

Punk vs. Lesnar, Austin vs. Hart, Edge vs. Cena, Andre vs. Hogan, and the like have all established the kind of "all-time" context born of eras passing and of the hours being spent by fans, pundits, and WWE itself talking through the short and long-term ramifications of each situation. The closer you get to present day, the harder it becomes to watch, for example, Triple H vs. Seth Rollins at *WrestleMania 33* and attempt to place it amongst history; that difficulty is in combination with some of the other unique challenges – an increasingly critical audience, a far too scripted product, a promotion that largely reserves the grandest stage for top stars of the past, etc. – that modern performers face in creating the kind of memories that did their forebears.

Make no mistake about it; The Architect vs. The King of Kings had all the makings of an iconic clash between student and mentor. With Rollins, Triple H received a mulligan for solidly unspectacular battles at past WrestleManias against his former protégés from Evolution; with Triple H, Rollins earned his first opportunity at a feature-length performance at "The Show of Shows." Between them, there was oodles of history, behind-the-scenes in the fledgling Triple H-developed project that became

NXT and on-screen as leader and pupil in The Authority. An untimely injury to Rollins proved a blessing-in-disguise, adding a riveting arc in the finals months leading up to *WrestleMania 33*, which provided 75,000 fans, a gorgeous open-air setting, and (to that point) the largest combined audience ever to witness a "Showcase of the Immortals", helping to boost the Rollins vs. Triple H profile. In terms of fluid storytelling, psychology, selling, emotional twists and turns, intangible qualities like cool entrances, and a satisfying climax, it delivered.

All the while, a thorough evaluation designed to determine whether or not it was worthy of Top 100 inclusion – and, if so, how highly ranked it should be – has to reconcile the fact that a significant percentage of the more critical viewership did not even think Triple H vs. Rollins was better than Shane McMahon vs. AJ Styles (a fringe Honorable Mention) from the same show, citing a variety of things that WWE could have done better, such as The Architect's initially anemic shift in character to a protagonistic role and the less than liberal use of hardcore elements given the nature of the "Non-Sanctioned" stipulation. Even if, from bell-to-bell, it was as intelligently worked as any match this decade, its faults were as much in the hindsight-spotlight as its strengths.

Careful inspection of Triple H vs. Rollins in comparison to its historical peers revealed its rather obvious Top 100 candidacy – it is an absolute joy to watch on replay, full of the sorts of little things that separate great matches from those that are very good (i.e. Rollins masterfully favoring his knee without overselling for the bout's duration, Stephanie McMahon's muted but highly effective role on the outside, and the more subtle introduction of The Game's dreaded sledgehammer, among others). Reappraisal as the years pass will ultimately decide if it should move up or down the list, but gauging its ability to stand against the already-established of the greatest ever conversation is an exercise in trusting that, eventually, even more critical eyes will be able to judge it for what it was instead of what they had wanted it to be and, thus, draw similar conclusions about it as are drawn on these pages.

Vince McMahon certainly had a glowing opinion of it, telling Rollins afterwards, "Unbelievable performance...you'll be proud of that when you look back, I'll tell you that."

Historically, much of its reputation will likely hinge on what kind of legacy Seth Rollins is able to forge. His accomplishments already put him in an elite class of the WrestleMania Era but, as of 2017, he had yet to ascend to that rare echelon of talents who consistently resonated on a visceral level with the majority of the audience, despite clearly being one of the cornerstones of his generation and having had a longer tenure as a headliner than anyone else who debuted this decade. If his own legend continues to grow, so too will the story of his split from and feud with The Cerebral Assassin likely become legendary. Few sagas in WWE lore build for three years to a climax, much less an excellent match on the grandest stage; from The Shield vs. Evolution to when Rollins "bought in" / sold out to The Architect's emergence as "The Man" under Triple H's tutelage to Rollins getting injured leading to The Game's violent revocation of his endorsement to the WrestleMania-hosted vindication of "The King Slayer," Rollins vs. Triple H was a modern epic.

Maybe it never ends up possessing the wider resonance of even one of its more contemporary peers, like an AJ Styles vs. John Cena or Daniel Bryan vs. The Authority; however, Rollins vs. Triple H is an utterly outstanding match that should age incredibly well, perhaps even better than some of its peers that were celebrated to a greater extent in the moment.

<u>#85</u>

The Road Warriors vs. The Midnight Express
Scaffold Match
Starrcade: The Skywalkers
November 27, 1986
<u>Top 5 All-Time at Starrcade</u> / <u>Top 5 Match in 1986</u>

Starrcade '86 was the rare glory year edition of the NWA's leading annual super-card not to be carried by Ric Flair as the leading man, but that it still stands as one of the signature events in Starrcade history and one of the most financially lucrative in NWA lore is testament to the success of the night's primary selling point – the Sky-Walkers Match – and the participants, The Road Warriors (with Paul Ellering) and The Midnight Express (with Jim Cornette).

Whenever Jim Crockett Promotions and the National Wrestling Alliance come up in situations where they have to be compared to the WWF, the business of Starrcade vs. WrestleMania is at the forefront of the analysis, often rendering the achievements of WCW's precursor far inferior to Vince McMahon's top special event franchise. While that is a valid point, it does not accurately capture the strength of the JCP-led NWA brand or the drawing power of the top-tier members of the roster during that period.

Hawk and Animal, for instance, are considered the biggest box office attraction of any tag team in history and one of the top main-event-level draws of the 1980s. They achieved their standing by selling out crowds in Georgia Championship Wrestling at the end of the territory era, then in the American Wrestling Association at the tail of its long-term peak, and finally in the NWA. When they came to the WWF in 1990, they were far more akin to a Ric Flair signing than a Steiner Brothers-like acquisition, huge stars who would immediately be pushed to the top and elevate their division along the way. *Starrcade '86* was arguably their pinnacle achievement.

The concept was simple: take two of the best tag teams in the world and have them fight atop a platform twenty-some-odd-feet above the ring, with the winning team being the one that knocked its opponents back down to the ground. "I don't know too many guys who were happy about being on top of a three foot wide fireman's scaffold 30 feet above the ring," Animal said on The Road Warriors WWE-produced documentary. "We just wanted to do the match," remarked their Hall of Fame manager, Ellering. "Hawk broke his leg three days before the match, cut the cast off in the back before the match, and I taped it," continued Animal. Cornette, in a shoot interview, added, "I thought I was going to die. We were the crash test dummies, [but] we were the featured match at Starrcade."

It carried a palpable sense of danger that not even Hardy on a ladder or Foley on top of the Cell could equal. If you can put yourself in the mindset of a fan seeing something of its kind in 1986, long before death-defying leaps became commonplace in the 1990s through ECW and the WWF, you can better appreciate the feeling emitted by the Scaffold Match that one wrong move could have meant not just horrific injury, but paralysis or even death, a feeling only amplified by one of the rails breaking two minutes into the match, Bobby Eaton nearly suffering a terrible fall, and Cornette's eventual plummet to the canvas that legitimately shattered his knee. There is a discomfort to watching it, a feeling that something terrible happening seems more probable than possible, on par with watching a man try to corral a crocodile.

Aesthetically, it has been criticized in hindsight for being boring but, if properly contextualized, the 7-minutes of match time is carried initially by the payoff of first seeing them climb the structure, later by the rather swiftly-stimulated visual appeal of seeing them dangle from the bottom of the scaffold like a high-wire circus version of the monkey bars on a playground, and finally by the climactic falls to the mat by Eaton and Dennis Condrey. If you fail to gasp when The Midnight Express rapidly descend from such heights, then you have missed the point of the experience. Should you count acrophobia among your list of fears, the energetic release on initially viewing the finish is comparable to being on a roller-coaster when the ride has ended or getting to the bottom of a gigantic water-slide. Enthusiasts who favored The Road Warriors could have been expected to emote as much relief that it was over as they would elation for their heroes' victory.

It was an unbridled success. If you wonder why it ranks this low, it simply does not retain much in the way of rewatchability; much of its allure is gone after seeing it once. Those conversely wondering why it ranks so highly (or at all) should recognize its intangible qualities, such as its innovation and the classic involvement of Cornette, as well as the novelty of the gimmick in general; though not invented by Hawk, Animal, Condrey, and Eaton, the Scaffold Match was popularized at *Starrcade '86* and was the stimulus for maintaining the prior year's Starrcade attendance record of 30,000 across two venues and increasing the closed-circuit viewing audience by 57% over the peak of Flair vs. Dusty Rhodes in 1985.

#84
Chris Jericho vs. Triple H
Monday Night Raw April 17, 2000 to Fully Loaded 2000; WrestleMania X8 to Judgment Day 2002

#1 All-Time Last Man Standing Match / Top 5 Match in 2000

It is not often that a WrestleMania memory is detrimental to the case of a candidate for the Top 100 matches, rivalries, and stories in modern pro wrestling lore but, thanks to a horrible storyline leading up to a good but not great match at *WrestleMania X-8*, Chris Jericho vs. Triple H is a rivalry that has been historically hindered instead of enhanced in the minds of many by its association with "The Show of Shows."

Compared to its peers, its resume is very impressive and includes such accolades as one of the most underrated moments in Monday Night Raw history, a fantastic Last Man Standing Match (in only the second version ever for the gimmick), one of the Top 5 standard tag team matches of all-time (Jericho/Benoit vs. HHH/Austin), a WrestleMania main-event, and a very good Hell in a Cell Match.

In revisiting and researching HHH vs. Y2J, one of the resources stumbled upon for match-by-match guides of each of wrestling's top feuds was a website called CageMatch.Net. Among its various features is an opportunity for fans to vote using a 1 (worst) – 10 (best) scale on the numerous aspects that shape individual rivalries. The voting application seemed to pretty accurately reflect at least the perception that a lot of the greatest sports entertainment conflicts possess, specifically in terms of how they rate against each other. The soon-to-be covered Lesnar-Taker saga, for instance, scored an aggregate 8.5 (out of 10), suggesting that it was a rivalry held in high regard. Jericho vs. Triple H, on the other hand, holds an aggregate score of 4.75 (out of 10).

90

Two comments on the rivalry's overview page poignantly showcase the general sentiment about the multi-year Ayatollah-Game story. The first calls it, "A rivalry that frequently halted Jericho's momentum, and usually made him look like a complete chump. Especially grating in 2002. Poor Jericho didn't have much of chance; he got thrown into the meat-grinder." The other points out that, "The stuff between these two guys in 2000 was really awesome. Unfortunately, everything from that point on was mediocre at best. *Fully Loaded 2000* was the peak of the conflict between these two men."

One would think those statements to be generally agreed upon throughout the diehard wrestling fanbase. The bottom line is that they are both largely correct. Though Triple H vs. Jericho was indeed one of the very rare match-ups to have ever been the final bout at a WrestleMania and justifiably earns historical credit for it, their interaction in the ultimate pay-per-view main-event never lived up to the standard that they had set when they were engaging in show-stealers from the upper mid-card.

We live in a world that tends to dwell on the negatives, a fact that has notably extended into the generally held mindset among the most enthusiastic followers of WWE; it makes it unsurprising that the best part of the rivalry – beginning with Y2J's amazing one-night Cinderella story to win the WWF Championship on the April 17, 2000 edition of Raw – would take a backseat to Jericho's ill-fated swerve to later join forces with Stephanie McMahon during her falling out with Hunter on the Road to *'Mania X-8*. It also makes it unsurprising that their match at *Fully Loaded 2000*, one of the best matches in each of their careers, would be overshadowed by the historical footnote otherwise known as the main-event that should never have been, given that it took place on the same card as the iconic Hogan vs. Rock match.

Viewed with the glass half full, the Last Man Standing Match rates as one of the two greatest in the history of the gimmick. It was a marvelous example of just how incredible Triple H was in 2000/2001; he was relentless in his assault, a more vicious and sadistic version of his idol, Ric Flair, who would have been proud of the way that, contrary to the way Hunter basically mowed through Jericho two years later, HHH put over Y2J without losing to him and basically helped turn him into the star that he became. *Fully Loaded '00* was also the first opportunity in Jericho's career to exhibit the qualities that made him so much like Shawn Michaels in the ring – resilience mixed in with flamboyance and elite athletic skills that could shorten the gap in physical stature. Y2J is the Kobe to HBK's MJ. The match was brutal, it was smart, it was devoid of those incessantly unnecessary referee counts after moves like bodyslams and backdrops; it was a bonafide classic.

A mixed bag it was, but Jericho vs. Triple H deserves to be remembered more for what it did accomplish than what it did not.

#83
Edge and Rey Mysterio vs. Kurt Angle and Chris Benoit
WWE Tag Team Championship Tournament Finals
No Mercy
October 20, 2002

#1 All-Time Standard Tag Team Match / Top 5 Match in 2002

Tag team wrestling has had a tendency throughout its existence to play a secondary role to the singles divisions. One particularly noteworthy period from the NWA just referenced and another from WWE lore that will not be touched on until much later provide inarguable exceptions, but promotional focus has notoriously waxed and (mostly) waned for wrestlers striving for accolades of a team-oriented variety, especially in WWE. To produce something truly great on the 20'X20' canvas, wrestlers need opportunity; and most of the opportunities are afforded to singles title bouts and one-on-one grudge matches.

In both aforementioned instances exempt from the usual trend, special attraction status for tag teams during those periods was aided by gimmicked payoff matches. To get noticed through merely standard tag team wrestling has proven a far more daunting task historically. Among the Honorable Mentions, three excellent standard tag team matches were discussed from 1990, 1991 and 2001 respectively, each serving as examples of how duos could achieve a level of success on-par with the more creatively engrossing stories told by their singles counterparts. When it comes to pure tag team wrestling, though, the gold standard for the WrestleMania Era is Edge and Rey Mysterio vs. Chris Benoit and Kurt Angle from *No Mercy 2002*.

With Angle anchoring the match through a uniquely dynamic issue with Benoit, as well as on-going rivalries with both Edge and Mysterio that were already highlighted in this book, the story is strong enough to compare well to the iconic tag match from Raw in 2001. It also meets the innovative standards set by its peers from the early 1990s. Where it sets itself apart is in the unmatched athleticism of its combatants and its practically flawless execution; it also features a more coherent presentation and out-of-your-seat-worthy false finishes.

It should come as no surprise...

Mysterio, Edge, Angle, and Benoit were four members of what was known at that time as the "Smackdown Six," which earned its moniker on the merits of the incredible matches that they were having every week. When WWE was done tinkering with the rosters after the brand extension and had settled on some measure of consistency in the late summer of 2002, the Paul Heyman-led Thursday night show coalesced into one of the best in-ring periods of all-time, letting its wrestling do most of the talking and allowing its workers to build the brand's reputation through a nearly unrivaled consistency of performance. Edge and Angle were the mainstays, having torn down many a house from April to June right after the split; Mysterio made his WWE debut on Smackdown in July, the same month that Benoit joined the roster. Along with Los Guerreros (Eddie and Chavo), they formed the foundation of what became the newly christened WWE Tag Team Championship division exclusive to Smackdown; there have been more popular eras in tag team wrestling history, but one could certainly argue that there was never one better than theirs.

Any combination of the "Smackdown Six" in tag or singles competition was marvelous, but the piece de resistance in 2002 was the WWE Tag Team Tournament Finals. The amazing chemistry that they had all developed with each other, week-to-week, provided a launching pad off of which the duos painted the pure tag team wrestling masterpiece.

2002 was an historic year that produced two of WWE's all-time greatest matches. Rock and Hogan had their titanic clash for the ages at *WrestleMania X-8* and HBK made his comeback in glorious fashion at *Summerslam '02*, so how impressive is it that Edge and Mysterio vs. Benoit and Angle still ended up Match of the Year on a few notable ballots? In the context of this conversation, it seems fitting that the greatest tag team bout ever also finds itself sitting among the clouds as one of the Top 100 with other matches, stories, and rivalries that have earned mythical status.

#82
Sting vs. Vader
Great American Bash 1992 to SuperBrawl III
Top 10 Match in 1992 / Match of the Year in 1993

Due to the unheralded period during which it took place in World Championship Wrestling, the series of matches between Sting and Vader appear, on paper, to be difficult to compare to the finest offerings from The Nature Boy or to WrestleMania main-event feuds of sports entertainment lore. Compare them head-to-head, however, and Sting vs. Vader is really a Top 75-level rivalry held down by its association with what is typically regarded as an uncreative and dreadful economic time for WCW. Held to the standard of its peers, as it should be in a situation that calls for it like this one, Sting vs. Vader was neither an example of pro wrestling creative writing at its even above-average nor was it a box office attraction, but good Lord their matches tore the house down and their in-ring run together from the summer of 1992 through the winter of 1993 was one of the oft-forgotten highlights of WCW history, post-NWA heyday and pre-Monday Night War.

As of 1992, Sting was WCW's top star. In the sense that Ric Flair was the measuring stick of NWA/WCW, Sting was a highly atypical alpha male; he was the babyface champion of a predominantly heel-driven company, he was a good but not great wrestler, and he was a solid but not spectacular interview. If analogized with the *Rocky* film franchise, Sting was Balboa, the very popular but just as unlikely brand ambassador in his promotion, while Flair was Apollo Creed, the far more charismatic, skilled, and subsequently revered legend of the ring. By circumstance, Sting had managed, both on-screen and in reality, to supplant Flair as "The Man" in WCW and had gone onto enjoy success against a host of less-heralded talents.

Then, along came Big Van Vader, the mastodon who had mauled his competition abroad and was ready to come home to claim one of the top prizes in world, the WCW Championship. Like Clubber Lang did to Balboa in *Rocky III*, Vader annihilated Sting, bludgeoning and bruising him en route to winning Sting's title at *Great American Bash '92*. The Stinger had vanquished his seemingly greatest foe in Flair two years prior at the same event and, just when it seemed like the Sting Era was getting into a groove, Vader unceremoniously knocked him off the top of the mountain.

When they met again at *Starrcade '92*, Sting had clearly regained the eye of the tiger, summoning the strength and resolve necessary to go move-for-move with the super-heavyweight. It was the match that took Sting-Vader into the all-time discussion. Vader and Sting were each other's greatest opponents, never looking better in the roles they were best-suited to play as in-ring performers, with tons of big moves that looked ever so impressive due to their ideal size dichotomy and non-stop action that made their matches seem like those all-punches, beat-the-tar-out-of-each-other-style fights in the *Rocky* films. The World Heavyweight Championship was not the prize (it actually was in only one of their three matches), replaced by an unsurprisingly never repeated "King of Cable" concept, but the manner in which they fought each other was brutal and worthy of the title.

Vader did things that no super-heavyweight should have been able to do. He was billed at 450lbs, so watching him crash down from the top rope gave the impression of severe shortness of breath and several painkillers the next day for The Stinger. Somewhere along the line, Vader cast aside the early WrestleMania Era tendency to ensure that big men worked like giants even if it muted some of the athletic feats of which they were capable and used his dynamic physical gifts to both wow audiences and deliver incredibly impactful aerial assaults that realistically could have wiped out his opponents.

"The White Castle of Fear" title applied to their conclusive Strap Match at *SuperBrawl III* was as silly as The Italian Stallion's post-fight patriotic speech at the end of *Rocky IV*, but it was an amazing match that took the brutality from December up to the next highest notch. Though the gimmick was too infrequently employed to rank against its peers for a more official bullet point on its curriculum vitae, Sting-Vader was the greatest Strap Match ever wrestled; hopefully the 1993 Match of the Year award is adequate compensation. Vader took the reins from Sting that year as WCW's #1 star, setting the traditionally heel-centered promotion back on its typical course.

Sting and Vader were vital to each other's careers, in different ways. Vader carried the momentum from their matches to the best year of his career, featuring a 285 day reign as WCW Champion and an impressive list of great matches. Though Sting obviously had far more famous feuds during WCW's financial resurgence in the late 1990s, the Vader series featured the matches of his life; Vader laid some serious whippings on Sting, the Clubber Lang-types that pushed The Franchise to up his game and also the Ivan Drago-type that confirmed like never before his grit and determination. Without their rivalry, they both still would have been icons, but their matches best showcased what made them iconic.

#81
The Rock vs. Chris Jericho
WCW Championship and Undisputed WWF Championship
No Mercy 2001 to Royal Rumble 2002
Top 15 All-Time at Royal Rumble / Top 15 Match in 2001 / Top 10 Match in 2002

The Rock vs. Chris Jericho rivalry was unusual. Rare are the pro wrestling storylines that start with such an iconic moment as a debuting Y2J's millennium countdown clock ticking down to its final seconds during the middle of a Rock promo, only for the in-ring payoff to not materialize until two years later. Had the same thing happened in August of this year instead of August of 1999, fans around the world would have been fantasy-booking Rock vs. Jericho to headline pay-per-views from September to Survivor Series in November. Unfortunately, Y2J got off to a rocky start in his WWE career and it took him roughly two-thirds of a year after his debut to get into a groove, thanks mostly to a feud that will soon be discussed.

By the summer of 2001, Jericho was becoming a bonafide main-event-caliber star. When he and Rock began teaming together against members of the WCW/ECW Alliance and notably aimed their mutual mastery of trash-talking at Stephanie McMahon, one could see the chemistry yet again on display with their interactions and not help but wonder how it would translate when they were squaring off in the ring against each other. As the tension between them grew, so too did the anticipation for their eventual matches.

It would be safe to say, then, that based on the quality of their matches in 2001 and 2002, it was worth the wait.

Each match featured very high stakes and each reflects today as carrying an added historical weight. *No Mercy 2001* was site of the first of their three PPV encounters; on that night, Jericho – in just the second headlining title bout of his career to that point – defeated Rock to win the WCW Championship, which he ironically never got anywhere close to capturing while employed by WCW. The second match, at *Vengeance 2001*, was of course the penultimate victory on the night that Y2J became the inaugural Undisputed Champion, again winning the WCW Title from Rock and immediately after defeating Steve Austin to win the WWF Title. Finally, *Royal Rumble 2002* played host to Jericho beating Rock in what most believe was the finest outing of his initial run as champion.

The Jericho-Rock series offered two important lessons:

Lesson #1 – Y2J vs. Rock matches were a consistent example of the critical advantages of in-ring chemistry. Both Jericho and Rock had wrestling styles that meshed well with a lot of different types of opponents. Though each had great chemistry with other superstars, many with whom they combined to produce far more famous matches and rivalries, they had just as strong a chemistry with each other.

As Samuel 'Plan notes in *101 WWE Matches To See Before You Die*, "What is always fun about Rock / Jericho matches is that a viewer will always get the very real impression that the two of them enjoy the work they put on together and that enjoyment translates into their prototypical pace." Theirs were matches equal parts explosive, like one might expect from Rock's matches with Austin, and fluid, like one might expect from Jericho's matches with Rey Mysterio. The result is that, as 'Plan further expresses, "Before you know it, you've witnessed twenty minutes of action that feels like ten." All three bouts remain incredibly rewatchable.

Lesson #2 – The Rock proved the value of not being an overly egotistical top star. Many of the all-time greats, particularly those who occupied the #1 spot in their promotion's hierarchy, wound up becoming famous for their lack of inclination to put others over when the time was appropriate. Rock's greatest rival, Austin, became notorious for walking out of the company when asked to lose to Brock Lesnar on Raw; Bret Hart became infamous for failing to put over Shawn Michaels on his way out of the WWF at *Survivor Series* (and proceeded to get "screwed"); Hulk Hogan might be the worst of the lot, having reportedly exercised his WCW creative control on numerous occasions to avoid losses. Almost every top star has a story of deciding not to put someone over, but no such story exists about The Rock (and it would probably be fair to say that no other tippy-top star in history would have signed off on losing to The Hurricane, as did Rock in 2003).

Jericho had gotten close to reaching the summit of the WWF's hierarchical Mt. Everest before October 2001, but not until The Rock came along did someone of extraordinary standing come forth who was willing to allow his shoulders to be counted down for three seconds and to subsequently give Jericho the boost to the top of the mountain. It may never have been clean, but protection in defeat is a gift from wrestling's God (Vince) earned through drawing money as "The Man." The fact remains that Jericho was 3-0 against Rock.

They were perhaps a better back-story away from vaulting up this list, but Jericho's original championship run is widely panned among wrestling historians, coming under fire for its creative shortcomings. Between what their feud meant for Jericho and their in-ring chemistry, however, they undoubtedly earned a spot on the list.

#80
Sting vs. Ric Flair
NWA World Heavyweight Championship
Clash of the Champions
March 27, 1988

Top 10 All-Time TV Match / Top 5 Match in 1988

The stones you have to possess to go toe-to-toe with Vince McMahon...

As much as Sting is deservedly remembered as one of Ric Flair's greatest opponents, it is not necessarily the wrestling itself that historically stands out about their most famous match, but rather what it represented in the prelude to the Monday Night War. For five straight years, the owner of the World Wrestling Federation had run roughshod over the professional wrestling industry, doing whatever he pleased en route to putting the vast majority of his competition for nationwide supremacy in sports entertainment out of business.

The scrappy National Wrestling Alliance, spearheaded by Jim Crockett Promotions, and their incredible, all-time great World Heavyweight Champion, Ric Flair, was the only viable game left in town other than McMahon's WWF by the spring of 1988. Every time that the NWA had tried to gain some momentum and throw a punch in the fight after rounds of getting knocked down and nearly out, McMahon would duck and counter swiftly and powerfully. However, on the night of *WrestleMania IV*, Crockett landed his punch in the form of the very first *Clash of the Champions*, aired for free on TBS: The Superstation, and headlined by Flair's defense of the World Title against the up-and-coming, increasingly popular not-yet-icon known as Sting.

A 5.8 cable television rating with a 7.8 final quarter hour during the main-event made *Clash of the Champions* a huge success for the NWA. Even though it proved little more in the grand scheme

102

of things than a glancing blow that got Crockett knocked out cold in response – the cable companies were so upset at the loss of revenue that they could have earned from *WrestleMania IV* that they explicitly told him never to pull a stunt like that again (a net win for McMahon), and then Crockett had to sell out to Ted Turner to avoid going under – the NWA had still delivered its counter-punch with gusto. Crockett and Flair had grown quite accustomed to being economically upstaged by the WWF at every turn, so it sure had to have been sweet to stick it to them, if but only for a single night.

The 45-minute time-limit draw, which awarded the match to Flair by judge's decision, made Sting into the star who would eventually be referred to as WCW's "Franchise." Without *Clash of the Champions*, Sting likely never would have been able to enjoy the spoils of being a major part of the winning side for two straight years during the Monday Night Wars; it built the foundation for his legacy.

It was also one of the five quintessential Ric Flair matches that best exemplified why Naitch is so revered, each featuring the long-form wrestling style that made him famous for his cardiovascular conditioning (the others include his bouts with Barry Windham, Lex Luger, Ricky Steamboat, and Terry Funk). Matched up in a head-to-head analysis with shorter compositions like Rock vs. Jericho, Flair's finest won handily, endurance and historical relevance trumping even better chemistry.

Among the things that made his matches with Sting (and Luger too) so memorable was that, for Flair's outstanding heel persona, The Stinger was a different sort of opponent, a new age hero cut from a mold similar to what had become so popular up north in the WWF. Sting was even billed from the same town as Hulk Hogan (Venice Beach, California). A mystique around The Stinger developed quickly and it was something that he carried with him throughout his career no matter the incarnation (blonde surfer or dark Crow). People who reference their desire to have seen Sting wrestle Undertaker often cite their respective auras as part of the reason. Flair had most prominently faced more naturally relatable protagonists prior to 1988, so it was an interesting change of pace to see him trying to overcome more of a comic book-type.

Anyone who had ever seen Flair's battles with Nikita Koloff would have recognized the way that Flair sold for Sting, but one of the most important things about The Stinger was that he was built up as larger-than-life rather than just another menacing monster. The face paint, much as it did for Sting's old running mate, The Ultimate Warrior, added a little something extra to his persona. Flair, then, to counteract his super-hero opposition, had to become more of a super-villain, accentuating as much as he ever had before his cunning. If Sting was Superman, then Flair was Lex Luthor and the Figure Four leg lock was Sting's kryptonite.

Flair and Sting would go onto wrestle numerous times on a variety of special occasions, often involving the World Championship, but none ever quite so prominently captured the magic on display on March 27, 1988 at the Greensboro Coliseum.

#79
The Rock vs. Kurt Angle
WWF Championship
No Mercy 2000 through No Way Out 2001

Top 10 Match in 2001

During the summer of 2000, Kurt Angle began his ascent toward the main-event level at which he would remain for the vast majority of the next six years. Winning the King of the Ring tournament undoubtedly aided his cause and some might argue that it was his love triangle storyline with Stephanie McMahon and Triple H that pushed him over the top, but it was his rivalry with The Rock over the World Championship that truly confirmed his elite status in the WWF hierarchy and allowed him to blossom into the all-time great that he would soon become.

To rewatch the pair of pay-per-view title matches between Angle and Rock, wrestled four months apart, is to revisit Angle's incredible progression as a performer. In the bout that began his first championship reign at *No Mercy 2000*, the hallmark traits of the Attitude Era's main-event style were unmistakable. There were many instances in which that style served only to enhance what would still have otherwise been a classic wrestling match had a stricter adherence to the rules been utilized; in others, it was a formula that, being as full of tactics more readily capable of eliciting crowd response as it was, allowed for less experienced headliners – like Angle as of October 2000 – to not have to bite off more than they could chew before they were fully ready. Angle had shown in previous featured-bouts against Triple H and Undertaker a rare acumen for rapid adaptation to the WWE main-event wrestling style, but short-cuts like heavy-interference, beyond-the-ring-brawling, and free-wheeling use of weapons gave Our Olympic Hero a security blanket against Rock in his very first pay-per-view show-closer should the learning curve have proven too steep.

Of course, the learning curve was not too steep for Angle. Thanks in part to his natural in-ring chemistry with Rock, Angle surpassed expectations in the biggest opportunity of his career to that point. Theirs was a match that put to good use its No-Disqualification stipulation, which ultimately allowed Rock to lose the title amidst shenanigans and simultaneously set-up Angle as an underhanded champion reliant on considerable help to win; performance-wise, however, Angle did not look out of place.

The Rock had a tendency, one for which he does not often enough receive credit from pundits, to bring out the best in the wrestlers that he worked with. Even when he was not getting his shoulders pinned to the mat, he still elevated his opponents by providing them with a platform to execute their game (in the ring and on the microphone) to the best of their abilities in front of one of the most raucous crowds that they would ever experience. Versus Angle at *No Way Out '01* is perhaps the quintessential example; Our Olympic Hero walked in as WWF Champion with his chance at advancing to the main-event of *WrestleMania X-Seven* on the line, lost the title, and wound up looking as good as he ever had before. Was it any surprise that, from that point forward until the day he left in 2006, he was considered one of the five best wrestlers in WWE?

Instead of an Attitude Era-style headliner, the PPV rematch was a preview of the highly athletic form of main-event wrestling that WWE would employ as they transitioned into a new era. Typically kept under the 20-minute mark and frequently dipping closer to 15-minutes in length, these faster paced headlining matches became commonplace for a couple of years and were so content-laden that if you blinked you would often miss one of the key psychological aspects of the story, much less a signature move that might have signaled the three count or tap out. Angle and Rock best put that style to use. The Great One would later utilize it against Chris Jericho and Brock Lesnar and would modify it to historically great success versus Hulk Hogan. The Olympic gold medalist made that style his own in renowned efforts against Lesnar, Chris Benoit, Edge, and Rey Mysterio; Paul Heyman made Angle and his style the backbone of the highly-appreciated Smackdown Six Era.

No Way Out should be remembered as the start of the incredible part of Angle's career. By that point, he absolutely had no need for any potential short-cuts in his matches. Written all over his face from the opening bell onward was an intensity that said as much about his real life competitiveness and determination as it did his character's increased confidence and disdain for his opposition. As clearly as his character was saying through his facial expressions, "I will not lose this title because I'm better than The Rock," the real life Angle was saying, "Before I drop this title, I need to prove that I belong right back in this spot again soon."

February 25, 2001 will go down in history as the night when one of the greatest matches in WWE lore happened between two of the greatest superstars ever...Triple H vs. Stone Cold Steve Austin: Three Stages of Hell. Understandably, it casts a shadow over Angle vs. The Rock, which accordingly deserves the moniker of one of the greatest matches ever wrestled, also between two of the greatest superstars of all-time, that nobody talks about.

#78
Bret Hart vs. Diesel
WWF Championship
King of the Ring 1994 to Survivor Series 1995

Top 25 All-Time at Royal Rumble / Top 10 All-Time at Survivor Series / Match of the Year in 1995

Among the more fascinating sub-plots of the WWF's so-termed "New Generation" period in the mid-1990s was the regularity with which Vince McMahon and company unsuccessfully tried to replace Bret Hart as their top star before ultimately going back to the well with The Hitman as the WWF Champion.

One of several fresh faces circa 1993-1996 asked to take the reins from Bret was "Big Daddy Cool" Diesel, who many have argued became a case of much too fast, much too soon. He burst onto the scene in the winter of 1994 and, within several months of his debut as a bodyguard for Shawn Michaels, was headlining a pay-per-view with Bret's WWF Title on the line. Later in the year, Hart controversially dropped the title to Bob Backlund so that the aging veteran could transition the belt to Diesel, whose ensuing run with the gold did not go particularly well. For as big a draw as Kevin Nash became when he joined WCW and formed The New World Order with Hulk Hogan and Scott Hall, he was a notoriously weak-drawing champion for the WWF during one of the worst financial years in its history. Nearly a year after winning the title, in what would become an all-too-familiar story for Hart, Nash's 358 day reign was ended by The Hitman.

That was the pattern: Bret would win the title, the WWF would eventually replace him thinking it had potentially found its next Hogan, and then Bret would be asked to re-stabilize business after the experiment failed.

Between June 1994 and November 1995, Hart and Nash had three PPV title bouts that, in addition to being quite possibly the finest examples of a technical wrestler against a much larger athlete in the WrestleMania Era, take on an interesting context when replaying them with knowledge of the WWF's strong desire to make Diesel into something he was not and its subsequent return to Bret as the status-quo champion.

Their first encounter at *King of the Ring '94* doubled as Diesel's initial foray into the main-event spotlight and, though clearly a work-in-progress, he was also clearly talented. More so than a break-out night for Nash, it was a true showcase for The Hitman's vast array of in-ring abilities; Bret's creativity was on full display, his counters of Diesel's major offensives authenticating his reputation as a wrestling genius with a knack for making the little details count toward the substantial critical achievement of his matches, especially when saddled with less-experienced opponents.

Interestingly, their original showdown did not have a definitive winner, as if the WWF was already thinking that Diesel was too valuable a commodity to lay down for The Hitman. Yet, their second featured match at *Royal Rumble '95* ended inconclusively as well; even when presented with an obvious opportunity to put Diesel strongly over Bret, the WWF's clear desire to get their new babyface champion over did not trump their decision to keep their former torch-bearer in a 1A sort of position (just in case).

The rematch was seemingly an Attitude Era precursor, its rules pushed to their limits without disqualification until all hell broke loose and there was no other choice but for the referee to call for the bell. Hart, exemplifying the ultimate team player that he was prone to be during his heyday, told Nash behind the scenes, "Let me be the aggressor, yet keep [you] strong." Diesel was struggling to fully connect with the audience after such a quick push to the top, despite having become a much more polished performer. The world was changing and the dominant big man inorganically leading the charge was not especially well-received; there was a natural tendency even then to go against the grain and boo Diesel. "All I would have had to do to turn him heel was to have started selling dramatically, but I didn't operate like that," Bret noted in his book, another fact that in hindsight makes an already first-rate match that much more engaging.

Survivor Series '95 played host to their third and perhaps their most highly regarded clash. By then, Diesel had failed to meet Bret's standard so, on that night, the WWF put the title back on Hart and started preparations for his next replacement (Shawn Michaels).

The No-Disqualification Match was a beautiful fight that saw both men well execute psychologically-sound game-plans to incapacitate each other in ways that played to their respective strengths. It also memorably gave rise to the prominent trend still popular today of main-event matches featuring a crash through the Spanish announce table. The spot (and the finish stimulated by it) was the culmination not just of a great WWF Championship bout, but of one of the most underrated rivalries of a virtually forgotten era (The New Generation) in modern pro wrestling lore – one that characterized the internal competition for the top spot in the WWF and the at times frustrating creative process that often appears to shun what gets over naturally with wrestling's core audience in favor of that which *might* hold the promise of capturing more casual fan and/or mainstream attention.

#77
Kurt Angle vs. The Undertaker
World Heavyweight Championship
No Way Out
February 19, 2006
Top 5 Match in 2006

This was the greatest WrestleMania match to almost but never actually happen at WrestleMania...

Kurt Angle vs. The Undertaker at *No Way Out '06* was among the best matches of the 2000s. The bell-to-bell action was nothing short of incredible, as one might expect of a bout for the World Championship featuring two of the greatest in-ring performers ever in their primes. There was one particularly sublime sequence that saw Angle counter Undertaker's Tombstone Piledriver attempt into position for his own version only for Undertaker to counter back into the set-up for the Tombstone before Angle finally escaped by grapevining Taker's leg and rolling him forward, right into the Ankle Lock. Something was missing, though, that kept it from being as memorable as possible: the type of atmosphere that could have been afforded it by the grand *WrestleMania 22* stage in Chicago six weeks later.

The original plan was for The Deadman and Our Olympic Hero, anchors of Smackdown since the 2002 brand extension, to have their very first pay-per-view one-on-one match since Angle rounded into one of the Top 15 stars of the WrestleMania Era, and to feature it at "The Showcase of the Immortals" in 2006. It was expected to continue the prior years' trend of inter-promotional matches, as Angle was moved to *Raw* in mid-2005, but the World Heavyweight Title scene was thrown into chaos when Batista had to undergo surgery shortly before *The Royal Rumble*. An audible was called to move Angle back to Smackdown so he could assume Batista's position as the champion, unfortunately bumping the long-awaited showdown between The Phenom and the Olympic gold medalist to the February PPV with just three weeks of hype behind it.

It has always struck as odd that, rather than shift the title plans for 'Mania 22 to Angle vs. Taker, WWE instead opted to move Angle into the title plans and opt out of an almost guaranteed Top 15 all-time 'Mania match; or to at the very least have just allowed Randy Orton and Rey Mysterio, the other two participants in the Triple Threat Match in which Angle defended the title at 'Mania 22, to compete for the championship by themselves. Arm-chair booking the past is a tedious exercise in most instances, but watching such an awesome effort be reacted to by the Baltimore crowd for No Way Out as if it were an average main-event, consequently lending it virtually no sense of occasion despite that the occasion was so extraordinary...one cannot help but imagine how history would remember Taker vs. Angle had the impressive buyrate for 'Mania 22 added an economic legacy to its reputation, had the aura that always surrounds WrestleMania given it that extra special historical boost, and had the Chicago audience in All State Arena on April 2nd (one of the most passionate crowds of all-time) been able to add its enthusiasm to the presentation.

Take the exact same match, tweak the finish to continue The Phenom's WrestleMania undefeated streak, and plop it at the top of hour number three at WrestleMania 22 and odds are we are talking about Taker vs. Angle as one of the Top 25 matches of all-time.

Now, that said, it is still a match very much worth celebrating. Undertaker was never a technical wrestler, but he could wrestle technically. It was not often in his career that The Deadman was afforded the opportunity to have a more technically-oriented match; wrestling Angle gave him the best chance to exhibit the full of range of his capabilities in that regard. There was something very appealing about seeing a near twenty-year veteran at that point wrestle like he had something to prove.

It was a situation in which both parties were immensely reverent of each other. The respect between Michaels and Flair, Perfect and Hart to be alluded to in upcoming entries is one of the aspects of professional wrestling that can yield top notch chemistry in the ring. There was also that level of respect between Angle and Taker. Tazz, on commentary with Michael Cole that evening, spoke on the air about a conversation he had with The Deadman about three years beforehand, during which Taker said candidly that he thought Angle might be the best he had ever seen. In 2005, Angle commented on a WWE Home Video production about The Phenom that Taker was the best of all-time. How that translates to the give and the take, the ebb and the flow seen throughout the course of a match is a mutual desire to work together toward creating a legendary work of art and careful crafting by two men very much in-tune with one another's characters. As a result, the pair was able to concoct that rare kind of magic that only the best of the best have managed.

For Angle, it will go down as the last truly great match of his WWE career. Not only by pinning him but also by repeatedly countering Taker's finishing moves, Angle perhaps never looked like a bigger star than he did on that night. For Undertaker, it will be remembered as the first of his nearly unprecedented run of Match of the Year candidates from 2006-2013 and, considering it was once scheduled for 'Mania, the unofficial beginning of his vaunted "Streak within the Streak."

#76
Greg Valentine vs. Roddy Piper
Dog Collar Match
Starrcade
November 24, 1983

<u>Top 10 All-Time at Starrcade</u> / <u>Top 5 Match in 1983</u>

The stature or influence of a match, rivalry, or story can be the primary factors in determining their place among the greatest of all-time, but so too can a match forge a singular legacy that stands alone in an instance completely unique to any of its peers. On the night that wrestling as we know it came to be at *Starrcade '83*, Roddy Piper and Greg Valentine went to battle in a Dog Collar Match so bloody, brutal, and dangerous that no one in mainstream North American wrestling ever tried it again.

It was an incomparable match and, as such, is very difficult to evaluate against other incredible matches. Frankly, it holds up only reasonably well in head-to-head comparisons. Yet, it might actually be the most real looking pro wrestling match of the entire WrestleMania Era, so it unquestionably belongs among the Top 100. In an industry lambasted for its pre-determined outcomes and endlessly flagged with the nauseously aggravating label of "wrestling is fake," Piper and Valentine beat so much hell out of each other that it felt a lot more like an actual fight at times, one of its few ties to what has become known as sports entertainment being The Hammer's Flair-esque over-exaggerated selling. Absent was the tit-for-tat of grappling holds and signature moves, replaced by constant swings in momentum that one might expect to see in a playground fight; well, you know, the kind of fight that involves being tethered by dog collars and a rather large steel chain.

Stunning remains the visual of seeing two men standing in opposite corners of the ring with a huge chain attached to the collars latched around each of their necks, pulling back as hard as they could in a perverse game of tug-of-war that makes your spinal cord injury-specialist author recoil at each sight.

Piper, as one might can imagine, was totally believable as the intensely angry, revenge-seeking protagonist, his facial expressions telling much of the story. It was a severely personal rivalry over the United States Championship that culminated in this match, after all; sheer barbarity was a logical response in an early 1980s wrestling storyline that supposedly cost one of its participants up to three-quarters of his hearing in one ear.

They made full use of their environment. The chain was weaponized in every which way, most notably around the ears, eyes, and throat, and even inside the mouth like a sadistic bite guard. Also used for striking, the chain in story was responsible for a deep laceration across Valentine's forehead and, adding to the realism, a cut on or in Piper's left ear. Bleeding from the ear has been a virtual novelty in purposeful pro wrestling blading (presuming Roddy's ear bled according to a plan). The Hot Rod sold it so well, staggering about as if he had been stricken with vertigo, that his heroic attempt to both regain his footing and take out his rival was borderline epic. Piper wildly swung the chain, sending it bunched together and pounding into Hammer's body; it watches as similarly cringe-worthy as a hard fall from a Ladder Match stunt or one of Mankind's unprotected chair shots at *Royal Rumble '99*.

Valentine too deserves a lot of credit for his role in the Dog Collar Match's success. Though featured as one of *The Greatest Wrestling Stars of the '80s* (a WWE DVD production), the Hall of Famer has not been afforded the historical glorification that have many of his contemporaries, but The Hammer was an exemplary pro wrestler, as exemplified by his superstar-confirming performance at *Starrcade '83*. A few weeks later, he had signed to work with the WWF as one of the foundational pieces of Vince McMahon's national expansion.

Against Piper, Valentine was efficiently vicious, relentlessly attacking Roddy's ear (biting it even) and delivering such impactful blows to the head that it made his follow-up Sleeper Hold seem like a sure-fire victory was in the bag. You will struggle to find anyone who has ever sold a Sleeper Hold better than Piper did on that night, leaning in such a believable way that it really did seem as though his carotid artery was being obstructed by Valentine's thick forearm.

In terms of the pure elements of in-ring success alone (selling, psychology, and execution), not many matches are better than Valentine vs. Piper, which owned the vaunted Flair-Race bout from the same card if not in prestige than certainly as more critically triumphant in hindsight. The Dog Collar Match remains a master-class in how wrestlers become emotionally consumed by their characters and how they allow their stories on the 20'X20' canvas to be physically informed by their ability to interact with one another in the context of their rivalry. An amazing camera shot showing the ring from above with buckets of their blood staining the mat evidenced their commitment to the authenticity of their performance.

The fact that this match is arguably the most realistic fight of the entire era and that it took place on the very first night of the era in question truly speaks to how the industry has changed over the last thirty-plus years.

#75
John Cena vs. Triple H
WWE Championship
WrestleMania 22
April 2, 2006

Top 40 All-Time at WrestleMania / Top 5 Match in 2006

When discussing the greatest WrestleMania main-events of all-time, contextualizing their long-term impact on WWE as well their quality, Triple H vs. John Cena at *WrestleMania 22* is not typically one of the first that comes to mind.

Perhaps it should be.

Certainly, from an in-ring standpoint, it was not a match that reached staggering critical heights given the limitations of its still inexperienced defending WWE Champion. It has been well-documented that Cena had his shortcomings as a wrestler when he was first given the ball and tasked with becoming the #1 star. As a worker, he needed another year beyond his showdown with Triple H to carry his end of a classic standard one-on-one bout.

Nevertheless, Cena vs. HHH was a praise-worthy achievement. It had a simple game plan and was executed very well. The Game was the incumbent owner of wrestling's prestigious moniker, "The Man." Cena may have held the top title for all but three weeks of the previous year, but Triple H was main-eventing his 3rd WrestleMania in a row and his 4th in the last five since the Attitude Era ended. He carried WWE's flagship brand during a key transition period in wrestling history. Cena emerged as the superstar most likely to dethrone The King of Kings, creating a dynamic that upped the historical ante. Triple H, then, wrestled the match like one might expect of a grappler so battle-tested; Cena, meanwhile, wrestled like one might expect of a still-learning but clearly worthy talent. The match eclipses many of

117

its more aesthetically nuanced peers because of its adherence to the basics – a story so uncomplicated, but so well told.

Of course, the intangible element that allowed such a simple tale to excel was the audience. Everyone in Chicago that night was completely invested in the match and its outcome. WrestleMania has become well-known for its melting pot crowds full of diehard fans from all over the world; combine that with Chicago's reputation as a top WWE market famous for some of the most passionate fans in the world and *WrestleMania 22* surely goes down as "The Show of Shows" with the craziest fans this side of Toronto's for *WrestleMania X-8*. Similar to the role they played for Rock vs. Hogan, the live attendees had as much to do with the memory created by Cena vs. HHH as the wrestlers, commentators, or production crew.

The reaction was unique. John Cena got vociferously booed. He certainly had his fans, but the loud, boisterous voices of the teenage to adult males largely drowned out The Chain Gang (as Cena's fans were then known). The trend toward jeering The Champ had begun the previous fall, but it was popularized at 'Mania 22. Ironically, Triple H had been public enemy #1 of the so-termed vocal minority since 2002; it once seemed implausible that someone would become more hated by that community of fans than him. For Cena to become that guy was ironic in and of itself because it was the teenage to adult male contingent that first took to him when he was crushing it with his rapping gimmick. When he adapted from Eminem to Superman, though, that crowd turned on him.

Plenty of matches have earned reactions that were not reflective of the face-heel dichotomy portrayed on WWE TV. What made the Cena vs. Triple H example different – what made it a watershed moment – was WWE's lack of response to it. Hogan was given the hero's welcome in Toronto four years earlier despite being the antagonist and Rock was booed out of the building despite being the #1 hero in the company; Hogan was quickly turned babyface and Rock was turned heel within a year.

When Cena and Triple H were treated similarly in 2006, WWE did turn HHH, but it was pretty clear that Hunter got cheered at *'Mania 22* mostly because he was not Cena. To the people relentlessly booing Cena, however, WWE said with their lack of action, "Go ahead." They kept pushing him as the lead protagonist on their programming and he became one of the biggest stars ever, even though to a huge portion of the audience, he was – for all intents and purposes – the top heel.

That was a game-changer. From that point forward, WWE embraced the vast array of preferences within their fanbase and essentially decided to do what they wanted to do and encourage the WWE Universe to concurrently do whatever it wanted to do. Cena sold a ton of merchandise to kids and was a great ambassador for WWE across various outlets and business was running strong, so WWE did not care if other sects of the audience booed because, to them, the positives of staying the course with Cena's persona outweighed the negatives. Good guys and bad guys are now as subjective to the individual fan as ever before and a pillar of pro wrestling storytelling has become perplexing. It is a strange, fascinating world in which we live.

John Cena vs. Triple H is representative of a foundational shift in the WWE product. It was also one of the rare "passing of the torch" moments in pro wrestling lore. Given the ego inherent to the pro wrestling industry, situations in which the Ric Flair-inspired adage "To be The Man, you've got to beat The Man" was put to literal use have been few and far between. Tapping out Triple H in the *WrestleMania 22* main-event made John Cena "The Man."

#74
The WWE Women's Revolution
NXT Takeover: Arrival to WWE Roadblock: End of the Line

Top 40 All-Time at WrestleMania / Match of the Year in 2015 / Top 5 Match in 2016

Women's wrestling has been a consistently major contributor to the WWE product for several years now, but it was such an afterthought for so long that it is still awe-inducing to think of how far it came during the so-termed "Women's Revolution." The Stratus vs. Lita rivalry was the rare exception to an unwritten rule throughout the WrestleMania Era (prior to 2015) that women had a ceiling as high as a tin shack's compared to the mansion's roof height of the men's; and, even if exceptional like Trish's match with Mickie James at *WrestleMania 22*, the best women's match would be no better than a good men's mid-card bout.

At *NXT Takeover: Arrival*, the WWE developmental brand's first special and the inaugural live event to stream on the WWE Network, fans became privy to a fundamental shift in women's wrestling that Triple H, NXT's founder, had been quietly spearheading. That night's title match between Paige and Emma was simple and well-worked, but what stood out was both the presentation and the 13-minutes afforded it so that they could achieve a higher quality and tell a more thorough tale. Bear in mind that Trish's retirement match was only 11-minutes long.

Later in the year at *Takeover: R-Evolution*, Charlotte Flair and Sasha Banks were afforded a similar opportunity and had what could quite comfortably be classified as, to that point, the greatest women's match ever under the WWE umbrella on account of superb storytelling, character commitment, and execution. Then, the next step was taken at *Takeover: Rival* with a Fatal Four-Way Match fueled by high octane pacing and intricate sequencing between Charlotte, Sasha, Bayley, and

Becky Lynch that proved women could do what the men could do if just given the chance; the participants became known as "The Four Horsewomen" in homage to Flair's connection to her father's famous stable. Sasha and Becky upped the ante yet again at *Takeover: Unstoppable* in a match two-minutes longer than anything else on the card; it felt like a main-event and its unequivocal show-stealing status suggested it could have been. These matches all had distinctly unique auras to every other women's match that preceded them.

Time and consistent attention had been so lacking for so long in WWE for women's wrestling but, with increased bell-to-bell time and steady creative focus, the NXT women's division kept proving that they deserved even bigger opportunities.

Banks vs. Bayley at *Takeover: Brooklyn*, which sold out the same venue that would host *Summerslam '15* the next night, was the brightest shining moment yet, doing for the perception of women in WWE what Ronda Rousey's dominance had done for women in MMA: legitimized it. It was a truly remarkable achievement that showcased how women could reach "Match of the Year" caliber heights. That evening, Triple H had said, in reference to Banks vs. Bayley, that he did not "put women in the main event," but that they "were the main-event." On the strength of their initial encounter, Hunter put them in an actual show-closing match at *Takeover: Respect*.

In the first-ever women's Ironman Match, Bayley and Banks put together another stunning story that won the *Pro Wrestling Illustrated* Match of the Year award. They each took full ownership of their characters, with Banks definitively stamping herself as one of the shrewdest antagonists in modern WWE, male or female, using whatever means necessary to come across as an unlikable bitch, even going so far as to snatch the headband off of a young Bayley uber-fan at ringside, wearing it around to add insult to injury.

The "Revolution" was given its official tagline less than a month from *Brooklyn*, as WWE began slowly incorporating the NXT philosophy on their main brands, initially peaking with the retirement of the "Divas" label during the first women's match in WrestleMania history to be regarded as the bout that stole the show. Slightly outdoing the now-underrated Bayley vs. Asuka from the Friday before *'Mania 32* at *Takeover: Dallas*, Banks, Flair, and Lynch – based on their headlining-caliber entrances and performances – made it feel possible that women could one day main-event "The Show of Shows," which would have been a laughable statement two years earlier.

Flair and Banks would go onto replicate the success of the classic Sasha-Bayley feud from NXT on a much grander scale, trading the Raw Women's Championship back and forth six times in five months and collecting on the third and fourth Monday Night Raw main-events in the history of the women's division, the first-ever women's Hell in a Cell Match, the first-ever women's match to main-event a WWE pay-per-view, the 2016 TV Match of the Year, and ownership of the greatest women's rivalry in WWE lore. Their success brought a level of equality to professional wrestling that some never would have thought possible for WWE proper and it now seems like the sky is the limit.

The "Women's Revolution" is a story still evolving through all the women mentioned plus the likes of Alexa Bliss and many others. That a future edition of this book featuring a revised list could conceivably highlight the likes of Banks vs. Flair by itself and numerous women's rivalries from 2018 on is a wonderful thing. *Viva la Revolution!*

#73
The Rock 'n' Roll Express vs. The Minnesota Wrecking Crew
Steel Cage Match
NWA World Tag Team Championships
Starrcade
November 27, 1986

Top 10 All-Time Steel Cage Match / Top 10 All-Time at Starrcade / Match of the Year in 1986

From Steve Austin's favorite era in wrestling (Jim Crockett's NWA in the mid-to-late 1980s) comes Stone Cold's all-time favorite match.

"Unheralded" might be the most appropriate term to describe it but, head-to-head against more heralded peers, it outperforms its understated status all the way to the Top 75. Broken down to the variables that shape the rankings, Arn and Ole Anderson challenging Robert Gibson and Ricky Morton for the NWA Tag Team Titles at *Starrcade '86* offers prime examples of dedicated selling, top notch psychology, and complete commitment to the story of a dominant force unyielding in its desire to break the underdog, in the process earning one of the most distinctly invested crowd reactions of the WrestleMania Era's first decade.

It may come as a surprise to many that this match even made the list or that it is Austin's favorite; Vince McMahon's hype machine has never gotten behind it and, unlike other NWA matches previously discussed from that era, it does not feature a wrestler generally regarded as a WWE legend (though obviously Arn, Ricky, and Robert are all WWE Hall of Famers due mostly to their contributions beyond McMahon's sports entertainment empire). Perhaps, then, some brand equity of sorts needs to be established before further reinforcing the match itself's placement in the countdown.

The Minnesota Wrecking Crew, as prominent members of the original Four Horsemen, need no further introduction, but it should be stated more definitively for proper historical perspective that The Rock 'n' Roll Express is one of the greatest tag teams of all-time. On four separate occasions, they held the NWA Tag Team Championships; they were incredibly popular, especially with women – Jim Cornette said in the documentary, *Rock 'n' Roll Never Dies*, that "[Gibson and Morton] had more sex on the way to the ring than I had in one month"; they headlined sold-out house show tours throughout the Carolinas with barely a top-level star underneath them in a year (1986) when the NWA combined to sell 2 million live event tickets (a feat not accomplished by WWE since the Attitude Era).

Make no mistake: The Rock 'n' Roll Express having to defend the NWA Tag Titles against The Andersons was a big deal. The Horsemen rose to prominence in 1986 and, given the reputation that they were quickly developing, it would have surprised no one had they walked out the new champions after facing Gibson and Morton. Rock 'n' Roll was a resilient duo who helped inspire the style of The Rockers and Hardy Boyz as smaller, faster athletes who gained in heart what they lacked in strength. Arn and Ole, though, came into *Starrcade '86* like a powerhouse college football team full of NFL prospects, rendering Gibson and Morton the equivalent of a lowly finesse-based team from a tiny conference hoping scheme and luck could give them a puncher's chance.

The Steel Cage Match at *Starrcade* was decidedly old school. It was not wrestled under Tornado-rules, so each non-legal participant had to stand on the apron despite the presence of the cage. Other than an adherence to the standard use of tags, however, it watches as novel to 99% of the WrestleMania Era; like Cena vs. Lesnar in 2012, it was total annihilation in a wrestling ring with the exception of the ending.

Ricky Morton, in an appearance on Austin's podcast in 2015, said that Ole Anderson legitimately did not much care for smaller wrestlers, thinking them not believable as opponents. He told the story of one of their first in-ring encounters and how, after walloping Ole over and over again merely for the veteran to no-sell, Morton went into the center of the ring and took an un-assisted bump; when an incredulous Ole asked him what he was doing, Morton responded, "Well, you wouldn't go down, so I thought I would."

Ole's attitude softened when his respect was secured, but he wrestled The Rock 'n' Roll Express like a determined Alabama team would play football if Jacksonville State was their opponent. He and Arn were in total command virtually the entire match, with but a few sporadic flurries of offense coming from the champions. Just when you thought Morton was going to save the day, The Andersons quickly stopped him dead in his tracks; just when you thought Gibson was going to initiate the Rock 'n' Roll retaliation, Arn and Ole cut him off before he could muster an iota of momentum. Yet, when all hope seemed lost, the beaten, bloody, and nearly broken Express took advantage of the tiniest of openings and got the surprise win out of nowhere.

It almost made for uncomfortable viewing at times. Unlike most high profile tag team bouts, this one teased but never delivered the formulaic "hot tag" around which team psychology in professional wrestling matches has largely been built...it literally *NEVER* came. It really is a fascinating match to re-visit that probably could not have taken place at any time (or much further) after 1986. Thinning was the veil protecting the sport's scripted nature, but it was still thick enough for such a one-sided affair to work as well as it did given the character dynamics of the era.

<u>#72</u>
Hulk Hogan vs. "Macho Man" Randy Savage
WWF Championship Match
WrestleMania V
April 2, 1989
<u>Top 10 Match in 1989</u>

THE MEGA-POWERS EXPLODE!!!

The Top 100 began with a great match that told a captivating tale on the night despite having very little story behind it. #72 presents a somewhat opposite scenario, in which the payoff itself was more or less standard-fare, but the rivalry leading up to it was so memorable that its in-ring shortcomings, while not forgiven, can be somewhat glossed over, its spot in the all-time hierarchy affirmed by its well-earned place on the pedestal of iconic WWF feuds.

Before they "exploded," Hulk Hogan and "Macho Man" Randy Savage were leading the charge like Batman and Robin for Vince McMahon's quest to put his once northeast regional territory on the global map. *WrestleMania III* was a legendary night for both Hulkamania and Macho Madness, as Hogan retained the World Championship in arguably the biggest main-event ever and Savage basically invented the concept of stealing the show in his Intercontinental Title defense against Ricky Steamboat. By 1987's end, Macho's popularity was beginning to rival Hogan's, leading the two powers to combine in a partnership understandably labeled as "Mega."

The Hulkster's assist (amidst heavy interference) of Savage winning the World Championship in *WrestleMania IV*'s title tournament final sealed the deal; The Mega-Powers would spend 1988, as Hogan once famously said, "[Doing] anything to win together, brother!" The inaugural *Summerslam* and the second annual *Survivor Series* were built around wrestling's comic superhero team come to life defending the virtues of good against evil forces like giants and money. No combination of antagonists could possibly have stood in their way. However, what neither counted on was that their undoing would come courtesy not of an evil villain, but from the villainous evil still lurking inside The Macho Man.

It was a fascinating story. For the first few years of the WWF's foray into North American mainstream consciousness, the mythology of their financially-booming, family-friendly product had mostly been built by simple, black and white examples of heroism; the All-American Sgt. Slaughter destroying the dastardly Iranian Sheik, for instance, and then Hogan overcoming the maniacal Piper, the back-stabbing Orndorff, the manipulative Heenan (with a manipulated Andre), and the Lex Luthor of wrestling, The Million Dollar Man. The unraveling of the Hogan-Savage relationship, conversely, was one of the first WrestleMania Era instances of how effective it could be to dig deeper into the human psyche, showcasing the creative potential of professional wrestling for all the world to see and simultaneously allowing art to imitate a more intricate part of life, as would become a more common trope for storylines in future years. The Mega-Powers, you see, were undone by a misunderstanding (or maybe not, depending on your perspective) regarding The First Lady of Wrestling.

Savage's well-documented real life insecurities often manifested themselves in his relationship with his actual wife and on-screen manager, Miss Elizabeth. She was storyline-responsible for bringing Savage and Hogan together in the first place. It was ironic that she involved Hogan in Savage's life to protect Macho Man from further physical attack and that the ensuing friendship was torn apart because of Savage's reaction to Hogan protecting Elizabeth from physical harm. The manner in which Macho perceived Hogan's intentions toward her was the breaking point for his character, but in his memorable interviews leading up to their showdown for the World Championship at *WrestleMania V*, it felt very much like his character's comments were the true feelings of the man behind them.

Hulkster told a great story in Savage's post-humus WWE documentary about the night that they filmed the duo's break-up on *Saturday Night's Main Event*. He said that during a take of the classic segment, Macho accused him of touching Elizabeth's breasts. As Hogan vehemently denied it, Savage got all riled up, prompting the attention of the NBC executives on hand. However, rather than allow cooler heads to prevail, Dick Ebersol (one of the network's top dogs), urged the cameras to keep rolling and for another take to be filmed, hoping to capture some of the legitimate tension. We all know how well that turned out. It was awesome!

The Savage-Hogan rivalry was a brilliant example of the hottest feud going capturing the attention of the audience on many emotional levels, not black or white but within real life's shades of gray. Hogan's comments during his unforgettable pre-match promo on the night of the title bout could be construed by some as the perspective of a man clearly in the right, while others could just as easily see the comments as self-righteous instead. Ditto for Savage. It had a different vibe than the other major angles of the era, feeling more authentic on TV. It was magic.

Some interpretative freedom reveals another interesting aspect to consider in hindsight. The Macho Man was an underdog with a chip on his shoulder who was obsessed with being the best, a perfectionist who would settle for nothing less than his very best on the microphone and in the ring; he would have been the internet's favorite wrestler had he come about in the digital age. He was a very well-sculpted athlete, but he was noticeably smaller than his primary competition to be the #1 star in the WWF. Smaller wrestlers today talk about making it in a "Land of Giants," but Savage quite literally made it – and made it big – in a "Land of Giants." It legitimately bothered him that, when he was the World Champion throughout 1988, he was still sharing the spotlight with Hogan. Reflecting back, you can see that Elizabeth was also in many ways the storyline-vehicle for Savage to vent his real frustrations of being labeled but not treated as the top guy.

That the payoff at *WrestleMania V* was little more than a stereotypical Hogan match is borderline irrelevant. Sure, in all likelihood they could have had a match on the level of Hogan-Warrior or Savage-Warrior and, had they, this rivalry would be in the Top 10 all-time, but the fact remains that they concluded their feud properly and definitively on the grandest stage to massive economic success. Had *WrestleMania V* taken place in a football stadium, then more than tripling the actual attendance combined with a pay-per-view buy record for wrestling that stood for a decade and still ranks 16th all-time would have amplified Savage vs. Hogan's stature.

"The Mega-Powers Explode" remains one of the greatest storylines in wrestling history.

#71
Rey Mysterio vs. Chris Jericho
Intercontinental Championship
Judgment Day 2009 to The Bash 2009
Top 5 Match in 2009

Over the course of their short and sweet saga, Rey Mysterio and Chris Jericho dazzled with a brand of action so eye-popping that it elevated their feud above several more historically vaunted rivalries in the all-time discussion despite the fact that it was a decidedly mid-card affair featuring not a single snazzy hype video production recapping its rather enthralling television happenings (not even for the payoff match).

Many things stood out about the Intercontinental Championship bouts between Mysterio and Y2J – great storytelling, innovation, and some of the finest character work of Jericho's career just to name a few – but perhaps their defining attribute was the diversity in their move-sets utilized to keep all three of their pay-per-view matches (in the span of six weeks) fresh, each one building so well off of the previous that none of the efforts felt repetitive. Their series of matches were shining examples of the variety that two opponents can put on display when working together across multiple PPVs.

There is something brilliant about the escalation of in-ring performances through rematches. In all, there were over twenty-five different variations of Jericho and Mysterio's signature sequences executed in their PPV trio. That the style in which their matches were worked was reminiscent of Mysterio's bouts with Dean Malenko in 1996, carrying with them an inherently higher level of intricacy and degree of difficulty, only amplifies the achievement.

A few noteworthy occurrences included the vast array of counters to the 619 (catching his legs into the Walls of Jericho, a spinning Argentine Rack Backbreaker using Mysterio's momentum running toward the ropes, and – best of all – fluidly plucking Rey's mask right off of his face); a Mysterio roll-through counter of a sunset flip into a head kick further countered into the Walls; an attempted spinning Argentine Rack Backbreaker by Jericho countered into a spinning DDT; a Codebreaker counter of a springboard cross body attempt; and, finally, the brilliant climactic sequence of their last match that saw Mysterio connect with the 619, only for the ensuing springboard splash to be countered into the Walls of Jericho, which was then countered into a series of pin attempts ended by Jericho snatching off Mysterio's mask only to find that he had been wearing two masks!

Story was not sacrificed for aesthetics, however, and the escalatory nature of the rivalry could to some be considered the strength of the feud ahead of the in-ring nuance. The first match, at *Judgment Day*, developed from a simple beef, with Jericho unhappy about Mysterio's involvement in costing him a shot at the World Heavyweight Championship. Y2J insisted that there would be no 619 used against him and yet, despite his crafty counters to it, a 619 around the ring post on the outside was Jericho's undoing; he had underestimated Mysterio, failing to unleash his full arsenal (including the Lionsault). The second match, at *Extreme Rules*, was more intense and more personal. In the weeks prior, Jericho had impersonated a Mysterio fan in the front row and viciously assaulted Rey as he made his entrance; then, during the match, he made clear his intention to remove Mysterio's mask, which of course he eventually so cleverly did, stimulating his capturing of the Intercontinental Title.

The PPV payoff featured a high stakes situation: the Intercontinental Championship against Rey Mysterio's mask, which for the Ultimate Underdog basically meant that his career was on the line. Anyone who recalls Rey's baby-face from the dying days of WCW understands that, without his mask, Mysterio was not a viable superstar; without his mask, he was Peter Parker instead of Spider-Man.

During the build-up to *The Bash*, Mysterio had sat among the swaths of mask-donning fans in the crowd and attacked Jericho in retaliation for the previous month's assault. By the time that he had outwitted Y2J by wearing two masks and thwarted his attempt at yet another disrespectful robbery of his gravitas in the payoff's waning moments, Mysterio had thoroughly and utterly one-upped Jericho.

Simplicity ruled the feud, in the end the plucky hero making the villain rue the day. Creativity hallmarked the storyline, the attacks from the crowd and the mask removal two of the most memorable plot points of 2009 (and beyond). Ingenuity characterized the wrestling matches, the visual artistry on display some of the finest of the century. The composite result was Top 75-worthy.

#70
Matt Hardy vs. Edge (with Lita)
Summerslam 2005 to Monday Night Raw
October 3, 2005

Top 10 All-Time Cage Match / Top 10 Match in 2005

The legacy of the Edge-Lita-Matt Hardy love triangle is its implications on WWE in the 21st century. It was their art imitating life scenario that taught WWE and its fanbase the sheer power of the internet. There should be no questioning the quality of the professional wrestling matches that came of their uniquely publicized situation, but it was the impact of social media (before the phrase was even popularized) that helps place Hardy vs. Edge just inside the Top 75.

Insider information about wrestling was once limited to written publications known as dirtsheets. The globalization of the internet and the new standard that it set as a worldwide communication tool put wrestling's backstage happenings out there for everyone to see. By the early-to-mid-2000s, it was increasingly common for diehard fans to be heavily influenced by news and rumors read on the web. *WrestleMania XX* in 2004 provided an example of the phenomenon, as audience members in-the-know mercilessly booed Goldberg and Brock Lesnar, both of whom were leaving WWE after their headlining match against each other.

Later that year, Matt Hardy had knee surgery and was forced into extended recovery. His long-time girlfriend, Lita, with whom he had portrayed the WWE's most beloved couple since Miss Elizabeth and Macho Man on-camera, began traveling from town-to-town with their mutual friend, Edge. What started as platonic evolved into romance. Hardy found out, eventually vented his frustration about the affair online, and was released from WWE as a consequence. Edge and Lita, meanwhile, were forced to endure the locker room drama while still gainfully employed.

The fallout of the story behind-the-scenes was covered extensively on the internet. Sure enough, fans who related to getting screwed over by their friend and their significant other started expressing their feelings at live WWE events. The movement started quietly at first, a smattering of chants by a small pocket of the attendees. Rapidly it grew to a point where nary could an Edge or Lita segment on TV occur without a thunderous "You Screwed Matt" or "We Want Matt" chant erupting. It reached uncomfortable depths for Lita, who was the target of many vulgar insults. A creative decision was made to pair Edge and Lita on-screen to take advantage of the heat.

An outpouring of support for Hardy led to WWE making the business decision to rehire him. The ensuing feud between Edge and Matt was one of the landmark storylines for what would become known years later as the "Reality Era." Taking full advantage of internet-fueled passion, Hardy initially came back unannounced in worked-shoot spots (part of the show but presented as unscripted). He called Edge by his real name (Adam), which just was not done back then in that context; he referenced the independent shows that he would be working for Ring of Honor (ROH), which had never happened either. When Hardy's return was made official, the promos exchanged between the trio were quite candid as all parties vented their very real frustrations; no verbal punches were pulled. It was really quite riveting to watch.

During the four matches that they had across the late summer and fall of 2005, the chemistry that had always made Edge and Hardy an engaging in-ring pairing remained, but the additional dynamic of real life betrayal and retribution created a concoction that took both of them to the next level in their careers. It was the rivalry that saw Edge, in particular, put all of the puzzle pieces together en route to his highly decorated main-event run.

Though Edge would win the feud in a Ladder Match on the USA Network Homecoming Edition of Monday Night Raw in October, it was a few weeks beforehand at *Unforgiven* that the saga hit its crescendo.

Naturally, the emotional climax for a TV narrative about infidelity is payback. Yet, beginning with their first match at *Summerslam '05*, Edge was presented as the superior man who was perhaps not in the moral right, but whose obvious Machiavellian traits made him an understandable associate with whom Lita would do wrong. Even with Hardy seemingly giving Edge his best shot in a brutal Street Fight on Raw, the no-contest ending implied that Matt could beat him up but that he could not defeat him.

At *Unforgiven*, in the best WWE Steel Cage Match of the 21st century, Hardy, Edge, and Lita told their story wonderfully. They played off the *Summerslam* bout very well, with Matt re-establishing his role as the protagonist who seemingly could not measure up to his enemy. In this instance, though, he was able to overcome the massive beat down and gain revenge. Hardy gave Lita a Twist of Fate and pinned Edge following a leg drop from off the top of the cage; accordingly, it was all the more rewarding for Matt and his supporters to have had to wait to see the comeuppance delivered.

Today, it is commonplace for real world affairs to be utilized in WWE storylines but, fifteen years ago, WWE was still trying to find a way to exist in a world where the internet lifted the veil on their business for anyone across the globe who wanted to see behind it. The way that the Hardy, Lita, and Edge saga was handled saw WWE take a big step forward into the modern history of the industry.

#69
CM Punk vs. Jeff Hardy
World Heavyweight Championship
Extreme Rules 2009 to Summerslam 2009
Top 15 All-Time Ladder Match / Top 15 All-Time at
Summerslam / Top 5 Match in 2009

Storytelling at perhaps its modern best occurs when two philosophies are pitted against each other that are relatable, even when the lines between good vs. evil are still clearly drawn. Erik Killmonger vs. T'Challa in *The Black Panther* is one of Hollywood's finest recent examples. One of the elite instances in pro wrestling lore occurred when the idealistic CM Punk fought over the World Heavyweight Championship during the summer of 2009 with the devil-may-care Jeff Hardy. Their lifestyles and personalities were polar opposites and it made for an awesome rivalry.

June that year kick-started what many fans came to call the first "Summer of Punk" in tribute to the rise of the Second City Saint as a "can't miss" act on WWE television. Though he had previously enjoyed mild success, winning the Money in the Bank Ladder Match at *WrestleMania XXIV* and cashing in three months later to become World Heavyweight Champion, he was a reasonably popular but rather bland babyface whose run near the top was forgettable. When he won Money in the Bank for a second time at *WrestleMania XXV* and cashed in again to become World Champion, the more organically antagonistic side of him emerged, and he began to thrive. In his first run with the title, he was a wrestler with a gimmick; he was the guy whose only vice was wrestling. During his second reign as champion, he developed a character; he slowly became the irreproachable, "Straight Edge" preacher whose choices made him better than you.

Some might think of the time between June and August '09 instead as "The Summer of Hardy." The youngest of the Hardy brothers had been a major star for most of a decade and had finally reached World Championship status by December 2008. His feud with Edge, full of twists and turns for six months, had culminated in a Ladder Match at *Extreme Rules* on June 7th. Hardy finally defeated The Rated R Superstar one-on-one to win back the title, but then Punk unceremoniously "cashed in" at his expense.

It was a perfect storm. Hardy scratched and clawed on the biggest stage in the world for years, working his way up from enhancement talent to tag team legend to Intercontinental Champion to World Heavyweight Champion. It is arguable that The Charismatic Enigma was never better or more popular than he was that summer and Punk's decision to wield the Money in the Bank contract heelishly at his expense was a stunning twist of fate to what seemed like Hardy's "moment." Then, once Punk got into a groove as the same type of ironically virtuous villain that had made him a legend on the independent wrestling scene, the natural dichotomy between their polar opposite ways of living became as much a central theme for their storyline as did the World Heavyweight Title.

The fanatical sect of a certain group of people can be very self-righteous. You see it with sports fans who develop unhealthy obsessions with their teams or staunch believers in one very narrow-minded religious school of thought. Substance abuse being a big problem in our world, a split has manifested that pits on one extreme side those that are addicts who over-indulge in drugs and alcohol and find ways to rationalize it, and on the other side those who abstain completely and constantly remind you of it. In real life, Hardy had a well-established track record of vacillating somewhere between recreational use and outright abuse. Punk, meanwhile, lived the "Straight Edge" lifestyle and became known as an occasionally moody prick, coming across like he believed everything he said in his promos about how he chose to live with every ounce of conviction.

Playing off of Hardy, Punk had the wrestling world hanging on his every word. "It's easier to be weak like Jeff because you sure can't be strong like me," he said in one of his brilliant promos. "I have to get rid of you so they stop living in your moment and they wake up and start living in my reality," he poignantly pointed out in another. Although Jeff's known-habits were morally questionable, Punk was coming across as the guy who spray paints someone's car with the words "Go Home Drunk Idiots" while the owner has one beer at the bar with his wife; he did it as only the best heels can, by striking the right emotional chords.

Their trio of pay-per-view matches told a flowing tale of redemption and relapse. In the ring, Hardy wrestled like he lived his life: "in the moment," claiming that beating Punk *his way* to win back the title was his salvation. Punk was far more calculated and methodical, tempting Hardy into the kind of environment – a TLC Match at *Summerslam '09* – about which Jeff once said, "My main concern is going out there and doing the one thing that people are going to remember more than anything." In a title bout that closed out the second biggest show of the year as reward for their on-screen efforts, they tore the house down with one of the best story-driven Ladder Match-variants ever, still brutally physical but equally as clever. Hardy could not help himself; during the climax, he climbed a ladder set-up near Punk's prone body on top of the announce table and Swanton Bombed away his final reign as World Champion.

Summerslam '09 turned out to be Hardy's Mt. Everest climb, his rivalry with Punk the summit of his singles career. He never ascended so high again. Punk climbed higher and represented in the minds of many the peak of the Reality Era opposite foes diametrically opposed to what he stood for to wrestling fans, but the natural extension of himself that shaped his Straight Edge Savior persona never met a more perfect match than The Charismatic Enigma.

#68
Chris Jericho vs. Chris Benoit
WrestleMania 2000 to Royal Rumble 2001

Top 15 All-Time Ladder Match / Top 10 All-Time at The Royal
Rumble / Top 10 Match in 2001

The Rock vs. Triple H and Shawn Michaels vs. Bret Hart are two
of the landmark examples of rivalries fought initially from the
bottom of the card all the way up to the top in WWE lore. Chris
Jericho vs. Chris Benoit does not often get mentioned in that
category but, even if their feud cannot equal the historical
relevance of such peers, it certainly could be said to have been a
more overt wrestling-characterization of the phrase, "coming-of-
age." When they began working together roughly six and three
months respectively removed from their debuts, they were
relatively unknown WWF commodities scratching and clawing
to duplicate and build upon their WCW successes but, by the
time they had concluded their on-again, off-again feud a year-
and-a-half later, they were each main-event tested and Vince
McMahon-approved.

Transitioning to the "WWE-style" was notoriously hard on many
of the former WCW stars, particularly during and immediately
following the Monday Night Wars, with all its requisite extra
scrutiny on talents who had made the jump. Jericho was
perhaps the most prominent to have struggled, drawing the ire
of the boss early and often. "You're green as grass and it's
embarrassing," Jericho recalled McMahon telling him during a
private meeting in his second book *Undisputed*.

Y2J and Benoit's triple threat match at *WrestleMania 2000* also
involving Kurt Angle was a prime showcase of the steep learning
curve that they were experiencing; they each displayed flashes of
the wrestlers that they would become in WWE, but timing issues
were aplenty.

Spinning off from that three-way scenario, however, was the beginning of their yearlong rivalry. In April, at *Backlash 2000*, Jericho and Benoit wrestled for fifteen minutes with the Intercontinental Championship on the line. It was a marked improvement over anything that either man had done to that point in the WWF and was a throwback to the quality that both had shown themselves capable of producing during the height of Monday Nitro. The following month in a Submissions Match at *Judgment Day* also with the IC Title at stake, they again delivered.

The WWE-style is best described by its production, psychology, and symmetry; what the wrestlers are going to do, why they are going to do it, and how best to execute the details are all discussed in the days and hours leading up to a match. Neither Jericho nor Benoit had ever lacked for talent, but far less went into their matches in WCW ahead of time; they were given a finish and they figured out the rest from bell-to-bell. *Backlash* and *Judgment Day* were efforts that made obvious the strides they were making in the art of crafting their matches, so much so that their feud was paused before *Summerslam* so that they could prominently clash with the alpha and omega of the year 2000, Triple H and The Rock, at *Fully Loaded* in July.

Jericho and Benoit passed their headlining tests with flying colors. Subsequently, their Two-out-of-Three Falls Match at *Summerslam* (no IC Title involved) watched more distinctly like a battle between two men well on their way to becoming two of the Top 30 stars of the WrestleMania Era and less like the work of two aspiring talents trying to ingratiate themselves in a brave new world. By the time *Royal Rumble 2001* had come around, Benoit had won back the Intercontinental Championship, Jericho had made it his business to regain it, and their scheduled encounter felt like the biggest match for the WWF's second oldest singles title since Rock and Triple H classically fought over it at *Summerslam '98*.

The Intercontinental Title had actually not been up for grabs in a Ladder Match since Rock-Hunter and, though many a Ladder

Match had taken place in between that built the gimmick's reputation as a stunt-brawl (see the rise of the Tag Team Ladder Match and TLC), Jericho and Benoit returned the genre to its HBK-Razor roots. Theirs was a utilization of the stipulation that was incredibly hard-hitting (see Jericho's chair shot to Benoit's head as he was diving to the outside) and innovative (see Jericho's Ladder-assisted Walls), but it was also more cerebral in its performance. Fans who better appreciate the little things might agree that, because of their efforts in the story-driven sub-genre of the gimmick, Jericho and Benoit are both underrated masters of the Ladder Match.

Tensions between them had been escalating higher for nearly a year, with Jericho losing all three previous one-on-one pay-per-view matches to Benoit. It has been rare that an IC Title victory this century has felt of similar consequence to its brethren from the 1980s and 1990s, but Jericho's cathartic win counts among the few.

They would go on to form an unlikely and extremely successful duo, would Benoit and Y2J, which would segue to another triple threat match with them as two of the three participants, this time for Steve Austin's WWF Championship. At their next two January Classic appearances following their all-time classic Ladder Match in 2001, Jericho would successfully defend the Undisputed Title and then take a key step toward his all-time classic *WrestleMania* match with Shawn Michaels, while Benoit would go onto have the match of his life against Angle for the WWE Title and then become just the second man to win the Royal Rumble Match as the first entrant.

Unquestionably, Jericho and Benoit came-of-age, from WCW projects to bonafide headliners, fighting each other.

#67
Team Austin vs. Team Bischoff
5-on-5 Elimination Tag Team Match
Survivor Series
November 16, 2003

#2 Survivor Series Elimination Match / Top 5 All-Time at Survivor Series / Top 10 Match in 2003

In the two post-comeback classics that Shawn Michaels performed before *Survivor Series 2003*, he had shown only glimpses of his full range of capabilities. To take nothing away from either match, the Non-Sanctioned bout against Triple H at *Summerslam 2002* achieved its unforgettable status by fully utilizing the opportunities afforded to it by the Street Fight gimmick; and the dream encounter between HBK and Y2J at *WrestleMania XIX* was really more of a Chris Jericho match. Michaels himself admitted to not being completely "back" after the Seattle show-stealer. "I was getting closer to feeling like I was the performer I had been before injuring my back," HBK noted in his first book. "I was not the Showstopper yet, but I was getting close."

Fifteen months after his comeback began, he entered the ring in Dallas, Texas for what promised to be perhaps the most psychologically engaging traditional Survivor Series match ever. Steve Austin's career was on the line. Jim Ross called the occasion, "The biggest match that Austin has never wrestled in." HBK and Stone Cold had not crossed paths on television since *WrestleMania XIV*, when The Rattlesnake had ushered in the Austin Era while simultaneously slamming the door shut on the Michaels Era. One of Austin's catchphrases was "Don't Trust Anybody," and yet here was Stone Cold being forced to trust that his career-threatening match would be won by a man who had every reason to purposefully lose and to simultaneously slam the door shut on Austin's career.

Pro wrestling matches are a fascinating blend of real life and on-screen character motivations. In any given performance, then, a unique dichotomy exists with what we are watching. The HBK persona, for instance, could have – at *Survivor Series 2003* – tapped into past prejudice held against the man who had, in WWE's fictional universe, defeated him in his final match and took his coveted World Championship. The man behind the persona, however, had made his name on giving absolutely everything he had to his opponents. "My back was shot, I was hooked on pain pills, and my spirits were shattered," he would say years later about his status going into the *'Mania XIV* main-event. He was unable to give Austin his best in 1998, but this match in November 2003 gave him a mulligan. Michaels made the most of it.

Shawn Michaels improbably came back from retirement at *Summerslam '02*. The Showstopper truly came back at *Survivor Series 2003*.

Michaels became the last remaining member of Team Austin when Team Bischoff still had Chris Jericho, Christian, and Randy Orton in the fold. Already facing a 3-on-1 disadvantage, HBK was launched into the ring post. When the camera re-focused on him, he was wearing one of the greatest versions of the crimson mask in WWE lore. He bled buckets and fought valiantly in the face of certain defeat to save Austin's career. He delivered Sweet Chin Music out of nowhere to eliminate Christian and desperately countered the Walls of Jericho into a pin-securing roll-up to eliminate Y2J. With only Orton left for Michaels to overcome, Bischoff and Austin both got involved in the proceedings, allowing the Legend Killer's stablemate, Batista, to swoop in and help Orton snatch victory right from HBK's grasp.

Samuel 'Plan, in his fantastic book *101 WWE Matches To See Before You Die*, wrote about the climax that "As Austin's music had for years started with the shattering of glass, his era ended with the shattering of a dream, courtesy of a hard and stark reality; Austin's forced departure was the reality, Shawn's miracle effort to prevent it the dream." A "miracle effort" well describes HBK's incredible performance.

As much as the second half of Team Austin vs. Team Bischoff was essentially a Shawn Michaels match, its legacy was forged by all thirteen men who played a role in it becoming the blueprint for how best to execute the Elimination Tag Team gimmick. Austin, HBK, Rob Van Dam, The Dudley Boyz, Booker T, Bischoff, Y2J, Christian, Orton, Mark Henry, and Scott Steiner (plus Batista, who was not officially in the match) all had the chance to showcase their abilities in a story with very fluid, non-stop action and numerous momentum changes. Orton, who had foreshadowed that it might be his night earlier in the show when he attacked the owner of the Dallas Mavericks, was particularly noteworthy in his performance. Jericho, meanwhile, was outstanding, and it should not be forgotten that this was as much his storyline crusade to oust Austin from his then-Raw General Manager position as it was Bischoff's.

Its quality should come as no surprise, in hindsight; nine of the ten men who comprised the teams are in the Top 60 of the WrestleMania Era (and Henry is a former World Heavyweight Champion), Austin is Top 10 and Batista is Top 20. Other than the WWF vs. WCW/ECW Alliance match in 2001, Team Austin vs. Team Bischoff was the most star-studded Survivor Series match of all-time.

So, the obvious question is why was it not also the greatest? Simply put, it may have provided the blueprint for Survivor Series matches, but eleven years later that blueprint was utilized to create something greater that may not have been anchored by a performance as brilliant as HBK's in 2003, but that enabled the rest of its competitors to shine brighter and allowed its similarly emotional high points to be better processed and absorbed by the audience.

#66
Shawn Michaels vs. Ric Flair
Career-Threatening Match
WrestleMania XXIV
March 30, 2008

Top 30 All-Time at WrestleMania / Top 5 Match in 2008

If there was a single word that best characterized WWE on March 29-30, 2008, it was "passion." Ric Flair was inducted into the Hall of Fame on Saturday and retired at the end of one final classic match at *WrestleMania XXIV* on Sunday. It is difficult not to get sentimental when recalling those events mainly because Flair himself was so outwardly emotional.

To date, he has been the only wrestler in WWE history to be given the Hall of Fame nod and a retirement match on the same WrestleMania weekend. It created a uniquely affecting dynamic that makes Flair's Hall of Fame speech requisite viewing in order to best appreciate his match with Shawn Michaels the following night. Watch it today and you will feel through the screen what it meant not only to him but to everyone in attendance. As he stood at that podium for an hour-and-a-half reflecting on all the people who played key roles in his life as a pro wrestler, it made you hope that one day something that you have done will have meant as much to you as being "The Nature Boy" meant to Ric Flair.

Triple H, in his introductory remarks prior to inducting his idol, aptly stated, "What made Ric Flair is his passion; his passion for life, his passion for this business. Ric Flair eats, sleeps, and breathes this business." Never was that more apparent than in the Citrus Bowl the next night when, in the closing moments of what was billed his "Career-Threatening Match," Flair started sobbing. During the Hall of Fame, he had barely held it together emotionally, tearing up on numerous occasions. When HBK's boot began stomping in the corner, "tuning up the band" for

145

Sweet Chin Music, the gravity of the moment gripped Naitch by his heart and he broke down.

No wrestler ever put more of himself into his craft than Richard Morgan Fliehr. His self-worth was wrapped up in being Ric Flair. What we saw when he fell apart at the end of that match was a man super-kicked into a phase of his life that he was not ready for. On Michael Jordan's 50th birthday, *ESPN The Magazine* did a feature on him in which he revealed that he still thought about getting down to his playing weight and making another comeback; MJ has never been able to let go of being a basketball player. Ric Flair, in some circles regarded as the Jordan of the squared circle, was not prepared in 2008 to let go of being a professional wrestler.

Ironically, a phenomenal film was released later that year called *The Wrestler* and, during the climactic scene, lead character Randy "The Ram" Robinson – who, like Naitch, reached his peak in the 1980s yet was still active into the late 2000s – tells the people attending a show to see him, "You know what? The only one that's going to tell me when I'm through doing my thing is you people here." You get the impression that Flair felt the exact same way; that he would have been fine dying in the ring. WWE did the right thing by him in trying to usher in the end of his in-ring career, but to the final three count of his last WWE match, Flair did everything he could to show the world that he could still perform at a higher level than the vast majority of his younger peers.

A straight wrestling match involving a 59 year old should have no business in the Top 100 of an analytical countdown of the greatest matches of the WrestleMania Era, but it is Ric Flair we are talking about. He "walked that aisle" surrounded by a beautiful setting and 74,635 people in a gorgeous robe that would have made his late seamstress, Olivia Walker, proud. Thanks in large part to Shawn Michaels, it was the best match Flair had wrestled in almost 15 years. More chants of "WOOO" were heard live that night than ever before. Flair was bathed in adoration as he hugged and kissed his family sitting at ringside and walked up the ramp one last time. What a way to go out...

All the credit in the world goes to HBK for scripting such an amazing tribute. He would later admit to demanding from Flair that he allow him full control over the match. Michaels was representing every fan who ever paid money to see The Nature Boy wrestle; he had a vision for what the last match in the career of arguably the greatest ever and inarguably one of the Top 5 of the WrestleMania Era should look like.

Mr. WrestleMania more than lived up to his reputation that night, guiding the retiring icon through a work of art that felt like a vintage Flair match from start to finish mixed with the brand of dramatic storytelling that HBK had become famous for in his post-comeback run. All that you could hope to see from one of The Nature Boy's matches was included; finally connecting with the flying cross body block to the "Dirtiest Player in the Game" tactics and everything in between. And when the time came to bring it home, Michaels noticeably looked at Flair and told him, "I'm sorry, I love you." Seconds later, it was over. Passion personified...

#65
Christian vs. Randy Orton
World Heavyweight Championship
May 6, 2011 Smackdown to Summerslam 2011

<u>Top 20 All-Time at Summerslam</u> / <u>Top 5 Match in 2011</u>

It took seventeen years for Christian to finally win the World Heavyweight Championship in WWE. A great many thought he never would, but he became one of those rare, special cases of the long-time veteran mid-carder breaking the proverbial glass ceiling. The victory over Alberto Del Rio and the quite genuinely emotional embrace with Edge afterward were opportunities for wrestling fans to watch someone's dream come true, but Christian's fairy-tale ended two days after he won the title (five if you add in the three days until Smackdown aired).

Imagine that for a moment. In some ways, we have all been there. Just when that ultimate goal has been achieved, something happens to yank the rug right out from underneath. Captain Charisma held the belt long enough to see "Christian" engraved on the plate they attach to the championship, and then he had to hand it over to Randy Orton presumably without any guarantee from Vince McMahon that he would ever get it back. A long-time Christian fan emailed that weekend, "I feel like I've been punched in the stomach, like Everton won the Premiership on Sunday and had it vetoed on Tuesday."

Christian's attempt to regain the title a few weeks later was equal parts thrilling underdog story and phenomenal display of in-ring chemistry. At *Over The Limit '11*, he and Orton had a remarkable match, countering each other's signature moves numerous times and producing out-of-your-seat-worthy false finishes, the ones nearly earning Captain Charisma the victory especially gut-wrenching for his "Peeps." It was such an intelligent performance. If the title change on Smackdown was psychologically presented as Orton the ever-confident predator against Christian the reluctant-but-capable new champion, then the rematch on pay-per-view was Orton at his babyface best, still showing traces of the vicious Viper but with more respect for his prey versus Christian, the challenger desperate to prove that he could still win the World Title even if there was no ladder involved.

Though he came ever-so-close, Christian failed to win back the championship. Overcome with emotion, he snapped on an ensuing episode of Smackdown and blasted Orton with the title belt; that is to say that he physically snapped, as his actions may have drawn the ire of the champion but, in knowing that Orton would retaliate, also afforded him one more chance at the championship against a weakened titleholder. At *Capitol Punishment*, The Apex Predator – still fully recovering from a concussion caused by Christian's belt-shot – was not 100%, seemingly giving the challenger a distinct advantage. However, at the conclusion of another hotly contested match full of the twists and turns fans had fast come to expect when they saw "Christian vs. Orton" on the marquee, The Viper struck with the RKO and pinned Captain Charisma yet again. Another opportunity for Christian and another failure.

Or was it? Christian's foot was clearly positioned underneath the bottom rope during the three-count that gave Orton the victory. Though definitively pinned, the technicality offered the challenger a glimmer of hope that he yet still may have one more chance to prove that he could beat The Viper.

In the weeks leading to *Money in the Bank*, what had begun as a competition between respectful rivals was reduced to despicable levels when Christian brought in a lawyer and added a clause in the rematch contract that gave Orton a fundamental disadvantage – should he get disqualified or should the referee make another mistake, Captain Charisma would automatically win the title. It was a cheap heel tactic, but its executor was excellent and his plan to regain the World Championship by any means necessary proved effective. Incredibly, he transitioned from the man everyone wanted to win to the man many wanted to lose in a matter of a couple months.

Just different enough from the previous three matches and featuring continually evolving character dynamics so as not to feel repetitive, the fourth bout in the series ended with the beginning of Christian's second reign as World Champion. In a brilliant bit of irony considering Orton's Legend Killer tendencies of 2003, Christian spit in his face, igniting a fury that led to The Viper gifting the title to his challenger thanks to a blatant low blow and then assaulting him with two RKOs on the announce table.

Summerslam 2011 played host to the payoff match, contested with No Holds Barred. Watched separate from the previous bouts, it was a very good performance worthy of headlining the second biggest show of the year; within the context of the entire saga, it was exemplary. Not only was the storytelling tremendous – how it brought Edge back into the fold pre-match and how it touched on the emotional twists of the overall feud – but it also served as a reminder of how to work a no-rules gimmick utilizing simplistic creativity absent the hardcore stylings of blood or flaming tables.

Every truly great series of matches features nuance in the sequences of moves performed, moments that, as with Mysterio vs. Y2J, play off of the key points in previous encounters –logical progressions in a physical game of chess. Only a rare class of wrestlers can string together four consecutive PPV matches without the rivalry becoming stale; with all due respect to Orton, it really was Christian who made the entire storyline so interesting. Because of the era-starting efforts of The Second City Saint, that time in 2011 is often referred to as the second "Summer of Punk." That many fans would still refer to it as the "Summer of Christian" is a testament to Captain Charisma's versatility, and of course his in-ring chemistry with Orton.

#64
Ric Flair vs. Terry Funk
WrestleWar '89 to Clash of the Champions IX
Top 5 Match in 1989

November 15, 1989 will forever be known as the night when either Terry Funk or Ric Flair would have to say to the other man two words consisting of five letters: "I Quit."

Back on May 7th, Flair had just regained the World Heavyweight Title to conclude his marvelous series with Ricky Steamboat when Funk entered the scene from his ringside judge's position to congratulate the new champion and put his name in the hat as the first challenger. Politely, Flair reminded Funk that there was a Top 10 ranking for contenders and that, legendary as he was given his status as a former NWA titleholder (for 424 days in the mid-1970s), Funk might have to wait. His pride wounded, Funk snapped and put Flair out of action for over two months with a piledriver onto a table. Echoing the words of Bubba Ray Dudley, "This was one of the most memorable things ever seen on television" to many fans of the time. Stuff like that just did not happen back then and it served as the inspiration for Dudley to famously incorporate the use of tables as regular weapons in his matches.

Sympathy for Flair was rampant and, for a character not particularly relatable, his ability to come across as the injured star athlete struggling with the sands of time was impressive and gave added fan motivation to an already increasing desire to cheer him for just being awesome. So typically brash and loud, his interviews successfully translated to the audience a humble tone throughout mid-to-late 1989. In the ring, the matches with Funk were some of the rare moments in Flair's career when his babyface exploits were close to on-par with his classic villainy; he was able to scale back his natural bravado to very effectively portray the comeback kid and keep the crowd in the palm of his

151

hand all the same as if he were leading the charge as the antagonist.

Funk was really the one who pushed Flair to a different sort of high point in his career; nothing on Naitch's career resume quite resembles the Funk feud. "Middle-aged and crazy, but crazy like a fox," Funk said of himself and, when he turned up the volume on that personality, it was one of the most fascinating portrayals in pro wrestling lore, as good a maniacal villain as Flair was an elitist heel. He was 45 years old when he came back to WCW from doing small parts in cult-classic movies such as *Road House* and *Over The Top*; perspective-laden as many wrestlers are during that stretch of their lives, Funk seemed to relish the chance to engage his industry's best wrestler.

One never knew what exactly Funk might do; that was part of what made him special. His match with Steamboat at *Clash of the Champions VII* ended with a prophetic blast to The Dragon's head with a microphone, reinforcing that he could snap and become exceptionally dangerous at a moment's notice. At *The Great American Bash*, site of the initial Funk-Flair showdown, Funk was escorted to the ring by a swarm of security guards, suggesting just as it did for Goldberg in the late-1990s that The Funker was not someone to be messed with; during the bout, he reinforced that notion by busting Flair open with a branding iron. In September, he attacked Flair again, this time wrapping a plastic bag over his head in an attempt to suffocate him; the visual was not exactly PG, given that Flair was already bleeding from a previous head-wound. All the while, when he was not losing his mind, he was frequently reminding of his sharply-tuned overall wrestling acumen, particularly his affinity for taking a beating.

The story leading up to and through *Clash of the Champions IX* was certainly one for the ages that wrestling historians have continued to hold in high-esteem all these years later. As rivalries go, it can go toe-to-toe with any feud from any era; and the matches within their saga have mostly passed the test of time. Its strengths many and its weaknesses few, it did a lot of things differently than its WrestleMania Era peers, which play into its place in the pantheon and make it challenging to rank. Nevertheless, The Nature Boy was as believable as a babyface as he ever would be, The Funker had as transcendent a six-month run as anyone ever has, and their payoff match was as gripping as any of the decade's finest.

By the time the "I Quit" Match happened, "integrity and [their] very man-hood" were on the line in place of the World Title. They had, from May to November, convinced fans of the sport just how much they hated each other and they expertly crafted a pay-off match that progressively built to a fitting end for their lengthy struggle.

<u>#63</u>
Shane McMahon vs. Kurt Angle
Street Fight
King of the Ring
June 24, 2001
<u>Top 10 Match in 2001</u>

No match moved up the Top 100 list during the ranking process as often as the Shane McMahon vs. Kurt Angle Street Fight. It scored fairly well against its peers in 2001, but not well enough to give it anything more than a spot on the fringe, near the cut-off close to the Honorable Mentions, in the early research phases. Then came the next viewings, putting it head-to-head opposite no-brainer choices in the Top 75 and, as a result of its brutality and entertainment value, it ultimately climbed closer to the Top 50.

Until recent years, Shane's matches, by comparison to his father's, were primarily confined to the high profile mid-card category. Consequently, his feuds against the likes of X-Pac, Test, Kane, Angle, and others lacked the epic aura, if you will, that the vast majority of the Top 50 possessed. Really, along with a pretty quiet crowd response, that historically subdued storyline-verve is the only thing that Angle-McMahon lacks. The Street Fight was a tremendous bell-to-bell performance that comfortably rates as the superlative in Shane's body of work (challenged only by his match at *WrestleMania 33* with AJ Styles) and should undoubtedly make any conscious countdown of Angle's greatest too.

For Angle, it represented to his career what *Mind Games* was for the perception of Shawn Michaels. Not that it was difficult to take him seriously, as the 1996 gold medal gave him legitimacy that all the money in the world could not buy; it was just that, much like HBK in the mid-1990s needed the bout against Mankind to show he was tough, Angle needed the match with

154

Shane to overtly express that not-yet-displayed extra "You've crossed me so now I'm going to kick your ass" gear. Intensity had been one of his persona's "Three Is," but there was something inescapably goofy about him that made what he did to Shane – bullying him and ruthlessly throwing him into and through the glass panes of the pay-per-view set – necessary for the completion of his character CV; at no point beyond that match did there ever seem to be a question again about Angle's place among the most well-rounded stars in the industry.

The fight's signature sequence at the top of the entrance stage was an accident, interestingly enough. "Unfortunately, whoever was responsible for getting the glass, got the wrong glass," Angle once said. "It was supposed to be [easily breakable] sugar glass, and it was Plexiglas. When we did break it, we both got bloodied up. There wasn't even supposed to be any pyro that night because they were afraid the sugar glass would crumble." Bruce Prichard, on-screen known as Brother Love and one of Vince McMahon's advisers circa 2001, described the backstage scene during that stretch of the match as "one of the most uncomfortable moments of my life" and that Vince was "cursing and yelling" at him to signal the referee to prevent further incidents when the first pane failed to break and Shane landed hard on top of his head.

Angle has had a tendency to deflect much of the credit for the bout's success to McMahon, thanks in part to his bumping. He has posited, "It was Shane's match. It was his time to shine. I knew I was going to have many other nights, Shane wasn't. Whatever I could do to please him, I was going to do."

For Shane, who joins Mick Foley and Jeff Hardy among WWE lore's premier stuntmen, *King of the Ring '01* was more than just another vehicle for him to put his body at risk to satisfy his daredevil urge. "Growing up in the [wrestling] business and witnessing amazing matches," Shane stated in a 2016 interview, "I always hoped that I'd have an opportunity to even scratch the surface and even attempt to have one of those matches." His average one-on-one match length (from 1999 to 2009) was 11 ½ minutes. Angle was hitting his initial career peak at the time and was a bonafide main-event player who commanded show-making opportunities; at 26-minutes, McMahon's match with Angle represented his best-ever chance to have the classic he sought to perform. Success has been commonplace in sports entertainment for the McMahon family but, thanks to the Street Fight, Shane owns the title for the most enthralling and memorable battle involving a non-wrestler in WWE history.

Frankly, Angle vs. Shane has proven itself to be, simply put, one of the most fun matches of all-time and, as such, is infinitely re-watchable. The movie, *Jaws*, sits in a similar position in the American Film Institute's 2007 list of Hollywood's greatest films as Shane vs. Angle does here. What the match shares with the film is that, broken down into its component parts, it probably does not belong in the Top 50. However, ask any movie-buff if they would watch *Jaws* on TV some random Saturday afternoon ahead of the superiorly ranked films and, they might not all choose it, but you can pretty much guarantee that nearly everyone would at least have to think about it; Shane O Mac fighting for his life against Our Olympic Hero induces the same internal conflict among wrestling fans when asked a similar question about watching the Street Fight at *King of the Ring '01* instead of the matches, rivalries, and stories to follow on the coming pages.

#62
John Cena vs. Umaga
Last Man Standing Match
The Royal Rumble
January 28, 2007

#2 All-Time Last Man Standing Match / Top 10 All-Time at Royal Rumble / Top 5 Match in 2007

Anyone who followed WWE through John Cena's unprecedented run as the industry's biggest star knows of the common refrains that accompanied his matches, among the many of which were chants from the audience of "You Can't Wrestle." Cena's in-ring abilities were under the microscope from the outset, due in part to the physically-awkward manner that he moved around the canvas. He was a Division III All-American (football) offensive lineman, so his athletic-gait was built for pushing people around instead of gracefully bounding to and fro.

Professional wrestling has often been compared to ballet, which combines storytelling with aesthetically-pleasing movement. Where that analogy falls short is that the object of the performance in sports entertainment is not limited to the equivalent of physical poetry; in other words, not every wrestling match has to look as pretty as Michaels, Angle, or Flair made it appear, fortunately for John Cena, in his early days as a headliner especially.

Though Cena, before *WrestleMania 23*, had a tendency to look the part of an offensive lineman on the basketball court when he was wrestling standard singles matches en route to his development into a bonafide all-time great, he knew the game; inelegant as he may have been, he was very competent. He had the ability to translate his charisma into the combat aspect of sports entertainment and he was strong enough to do anything that anyone could ever ask of him in a match. Cena went on to earn praise for the bell-to-bell work during his prime years but, even earlier on, he had outstanding performances that hold up incredibly well against his later standard. Especially when the rules were de-emphasized in brawling atmospheres, one thing that without question Cena could do to achieve widespread respect before his physical maturation was throw down in a knock-down, drag-out fight.

And he and Umaga had a hell of a fight!

Umaga was a very well-presented monster heel who debuted on the post-'Mania Raw in 2006 and went undefeated until losing to Cena at *New Year's Revolution '07*. A member of the famed Anoa'i wrestling family (The Rock, Yokozuna, Rikishi, and Roman Reigns, among others), The Samoan Bulldozer was a swift-moving super-heavyweight known for his striking. Adding to his presentation was Armando Alejandro Estrada, whose engaging, Cuban-accented introduction of Umaga is one of the era's too-often-forgotten soundbites.

The Last Man Standing stipulation was added to their rematch for the WWE Championship on account of Cena scoring a rather resourceful-but-indecisive win to hand Umaga his very first loss. With no restrictions in place at *Royal Rumble '07*, they beat the tar out of each other; the Samoan was blasted right in the face with the ring steps, which Cena had thrown at him from the squared circle to the floor; Cena was busted open when he could not maintain Umaga's weight for an FU and fell head-first into the steel steps; Umaga had his head smashed in between the ring post and, courtesy of Cena, a TV monitor; Cena landed hard on his neck and shoulder when taking Umaga's Samoan Drop; in probably the most enduring moment of the match, Umaga ran across two announce tables and crashed through a third when he missed Cena with a diving splash; finally, following a thunderous FU, Cena wrapped the ring ropes, which Estrada had loosened in one corner to help Umaga fashion a spike out of the metal part of the ring that connects the turnbuckle to the post, around Umaga's neck and, according to WWE folklore, legitimately choked him out (in a modified STF) before getting the decisive ten count. It was an unforgettable war.

WWE's romanticized relationship with WrestleMania has prompted fans and peers alike to point to the Shawn Michaels matches in April 2007 as Cena's in-ring turning point, but *Royal Rumble '07* likewise cannot be understated in its importance to Cena's career.

The significance of the Umaga match to John Cena lore (and, thus, WWE history) is two-fold. First of all, it was one of the greatest brawls of the 21st century, a Last Man Standing Match that stands the test of time as one of the preeminent versions of the genre in addition to being one of the ten greatest matches overall at The Royal Rumble. Second, it was the match that allowed him to show the world that he did not need the assistance of a tenured veteran to maximize the potential of a high profile performance. When he became #1 Contender to the WWE Championship at *No Way Out '05*, the list of wrestlers with whom he was paired for the next two years included Angle, JBL, Jericho, Christian, Edge, Triple H, RVD, Booker T, and Big Show, each of them Top 50 selections in *The WrestleMania Era*. The Umaga series in January 2007 was Cena in a sink-or-swim situation and, at *Royal Rumble*, he swam a few laps.

<u>#61</u>
Brock Lesnar vs. Undertaker
Unforgiven to No Mercy 2002; WrestleMania XXX to Hell in a Cell 2015

<u>Top 10 (x2) All-Time Hell in a Cell Match</u> / <u>Top 10 Match in 2002</u> / <u>Top 10 Match in 2015</u>

Featuring one of the most infamous and historic moments in modern pro wrestling lore as well as a pair of Top 10 Hell in a Cell matches, Brock Lesnar vs. Undertaker, it could be argued, deserves to be ranked higher than #61. However, theirs was always a mixed bag of a rivalry, marred as it was by questionable creative decisions in their television storylines and the controversial response to the finishes in most of their six featured pay-per-view bouts. Before Autumn 2015, in fact, their original Hell in a Cell from 2002, the best match in their on-again, off-again saga from both the first and second parts of Brock's WWE career, began phase two of the research process at #92. It was the strength of their second Hell in a Cell in 2015, one of the most underrated matches in an era full of great ones, that elevated the feud to its current position.

In the bloodiest brawl in WWE since 2008's Michaels vs. Jericho non-sanctioned fight prompted changes to the rules on intentional bleeding, Taker vs. Lesnar at *Hell in a Cell '15* was precisely the modern slugfest – complete with The Phenom's crafty machinations of believably unsettling the Beast Mode routine – that many had hoped for both when they wrestled two months prior in the main-event at *Summerslam '15* and roughly nineteen months prior in a marquee match at *WrestleMania XXX*. It was a smartly worked battle that capitalized on the chemistry that its combatants had built in the early 2000s and it was enhanced by its original use of the exposed wood beneath the padding that covers the canvas during the climax.

The greatest rivalries do not rest on the laurels of their biggest moments. Lesnar vs. Taker was never short on noteworthy happenings, but while the imprint they left on WWE history is certainly more substantial than that of the Angle-Shane Street Fight, without the requisite work in the ring those moments would have deserved their attention on a separate list than this one. Such is the dynamic at play when ranking Taker vs. Lesnar, weighing the glorious against the notorious.

Summerslam '15 had ended in an over-booked mess (thanks to a "rogue timekeeper"); *WrestleMania XXX* had provided one of the most shocking moments in WWE history when Lesnar ended Taker's vaunted undefeated streak on "The Grandest Stage Of Them All," but the first twenty-five minutes and nine seconds that preceded the three-count were painfully disappointing (thanks to Taker suffering an early match concussion); rewinding the clock to *No Mercy '03*, the last PPV meeting between the two before Lesnar left WWE for eight years was agonizingly bad (thanks to it being handicapped by a "Biker Chain" stipulation). Their overall story needed that fitting, high-quality conclusion provided by their second foray into Satan's Structure to get their rivalry over the hump and deeper into the Top 100.

Make no mistake, however, that their rivalry would not have been able to crack the Top 75 without their first Hell in a Cell match. Back in 2008, WWE released a DVD set that anthologized the gimmick and afforded the chance to sequentially view each version to that point. Some iterations truly struggled in comparison to the ones most famous for their death-defying stunts, but Lesnar vs. Undertaker at *No Mercy '02* stood out as tremendously gory and, thanks to starting the trend of keeping the entire match within the confines of the Cell, was possibly the version that best captured the original intent of putting a roof on the structure. Unlike some of its peers that also kept the entire presentation in-house (including the vast majority of the Cell matches since the bleeding rules changed), Taker vs. Lesnar never failed to hold attention; vicious chair shots, tons of blood, Paul Heyman's effective complimentary role on the outside, and generally brutal physicality were plenty enough to offset the lack of a fall off the Cell or a fight on top of it.

One unmistakable quality of the Taker-Lesnar feud was its intent; the purpose was always, no matter in 2002, 2003, 2014, or 2015, to showcase Brock as the unstoppable monster and it irrefutably accomplished that goal. Lesnar earned a lot of credibility from stepping into Undertaker's "yard," taking everything that one of the most dominant stars ever could dish out, and leaving The Deadman longing for previous decades after being a victim along Lesnar's destructive path. Brock would not have become the star that he became without Undertaker and, though the historic moments and Hell in a Cell matches may not have left a mark indelible enough to move their rivalry into the Top 50, Taker vs. Lesnar did indeed make an impression.

#60
Ric Flair vs. Hulk Hogan
WCW Championship
Bash at the Beach
July 17, 1994

Top 5 Match in 1994

It is understandably difficult for many of the preceding entries to hold a historical candle to the first true "dream match" of the WrestleMania Era, no matter how much bigger it could have hypothetically been. WCW pulled the trigger on what was still regarded by many in 1994, when both wrestlers were past their physical primes, as the biggest match in pro wrestling history: Ric Flair vs. Hulk Hogan.

As good as it was – and it has had a tendency to be underrated over the years – it remains difficult to watch it without wondering how it might have looked in front of 62,167 at the Hoosier Dome in Indianapolis two years prior.

It is a fascinating exercise, looking back at certain periods throughout the last few decades and searching for reasons why various things panned out in the manner in which they did, scenarios on which fans often reflect and wonder, "What if?" Among the most commonly pondered and speculated about is, "What if the WWF had stuck with the original plan of Hogan vs. Flair at *WrestleMania VIII*?"

Numerous reasons have been given, from creative differences to egomaniacism. WWE has maintained in the nicest way possible that, as Jerry Brisco said on the documentary *The True Story of WrestleMania* regarding several pre-'Mania live events headlined by Hogan vs. Flair, "None of them seemed to be the attraction that we thought they were going to be." The Nature Boy himself even admitted in his book that they were unable to sell-out WWE's top market at the time, New York City's Madison Square

Garden; back then, such a thing carried a tremendous amount of weight in Titan Towers.

Enthusiasts around the world are to this day in agreement, however, that it was a massive missed opportunity not to push forward with the match. "It was forbidden fruit, the impossible dream, the battle no one thought would ever happen," Flair said of his clash of historic titans with Hogan. Throughout the 1980s, Hogan had reigned supreme as the WWF Champion, drawing the kind of money that Flair could never have hoped to equal. During the same period, Flair had ruled the NWA as its champion, becoming the landslide winner among aficionados as the Wrestler of the Decade on the strength of performances that Hogan could never have hoped to equal.

The top guys from each of the two remaining promotions left after the demise of the territory-based model surely would never end up in the same company. The phrase "dream match" is thrown around too often these days, but when Flair left what had by then become WCW in 1991 to work for Vince McMahon, something that fans had literally only been able to dream about prior to was there for the booking. And yet they passed...

Eric Bischoff, Ted Turner, and WCW did not miss the chance when the dream was offered another opportunity to be realized two-and-a-half years later. Improbable as it may have been, a series of events led to the ultimate WWF guy at the time in Hogan signing with WCW in June 1994. On Independence Day (USA), the Hulkster was thrown a ticker-tape parade. Less than two weeks later, Hogan vs. Flair finally happened.

It worked out well for WCW. Flair was coming off a triumphant return to the company in 1993, capped off by a huge win over Vader in a Title vs. Career match in the main-event of *Starrcade*. He was running pretty hot when Hogan arrived, so they both carried a great deal of momentum into their initial encounter (maybe even more than they would have in the WWF for *'Mania VIII*). They added pomp and circumstance to the presentation by involving Shaquille O'Neal and having Mr. T accompany Hogan to the ring; American Wrestling Association legend and WWE Hall of Famer, Nick Bockwinkel, then serving as WCW Commissioner, was at ringside; Michael Buffer was there for the introductions. Sure, it deserved all the dressings that only WWE and its WrestleMania stage could have provided, but WCW did its best. The allure of the dream becoming reality doubled WCW's previous-best pay-per-view buyrate and jam-packed the Orlando Arena.

Beyond the confines of the WWE ring, Flair and Hogan ditched much of the classic Hulkster formula, opting instead for the much more critically-acclaimed Nature Boy formula; as a result, their match featured a lot of back and forth action and several teases of their famous finishing sequences leading up to a meatier climax as opposed to the stereotypical style of Hogan getting beat-down for the bulk of the match and then making his miraculous comeback. Sherri Martel's involvement as Flair's manager was one of the forgotten aspects of the match's success, as she replicated a lot of what she famously contributed to Ultimate Warrior vs. Randy Savage in 1991. All in all, it was a thoroughly engaging piece of work.

They went onto have several other matches that exemplified the law of diminishing returns in wrestling, but their first encounter successfully captured the magic of the occasion and should be fondly remembered for it.

#59
Seth Rollins vs. Dean Ambrose
Money in the Bank 2014 to Hell in a Cell 2014; Payback 2015 to Money in the Bank 2015

Top 20 All-Time Ladder Match / Top 15 All-Time Hell in a Cell Match / Top 25 All-Time at Summerslam / Top 10 Match in 2014 / Top 10 Match in 2015

There was something different about The Shield that you could see from the outset. So many new talents had come up through the ranks in the latter part of the 2000s and right after the turn of the decade that had lacked that unmistakable, potentially era-defining star power that Seth Rollins, Dean Ambrose, and Roman Reigns exuded immediately. Oozing through their body language was what Ambrose once phrased as their "screw everybody" attitude upon arrival to the WWE main roster.

Within months of their debut, they were being talked about as cornerstones for a new generation and, together, they became one of the hottest acts in the game. "The goal from day one," according to Ambrose, "was to take over the business." They began to truly realize their goal through the first six months of 2014, peaking with a clean sweep of Evolution in a Six-Man Tag Team Elimination Match at *Payback*.

On the next night, though, the shockingly unthinkable happened: Rollins turned on his brothers, joining forces with the era's epitome of evil in the Stephanie McMahon and Triple H-led Authority and blossoming as a singles star under their tutelage.

Consequently, an incredible two year, on-again/off-again story would develop between Rollins and Ambrose that has the potential to become the Hart vs. Michaels or Rock vs. Triple H of its time. The Lunatic Fringe took The Architect's betrayal most personally and, while Reigns set forth on a journey to cut off the serpent's head (HHH), Ambrose took the fight to Rollins.

At *Money in the Bank 2014* during the titular Ladder Match, Rollins jockeyed to position himself with the contract that would eventually earn him what is destined to be one of the top highlights of his career – his cash-in at *WrestleMania 31* at Roman's expense to become WWE Champion. Ambrose fought tooth and nail to prevent him from ever getting his hands on the briefcase in the first place, but interference from The Authority thwarted the initial stage of his revenge plot. At *Summerslam '14*, Authority involvement once again disrupted Ambrose's attempt at giving Rollins a strong measure of comeuppance. Two months later at *Hell in a Cell* in the titular main-event match, at the moment that it appeared Ambrose was finally going to serve Rollins ultimate justice, intrusion from a different source (Bray Wyatt) cost The Lunatic his chance once more. It was captivating.

With The Authority backing his play, Rollins was elevated to main-event heights in the opening half of 2015. Ambrose re-engaged him in May and looked to have dished out what would have been for Rollins the coldest form of retaliation in taking his WWE Championship; he beat him fair and square at *Elimination Chamber*, but a last second swerve altered the result to a disqualification victory, offering The Architect an undeserved reprieve. To his credit, Rollins needed no assistance to defeat Ambrose in an epic, grueling Ladder Match at *Money in the Bank 2015*. However, one year later, after Rollins had returned from injury to earn the best win of his career in defeating Reigns to win back the championship that he never lost, Ambrose – who had won the Money in the Bank Ladder Match earlier in the show – cashed in his contract and finally beat Rollins.

The dichotomy between them was fascinating, in part because many had pegged Ambrose as the natural breakout heel of The Shield thanks to his character's history of maniacism on the independent scene, while an equal number thought Rollins to be an ideal babyface for modern times due to his incredible athletic talents, a Bret Hart-sized guy who could do everything that Shawn Michaels could do and more. Yet, as they became more deeply entrenched in their story, Ambrose displayed that the same charisma so popularly used to predict his future as an antagonist was making him a perfect anti-Authority protagonist, while Rollins managed to consistently incite the WWE fanbase's ire with few peers. They seem destined to reverse the hero-villain dynamic someday and pen another marvelous chapter in their saga.

To date, Rollins vs. Ambrose has been a rivalry hallmarked by great storytelling and redesigning certain wrestling genres, such as the Lumberjack, Ladder, and Hell in a Cell matches. Their involvement in 2014 was largely responsible for arguably the best Money in the Bank Ladder Match since the original; in unquestionably the best Lumberjack Match of all-time, the pair bucked the traditions of the so-termed "human cage" and brawled all around the Staples Center; in one of the best modern examples of how best to execute a Hell in a Cell Match without the possibility of blood-soaked violence, Rollins and Ambrose battled on top of the structure and tumbled off of the side of it through the announce tables; their 2015 Ladder Match may quite possibly be remembered in the years to come as the Bret-Owen at *Summerslam '94* of Ladder matches, a version of the gimmick that perhaps best exemplified the instinctive strategy of retrieving a hanging title from a hook. Hopefully there is more where all of that came from.

Rollins stated in 2014 about The Hounds of Justice, "We had gone as far as we could possibly go as a group; and my ultimate goal is to be THE very best...to be the standard bearer." That Ambrose or Reigns could have just as easily said the same, one has to admit that, as amazing a faction as was The Shield, it has been and probably will continue to be even better watching them fight each other for the top singles spot.

#58
Batista vs. Triple H
World Heavyweight Championship
WrestleMania 21 to Vengeance 2005
Top 10 All-Time Hell in a Cell Match / Top 5 Match in 2005

When it comes to great stories in professional wrestling history, Batista slowly losing patience with his role as Triple H's enforcer in the faction of the 2000s, Evolution, and ultimately sparking a rivalry with his mentor that led to the main-event of *WrestleMania 21* and one of the most underrated matches of the decade ranks pretty high up there.

Triple H, with the exception of the two month period in 2003 when Rock and Austin came back for WrestleMania Season, was the biggest star in the business for about three years. His "era," if you will, is not often talked about, perhaps due to a lot of unpopular creative decisions in the years that immediately followed the vaunted Attitude Era, but The Game had done his very best to replicate for WWE what Ric Flair had been able to do for the NWA in the 1980s: lead the company as its heel measuring stick, putting over the guys who really earned it and seeing if any of them could catch on and supplant him as "The Man."

Evolution was Hunter's version of Flair's late 1980s Four Horsemen. Stocked with past, present, and future star power, Evolution existed to initially keep Triple H strong at the top of the card and to later give The King of Kings new opponents who could vie for his crown. Randy Orton, front and center in the eyes of many as the obvious one that WWE saw as the breakout star of the group, was the first to try and seize the throne, but one of those aforementioned creative decisions doomed The Legend Killer from fulfilling perhaps his full potential. Batista, meanwhile, stayed mostly in the background, quietly honing his skills.

169

Then, what reflects in hindsight as a fairly subtle tide-turning moment happened about a month away from the calendar flipping to 2005. Shortly after *Survivor Series '04*, where interestingly there was a prominent sign during the Team Orton vs. Team Triple H main-event that read "Ha Ha! Batista Can't Get Over," a backstage segment saw The Animal merely glance longingly and intensely for just a few seconds at Triple H's World Heavyweight Championship belt.

To have been a fly on the wall wherever Vince McMahon was when he heard how much the crowd responded to that seemingly fleeting piece of television...

Batista sure never had any trouble getting over after that. In the months that followed, they produced an excellent, long-term story. The tension began to rise right as the New Year began, with Batista looking to take the next step in his career, but Triple H stifling his progress and clearly recognizing that his control over The Animal was waning. The Game purposefully avoided having to wrestle Batista in an Elimination Chamber title defense and then did everything in his power, including staging a faux-attempt at a hit-and-run, to influence him to challenge for the WWE Championship over on Smackdown after Batista had won the 2005 Royal Rumble Match.

The contract signing that revealed Batista's decision regarding which title he would pursue drew one of the highest quarter hour TV ratings in a long time and his ensuing match with Triple H on the grandest stage popped the strongest WrestleMania buyrate in between historic pay-per-view-juggernauts *WrestleMania X-Seven* and *WrestleMania 23*, getting Batista's main-event run off to a really good start at the box office and giving Triple H's drawing power, post-Attitude, a verifiable credibility boost. They both earned that recognition on the back of a tremendously well-performed and well-booked saga.

HHH went onto put over Batista at three straight pay-per-views, solidifying his former protege as one of the biggest stars to have come along in several years and as a cornerstone of the next half-decade in WWE. The Game deserves a lot of credit for it too. By the time that their rivalry wrapped up at *Vengeance* in June, not only had Hunter elevated Batista as firmly as anyone was elevated by another star throughout the 2000s, he had essentially completed Batista's top guy training by teaching him many a lesson in how to work a feature-length main-event match. The Animal was not a particularly accomplished wrestler when he caught on with the audience; he was competent but little more, as exemplified by his serviceable but not overly memorable matches with Triple H at *WrestleMania 21* and *Backlash '05.* The Hell in a Cell blow-off to their feud, though, seemed to be when everything clicked for Batista for the first time and, up until the Undertaker series two years later, it remained the lone match in The Animal's body of work that showed him fully capable of meeting all headlining-superstar expectations.

You will not find many bloody brawls in the WrestleMania Era that were much better than Batista and Triple H's Hell in a Cell Match. Of all of The Game's main-events during his modern-Flair run, not a single one more definitively showcased the influence of his idol. It was a very Nature Boy-esque performance and should rightfully go-down as one of the greatest matches of his career. To be honest, it should also be recognized as the best match of Batista's career, even if the Taker series simultaneously merits its accreditation as The Animal's turning point as a performer.

All in all, if you couple what the rivalry achieved economically with the upper end of what it achieved critically, there is little question that Triple H vs. Batista belongs here.

#57
Randy Orton vs. John Cena
Summerslam 2007 to No Mercy 2007; No Way Out 2008 to WrestleMania XXIV; Summerslam 2009 to Bragging Rights 2009

Top 25 All-Time at Summerslam / Top 5 Match in 2007 / Top 5 Match in 2009

By *Summerslam '07*, some sixteen months after defeating Triple H, John Cena had confirmed himself as the leader of a generation. Three years prior, it had seemed like it might be Randy Orton who would be leading WWE into the future. At *Summerslam '04*, Cena first confronted him in a memorable backstage segment just hours before an RKO out of nowhere made Orton the youngest World Champion in WWE history, but a series of immature personal patterns and lousy professional booking decisions stymied The Legend Killer's potential to be the face of the franchise, leaving the door cracked for Cena to kick wide-open in 2005 and beyond.

Even before their initial interaction began their paths to battling each other, they always seemed to be linked together by their era; they started together in OVW, debuted for WWE in mid-2002, were split by brands, became the burgeoning stars of their respective rosters, and hit their initial career peaks within eight months of each other. When Orton announced his #1 contendership to Cena's WWE Championship at *Summerslam '07* with a ring-rattling rendition of his signature move, it was five years in the making. That night in East Rutherford, New Jersey, Cena and Orton became the only pairing from the post-Attitude Era in the 2000s to main-event a Big 4 pay-per-view together without the assistance of a superstar who started in the 1990s; and they delivered.

Their rivalry blossomed over the next two years and came to be defined not as one of those feuds that is necessarily special because they pushed each other to new limits like an Austin-Rock or Hart-Michaels, but special instead because they provided each other, through character contrast and natural chemistry, with a proper platform on which to best showcase their individual abilities.

So much about each star made them ideal foils; Orton was groomed for success from the word go and had an innate talent for wrestling exemplified by how graceful and effortlessly he utilized his physical gifts around the ring, while Cena was the least heralded member of their famous rookie class, had to work his way up by organically discovering a gimmick that connected hugely with the fans, and developed as a wrestler despite a very awkward athleticism; Orton, at his finest, has proven to be an artist inside the squared circle, immersing himself in his character like few in the modern era through pronounced body language and expression, while Cena is far better described as the sports entertainment equivalent of a performer in a blockbuster action movie. They were made for each other, and WWE revisited their feud years after its shelf-life had expired because of it.

When they re-engaged over the WWE Championship ahead of *Summerslam '09*, it was in the midst of Orton's career year; Cena may have been the unquestionable #1 guy in the company, but there was not a better pro wrestler on planet earth in 2009 than Randy Orton. The Viper swallowed the cocky Legend Killer and spit out in its place one of the most sadistic villains WWE has ever produced, as cold and calculating as his mentor, Triple H, and as deranged as Mankind.

Across four title bouts on PPV in two months, their story became the stuff of modern legend.

The basic theme in all of their matches was dissection, with Orton dominating, picking apart the entire Super Cena routine, and stopping numerous bursts of comeback dead in their tracks with silky-smooth precision. With all due respect to Cena, who can indeed count his matches with Orton among the Top 15 collections on his resume, the Orton-Cena series chiefly put on display Orton's phenomenal ability to act out his persona on the WWE stage. Their "I Quit" Match was, to the wrestling psychology aficionado, as unforgettable for The Viper's psychotic behavior as Mankind and The Rock's nearly unparalleled violence was to the enthusiast of hardcore wrestling. In the "Anything Goes" Ironman Match that ended the iconic part of their story, Orton offered perhaps the most Oscar-worthy presentation of his life, completely and utterly (and brilliantly) lost as he was in the fiction; he even tried to "blow up" Cena with entrance ramp pyrotechnics, managing to be believable in an otherwise unbelievable situation.

In hindsight, it almost seems strange that they did not main-event WrestleMania together in 2008 or 2009, much less not even meet in a one-on-one match at "The Show of Shows." They almost headlined when Cena shocked the world and won the '08 Rumble Match, but they shared the spotlight in a Triple Threat at *WrestleMania XXIV* and then did not renew their rivalry in 2009 until after *WrestleMania XXV*. Still, theirs was arguably the defining feud of that period in WWE history; over that span, Orton was never bigger or better and Cena became one of the biggest stars in industry lore.

#56
Hulk Hogan vs. Andre the Giant
WWF Championship
WrestleMania III to WrestleMania IV

Andre the Giant vs. Hulk Hogan set a WWE attendance record that stood for almost thirty years of 93,173 at the old Pontiac Silver Dome outside Detroit, Michigan; it set an untouchable television ratings record with a 15.2 (good for 33 million viewers) for the February 1988 NBC special, *The Main Event*; it set an also untouchable record for pay-per-view buyrate – the percentage of homes with PPV capability that ordered the show – with a 10.2 for the WWF Championship match at *WrestleMania III*. Hogan vs. Andre captivated the world more so than any one single match ever had before or ever has since.

Thirty years is a long time, however, and the further removed we are from the peak of Hulkamania, the more arguing that occurs over the rivalry that not only segued WrestleMania from its inception as a celebrity-driven show featuring wrestling into a wrestling show featuring celebrities on the strength of Hogan and Andre's larger-than-life personalities, but also spawned WWE's second yearly pay-per-view franchise, The Survivor Series, as well. In growing numbers, younger generations of wrestling fans flat out do not get what the hype was all about.

Perhaps they were conditioned on The New Generation and expect a certain in-ring quality that Andre vs. Hogan could not possibly live up to in hindsight since it was wrestled in a different era and in a promotion that did not yet demand such a high standard. Or maybe they were introduced to pro wrestling during the Attitude Era or beyond and have views of clashes between historic titans shaped by an abundance of signature spots and finishing moves to which a basic superhero scuffle like Hogan vs. Andre aesthetically pales in comparison. Whatever the reason, they dislike the match at *WrestleMania III*, in particular, and have heaped upon it descriptors that spark ardent retorts from its defenders.

These critical fans are joined by pre-WrestleMania Era WW(W)F and NWA/WCW enthusiasts, as well as a pocket of pro wrestling analysts and historians; respected journalist, Dave Meltzer (of the famous original dirt-sheet, The Figure Four Newsletter), actually critically-rated the match *negative* four-stars.

Truthfully, they do have a point. Though the feud was top notch, with Hogan's long-time nemesis, Bobby "The Brain" Heenan, coercing Andre to the dark side, and though the crowd was completely invested, the action was compelling and dramatic for what it was, and the atmosphere was among the most incredible in wrestling lore, there just was not much there from bell-to-bell as compared to its peers that also stake claims to all-time greatness. That Andre could barely move at that point in his life due to a disease that was supposed to have killed him by 1987 should of course be taken into account, but you cannot watch wrestling in a bubble, especially when performing broad historical examinations; the fact of the matter is that a Hogan-formula match featuring a 500-pound man who could barely walk did have significant limitations.

Still, listen to the way that several of John Cena's generation of stars speak of Hogan vs. Andre with such "this is why I got into this business" kind of reverence. There can be no denying the impact that Hogan vs. Andre had on the industry. It was the *biggest* wrestling match of all-time; that should go without saying and virtually without challenge. Steamboat and Savage may have been a *better* match and men like Bret Hart may have sparked a priority shift toward a consistently higher standard of in-ring performance, but WWE as we know it was born when, as Gorilla Monsoon classically called on commentary, "The irresistible force" met "The immoveable object" and when Hogan slammed Andre; and that is, of course, why Hogan vs. Andre had to rank near the Top 50.

#55
Bret Hart vs. Mr. Perfect
Intercontinental Championship
Summerslam
August 26, 1991

Top 15 All-Time at Summerslam / Top 5 Match in 1991

The 1990s produced the majority of the most talked about Intercontinental Title matches in history. It could certainly be argued that Bret Hart vs. Mr. Perfect has become the one from that list which has received the least amount of hindsight-publicity, filed away as the predecessor of The Hitman's pair of classics eight and twelve months later versus Piper and Bulldog respectively and often positioned behind the progenitors of the Ladder Match. Maybe that is not an entirely fair assessment, but does it not seem like this match is the fourth or even fifth match in the conversation in this day and age, despite the fact that it is just as good?

"It was a clinic," Hall of Fame former 5-time holder of the title, Edge, once said about the match. "It was hard-hitting, action-packed, and fast-paced, but also told a story. At that point in WWE, that wasn't seen a lot." Really, the only other time that it had been so prominently seen was the archetypal bout that put the IC Title on the map in the first place, Steamboat vs. Savage. Mr. Perfect, real name Curt Hennig, helped build on the *WrestleMania III* foundation by making the championship "the worker's title" and, by 1991, nobody in the company was a better worker than Bret Hart, who won the title at *Summerslam '91* from Perfect and promptly became quite possibly the greatest Intercontinental Champion ever; he was certainly the titleholder with the most famous trio of IC Championship matches.

Because of Perfect's health at the time, the match wound up taking on the role of a "passing of the torch." Hennig's back had gotten so bad late in the spring of 1991 that he was set to move into a non-wrestling role by year's end, but he insisted on dropping the title to Bret and not simply giving a half-speed effort on account of his injury. There was a lot of real world mutual respect from the two of them being second generation wrestlers whose dads were well liked behind-the-scenes. Perfect's show of fortitude, perhaps a microcosm of the match overall, does not frequently enough enter the discussion with Michaels at *WrestleMania XIV*, Triple H on *Raw* in May 2001, and Angle at *WrestleMania XIX* as one of the gutsiest displays in pro wrestling lore. Hart was always greatly appreciative of the gesture, for it effectively kick-started his run to a Top-10-of-the-WrestleMania-Era resume.

Billed as "The Excellence of Execution vs. Perfection," it was inspirational to Edge and others. "It was a milestone match, especially for guys like me, because I was growing up watching that and seeing a different style, a style that I gravitated to and wanted to do if and when I got into this business."

Like Steamboat-Savage, it was the type of match that showcased to the WWF audience the entertainment to be found in a more athletic version of that era's more character-driven style. Both Henning and Hart were highly intelligent workers, so there was no absence of personality in their physical battles, but the concentration was, so to speak, more on the sport than the entertainment, less overtly theatrical than a Hogan or Savage or Warrior performance and more like a high profile NWA match with quicker pacing and better production value. It was matches like Perfect vs. Hart – and The Hitman's rise through the ranks to top level star – that helped shift the modus operandi for the WWF main-event to something far more immersive and critically acclaimed.

So, why the tendency to find it further down the list? It basically boils down to the historical weight carried by its peers. Bret's matches with Piper and Bulldog took place in front of massive crowds on nights better ingrained in WWE mythology, both elevating Hart to the forefront of the burgeoning New Generation; HBK and Razor's Ladder Match is legendary for a plethora of rather obvious reasons; and The Rock vs. Triple H Ladder Match had its finger on the pulse of a celebrated era, significantly advancing the careers of two of Attitude's titans. Hart vs. Perfect, by comparison, is very (but a little less) important to Hart's upward trajectory; is legendary, but not quite so fabled as HBK vs. Razor; and was a catalyst for a more intangible shift in the in-ring product as opposed to the unmistakable launching pad for two Top 10 all-time greats and a Top 25-level all-time rivalry that was Rock vs. HHH.

Nevertheless, as Hall of Famer Harley Race reverently said about them and their *Summerslam* match on Hennig's WWE-produced documentary, *The Life and Times of Mr. Perfect*, "[They both had] great heads for wrestling and when you put two great heads together for anything, it's going to come out well." Thanks to incredible chemistry that was second to none, the iconic Intercontinental Championship match came out very well and is quite deserving of its place just outside the Top 50.

#54
Ric Flair vs. Lex Luger
NWA World Heavyweight Championship
Great American Bash 1988 to Starrcade 1988; WrestleWar 1990

Top 5 All-Time at Starrcade / Match of the Year 1988 / Top 5 Match in 1990

As the NWA/WCW portion of the list continues, so grows the number of contributions to the Top 100 made by "The Nature Boy" Ric Flair. Already covered has been some of his most famous work, but there was something generationally-significant about his series in mid-to-late 1988 (and final featured match in February 1990) with "The Total Package" Lex Luger that helped make it perhaps the most underrated body of work in the pantheon of great Naitch rivalries.

The wrestling world had changed by 1988. Starrcades '83-'86 watched very differently than *Starrcade '88*. The WWF's complete dominance in the quickly quietening prelude to the Monday Night War between Vince McMahon and Jim Crockett was influential on the entire business, particularly because the NWA (the only real competitor to the WWF) was forced to adapt its signature booking style, switching the focus for Flair, who was successfully seeing them through the transition as still one of the top draws in the game, to rivals that better fit the mold of the modern pro wrestler (see Hogan and Savage).

Lex Luger, who looked like a Greek God, was the next in a long line of pro football players to become pro wrestlers, and he excelled at a rapid pace. After winning the *Pro Wrestling Illustrated* Rookie of the Year award in 1986, Luger replaced Ole Anderson in The Four Horsemen. He was smart, he could talk, and he could get it done in the ring; guided and molded by Flair, Arn Anderson, Tully Blanchard, and JJ Dillon, by the start of

1988, he was well on his way to backing up his nickname by becoming a truly total package of pro wrestling attributes.

When the Batista vs. Triple H feud was highlighted earlier, it was celebrated as one of the storyline-achievements of the 2000s; and it was inspired by the classic manner in which Luger was excommunicated from The Horsemen. Disagreements with the other members led the vaunted stable to turn on him, but the plot gloriously thickened even further. Luger sought out Barry Windham for help as the second generation star was coming off the pair of excellent NWA Title matches with Flair discussed among the Honorable Mentions. They teamed to defeat Anderson and Blanchard to win the Tag Team Championships on the same night that Flair wrestled his Top 100 match with Sting at the inaugural *Clash of the Champions*. However, in a shocking act of treachery during a rematch soon afterwards, Windham turned on Luger and accepted Lex's vacated spot in The Horsemen (the version that was inducted into the WWE Hall of Fame in 2012).

By the time that Luger had earned a shot at Flair's NWA World Title at the first *Great American Bash* to be offered on pay-per-view, there was a deeply-rooted story in place that put him in prime position to be Naitch's potential successor. Unlike the case between Sting and Flair in March, Luger and Flair had tremendous build-up to their title match at *The Bash*; as was the case with Sting when he wrestled Flair, Luger was clearly not yet the performer he would become, though he more than admirably carried his part of the match. Flair retained on account of the state athletic commissioner's ruling that the match be stopped due to Lex excessively bleeding.

For the last half of 1988, Luger scratched and clawed his way to the brink of the championship, with a rematch set for *Starrcade*. It was on that night in the Norfolk Scope in Virginia that he put on full display why he is one of the most criminally underrated wrestlers of the WrestleMania Era. Against the man whom Tony Schiavone, on commentary, aptly referred to as "Mr. Starrcade,"

Luger unleashed as complete an arsenal of power, speed, catch wrestling, and endurance as had been seen from a wrestler of his physical stature to that point. He even sold pretty well his "knee injury" (sustained during an expected attack from Flair to set-up the Figure Four), particularly during a superlative finish that saw Luger put Naitch in the Human Torture Rack, only for his "knee to give out," prompting him to fall onto his back as Flair seamlessly maneuvered into a pin cover with his feet on the ropes for the leveraged three-count out of nowhere.

It was the kind of performance that might make a curious fan reflect on *Starrcade '88* and ask, "Why didn't Luger win the title that night?" An exploration into the answer to that question is partly what shapes the generational-significance of Luger vs. Flair and also begs the additional question, "Why are inferior matches from inferior storylines held in higher historical regard than Flair vs. Luger?"

For all intents, Luger did not win the NWA World Heavyweight Championship from Flair because the behind-the-scenes political game was favoring Sting as Naitch's true successor in the long-term and was favoring in the short-term the big returning star from recent WWF fame, Ricky "The Dragon" Steamboat, with whom Flair would trade the title back and forth in early 1989. *Starrcade '88* was the first PPV under the World Championship Wrestling banner and Ted Turner's ownership, and it seemed like an ideal stage and time to strike while "The Total Package" was hot, but it would seem that Luger was simply a victim of creative tunnel vision.

It also must be pointed out that Luger, as intelligent as he was – Flair credits him as being responsible for bringing greater awareness to issues like verification of the house gate percentage owed the wrestlers and the logic gap in wrestlers not having health insurance benefits paid for by the promotions that ask them to willingly wreck their bodies – he never had much inclination to do much more than he was told. The tippy-top stars of the WrestleMania Era might have gone to bat for their cause in similar circumstances (Flair, at various points, certainly did), but Luger was self-professed not to have been wired that way.

Flair's storyline with Luger was excellent, but it never featured the historic crescendo of a title change which, in the case of Flair putting over Sting, has also been regarded as a torch-passing moment. Thus, Luger has basically been relegated to the category of "just another challenger to Flair" instead of being remembered as the young lion who pushed him to an in-ring level that he only reached with but a few others. There was also no ahead-of-its-time segment (i.e. a piledriver on a table) or gimmick match (i.e. "I Quit") to push Flair-Luger to the forefront of history alongside Flair vs. Terry Funk, even though most respected pundits rate Flair-Luger and Flair-Funk on a near-equal level and despite Flair-Luger taking place on more prominent stages and outdrawing Flair-Funk on pay-per-view.

So, allow this to permeate and revise the strange narrative that has devalued Luger, himself, and the Luger-Flair rivalry. The *Starrcade '88* main-event was as great a match (as defined by this book's thorough definition of the phrase) as was ever seen at NWA/WCW's premier event. Hindsight suggests, as Chris aka "Mizfan" from *WCW: The Legacy Series* has posited, that the late 1980s were defined more by Luger vs. Flair than Sting vs. Flair and that their match at *WrestleWar '90* was the last true NWA Championship match before Ted Turner fully re-branded a more distinctly WCW-style.

<u>#53</u>
The Rock vs. Brock Lesnar
Undisputed WWE Championship
Summerslam
August 25, 2002

<u>Top 15 All-Time at Summerslam</u> / <u>Top 5 Match in 2002</u>

Before he had earned the menacing modern nickname, The Beast Incarnate, Brock Lesnar was just the menacing Next Big Thing, a moniker that, when contextualized, really only applied for the five months between his debut on the night after *WrestleMania X-8* and the closing moments of *Summerslam '02.* By the time that Lesnar had dispatched of The Rock to become the youngest WWE Champion ever (25 years old), there was nothing "Next" about him. Rather, in a post-Attitude world in which The Rock was off to Hollywood on hiatus and Stone Cold had infamously taken his ball and gone home (interestingly over creative issues with being fed to Lesnar on Raw), Brock was nothing less than the #1 star in WWE – *The* Big Thing.

The match that coronated his newly minted position was nothing less than fascinating. Lesnar's mere presence sold to even the untrained eye that he was in the top one percent of all physical specimens in any sporting endeavor. The Rock, with his combination of size and stamina, had long been considered one of the most gifted athletes in WWE lore. Lesnar walked in the door and immediately assumed a position ahead of The Brahma Bull as wrestling's preeminent athlete. The build-up to their showdown at The Summer Classic was structured accordingly, sold as a battle between the two best athletes in WWE, only slightly accented by creative flairs of the shock-TV that hallmarked the era. "All I care about is being the absolute best," Rock stated; *Summerslam* offered him yet another stage on which to prove it. For Lesnar, it was about becoming #1 and affirming the top spot that, in his mind, he had already taken despite *Summerslam* being his first opportunity to headline for WWE.

In a situation quite similar to Vader's arrival in WCW, there was a distinct sense of inevitability to Lesnar's first title shot. How could he not win? Lesnar had torn through the WWE roster, demolishing all and sundry, most notably Hulk Hogan on Smackdown two weeks prior to *Summerslam*. Hogan had valiantly fought Father Time since his return earlier in the year and had been on a legendary nostalgia run that included the classic match with Rock at *'Mania X-8*, but Lesnar annihilated him and achieved his victory over the aging icon with a simple bear hug that left Hogan unconscious and bleeding from the mouth; and to think that Lesnar had almost mowed over Steve Austin two months prior. The result against Rock, as with Vader versus Sting, felt like a formality; the only thing left by match time was to see how courageous an effort The Most Electrifying Man in Sports Entertainment could muster.

Among the attributes that make Rock so special is his command of the moment. We saw it repeatedly throughout his WWE career and he has since used it to become one of the biggest box office-drawing actors in the world. During his peak wrestling days, he had the ability to maximize a performance under any condition, prominently in environments with crowds that turned on him and especially – and this is a rare quality among the Top 10 greatest wrestlers of all-time – when another star needed to be put over (this makes the third example cited already).

The line partially referenced earlier from the pre-match video package, "I want to be the absolute best that the industry has ever, ever seen," was one of Rock's mantras during 2002/2003 and, when he got into that state-of-mind for epic matches, few in history could rival his work. Shawn Michaels was the master at producing at the highest possible level when the lights were on brightest but Rock, as well as anyone else not named HBK in pro wrestling lore, saved his best for the occasions that mattered most. The Rock vs. Brock should rightfully be remembered as an epic WWE Title bout and *Summerslam* main-event, in large part due to the efforts of The Great One.

It was a match ahead of its time. Lesnar, upon returning to WWE in 2012, developed a signature style (identified as "Beast Mode" in the Honorable Mention section). Playing off his impressive MMA career, the method is predicated on Lesnar dominating 70-80% (or greater) of the offense, his opponent selling like crazy, and Brock bumping for short and often impressive bursts within a roughly 15-minute time-frame. It is a highly unique main-event format given its one-sided nature, but Lesnar's credibility borderline demands it. That style debuted ten years before it was popularized when Rock supplied a riveting 25% of the offense at *Summerslam '02* but largely found himself looking up at the lights after having been on the receiving-end of continuous suplexes and slams.

Underappreciated historically and perhaps overshadowed by arguably Summerslam lore's greatest performance in the match that preceded it on August 25, 2002, Rock vs. Brock was too important to the industry and too impressive in its overall presentation not to be celebrated for its achievements. Lesnar used it as a springboard to the rest of his life, in wrestling and beyond, becoming the world's most well-known sports celebrity to ever wrestle for WWE. Between Brock's career-defining moment, Rock's stellar character work, a big fight feel aided by a hostile crowd, a wonderful pace, and a tremendous finish, the *Summerslam '02* main-event is unequaled by over two-thirds of the WrestleMania Era.

#52
Eddie Guerrero vs. John "Bradshaw" Layfield
WWE Championship
Judgment Day 2004 to Smackdown July 15, 2004

Top 20 All-Time Cage Match / Top 5 Match in 2004

When Eddie Guerrero became WWE Champion in February 2004 and promptly engaged in a rivalry with Kurt Angle, there was a safe assumption made that his feud with Our Olympic Hero culminating at *WrestleMania XX* would be what was most remembered about his main-event run. However, that assumption was proven false thanks in large part to an unlikely rival emerging as perhaps the most definable foe of Latino Heat's Hall of Fame career, one John "Bradshaw" Layfield.

Out of left field and on account of heavy roster depletion, JBL transitioned from tag team afterthought coasting on his Attitude Era role-player reputation to Smackdown's newest main-event star in the spring of 2004. Opportunity knocked loudly and he answered resoundingly with a big-talking, gregarious, filthy-rich persona with far right-leaning political ideals regarding United States border-control to Latin America. WWE's Hispanic demographic was on the rise in accordance with America's, so Layfield's actions and hardline stance struck a chord with an ever-expanding sect of the audience. Plus, Eddie was so wildly popular in general that virtually everyone rallied behind him.

For Guerrero, whose family name was originally made famous in Mexico, JBL was the perfect foil. Eddie drove a low-rider during his entrance; JBL was driven to the stage in a limousine. Layfield's theme song featured the opening bell of the New York Stock Exchange; Guerrero's music promoted his "Lying, Cheating, and Stealing" catchphrase. Latino Heat was listed at 5'8"; Bradshaw was billed at 6'6." However, they did well not to rest on the laurels of their natural differences. JBL infamously laid his hands on Guerrero's mother, for instance, causing her to have a "heart attack" (props to the entire Guerrero family for top notch acting). Thus, by the time of their first WWE Championship match, Eddie was already out for blood.

JBL did indeed bleed for his sins during their initial encounter at *Judgment Day*, but a chair shot from Layfield prompted Guerrero to spill more blood in one match than any other performer in the WrestleMania Era; there has never been a more gruesome scene in WWE lore than Eddie fighting to stay conscious while pints of blood spilled down his body, less the proverbial crimson mask and more like a crimson suit. Overall, the flow and pace of the match was perfect for the story that they told. They kept the crowd engaged from the pre-bout video package until the pay-per-view faded to black without ever relying on stunt-spots or a plethora of finisher kick-outs. It compares so favorably head-to-head against its peers, instead, by way of its deeply-affecting drama.

Due likely to Eddie and JBL's prior statuses as mid-to-lower-card wrestlers and unquestionably to Smackdown's talent drop-off, *Judgment Day '04* produced one of the lowest PPV buy totals ever to that point, but for many reasons - including the blood, the character performances from both, the chemistry on display, and the overall storytelling - JBL vs. Eddie, Chapter 1, has become something akin to a cult classic and is truly one of the most underrated matches of all-time.

Random as it may have been, the rise of John "Bradshaw" Layfield was an undeniable success. He completed one of the unlikeliest of championship chases ever witnessed by winning the WWE Title at *The Great American Bash*. In another often-forgotten classic that contends in the historical competition for best-ever Bull-Rope/Chain/Strap Match, JBL controversially captured the coveted gold and infuriated not just the camp who opposed his extremist platform, but also the growing number of diehard enthusiasts to whom Layfield's sudden ascent inspired feelings that WWE was taking deliberate steps backward from allowing the best wrestlers in the world to maximize their achievements regardless of their appearance or size; to them, Eddie's triumph over Lesnar in February had reflected a philosophical shift and the switch to JBL as champion left them feeling like Marty McFly in *Back to the Future II*, waking up in an alternate 1985 to Biff Tannen running the town.

Nevertheless, JBL was tremendous in his role as he capitalized on the heat coming from multiple fronts to become the longest reigning WWE Champion in the history of the Smackdown brand. His nefarious victory to conclude the Bull-Rope Match was built pristinely from start to finish so that, when Guerrero had seemingly overcome the odds in JBL's chosen stipulation-bout only for Angle, then the acting General Manager, to use instant-replay to reverse the decision and award Layfield the title, it achieved maximum disappointment from the fanbase.

The payoff - an excellent Steel Cage Match on the July 15, 2004 Smackdown - served only to further instigate JBL's detractors, as he escaped with the title by the skin of his teeth thanks yet again to Angle's involvement and would go on to consistently headline for another three years. Guerrero, meanwhile, provided one of the top flashbulb moments of his career with a Frog Splash from off the top of the cage in what proved the end to his relatively brief stay at the summit. Yet, criminally underappreciated as it may be, the JBL-Eddie feud stands the test of time as the best story either of them ever told in a WWE ring and rightfully earns its place near the upper half of the WrestleMania Era's 100 greatest matches, rivalries, and stories. Should you disagree with its ranking, do yourself a favor and watch it again with a fresh perspective.

#51
Brock Lesnar: The Conqueror
WrestleMania XXX to WrestleMania 31
Top 10 All-Time at Royal Rumble / Top 40 All-Time at WrestleMania / Top 5 Match in 2015

Some like to say that wins and losses in professional wrestling do not matter.

This passage from *The WrestleMania Era* sums up well the falsity in that statement:

> In the two years that Lesnar had been back [between *WrestleManias XXVIII* and *XXX*], WWE had basically stripped Brock of his mystique. He lost that match to Cena in 2012. He lost to Triple H at *'Mania 29*. He struggled to beat CM Punk. When he returned, Brock was a God amongst men. By bell time of the Taker match [at *WMXXX*], he was most decidedly [human]. Such is why nobody thought it worth their time to even fathom that a mere mortal like Brock could take down the previously immortal Streak. It was for that reason that the match had garnered almost zero energy from the crowd before the finish. Yet, after those three seconds that handed The Phenom his first WrestleMania defeat, Lesnar was, once again, divine. The mythological status restored, Heyman's nicknames for Brock – "The Conqueror" and "The Beast Incarnate" – were no longer the savvy words of a master orator; they were the truth.

Brock Lesnar's defeat of The Undertaker was the catalyst for an enormously successful 12-month period that anchored two Summerslams, a Royal Rumble, and a WrestleMania, that showcased creative mastery of what The Conqueror could be, and that produced one of the most shocking results, one of the most fascinating main-events, one of the January Classic's ten greatest matches, and one of the quintessential versions of the previously-termed "Beast Mode" in-ring style that was also among the Top 15% of all-time WrestleMania matches. Had it avoided the unfortunate modern trend of following an incredible beginning and exhilarating middle of a story with no particularly definable end, it could have ranked even higher. Alas, Lesnar's path of destruction, particularly between the New Orleans and San Francisco-hosted WrestleManias, was as memorable as anything else in WWE this decade.

The ability to sustain the momentum of such a titanic achievement as ending The Streak was perhaps the defining trait of the story. Lesnar, in his rematch from *Extreme Rules '12* with John Cena at *Summerslam '14*, completely annihilated the WWE Champion. It was 16-minutes and 5-seconds of The Beast throwing Cena around like a rag-doll and then completing the job with an emphatic, conclusive victory. No prior main-event had ever been quite so one-sided from start to finish, so it was essentially the headlining version of a squash match, rendering Cena a glorified enhancement talent; Superman got run over by Doomsday.

For 224 days, Lesnar was the reigning, defending, undisputed Heavyweight Champion of the World, yet only showed up a handful of times. Part of the intrigue when he won the title was how a product that typically revolved its five hours of weekly programming and monthly pay-per-views around the primary narrative of the WWE Champion defending his title would function without the consistent physical presence of the titleholder. It was certainly novel, as well as polarizing. Lesnar only defended the gold three times in 7 ½ months. By comparison, Seth Rollins, the next in the lineage of WWE Champions, had defended on three separate occasions before he had reigned for even two months.

In Brock's absence, it was Rollins who emerged as WWE's focal point, and The Architect was inserted into the Lesnar-Cena rematch ahead of *Royal Rumble '15*. Candidly, the Legend of The Conqueror may not be remembered the same way without the combined efforts of Lesnar, Cena, and Rollins in that Triple Threat Match. Ending The Streak was undoubtedly the tale's greatest moment, but Brock's defense of the WWE World Heavyweight Championship at *Rumble '15* was its greatest match. The Beast-Mode style is predicated on Lesnar's dominance, so watching him impose his will against *two* elite superstars was, in and of itself, very engaging. Even more so than in one-on-one matches against Cena or Taker, the Triple Threat painted perfectly the picture of Lesnar as an unstoppable monster. There was also the element of Rollins and Cena attempting to neutralize Brock, which was like two Jedi feebly trying to take down a Sith Lord in Star Wars. The performance was a confluence of their personalities and in-ring strengths that they magnificently executed to the tune of one of the best multi-man singles matches you will ever see.

Two months later, the Lesnar story hit the final note of its crescendo. The Beast carried the company on his back that WrestleMania Season, famously breaking the news on ESPN of his re-signing another lucrative deal with WWE just days before *WrestleMania 31*. The coverage stimulated interest and ratings and served as the pillar for the establishment of a more concrete working relationship between sports entertainment's #1 brand and The Worldwide Leader in Sports. The media momentum translated to another blockbuster "Showcase of the Immortals" for WWE, headlined by Lesnar's title defense against the ever-controversial Roman Reigns. Brock took him to "Suplex City" – a catchphrase born of a taunt made during the match – and ultimately lost the title when Rollins cashed in his Money in the Bank contract to pin Reigns, ending a remarkable one-year run and proving that the right win at the right time absolutely matters, for it is undeniable that Lesnar would have been at least 50% less interesting had he not become the illustrious "1" in "21-1."

#50
Bret Hart vs. The United States of America
March 1997 to November 1997

Top 20 All-Time at Summerslam / Top 5 Match in 1997

A white-meat babyface in pro wrestling is defined as a good person who follows the rules and rarely if ever strays from the confines of a strong moral compass. Many fans have been rebelling against that kind of character for much of the WrestleMania Era; Bret Hart was realistically the last great white-meat babyface capable of earning the adulation of all parts of the fanbase until Daniel Bryan. In 1996, a shift that had been building for years cratered then-representatives of that brand of hero like Shawn Michaels and a young Rocky Maivia, forcing their turns to the dark-side and, as fate would have it, catapulting them to incredible success because of how well appreciated their villainous performances were to a growing, increasingly rebellious sect of the audience. By year end, not even Hart, the consummate orthodox hero, could maintain stable ground in such an outdated role.

During the most famous portion of his Top 10 all-time rivalry with Steve Austin, Hart began to vent his frustration with the growing fan-tendency to embrace the anti-hero. While, to many, the altered course in how the product functioned when good guys got jeered while the villains were cheered was considered a welcome shift, to Bret Hart it was more like an earthquake. On the Raw after *WrestleMania 13*, his frustrations boiled over, and he unleashed a lengthy monologue chastising American wrestling enthusiasts for behavior he thought unacceptable to his more conventional standards, all the while renewing his commitment to fans beyond the borders of the USA.

It was as sad as it was brilliant. Throughout 1996 up until March 1997, Americans despondently bore witness to the demise of the last traditional hero that our country's (and the world's) top wrestling promotion would produce for twenty years, as Bret slowly deteriorated into a whiny, entitled antagonist; that was the sad part. The brilliant part was that he managed to turn heel on a single nation; a lot of wrestlers had been successful denouncing the United States, but an equal parts anti-American and pro-everywhere-else persona was novel. From a character standpoint, it was by a comfortable margin the greatest thing that The Hitman ever did in his career and was, like his run atop The New Generation in general, undervalued historically for its ingenuity.

The further Bret's storyline progressed, the more heavily he leaned on his Canadian heritage. He reconciled with his all-time great rival / brother Owen, as well as with his rival / brother-in-law Davey Boy Smith and his former partner / brother-in-law Jim Neidhart. Together with Brian Pillman, who was sympathetic to their cause, they formed The Hart Foundation, the name from the classic Hitman/Anvil tag team adding a familiar feel to an otherwise highly unique and creatively provocative stable. Austin was initially their primary target, but moving toward *In Your House: Canadian Stampede* (in Bret and Owen's hometown of Calgary, Alberta), others began to experience their wrath as well.

Officially ending when the man behind the fiction was unceremoniously screwed in Montreal at *Survivor Series*, Bret's character's renowned arc peaked that summer. July and August of 1997 produced two of the most underrated matches in The Excellence of Execution's stellar body of work.

The *Canadian Stampede* main-event was just tremendous. The Hart Foundation vs. Austin, The Legion of Doom, Goldust, and Ken Shamrock produced a response from the Saddledome crowd nearly unequaled in the WrestleMania Era, strong enough to rattle the cameras from the vibration of the building. During the climax, Vince McMahon stated, "There has never been a match like this before." He was right; 25 straight minutes of non-stop action making full use of each of the ten combatants without ever utilizing customary team-oriented tropes like the hot tag was like nothing seen before it or arguably ever since. In regards to in-ring storytelling and the drama that it induced, it was just as good as its multi-man brethren such as the triumvirate of classic War Games matches or any Elimination Tag from Survivor Series history. Though Bret starred in the match, the performance of the night went to Owen; both he and Austin were sent to the dressing room with injured knees, only for both to return in time for the finishing sequence that saw The Rocket pin Stone Cold. One of the most aesthetically enjoyable matches ever, the 10-man tag was also psychologically-engrossing. It was a masterpiece.

A victory on Canadian soil fed right into *Summerslam* in New Jersey. Bret challenged Undertaker for The Deadman's WWF Championship and promised that, should he not win the title, he would never wrestle in America again. Adding oil to the water, Shawn Michaels – Hart's biggest career rival – was appointed the special guest referee and would not have been able to wrestle in the USA either if he had not fairly officiated the match. These were the three most enduring stars of The New Generation in Bret, Taker, and HBK; it was quite fascinating seeing them share the squared circle. The in-ring dynamics played out straightforwardly as a characterful technician vs. big man bout until the closing minutes, when two of the best ever cashed in on the investment they had made in steadily building their story across a near-half-hour match and delivered a flurry of activity, assisted by Michaels, that ended with Bret becoming champion and the start of the famous HBK-Taker feud.

It was all downhill from there. Though the months leading up to Summerslam were surely some of the proudest in Hart family history, the enhanced pride made the fall that much greater.

By December, Pillman was dead and only Owen remained under contract with the WWF, but the brilliance of The Hart Foundation's post-*'Mania 13* run should not go undervalued historically. It is a shame, honestly, Bret not staying in the WWF until the end of his career. He proved in 1997 that he could reinvent himself and, if ego had given way to wisdom (speaking of all parties), he could have contributed far more to the late 1990s than bad memories of a Screwjob...

#49

Edge vs. Chris Benoit vs. Christian vs. Chris Jericho vs. Kane vs. Shelton Benjamin Money in the Bank Ladder Match WrestleMania 21 April 3, 2005

Top 5 All-Time Ladder Match / Top 30 All-Time at WrestleMania / Top 5 Match in 2005

Though only time can reveal if the following statement will remain true, as of 2017, Money in the Bank had overtaken the Royal Rumble as the gimmick most likely to elevate new top-level stars. During the WrestleMania Era, winning Money in the Bank (MITB) has catapulted ten wrestlers to their first World Championship in WWE compared to Royal Rumble's seven; of those ten superstars, five of them confirmed their status as consistent main-event players through Money in the Bank compared to four headlining stamps of approval via the Rumble. Additionally, five other previously established top guys won another World Title thanks to Money in the Bank. The Rumble began directly setting up title opportunities in 1992, which means that MITB has produced more new champions and total champions in less than half the time.

It all began in 2005 with what has endured, on account of its quality and its impact, as one of the Top 50 matches ever. The brainchild of long-time WWE writer, Brian Gewirtz, and all-time WWE great, Chris Jericho, Money in the Bank shifted the focus of the Ladder Match from the mid-card, the gimmick's hierarchical home for the vast majority of its existence to that point, to the main-event. Intercontinental Champions had used the Ladder Match in the 1990s as a segue to legendary runs as headliners and the TLC Era duos had utilized the stipulation to reinvigorate tag team wrestling in the early 2000s; each exhibited the prospects of the Ladder Match to both advance individual careers and make otherwise mid-card acts marquee attractions,

197

so it seemed plausible that a direct line could be drawn between Ladder Match participants (mainly winners) and the highest echelon of WWE stars in the main-event like the Rumble had before it. Edge, a TLC veteran, was given the proverbial pen.

Edge was all-important in creating a legacy for Money in the Bank and his success is one of the primary reasons that the 2005 original should remain so highly regarded historically. His performance in the match at *WrestleMania 21* was, ultimately, opportunistic (not especially bold except for being the winner), but it was what he did as the inaugural holder of the contract for a World Heavyweight Title shot and his cash-in nine months later that crafted the MITB template. The Rated-R Superstar shined in 2005, climbing the last rungs of the proverbial ladder to capture the WWE Championship the same way that he had climbed the literal ladder to take hold of the contract-containing briefcase.

So much mystery surrounded the manner in which Edge would execute his guaranteed title shot. When Vince McMahon introduced him after the conclusion of an Elimination Chamber Match at *New Year's Revolution '06* and when he proceeded to dethrone then-champion, John Cena, it was just a tremendous moment for a variety of reasons. In addition to essentially achieving the upper limits of the Ladder gimmick's potential, it pushed the experienced mid-carder to the top spot he would occupy for six first-ballot Hall of Fame-stimulating years. Also, just as Shawn Michaels winning the '96 Rumble and fulfilling his "boyhood dream" at *WrestleMania XII* was a watershed combination of the Rumble-'Mania double that fans have come to associate with the allure of wrestling's preeminent season, Edge winning Money in the Bank and successfully deploying his contractually-obligated championship match in such dramatic fashion made the MITB winner and his/her eventual cash-in something that enthusiasts anticipate every year, hoping that WWE can catch lightning in a bottle again.

Complimenting Edge's prosperity as the initial victor, Money in the Bank 1 – the first-ever singles multi-man Ladder Match – has become the atypical original iteration of a genre (or, as in this case, sub-genre) to stand the test of time as the finest. Working in its favor was its cast of Ladder Match characters – Jericho and Edge, plus Christian and Chris Benoit, who had each already shown the ability to thrive in such an environment. The intricacy of executing pre-planned spot routines obviously came a lot easier to wrestlers who had already helped re-define what a Ladder Match could be. Those four, along with the intelligent presence of Kane, provided an extremely sturdy foundation, setting the stage for the ultra-athletic Shelton Benjamin to shine.

Benjamin might be the superlative athlete of the WrestleMania Era; and, if Edge was responsible for building the reputation of the Mr. Money in the Bank *moniker*, Shelton deserves credit for providing the human highlight reel that basically verified the Money in the Bank *Match* (and the singles multi-man Ladder Match in general) as a show-enhancing and later pay-per-view anchoring stipulation. He never won the briefcase, but it could certainly be argued that Benjamin's exploits in the first, second, fourth, and fifth editions (all at WrestleManias) popularized the MITB sub-genre in a manner similar to how Jeff Hardy's daredevil tactics popularized TLC. Money in the Bank made Shelton an unequivocal Ladder Match legend, that much is certain.

The Rabid Wolverine's role in the original bout's success cannot be understated either. Insomuch as Money in the Bank 1 was mostly a stunt-brawl – a 16-minute crash-bang attack on the senses – Benoit offered an added dimension of storytelling through his ability to sell the effects of Edge and Christian's assault on his arm and exhibit physical pain following a diving headbutt from off the top of a ladder. He was busted open the hard way and was forced to drag his limp arm by his side as he tried to climb toward the dangling briefcase and fend off The Big Red Monster, looking every bit the wounded warrior and gaining the appropriate sympathy for it until Edge whacked his injured arm and sent him careening back to the mat in the bout's climactic scene.

Most impressive about the original Money in the Bank is how well it compares to its peers in the Ladder Match genre overall, story-driven and stunt-brawl alike. If ever you sit down over the course of a day or a week and watch the best-regarded from the Ladder Match library, notice how well-rounded is Money in the Bank 1, particularly its blend of Benoit's dramatics, Benjamin's other-worldly athleticism, and the general creativity of the overall performance. That same stylistic mixture has rarely been replicated in its sub-genre, but should be studied as the blueprint whenever the gimmick is called upon.

When married with the sterling quality of its historic first outing, its star-making history is the intangible that boosts Money in the Bank's maiden voyage at *WrestleMania 21* securely into the Top 50. Pundits can argue the virtues of having crowned so many World Champions over a relatively short amount of time, but what cannot be argued is that Money in the Bank has made more World Title dreams come true than any other stipulation-based avenue.

#48
The Undertaker vs. Batista
World Heavyweight Championship
WrestleMania 23 to Survivor Series 2007
Top 30 All-Time at WrestleMania / Top 5 Match in 2007

When the first Money in the Bank Ladder Match aired, Undertaker's performances were rarely the most anticipated on the WrestleMania card. Though his win/loss record was perfect, his track record for match quality had for many years been spotty, granted that was mostly through little fault of his own. From The Phenom you could expect a spectacular entrance, but not always great wrestling. In 2007, however, Taker was paired with one of the biggest stars of the post-Attitude Era and the World Heavyweight Champion at the time, Dave Batista. Something magical proceeded to happen at Ford Field, what one half of the commentary team that night, JBL, would later call "a giant leap forward" for Batista and the start of perhaps the most celebrated run of matches of the 21st century (if not ever) – what in some circles has become known as "The Streak within The Streak" - for Undertaker.

The main ingredient for the recipe that concocted the magic at *WrestleMania 23* was heavy-motivation. "We had a lot of milestones with [that] match," Batista recalled in his WWE-produced documentary. "We thought we were going to be the main-event." In the two prior years since first winning the World Title at WrestleMania, Batista had never been defeated for the championship. Undertaker was, of course, undefeated at WrestleMania, 14-0 at the time to be specific. The Animal legitimately seemed a threat to break "The Streak," as it would have allowed his career to reach a new, even higher peak. Nonetheless, John Cena confirmed his ascent to being the tip top star in WWE in the main-event opposite Shawn Michaels instead. "We felt like we deserved better," Batista said. "[So], I really wanted to steal the show; I think Undertaker did as well."

Although the build-up to Taker-Batista was well done, expectations for the match were not particularly high. Batista typically shoulders the blame for he and Taker not getting the main-event spot in Detroit but, truth be told and though few would ever admit this, it probably had at least something to do with The Deadman too. The Animal, aside from his Hell in a Cell Match with Triple H, had never really rounded into form as an elite wrestler capable of continually validating his position with great storytelling, but Undertaker did not exactly have a sterling history for knocking it out of the park either, even though he was always so revered by his co-workers. When push came to shove, it would have been near-unanimously agreed that Cena and Michaels were the more bankable commodities at such a huge event.

Such was what made Batista vs. Taker plausibly the most pleasant surprise in modern pro wrestling lore. They had a fantastic match that had the wrestling world buzzing. After the match, Batista yelled backstage at the top of his lungs to his peers, "Follow that!" Only one match could have (HBK-Cena) and it is only debatable that it did. Batista vs. Taker remains to this day one of the greatest matches in WrestleMania history and *THE* greatest big man, powerhouse-style match in WrestleMania history. Hindsight reminds that it did not need to be the last match on the card to prove its point and establish its legacy.

It was not just that WrestleMania was arguably their night that earns a spot for their feud in the Top 50; 2007 was their *year*. Though other matches occasionally garnered more critical acclaim, the total body of work that Batista and Taker put together through four combined pay-per-view matches between April and November and a TV Match of the Year-contending Steel Cage Match on Smackdown in May earned them Rivalry of the Year honors. "To be able to keep [fan] interest and to keep them coming back, you have to have phenomenal matches and that's what they did," Triple H once noted in regards to the difficulty in having that many matches in big situations during a short time-period.

The entire program stands as a shining example of how a veteran star in Taker's position, with many years of quality booking behind him and a nearly unrivaled reputation with fans, can elevate a younger peer. Taker had so much equity built up with the audience that for Batista to not just hold a 2 win-1 loss-2 tie record over him but to go toe-to-toe with him in so many great brawls was the forever-stamp for The Animal's own credibility. Overpowering Triple H was an accomplishment of immense proportions in 2005; having a top-notch match with Undertaker at WrestleMania, being bloodied and so close to defeat only to draw in a Last Man Standing Match with The Phenom, taking everything The Deadman could dish out while locked with him in a cage and again dueling him to a draw, beating Taker clean in the middle of the ring with the World Title at stake, and never suffering another loss to him, not even inside Hell in a Cell? That was perception-enhancing and career-defining for Batista.

During their match at *Cyber Sunday*, site of Batista's clean win, Jerry Lawler mentioned on commentary how big a deal it was to have Undertaker, Steve Austin (voted the special guest referee for the bout by fans), and Batista in the same ring at the same time. Before the matches with Taker that spring, it might have struck fans as forced and/or odd to put The Animal in such esteemed company, but not after. The matches with Undertaker legitimized Batista's place in WWE lore, becoming the first line of defense in debates about his WrestleMania Era Top 25 candidacy; any attempt to shoot down his worthiness can be quickly countered with, "*WrestleMania 23* versus Taker."

"It opened up a lot of eyes and I finally proved myself to a lot of people," Batista has recounted about his awesome performance at Ford Field. In doing so, he provided The Phenom with a game dance partner en route to Taker's first consensus classic on the grandest stage. They both used it as a springboard, The Animal to the rest of his storied career and Taker to an unprecedented total of seven consecutive Match of the Year candidates at WrestleMania.

#47
Mankind vs. The Undertaker
King of the Ring 1996 to Survivor Series 1996; In Your House: Revenge of the Taker; King of the Ring 1998

Top 5 All-Time Hell in a Cell Match / Top 5 Match in 1998

In 2017, "The Doc Says" podcast teamed up with fellow LOP Radio personalities, from "The Right Side of the Pond," Samuel 'Plan (of *101 WWE Matches...*), Neil "Maverick" Pollock and Mario "Mazza" Rousetty, to create a career retrospective for The Undertaker ahead of what was thought to be his imminent retirement at *WrestleMania 33*. The general consensus was that The Deadman's rivalry with Mankind was very influential to the incredible run he would go on to have during the most celebrated years of his near three decade-long tenure.

When Mick Foley's darkest inner monster debuted after *WrestleMania XII* by attacking The Phenom, it set out to rip Taker apart physically, mentally, and in the win/loss column like nobody ever had before; and it was the best thing that ever happened to The Deadman, who had been little more than a "lumbering zombie, a very limited demonstration of the character," as 'Plan put it. Mankind did for Undertaker what neither Hulk Hogan, the WWF Championship, nor six straight years of top star-level booking could do: make Taker an interesting character beyond the smoke and mirrors of his gimmick. "The way that [he] brought Undertaker down to his level and how he was the only person that managed to take Undertaker to a place he had never been, it was a really interesting narrative," Maverick stated.

Though important to establishing his unparalleled persona, the at times laborious creative approach with Taker from 1990 through early 1996 was, combined with the lackluster quality of his opponents, limiting to his potential. For instance, he was one of the best athletes that WWE had ever signed but, sans for walking the ropes or his vertical leap-assisted diving clothesline, there were few overt displays of it. His matches with Mankind, starting with an underrated gem at *King of the Ring '96*, allowed him to showcase his in-ring talents to a greater extent. Also, there was nothing particularly relatable about a deceased mortician unlocking the powers of a mysterious urn wielded by his highly unusual cohort, Paul Bearer. He was like a shadow across the WWE Universe, ever-presently looming over an increasingly reality-infused sports entertainment scene.

"What's particularly interesting about the feud as it progresses," 'Plan added, "is how Mankind deconstructs the Undertaker character in almost every sense of the word - Paul Bearer turning on The Undertaker, his match style changing completely, [plus] instances when The Undertaker would come to the ring without the usual gear or skip an entrance altogether and appear in the ring." Working with Foley, noted by Maverick as "the most creative pro wrestling mind there's ever been" and splitting from his long-time alliance with Bearer opened the door for a lot more creative exploration of what Taker could be.

"[The rivalry] showed that a more athletic, a more out-going, a more humanized Undertaker was a good thing and that the character could still work without being the same caricature that it been up until that point," 'Plan inferred.

Few rivalries in professional wrestling history, though, have been as mutually beneficial as Mankind vs. The Undertaker. Perhaps best known for Foley's famous fall off Hell in a Cell, their on-again, off-again story spanning 2 ½ years "set Mick up perfectly as well," Mazza noted.

Undertaker was revered by his peers like only Andre the Giant before him by the time he had reached his 30th birthday and nobody had ever been given the opportunity to dominate a storyline against him. Foley made the most of his chance to be the first, as Mankind continually left Taker lying, defeated him cleanly and decisively in their initial pay-per-view showdown, beat him again in the first-ever Boiler Room Brawl at *Summerslam '96*, and "buried him alive" as well. Just as Foley would later be famous for confirming other major stars on the rise, Taker validated Mankind and offered him a launching pad to superstardom.

Of course, *King of the Ring '98* has historically usurped the rest of their feud. Mankind was launched from atop Hell in a Cell, crash-landing through the announce table where Jim Ross sat in bewilderment and uttered the famous call, "Good God almighty! Good God almighty! That killed him! As God as my witness, he is broken in half!" Combined with Foley's second fall - through the top of the Cell and onto the mat (knocking him out) with a chair chasing him down, blasting him in the mouth, and causing one of his teeth to become stuck in his nose - plus two additional bumps onto hundreds of thumbtacks, it was certainly the celebrated match in the Mankind vs. Undertaker library, eclipsing all of the other things that they achieved together.

"With that one move [from Cell to announce table], everything that I had accomplished during my thirteen years of wrestling became instantly obsolete," Foley once recalled. "For better or worse, that's the one thing I'll be most remembered for." The same can probably be said of his rivalry with Taker, who so benefited from the Mankind experience that it would be safe to call it the single most important feud of The Deadman's career. Let it from here on be honored as one of the greatest overall rivalries in WWE history too, for through it, as Mazza concluded, "They both enhanced their wrestling legacies."

#46
Hulk Hogan vs. Shawn Michaels
Summerslam
August 21, 2005

<u>Top 10 All-Time at Summerslam</u> / <u>Top 5 Match in 2005</u>

Hulk Hogan was a decidedly mortal 52 years old when he stepped in the ring with Shawn Michaels at *Summerslam '05* and, having just completed rehabilitation following a total hip replacement earlier that year, was fairly immobile for a man expected to work a 20-minute main-event. During his 2005 WWE Hall of Fame induction speech in April, though, fans had practically begged Hogan to do one more match, so WWE obliged by putting him in a tag team bout with Michaels as his partner to do most of the work. Of course, when the fans had pleaded with Hogan for one more match, what they really meant was one more *dream* match.

There is a certain expectation that comes with seeing two of the Top 10 stars of the WrestleMania Era facing off against each other; it is implied by a tag line like "Legend vs. Icon" that a match will be legendary/iconic and nothing logical like the advanced age or deteriorating condition of one of the combatants can fully deter those expectations, especially when that match involved Shawn Michaels.

During the aforementioned tag team bout a month after the Hall of Fame, Michaels got to see firsthand what Hogan was capable of physically. All that he could have realistically expected from Hulk in their eventual singles match was basic striking, minimal bumping, the big boot, and the leg drop. Go watch Hogan and Michaels vs. Hassan and Daivari from *Backlash '05* and see for yourself. To a far greater extent than he would have to three years later in Ric Flair's retirement match, Michaels was going to have to assume almost all of the responsibility for his ensuing match against Hogan living up to expectations.

The first thing that Michaels did was execute one of the most unforgettable two month heel runs in modern wrestling lore. After a shocking rendition of Sweet Chin Music charted his path for the Road to Summerslam, Michaels began channeling parts of his cocky persona from the mid-1990s into his act that most fans assumed had been long since buried. In one particularly memorable segment, HBK parodied a Hogan appearance on *Larry King Live*, mocking the Hall of Famer to no end. Perhaps fueled by the thought that Hogan had no intention of living up to an original agreement to a multi-match series that would have allowed HBK to successfully avenge his forthcoming loss at Summerslam, Michaels laid into the Hulkster, utilizing many of the politically-based stories that had soured Hogan's reputation through his WCW years especially; as mentioned in the Hardy-Edge chapter, the summer of 2005 really was like a Reality Era preview.

You would be hard-pressed to name a Summerslam match that was ever built-up better on television. HBK was phenomenal, arguably saving his best promo for the go-home Raw six days before the match. It was in Montreal, a place that despised Michaels for his part in the infamous "Screw Job" with Bret Hart in 1997, when HBK was at the peak of his notoriety. He held nothing back, even going so far as to tease The Hitman's return to live WWE TV. By the time he was done, after 7 weeks of brilliantly hyping the showdown, a huge part of the audience wanted to see Hogan give him comeuppance. Call it a throwback to a different era of his career but, with his head on straight and little more than creative satisfaction his primary focus, Michaels delivered as an antagonist as well in the summer of 2005 as he ever had during his heyday.

It would seem that the second largest number of people to ever buy a Summerslam on pay-per-view was evidence that HBK had done a fantastic job of hyping his bout with Hogan. If anything, the work that Michaels did before the match only increased the expectations for what he would produce during the match. Continuing with the theme that his character had established throughout July and August, he basically morphed into the crazy bump-taking, Mr. Perfect-esque wrestler that had earned him the respect of his peers in the early 1990s. Given Hogan's limitations, what other choice did he have but to offset Hogan's physical inadequacies by enhancing his own physical demand? He sold for Hogan like he did for the giants he became famous for making look like a million bucks a decade prior. It was over-the-top, but it was wildly entertaining and the match simply would not have been better than above average without it.

The interesting historical narrative written about Hogan vs. Michaels, however, is that HBK's strategy made Hogan look *bad* and that the match *suffered* for the so-called "over bumping." The herd mentality among more critical wrestling fans has adopted that line of thinking as gospel and has painted for many a classic encounter that had no business coming anywhere close to meeting the expectations for a dream match as instead a ridiculous display of egomaniacism. As Michaels would later point out in an interview defending his actions, he had replicated against Hogan the style that he had employed against Diesel to critical acclaim in 1995/1996 but was critically shamed for it in 2005. Try to imagine, if you will, what that match would have looked like without the manner in which HBK sold Hogan's offense.

Hogan vs. HBK's place on this list, make no mistake, is not *in spite* of the over-the-top selling from Michaels, but *because of it*. If you want to dive into the psychology behind it, Michaels bumped around in such a way that mirrored the amplification of the personal heights to which he had taken his feud with the Hulkster. As Hogan himself put it in one of his pre-match interviews, "[HBK] took this thing to a whole 'nother level dude." Why should Hogan's physical retorts have been sold any other way but to a similarly "whole 'nother level," dude?

For all intents, the format of the match was nothing more than the classic Hogan formula but, because of HBK's bumping, Hulk had the best version of the match which had made him a superhero to millions in the late 1980s at the ripe old age of fifty-two. Thanks to Michaels, Hulkamania got to really run wild one more time. Certainly, give credit where it was due to Hogan for turning back the clock in his own right, selling wonderfully for Michaels both with his body language and facial reactions as well as executing one of the best blade jobs ever to add a crimson element to proceedings, but how good was Michaels that he was able to coax a borderline-to-outright classic out of a wrestler who could literally do nothing more but punch and fall down before creakily lifting his boot up and then performing a leg drop?

The entire seven week run between super-kicking Hogan and losing to him at Summerslam was one of the most epic displays in the legendary career of Shawn Michaels and, for that, it narrowly earns its place among the Top 50 greatest matches, rivalries, and stories of the WrestleMania Era.

#45
The Undertaker vs. CM Punk
WrestleMania XXIX
April 7, 2013
Top 25 All-Time at WrestleMania / Top 5 Match in 2013

Perhaps the most memorable quality of the otherwise critically-panned *WrestleMania 29* card was that CM Punk unequivocally stole the show. So much success in professional wrestling lore has boiled down to right place and right time but, in regards to the industry's Holy Grail of closing "The Show of Shows," Punk's snub in 2013 was a case of right place and *wrong* time; every other star who ever had a year as strong as his 2012 main-evented 'Mania, but Punk peaked during the two year window when The Rock specifically came back to wrestle John Cena twice. Though Punk was so good that Rock modified his in-ring schedule to work an underrated (and economically fruitful) program with him too, The Second City Saint's best and most versatile year in WWE culminated in the final match of Undertaker's vaunted "Streak Within The Streak" instead of the final match of 'Mania 29.

History should now better appreciate the unenviable task that Punk was given when asked to combine with The Deadman to create a program in just four weeks that would end in a match at WrestleMania forced to follow six prior Taker outings at "The Show of Shows" which included two World Title wins, multiple candidates for greatest match ever, two main-events, and six consecutive utterly epic performances against four of the WrestleMania Era's Top 20 stars. Undertaker had managed something quite impressive in escalating further The Streak's reputation with Triple H after the HBK saga had ended; by the time he was 20-0, however, The Phenom had exhausted most of his character's creative potential, so it was going to be up to his opponent to coax something comparably engaging out of him.

CM Punk had routinely made magic for two years, so there may have been an assumption on the part of fans and management alike that he could very quickly turn nothing into the most heated feud of WrestleMania Season 2013, but that he did it nevertheless deserves appropriate praise given the unique and weighty circumstances. The death of Taker's long-time manager and rival, Paul Bearer, shortly after Punk had earned the chance to end The Streak, offered The Best in the World a new kind of chink in The Deadman's armor to exploit. Batista had tried to prove that he was on Taker's level, Edge wanted to replace Taker as WWE's "Phenom," HBK and Triple H both attempted to use Taker as a springboard to that ever so elusive next highest level of immortality; Punk added a new wrinkle to The Streak's most epic encounters, gnawing at Taker's raw emotions for Bearer and showing flippant regard in place of condolences. Punk attacked Kane, stole and carelessly bandied about with the iconic urn, and even had Paul Heyman imitate Bearer to set-up a sneak-attack that concluded with Punk pouring Bearer's "ashes" all over The Deadman.

Soulless was Punk's psychological assault on Taker. Maybe that was an example of art imitating life; the other four opponents in Taker's "Streak Within The Streak" talk of The Phenom with the type of admiration that has made Undertaker the successor to Andre the Giant on WWE's all-time most-respected list, but Punk has gone on-record in stating that he could not have cared less about wrestling The Deadman at *WrestleMania 29*, possibly stemming from the rumblings years prior that Taker's unflattering opinion of Punk's style of dress for a top star might have led to The Straight Edge Savior persona being downgraded to mid-card status after Punk's break-out summer in 2009. There was indeed a look of disdain on Punk's face as Taker made his way to the ring at Met Life Stadium; it was perhaps at least partially rooted in behind-the-scenes perception of reality and the slight of not being in the main-event as much as it was simply a character in the proverbial zone.

Motivational source material aside, it was all but a foregone conclusion long before the bell rang on April 7, 2013 that Punk-Taker was going to steal the show. The controversy that they stirred with the Bearer ashes angle on the go-home Raw before 'Mania had the wrestling world talking most about their match. They were then each given aura-enhancing entrances on the night, with a spirited rendition of Living Colour's "Cult of Personality" as memorable a live music instance as there has been in WrestleMania lore and Taker's walk through the grabbing hands of hell's minions symbolic of the pull of time bringing him closer to the end of his career. Punk wore Taker's signature color scheme and would further antagonize The Phenom by perfectly executing (once at least) the Old School tight-rope clothesline, as well as nearly ending The Streak by blasting Taker between the eyes with Bearer's urn. After four straight epically wrestled matches full of finishing blows unable to elicit finishes with HHH and HBK, Taker's match with Punk – in a similar manner to his match with Edge at *WM24* – demanded a greater fan attention to detail to maximally appreciate its triumph.

For both men, it was special. Taker had left his physical prime in Houston, Texas at *WrestleMania 25*, so for him to have a match *that* good with Punk without much in the way of excess, if you will, showed the world that he was still WWE's go-to wrestler when the lights were on brightest. Punk, meanwhile, offered what proved to be his parting shot to "The Showcase of the Immortals" franchise, forcing a night to be his that he and many pundits believed should have been his all along despite WWE not positioning it as such. They were like a vacuum that sucked all the energy out of the live audience, rendering even Rock vs. Cena 2 a match with lackluster crowd response. It was a true classic.

Frankly, it might have ranked higher had it taken place in a different year. It must be emphasized before moving ahead to #44 that the competition for 2013 Match of the Year between Punk-Taker and the two-headed monster from *Summerslam* – Punk-Lesnar and Bryan-Cena – was the most riveting of the entire research process, even more so than 1997 (Austin-Hart and the first-ever Hell in a Cell) or 2000 (HHH-Cactus and TLC); no other year produced quite the same miniscule discrepancy at the top. It was that triple threat, so to speak, which refined the year-to-year ranking model, with each member of the trio inching ahead at some point in time before the others moved in front of Punk-Taker partially on account of their respective standings in Summerslam lore.

Top 50 all-time is not too shabby, obviously. With an awesome performance, Punk validated his "Best in the World" status that night in front of over 80,000 people and on the grandest stage possible. *WrestleMania 29* should always be remembered as the night that Punk took Undertaker to his absolute limits and, even though he did not headline the show, had the majority of the headlines written about the show centered on him.

#44
Ric Flair vs. "Macho Man" Randy Savage
WWF Championship Match
WrestleMania VIII
April 5, 1992

Top 25 All-Time at WrestleMania / Top 5 Match in 1992

"Macho Man" Randy Savage holds several distinctions in the WrestleMania Era; he is one of its Top 10 overall stars and arguably its most uniquely charismatic figure; he is acknowledged by many as the original "Mr. WrestleMania" for his classic matches on the grandest stage. He is also one half of *the* most beloved couple in sports entertainment lore.

Miss Elizabeth and Macho Man were the Clark Kent and Lois Lane, Zack and Kelly, or Ross and Rachel of professional wrestling. Fans delighted in the success of their on-screen relationship; even the most quibbling enthusiasts would struggle not to admit at least a small rooting interest in Savage ending up with the First Lady of Wrestling.

Never before or since has a WWE romance evoked the sort of emotion that did Macho and Liz. Their reunion at *WrestleMania VII* – perhaps the most striking example of the soap opera element's effectiveness in sports entertainment – drew legitimate tears from many viewers; it was admittedly a spine-tingling sort of moment. When they tied the knot in the main-event at *Summerslam '91*, it was as Ted DiBiase aptly described it, "Like watching the prince and the princess get married."

Of course, before the nuptials and before they reunited on TV, they were married in real life the year before Macho Man's 1985 WWF debut. Miss Elizabeth was his manager and Savage, being a heel, was clearly shown to have been an overbearing figure in her life (most prominently in response to Hulk Hogan's affection toward Liz leading up to *WrestleMania V*). Ask many of their pro wrestling peers and they would tell you that what was seen on-camera was art imitating life. Macho was notorious for his insecurities about her. He would reportedly lock her in the dressing room when she was not accompanying him to ringside so that none of the other wrestlers could interact with her. Liz told Jimmy Hart that Savage once bought her 21 TV dinners for a three week road trip so she would not have to leave their house.

We bore witness in 1991 to the intensely passionate feelings that the Macho Man character could conjure toward Elizabeth on-screen when the "newlyweds" were subjected to the machinations of Jake Roberts. Savage found new life as a top babyface through defending his bride against a sociopath. Just when it seemed as though they were going to be able to move on from The Snake's brand of evil, though, Macho became #1 contender to the WWF Championship at *WrestleMania VIII*, and the defending titleholder at the time, Ric Flair, preyed on the Savage-Liz relationship in his own dishonorable way.

Flair, supported by his right-hand men Bobby Heenan and Mr. Perfect, insinuated that he had been involved with Liz before Savage was in the picture and that she still harbored romantic feelings toward him. The exemplary antagonistic trio promised to show a gigantic centerfold of her on the big screens at the Hoosier Dome if Flair retained the title. Take that into the context of the above; the wrestling world's vested interest in Savage and Liz + Macho Man's well-known fervor for his wife and his insanely jealous tendencies + the kiss-stealin' owner of "Space Mountain" legendary for his exploits with women. The sum of those aforementioned parts was one of wrestling history's most emotionally-charged matches.

The reaction to Macho Man's entrance at *WrestleMania VIII* powerfully emanated across the airwaves. Watched today, the thunderous response he got can suck you right into the story as if it were the early 1990s again. Savage and Flair crafted an ultimately cathartic tale wrestled in a style similar to Hogan vs. HBK. It was not a 50-50 match; Flair used Macho's retribution-seeking against him, warding off an opening onslaught to take control for a dominant stretch of the early run-time. The crowd was deflated by it, but their energy building up to Savage's initial comeback was palpable. When Macho Man took control, the audience went bananas. It has become a lost art, the ability of wrestlers to connect on those sorts of emotional crescendos.

Undoubtedly, one of the intangibles which aids in the impassioned storytelling and helps set this match apart is the commentary. Gorilla Monsoon and Bobby Heenan were an incredible pair in the booth; their investment in Flair and Savage as characters, with clearly defined roles on the moral spectrum, heavily assisted in portraying to pay-per-viewers then and DVD/Blu-Ray/WWE Network viewers now the stakes of the match both personally (i.e. Liz) and professionally (i.e. the title).

In execution, it was very much a classic NWA Flair match just with better, WWF-boosted production value. Mr. Perfect, acting as a ringside henchman as well as JJ Dillon ever did, slipped Flair the foreign object used to regain the advantage and then blasted Savage in the knee with a chair, kick-starting the build to the final emotional high of Macho Man overcoming near-crippling odds to roll-up Naitch for the three-count and regain the WWF Championship.

The entire presentation showcased champion and challenger at or near their best, in the twilight years of their respective primes. Though infamous for being subbed in for Hulk vs. Naitch, Savage vs. Flair pitted the man best known for being the world's greatest wrestler (Flair) against the man who essentially wrote the book on the modern WWE style of wrestling (Savage); they lived up to the hindsight hype. It was that historical narrative combined with the WrestleMania stage and the awesome commentary that allowed Savage vs. Flair to eclipse any ranking advantages held by its Top 50 predecessors.

#43
The Dangerous Alliance vs. Sting's Squadron
War Games Match
WrestleWar
May 17, 1992

#1 All-Time War Games Match / Top 5 Match in 1992

War Games was WCW's most celebrated special attraction match; if it was to WCW what The Royal Rumble Match is to WWE, then interestingly both editions most historically romanticized (for good reason) by their respective fanbases occurred within four months of each other. The Dangerous Alliance, arguably the most underrated faction in wrestling lore, versus Sting's Squadron was the match in which it all came together for the War Games gimmick and, as Chris aka "Mizfan" from the fantastic *WCW: The Legacy Series* stated in their podcast dedicated to *WrestleWar '92*, "People who love War Games...this [version] has to be the reason why."

There has frankly never been anything quite like it.

War Games '92 was still as violent as any match seen that year, living up to the reputation set by its predecessors, but it was also an extremely inventive performance. A generation of younger wrestlers and savvy superstars making their first appearance in the match was added to the mix of War Games veterans in what turned out to be the perfect recipe.

"For War Games to work you needed to have everybody involved not only want to win the match but legitimately want to exact as much pain and blood as possible out of everyone on the other team," Mizfan referenced about the participating characters in the presentation. "[They] want to be locked inside the structure so that they can tear each other apart. Everyone in this match did perfectly what they needed to do."

The match opened with an awesome duel between Barry Windham, still in his '87-'93 prime, and an emergent "Stunning" Steve Austin, who was peaking athletically at the time and had the match of his life to that point (plenty of blood was spilt throughout the proceedings, but nobody bled more than Austin); the incomparable "Ravishing" Rick Rude entered the fray and added a confident, steadying presence before Ricky Steamboat came in full of babyface fury, his greatest contribution unquestionably the creativity he put on display; Arn Anderson's veteran savvy was vital given his history in the earlier War Games, while Dustin Rhodes (pre-Goldust) provided exuberance typical of youth but likewise reminiscent of a really hot tag in a standard team format; Larry Zybszko, practically useless the year prior, played the same role but purposefully as ultimately the scapegoat for the losing team; Sting's late appearance as the powerhouse star was somewhat muted overall, but still had its very noteworthy moments, while Bobby Eaton's overall performance could not be understated, as he was integral to the effectiveness of the climax; Nikita Koloff offered an additional layer of emotional depth to the match when he officially settled his differences with Sting in one of wrestling history's best man-hugs; Medusa climbed to the top of the structure, prompting Sting to join her and attempt to quell her interference in an eye-popping sight that may have inspired Shawn Michaels and Undertaker to copy it five years later in the first Hell in a Cell; and, not to by any means be forgotten, Paul E. Dangerously's blueprint-sized game plan and ringside instructions took the over-dramatized strategizing that JJ Dillon had done in the early years to the next level.

Twelve current and future Hall of Famers made War Games '92 just about everything that you could ever want from a pro wrestling match.

In terms of pure elements, it was both brutal and smart (all involved sold their butts off, were psychologically locked in and immersed in the story told, and executed even the more difficult sequences expertly); intangibly, there was no shortage of innovation; in regards to memorable happenings, the five most engaging moments in War Games lore probably came from this one match, with the climactic Dangerous Alliance scheme in particular (borrowed years later in Cena vs. Umaga) boldly going where no match in the WrestleMania Era had gone before; the feud that the battle culminated was outstanding (The Dangerous Alliance rose to prominence as the top heels in WCW in late 1991 when they initially targeted Windham, Rhodes, and Sting and were a dominant force through the winter and early spring of 1992 as Steamboat and Koloff also drew their ire – War Games was perhaps only more appropriate in 1987); historically, it is not just the superlative version of War Games, but it is also one of the greatest matches ever in NWA/WCW period. It was truly an all-time classic.

"There are great little things on every level, in terms of wrestling and in terms of storytelling," Mizfan concluded. "It's a match where everyone comes out looking better than they did going in."

So, why not rank it higher? What makes the few matches ranked just ahead of it greater? Well, as *WCW: The Legacy Series* co-host, Mystic, countered, "[Though] all the moving parts were as awesome as could be, War Games as a match can only be so much."

A fair assessment of even the best remembered versions – like the 1991, the originals in 1987, and even the most dynamic of the lot in 1992 – yields reasonable critiques about the genre. As it progresses up to more competitors rather than whittles down to less, the camera work was rarely able to properly keep up with the action, often producing finishes that would happen mostly away from where viewers could see it. Visually chaotic might be a good description; it could be a bit of a mess, particularly when "The Match Beyond: Submission or Surrender" got underway.

From a comparative standpoint, it is also difficult to ignore that so many more people watched the next few matches listed, with double and triple the pay-per-viewers and three to a whopping thirteen times the live attendees. WCW matches have been tucked into relative obscurity and even though modern fans have access to matches like War Games '92 via the WWE Network, where would the incentive come from to seek them out? The more opinions there are, the more "popular" they can become. Hopefully, this book and podcasts like *The Legacy Series* will help establish a greater appreciation for WCW's contributions to modern industry lore.

It is true that many WCW fans from that period recall War Games matches as being better than they were, whereas many fans who did not see them in their heyday have a tendency to view them as overrated. Sting's Squadron vs. The Dangerous Alliance, though, is far from overrated.

#42
Team Cena vs. Team Authority
5-on-5 Elimination Tag Team Match
Survivor Series
November 23, 2014

#1 All-Time Survivor Series Elimination Match / #1 All-Time at Survivor Series / Top 5 Match in 2014

The Reality Era was given its name for its embrace of manipulating fan perception to blur the line between what goes on behind the camera and what is scripted to take place in front of it. The Authority was the perfect on-screen villainous leader for that progressive booking philosophy, transferring the perceived reputations of Triple H and Stephanie McMahon – backstage schemers with limiting viewpoints – from the internet to WWE TV. In recent years, WWE crafted several cerebrally-stimulating storylines using The Authority as a central figure.

WWE's modern creative process demands maturity; it is forced to develop more intricate stories that appease the diehard sect of the audience most integral to the WWE Network's vitality – the same part of the fanbase under whose skin The Authority so easily got. Emotionally engaging the "smart" fan can be challenging. To borrow an analogy from comic books, these fans often prefer the more psychologically dense, Batman-type arcs. All the while, WWE must not ignore the parts of their fanbase that emotionally resonate more with straightforward, Superman-like chronicles.

The best modern wrestling angles see WWE carefully weave themes from both creative approaches into one coherent drama. The Authority vs. Daniel Bryan is one of the greatest examples. Some people thought that Bryan was perceived by WWE management as a great wrestler who could never be the top star. He started off as an internet darling and had successfully won over the large majority of the fanbase by *Summerslam 2013*, but when The Authority brought his so-termed "glass ceiling" to TV as a storyline, Bryan's popularity exploded.

In Christopher Nolan's *Batman* trilogy, The League of Shadows maintained its presence even when not the primary villain; its leader was the foil in the first film, its existence was muted in the second film, and its themes were brought back for the final film. If *Summerslam 2013* to *Survivor Series 2014* was an analogous period in WWE, then the first act concluded at *WrestleMania XXX* with Bryan's glorious underdog triumph over the Triple H-led Authority and the second act ended at *Summerslam 2014* with The Authority's role less pronounced; the climactic third act, then, brought back to the forefront The Authority's tyrannical reign over WWE building up to and culminating at *Survivor Series 2014* with a truly remarkable Elimination Tag Team Match.

Team Cena vs. Team Authority may not have created the potent cocktail for organic hatred and ultimate catharsis among the modern fanbase that Bryan's saga did, but it utilized the expanded roster of talents afforded by the Survivor Series gimmick to integrate a diverse series of themes that appealed to various parts of the audience. The pre-pay-per-view television hype and the match itself saw a combination of nerve-grating opportunism from Seth Rollins, frustration from The Authority-squashed revolt by Randy Orton, betrayal from Big Show, anti-Americanism from Rusev, intrigue from former Wyatt Family members Erick Rowan and Luke Harper, anticipation from the resurgent Ryback's recruitment by both sides, and disgust from Dolph Ziggler being screwed out of both the Intercontinental Title and nearly the underdog heroism of defeating The Authority.

There was also a stimulating dichotomy at play with John Cena. Certain fans were placated by his position as the face of the resistance against the dastardly Authority; WWE's ultimate symbol of purity versus the ultimate symbol of wrestling's dark side. Other fans were perplexed. The Authority, for the first year of its existence, was an exceptional antagonist for a story featuring an anti-establishment babyface. Cena, though, *was* the establishment, his role almost like plopping Superman's character into a Batman story arc. So, how does one cheer the effort to tear down the wall of despotism while simultaneously cheering a man who benefits from the authoritarian regime? The beauty of the Reality Era was that WWE knew how to handle such complicated situations with maturity.

The extremely well-executed first 25-minutes of the Survivor Series match reflected all of the aforementioned diversity of themes. Then, Team Cena member, Big Show, knocked out his own captain and the narrative focus shifted its appeal. Wrestling's Man of Steel getting eliminated and leaving the underutilized-but-very-popular Ziggler to play the Survivor Series-classic 1 vs. 3 underdog role heightened the emotional stakes. Ziggler went on to pay incredible tribute to the famous Shawn Michaels comeback in 2003 and put on a performance that channeled the spirit of Daniel Bryan's story. Rollins arguably exceeded the impressive quality of Ziggler's outing, while Triple H provided phenomenal cerebral depth on the outside with both his actions and his expressions.

Just when you thought that the emotional roller-coaster was going to end with corruption winning the day, the long-awaited debut of Sting offered a final saving grace. The Stinger's arrival negated heavy Authority interference and allowed Ziggler to be the sole survivor, giving fans of all types multiple levels of emotional release. "It was awesome," Hunter would later note out of character. "[The fans] didn't see it coming; it was just larger than anything you could have anticipated. That's one of those goosebump moments." Any concern about Sting's fourteen year absence from the mainstream spotlight proved unfounded. "The reaction was unreal," Cena commented on Sting's WWE-released documentary. "Nothing is for sure until it happens; and when it happened, it was something special."

The inaugural WWE appearance for a legendary figure being handled so maturely was another example of the product's growth and provided a much-deserved spotlight for a man who, in all this talk of perception and reality, never would have signed with WWE had they not matured. Sting went onto have a legacy-enhancing run in the year that followed, but that moment at Survivor Series may have been his greatest. It was a major intangible addition to Team Cena vs. Team Authority's historical stature.

The claim that it is the greatest Survivor Series Elimination match ever, even eclipsing Team Austin vs. Team Bischoff from 2003, speaks to another of the Reality Era's defining traits: its habit of re-defining. As was discussed with Rollins vs. Ambrose, WWE and the foundational performers of the Reality Era did well to acknowledge the successes of industry history and tweak them to better fit contemporary conditions. In Team Cena vs. Team Authority, it was as if WWE identified everything that had worked in the previous two most successful versions of the Elimination Tag gimmick and blended the elements into an ideal amalgamation for November Classic lore. From WWF vs. WCW, it took the significant sense of occasion and epic length to allow for so many personalities to share the stage. From Austin vs. Bischoff, it adopted the fluidity of movement and dramatic conclusion. Its finished product was brilliant.

Team Cena vs. Team Authority is the greatest example of the longest-tenured PPV gimmick match in WWE history. Its depth of content equaled the sheer amount of memorable happenings in the pre-match build. In the end, Cena was not Superman; Ziggler seized the day; The Authority lost; and WCW's Franchise finally showed up. To top it all off, Triple H and Stephanie were fantastic after the match ended, mixing shock, disappointment, and rage with a crowd-pleasing temper tantrum. Its superlative achievement was accomplishing the near impossible in modern pro wrestling: it offered something for everyone.

#41
John Cena vs. Shawn Michaels
WWE Championship
WrestleMania 23 and Monday Night Raw
April 23, 2007

Top 30 All-Time at WrestleMania / Top 10 All-Time TV Match /
Match of the Year in 2007

John Cena is the LeBron James of professional wrestling. Like "The King" of the hardwood, Cena is one of the best ever, having amassed staggering statistical achievements on a resume worthy of the "greatest of all-time" conversation. However, there is a sizeable portion of both the basketball and wrestling fanbases that insist on tearing down their careers.

Call it the curse of being "The Man" in WWE during the most cynical period in modern world history, but critical enthusiasts are readily apt to poke holes in any supporting argument in Cena's defense. His relationship with the audience has just been that heated and, though the temperament has thawed thanks to his impressive ability to adapt his in-ring game to the more popular, indy-influenced style during this decade, there remains for many diehard fans a fairly disdainful attitude toward his work from 2005-2012, the time-frame that really built the bulk of his legacy.

No matter how strong the evidence used to reinforce his career as having been among the truly remarkable of WWE lore, the perception remains of Cena as an overbearing presence in the main-event, a limited performer with too few gears to be considered great, and an exemplification of why WWE was believed by some not to have been as good as it should have been in the post-Attitude Era. That perception has already, for those who feel that way, prevented Cena's unparalleled run at the top in WWE, like LeBron's in the NBA, from being appreciated as special and that perception may cause a Cena-heavy Top 40 in this book to be frowned upon. It is that perception, make no mistake, that has underrated Cena's pair of April 2007 matches with Shawn Michaels.

Cena will likely be the most polarizing Top 5 all-time greatest superstar to have ever lived; just as his reputation growing historically will raise the profile of his rivalries, the loud voices of his detractors will try to hold down some of his finest work. His matches with HBK, for instance, were the turning point in his career; his rival Edge referred to the *WrestleMania 23* main-event as Cena's "breakthrough performance" and the match "where he went to a different kind of realm"; the rematch on Raw in London three weeks later was the consensus WWE Match of the Year in 2007. Yet, Cena vs. Michaels may never get the credit for its accomplishments that it deserves.

If you look at it from the perspective of an HBK fan, it would be a fair assessment to state that John Cena does not make the cut as one of The Heartbreak Kid's top opponents; looking at the post-comeback years alone, 2007 with Cena was the weakest Match of the Year frontrunner that Michaels produced, but every last one of those other classics will be discussed shortly on these pages. The stories that HBK told with Cena were excellent in their own right; they were straight out of the playbook of The Icon's childhood hero, Ric Flair. If you ever wondered what Flair in the latter years of his prime vs. Cena might have looked like, Michaels vs. Cena painted you that picture. Their matches demanded more of us as fans, gradually building as they did the highs and lows, but a throwback to the National Wrestling Alliance was never destined to be received in quite the same way as an Attitude brawl, an ultra-athletic '02/'03 match, or a more modern "epic." Everything from the length to the pace to the psychology to the selling style to the near fall methodology was like watching a Flair match at Starrcade in the 1980s; and, in the grand scheme of things, that is a significant compliment.

Michaels quite clearly relished the opportunity to be in the focal point match primarily responsible for selling people on the biggest show of the year. To wrestle the new face of the company in the main-event – and in a one-on-one match – may not have equaled the emotions of the boyhood dream coming true, but adulthood dreams coming true feel just as cathartic if not more so, especially if they involve something you love that got taken away from you.

Those matches, though, will ultimately be remembered for John Cena. *WrestleMania 23* was the night that it felt like the John Cena Era had truly arrived, with no more appropriate highlight on the reel than The Champ's Ford Field-inspired entrance with the Mustang, after which Cena hopped out and walked down the ramp of that incredibly designed set with his infamous custom WWE Title belt over his shoulder; other than *WrestleMania XXVIII*, site of his first match with The Rock, it stands out as perhaps the most indelible of all his WrestleMania moments.

The weight on his shoulders that year was tremendous. WrestleMania was making its return to a stadium venue and Cena was unquestionably the biggest name in WWE on that card. Fortunately, "John Cena handles pressure better than almost anybody I've ever met in this or any other industry," Paul Heyman has been quoted as saying. "The more pressure that you put on John Cena, the bigger his shoulders grow." Original plans saw Cena matching up against Triple H again, but The Game went down with his second quadriceps tear, Michaels stepped in, and the kind of match expected of Cena in the biggest match of his life to that point instantly changed. As Heyman recalled, "If John Cena is truly going to carry WWE into the future, he's gonna have to hold his own with the man whose nickname [Mr. WrestleMania] is branded on the very show that Cena is now being enlisted to carry."

In a situation in which he had to deliver, Cena came through. He played very well the part at *WrestleMania* of a young lion fighting against an overwhelming disadvantage in big fight experience and seized the day (and the victory). Michaels expertly acted out his on-screen role of the cagey veteran presented with what could have been his final shot at WWE Championship glory on the grandest stage and wonderfully did his job as the man tasked with guiding Cena to his first feature length title bout unreliant on the bells and whistles that had hallmarked his previous standout efforts. The rematch on Raw was heralded as better than the original; it reversed the role of the aggressor (and the result) and can be easily identified as the match in which Cena earned his PhD in professional wrestling performance; the validity of JBL's nickname for Cena, "Big Match John," started with the HBK series.

The Champ vs. The Showstopper has a lot of things going for it in a "greatest ever" discussion. In addition to the above talking points, the Cena-HBK headlined *Mania 23* drew the second largest number of pay-per-view buys ever (assisted by Donald Trump) and a WWE.COM panel voted their Raw rematch the greatest match in the WWE flagship show's history, but its legacy hinges on how you feel about its importance to the career of the ever-controversial John Cena.

#40
Kurt Angle vs. Brock Lesnar
WWE Championship
WrestleMania XIX to Smackdown September 18, 2003

Top 35 All-Time at WrestleMania / Top 30 All-Time at Summerslam / Top 5 All-Time TV Match / Top 5 Match in 2003

"Amateur or professional, the competitive nature of an athlete never changes"

Those were the words of Jesse Ventura during his narration of 2004's *The Mania of WrestleMania* when discussing the rivalry between the most accomplished athletes in WWE history: Kurt Angle and Brock Lesnar.

Pro wrestling has had a lot of great athletes come through its ranks, many of whom excelled in amateur sports to varying degrees, but if we compare WWE to the NFL or NBA, then Angle and Lesnar possessed the skill sets most likely to translate to the highest possible levels of in-ring achievement – World Championships and WrestleMania main-events – and become the sports entertainment versions of Peyton Manning in pro football and LeBron James in pro basketball, the top prospects who come into the league and have to live up to the hype.

With all due respect, many of wrestling lore's greatest stars had nothing close to the athletic pedigree of Lesnar and Angle. Arguably the biggest star of all-time, Steve Austin, was a Tom Brady-type, a 7th round caliber talent who rose to his pantheon position without an ounce of the high-touting.

Much of the intrigue during the Angle vs. Lesnar feud in 2003, then, stemmed from their backgrounds and how the organic competition between the two would play out in the dramatic world of WWE, which has always been at its best when it finds

231

legitimate (real life) conflicts among foes that it can amplify for its viewing audience. For Rock and Austin, it was about being the alpha male; for Hart and Michaels, it was about career validation; and for Angle and Lesnar, it was about who was the best. As wrestling enthusiasts, there are a handful of reasons to invest in the stories told on the 20'x20' canvas, but what Lesnar and Angle brought to the table was unlike anything else in history. 99.9% of their peers had categorically failed in some form or another at one point in time; failed to make it in the NFL, failed to reach the pinnacle in WWE, or even failed to make it to WWE at all. Lesnar and Angle both climbed another sport's Mt. Everest and carried an expectation of immediate and immense success once they had begun to master their new craft.

It is fascinating to watch two entities who know how to win to that degree, be they individual athletes or teams, competing against other; and here is the thing – it does not happen very often. Angle vs. Lesnar was more like seeing the 1980's 49ers versus the 1990's Cowboys more than it was anything we have actually seen in sport. They were once-in-a-generation prodigies and they so happened to debut within 28 months of each other.

"There's a little envy; there's a little jealousy," Angle said in the Ventura-narrated documentary. "I'm an Olympic gold medalist, he's not. I'm a two-time national champion, he's not. Could he have done these things? Maybe, maybe not. I think we always wonder in the back of our minds, 'Who is better now?' I think it will always be like that as long as both of us are in sports entertainment." That aspect of their rivalry was in place from the moment that Brock showed up as a former NCAA Heavyweight Champion. All WWE had to do was sprinkle some sports entertainment flair on their feud and it was off to the races.

WrestleMania XIX was the perfect stage for them. They were ideal opponents, wrestling for the WWE Championship at an event proven to substantially bolster the historical reputation of anything that excels there, and they earned their main-event position that night, but bad timing put Angle in the predicament of risking permanent damage to his re-injured, formerly broken (friekin') neck and wrestling the match at around 40% (or less) healthy. "There is no second-string Kurt Angle that comes in and takes his place," Triple H said. "It's do-or-die. I don't think it becomes an issue of letting anybody down but yourself." Angle acquitted himself well in what proved to be his only "Show of Shows"-closer, putting in one of the two gutsiest performances of the WrestleMania Era (and out-performing the other to boot).

It was actually for Lesnar whom the match became most famous, though. As he describes in his book, *Death Clutch*, the notorious Shooting Star Press gone wrong was set in motion by John Laurinaitis, a former wrestler and long-time WWE executive who was the agent tasked with helping Lesnar and Angle put their match together backstage. Brock became one of pro wrestling's first YouTube sensations for being a near 300lb monster who could do a gainer off the top rope and land it perfectly half-way or more across the ring. Johnny Ace saw it and convinced Lesnar on the day of WrestleMania to do it against Angle. "Brock, you gotta finish the match like that. It's so memorable. It's your WrestleMania moment," he said. An exhausted wrestler and a sweat-soaked rope botched that plan.

As Larry Matysik, author of *The 50 Greatest Professional Wrestlers of All Time*, aptly described the moment, "Even [with the botch], the massive muscle package that is Lesnar catapulting through the air was mesmerizing."

Shamefully, though still great, their 'Mania match was not all that it could have been. They were given a mulligan at *Summerslam* when both were healthy, but outside interference and repeated disregard of a previously unwritten-but-understood rope-break rule convoluted a situation that did not benefit from over-booking.

The third time was the charm.

Angle vs. Lesnar III was as good as the match that stole the show from them at *WrestleMania XIX* and nearly as good as the match that stole the year from them back in January; it was also the best Ironman Match ever. Wade Keller, editor of *The Pro Wrestling Torch*, rated the match "five-stars" and felt it superior to Rock vs. Triple H, Michaels vs. Hart, and Flair vs. Steamboat [the 55-minute, 2/3 Falls Match]. Here were his extended thoughts:

> In the ring, these two took a match that is nearly impossible to perform flawlessly because of the enormous hole of time to fill and they managed to advance the 60 minute Iron Man concept to a previously unreached level. There weren't the extended slow spots or cheap bumpless stand-up floor brawling that has been used to fill time in past marathon matches. The drama, the psychology, the variety and impact of the moves, the playing into each wrestlers' signature spots and trademark styles, the placement of the falls and the final finish, the integration of their characters - most everything was better [than in the] other 'modern era' 60 (or near 60) minute matches.

Whenever the superlative effort in your series of matches, which include the main-event of WrestleMania and a Summerslam rematch with the WWE Title at stake, winds up being from a September episode of Smackdown, you should not be surprised if your rivalry fades historically and you probably are not going to feature too heavily deep into the Top 50 discussion. That said, Angle vs. Lesnar has never and may never be replicated in terms of the particular brand of hype surrounding it born of their athletic reputations.

#39
AJ Styles vs. John Cena
Money in the Bank 2016 to Royal Rumble 2017

Top 10 All-Time at Royal Rumble / Top 10 All-Time at Summerslam / Top 5 Match in 2016 / Match of the Year in 2017

No one who witnessed the AJ Styles vs. John Cena trilogy will likely forget it anytime soon.

Rewinding to 2016, it had become quite common, by the time they had initially interacted in a WWE ring, for Cena to be involved in high profile battles against representatives of the non-WWE pro wrestling scene. With all due respect to the other Cena opponents who originally made their names in smaller wrestling promotions before stepping up to the big leagues, The Phenomenal One was the biggest non-WWE wrestling star to emerge since WCW shut down its operations in 2001; so, even though a lot of the material that Styles used in the promos to set-up his matches with Cena was recycled, it felt reasonably fresh given the reputation of its orator.

Here was the best in-ring performer in the world, an incredible hybrid of Shawn Michaels and Bret Hart stylistically whose legendary matches in TNA segued to a highly decorated stint in New Japan Pro Wrestling when that promotion was hitting its modern stride, coming to WWE during an era in which all barriers for talents like him to instantly succeed had already been torn down. Cena, no longer creatively handcuffed, to a degree, by being the be-all, end-all star constantly in need of being booked strongly, had transitioned his focus to tearing down the proverbial house as often as possible. Motivation in the Styles vs. Cena series was therefore easy to come by, the former focused on establishing his WWE legacy and the latter healthily obsessed with expanding his historical footprint, including in the final phase of the rivalry adding a record-tying 16th World Championship reign to his resume.

Their first match together at *Money in the Bank '16* was reminiscent of Cena's *WrestleMania 23* encounter with HBK in how it painted such a clear picture of AJ's vast superiority between the ropes. Cena had very few counter-measures to combat The Phenomenal One's near-constant offensive onslaught, much of which was in itself counter to Cena's tried-and-true arsenal. The one-sided nature of it stood out in a time period in wrestling lore that had become so dependent on back-and-forth, critically-acclaimed action (the so-termed "50-50" match). It was like watching a matador constantly outwit a bull; Cena, of course, got in his licks, but the vast majority of the match featured Styles in the driver's seat, taking Cena anywhere he wanted him to go. That AJ was so dominant and that he still won, no matter the interference, contrasted the Cena formula of years past and made clear how serious a threat Styles had become in less than six months in WWE.

Part of the fascination in Cena's feuds over the years, particularly when he has wrestled talents that do not fit the mold of the classic WWE Superstar, has been to gauge the upper limits of a Cena opponents' future prospects by how well they were booked against him. The deeper into the decade we reached, the more frequently Cena tended to lose, but most of those losses were tainted; and many Cena foes that cheaply defeated him then went onto decisively lose most if not all of the rematches and consequently drop several rungs down the hierarchical ladder. Rare were both the opponents who beat Cena multiple times (like Edge or CM Punk) or who beat Cena clean (like Daniel Bryan). Styles went into his rematch against Cena at *Summerslam '16* attempting to join elite company and avoid tumbling down the WWE rabbit hole toward comparative mediocrity.

In the consensus 2016 WWE Match of the Year, Cena threw everything that he had at Styles, including variations of his move-set that had never previously failed to put away a rival (i.e. the "Super Attitude Adjustment" from off of the second turnbuckle); AJ would not stay down, though, eventually pinning Cena clean in the middle of the ring. The landscape had obviously changed, considering that Cena was in the midst of a part-time run and that WWE had become by 2016 a promotion in which someone like Cena and someone like Styles could be viewed on an equal playing field, but the fact remains that for the first time since Cena became "The Face That Runs The Place" in 2005, he lost consecutive matches to an opponent with at least one such defeat coming without distraction or plausible excuse; Styles even added a third consecutive pin of Cena in a Triple Threat Match at *No Mercy* two months later.

The *Summerslam* bout continued the trend that Cena began in 2015 of performing the majority of his matches, regardless of the setting, as if they were the main-event of a WrestleMania – a trend, by the way, that trickled down the card. It remains to be seen how increasing the volume of "epics," with their dramatic high points derived from kicking out of finishing moves, will affect the overall perception of that approach, both on the matches that took place during the period when epics were so much more common and on the epics from previous eras (see HBK vs. Taker); however, any stylistic criticism that may, in time, rise to prominence during analyses regarding all-time greatness should exclude AJ vs. Cena on account of the feud's over-arching achievements.

AJ capitalized on the momentum built from his pair of summer victories over Cena to win the WWE Championship from Dean Ambrose and to put the final touches on his 2016 WWE MVP candidacy. By *Royal Rumble '17*, Styles had become one of Cena's top rivals, the one guy that the golden boy seemingly could not defeat. Their third singles match on pay-per-view felt less like the co-headliner of the January Classic and more like the *WrestleMania 33* main-event come early, in part due to the escalatory nature of their on-going saga and in part due to the host venue packing in a very WrestleMania-esque 52,020 people. On that night, Cena earned his share of history with Ric Flair, becoming just the second wrestler to notch sixteen World titles on the back of a characterful performance that showcased the determination and poise of a man obsessed with rising to the occasion.

It was without question, especially from *Summerslam '16* on, an instantly classic rivalry the popular reception to which puts it squarely in the mix for a Top 30 all-time ranking. Just inside the greatest forty ever seems like a good starting point for its historical aspirations and, aided by its event-specific status as one of the ten best matches in Summerslam *and* Royal Rumble lore, it could conceivably reach much higher with the passage of time enabling the better establishment of long-term context.

#38
Eddie Guerrero vs. Rey Misterio, Jr.
Title vs. Mask
WCW Cruiserweight Championship
Halloween Havoc
October 26, 1997
Top 5 Match in 1997

As has been quietly demonstrated throughout the Top 100 to this point, the hierarchy that largely dictates roster positioning – from the mid-card to the headlining spots on which the financial health of wrestling events has historically depended – has made it much easier for a main-event-level match to earn more checkmarks on the attribute list of greatness than its counterpart from lower down the card.

This will be one of the final and most noteworthy exceptions.

Like Mysterio's later battles with Angle and Jericho in WWE, his 1997 WCW Match of the Year with Eddie Guerrero is one of the most epic bouts of all-time that was not intended to be epic. A tired replay of the Hogan vs. Piper feud of the mid-1980s was the television focal point of *Halloween Havoc*. Operating from a position not valued as highly by World Championship Wrestling, Eddie and Rey sought to make the very most of their 13-minute run-time and far out-kick the proverbial coverage of their angle. The slam-dunk of a Cruiserweight Championship match was assisted by on-air advocate and commentator for the division, Mike Tenay, whose words all these years later provide context otherwise missing in the absence of a pre-match hype video to set the stage.

For those less familiar with the build-up, here is a summary of the situation written by Daniel "Cynical" Adams, a Singer/Songwriter, 30+ year fan, and frequent social media sparring partner who considers Misterio, Jr. vs. Guerrero to be the greatest match ever:

> "Eddie had been the Mexican superstar full of spirit and sportsmanship, but he was growing increasingly frustrated by the success of the nWo and the fact that good guys were finishing last. So he turned heel to the shock of everyone not named Mike Tenay, [who] told anyone who would listen that Eddie was the first luchador in history to remove his own mask, thereby spitting on his heritage, and that he also turned on his tag partner. No one bought it because all they'd ever seen him do was behave honorably in WCW. Over the course of a few weeks, he got meaner, greasier, and more aggressive. He began to win more and more, but Rey was a thorn in his side. Finally, he granted Rey a title shot at *Havoc*, but demanded that Rey put his mask on the line."

Guerrero's character transformation combined with his well-established "best in the world"-caliber in-ring skills were what prompted the incomparable Bobby Heenan, also on commentary at *Havoc*, to state matter-of-factly about him, "We're talking about one of the most talented men in our sport, ever." Eddie could cut promos, he could act, he could fly, he could wrestle, and he could psychologically piece together a match like few others; he was able to add something on the character side of the cruiserweight division that set him apart. His feud with Misterio was, thus, a little different from the average game of one-upmanship that had become the norm for the cruiserweights.

His three rivalries previously discussed may have given the impression that 2004 was Latino Heat's career-year, but those who saw his personic shift in WCW might argue that 1997-1998, at a time when he was younger and healthier and hitting his villainous stride, was his definitive best.

Rey, meanwhile, had spent the year and change between the first in his classic series with Dean Malenko in 1996 and that fateful night in October 1997 opposite Guerrero becoming one of the most exciting, popular, and critically-acclaimed wrestlers in the world. The general American audience had no idea what a "high-flyer" truly was until it laid eyes on him; for a solid year, he dazzled the wrestling world with moves that they had never seen before. With ratings on the rise and buyrates up, never before had a global viewership been privy to that degree of fast-paced grappling. Misterio's prosperity was the catalyst for talents like Guerrero to maximally succeed in WCW despite smaller statures.

So, the "Title vs. Mask" stipulation only served to amplify a match that had a lot going for it prior to bell-time on account of Guerrero's growing reputation and Misterio's already-ingrained standing.

In what has been regarded as the peak of the WCW Cruiserweight Title, Misterio vs. Guerrero was an exercise in aerial artistry and at the same time a master-class in pro wrestling-psychology. Knowing the focus his nemesis would place on removing his mask during the match, Rey wore a bodysuit for the occasion that extended from his signature head-wear down to his feet, as well as eye make-up to keep further hidden any features that might be exposed should Guerrero expectedly tear away at the upper-most quadrant of his attire. Eddie controlled proceedings basically from start-to-finish, with Rey's spurts of perfectly timed and incredibly dynamic offense (see springboard moonsault from the top rope into a DDT) coupling with Guerrero's personality (facial expressions and body language, especially) to create an immersive experience eaten up by a Las Vegas audience that continually chanted "Eddie Sucks" in defiance of Latino Heat's dominant antics. Rey's Splash Mountain Bomb counter into a hurricanrana-pin for the three-count was the cherry on top of an absolutely fantastic match.

Of course, everything on this countdown is great, making it a legitimate question to ask what separates Misterio-Guerrero from similar mid-card matches. In this case, the answer came from the initial research phase, comparing the best of the best from each calendar to determine a year-to-year ranking. Consider that Title vs. Mask was up against, in 1997, two of the contenders for #1 overall in Bret Hart vs. Steve Austin and the original Hell in a Cell between Michaels and Taker and that, due to the level of innovation on display, Misterio vs. Guerrero was actually within striking distance of being their equal; again, it was an epic performance never intended to be epic that compares quite favorably to unquestionable, all-time epics. In the relative scheme of things, that has to matter, as does the fact that it provided top-notch entertainment that could be watched in half the time as those matches grander in scope and historical repute.

Guerrero-Misterio should therefore be a respected rather than controversial Top 40 choice, not just an exceptional mid-card match but simply an exceptional pro wrestling match, period.

#37
Shawn Michaels vs. Bret Hart
WWF Championship
WrestleMania XII to Survivor Series 1997

Top 30 All-Time at WrestleMania / Match of the Year in 1996

For better or worse, and mostly for worse, Shawn Michaels vs. Bret Hart defined The New Generation. Montreal cast a shadow over them and not even their genuine embrace twelve years and two months after "The Screwjob" could pierce the darkness enough to allow wrestling fans, especially those of us who lived it, to think of more positives than negatives when it comes to The Hitman's rivalry with The Heartbreak Kid.

"There's absolutely not one desirable thing about that," Michaels told Jim Ross in 2013 when asked about his role as the proverbial trigger-man in Vince McMahon's plot to get the WWF Championship off of Hart before The Excellence of Execution took his talents to WCW. The chairman swore that he would take the heat, but in spite of HBK merely being a good soldier for a notoriously persuasive boss, he knew from the start that much of the crap was going to roll downhill onto him and that many of his fellow wrestlers would quite possibly never be able to look at him the same way again. Some would say he then karmically suffered the back injury that ended the first phase of his career just two-and-a-half months later.

Ross lightly pressed Michaels in follow-up to the above comment and almost rhetorically asked, "Lowest point in your career," to which HBK promptly replied, "Easily."

Nevertheless, with Earl Hebner's swift call for the bell as Michaels locked Bret in his own Sharpshooter at *Survivor Series '97*, the career of one of the most honored WWF Champions of all-time was ended in one infamous instant. "When it happened, I was...devastated," Hart told J.R., barely able to speak as a result of getting so choked up, even at that time about sixteen years post-Montreal. "I can't even put it into words."

A broken heart is difficult to describe, but it causes deep anger and grief. "The Screwjob" was such a huge turning point in Bret's life. It sent him to WCW in the worst possible way; WCW creative completely botched his tenure there; his brother, Owen, proceeded to die in a horrifically tragic way when he fell from the rafters preparing for a special entrance at a WWF event; he was kicked in the head during a match with Goldberg that gave him such a bad concussion that he had to abruptly retire; and, finally, on the same day that he divorced the mother of his four children, ending an often rocky eighteen year marriage, he hit his head during a bicycle accident and instantly suffered a stroke from which he never fully recovered. "I loved the company," Bret would later say about the night that started his downward spiral in November 1997. "I felt so betrayed."

Whether you believe Bret was wrong not to willingly do the honors however McMahon wished (since he was leaving) or you think that "The Screwjob" was the most deplorable thing in wrestling history – or you believe both – the events of Montreal were the final words written in the Book of HBK vs. Bret, a rivalry that in addition to illustrious infamy gave us one of the best matches (albeit one also struggling to age well in hindsight) in WWE history: the Ironman Match.

In 2004, Michaels vs. Hart in the main-event at *WrestleMania XII* was voted by its peers "WrestleMania's Greatest Match." Let us begin the discussion of the Ironman Match, then, by talking about its perception in the years since, because no other Top 50 match, rivalry, or story has scored worse on time's test. Critics say that it was boring and that hour-long matches from back in the 1980s through to present day were far superior in their entertainment value. Though it was in many ways a masterpiece of its time that served as the other (non-Montreal) peak in a heated competition between Bret and HBK to lead The New Generation, that it has not aged gracefully and that you really do have to be in the right frame of mind to commit the time and attention necessary to fully appreciate it has to be reconciled.

Some of the more recent perceptional shift surely comes from the lack of heat from bell-to-bell. The crowd was indeed unusually quiet, but that was in part because the WWF audience was not conditioned for something like a 60-minute match; such a thing was better suited to the NWA-turned-WCW fanbase. Reverence for the wrestler who could perform an hour-long match was maintained throughout the 1980s by the more traditional thinkers of the NWA, but it was at a premium in the WWF thanks to McMahon's sports entertainment model attracting a legion of new fans who rarely saw a match go twenty-minutes until Bret's ascension to top star status. The Ironman managed the lowest decibel level out of any crowd for a Top 50 all-timer – that much would be difficult to dispute – but at least some of that had to boil down to awe for something that most of them had never seen before. Watching at home today, you hear the crowd chanting "This is Awesome" at The Shield and The Wyatts before the bell rings and you naturally assume it has to be more exciting; the opposite can easily be assumed when watching Bret vs. HBK.

That they were so evenly matched was the point of the Broadway (no falls, no finish). Bear in mind that Hart is the primary reason why more intricate, athletic, and exciting matches are prioritized in WWE today. Much of the intense respect that he garnered came from his being such an artist on the 20'x20' canvas, for bringing that superior artistic skill to the main-event level in the WWF and to another level overall, with all due respect to The Nature Boy. Michaels followed his lead and ultimately topped him before all was said and done, taking that added touch of showmanship from Flair's playbook and mixing in both a near unmatched athleticism and his own brand of artistry comparable to Hart's.

Sparked by a mutual quest to change the industry (even during a down economic period), Michaels and Hart were two men who played supporting roles in a land of giants in the 1980s rising above the highest level that they ever thought they could have reached to compete for the #1 spot in the worldwide leading sports entertainment company. Could the pace and flow of the Ironman Match have any better reflected their grind to the top or their game of one-upmanship for supremacy atop the apex?

So much about it remains remarkable. The HBK entrance is arguably the most iconic in WrestleMania and, by extension, WWE history; providing the audio soundtrack to its action was vastly underrated commentary from McMahon and Jerry Lawler; Hart's reaction to Howard Finkel's announcement, "This match...has been ordered to continue...under Sudden Death rules," is an awesome character moment from the 1990s; and, of course, HBK's emotional response to winning the WWF Championship for the first time while McMahon utters one of the Top 10 soundbites of the WrestleMania Era, "The boyhood dream has come true...for Shawn Michaels," is surely the most enduring aspect of the presentation.

Sadly, the overall rivalry is wrestling's greatest Shakespearean tragedy.

#36
Ric Flair vs. Dusty Rhodes
NWA World Heavyweight Championship
Starrcade 1984 to Great American Bash 1986
Top 10 All-Time at Starrcade / Top 5 Match in 1985 / Top 10 Match in 1986

"Dusty Rhodes, you're a country-talking fool. I'm the Nature Boy; I'm the dealer. You know why? Because this says so!"

"I'm the best-looking man alive! I'm not Dusty Rhodes, sitting in the control room with a David Allen Coe truck driver hat on; I'm not wearing blue jeans; I don't have on a funky t-shirt. I'm alligators [shoes] and Rolex watches! From head-to-toe, I'm the man!"

It should be made clear from the start of the conversation about the Top 25 all-time caliber rivalry between Ric Flair and Dusty Rhodes over the NWA World Heavyweight Championship that it joins another prominent feud to be discussed later as one of the greatest ever based mostly on the story that it told across two years rather than anything particularly noteworthy that it accomplished from bell-to-bell in the wrestling ring.

The pair of quotes listed above evidence the stark contrast between "The American Dream" and "The Nature Boy" - one a son of a plumber who had both wined and dined with kings and queens and slept in alleys and dined on pork and beans, the other a doctor's son who became a limousine-riding, jet-flying, kiss-stealing, wheel-dealing son of a gun (Woo!). Yet, they also exemplify the essence of the Rhodes and Flair story. So many matches, rivalries, and stories on this list are ranked where they are because of what the wrestlers involved did in the ring during payoff matches, but Rhodes vs. Flair is ranked where it is because of the opposing forces of who they were and, perhaps most importantly, the engaging qualities of what they said.

That goes against the general idea that the payoff is what really counts and everything else is the sideshow that leads to and promotes it. They changed the game. Interviews were important and always had been, but the modern promo in professional wrestling came to be defined by the consistent brilliance of their verbal duels; it could be argued that no series of point-counterpoint segments ever duplicated their display of microphone mastery from 1984 to 1986. The vast majority of the quotes that shaped their respective WWE Hall of Fame induction videos came from their rivalry.

Bottom line: some matches can be viewed on a compilation DVD like *The Essential Starrcade* and leave previously unfamiliar viewers with an understanding of that which made them special; Rhodes vs. Flair is unlikely to be considered among them.

The wrestling on display in even the biggest Flair vs. Rhodes match was very simple, with focus heavily on the psychologically sound and very storyline-appropriate strategy of going after each other's legs. The sequences were that incredible-to-look-back-on paradoxical combination of gritty and silky smooth. However, viewing Flair vs. Rhodes today is almost like watching a movie from the 1960s or prior in that what was done was *so* basic that it threatens to bore the modern fan who might expect more sizzle to the presentation given the rivalry's reputation historically. Flair vs. Luger offered better in-ring performances frankly, as did the vast majority of the rest of the Honorable Mentions and Top 100.

So, in order to best appreciate matches between Flair and Rhodes, you have to learn the context of their rivalry.

"What's causing all this? It's ten pounds of gold around one hell of a body, one of hell of a man. I'll tell you what's causing it; guts, fortitude – Dusty Rhodes, something you're very short on."

That they were arguably the two greatest talkers in history allowed them to establish a crystal clear delineation between their personalities and prompted the audience to pick sides, but when you read the three quotes thus far posted, you might get the impression that Flair was already the full-blown antagonist for which he is best known in wrestling lore throughout the saga with Big Dust. There was animosity between them surely; it stemmed from before the WrestleMania Era ever began, as it was Rhodes whom Flair defeated to win his first World Championship in 1981 and it was on the same night that Flair started his second reign, by taking the NWA torch from Harley Race at *Starrcade '83,* that The Dream made clear that he was next in line.

The Nature Boy was The Nature Boy. His life revolved around being World Heavyweight Champion and anyone who threatened his existence became the object of his ire. Coming out of the original *Starrcade*, though, Flair was a hero to the people; it just so happened that in walked the ultimate babyface in Rhodes at the same time. It created an interesting dichotomy necessary for contextualization; exemplified by their first spotlight match of the WrestleMania Era at *Starrcade '84,* they were initially respectful of each other, sharing a mutual desire to be the best and be the guy who holds the most prestigious wrestling championship. A cut above the eye halting The American Dream's quest to regain the World Heavyweight Title without such context misses an important part of Flair's evolution as a character and threatens to weaken such statements as "Dusty Rhodes vs. Ric Flair is one of the most complete and thorough stories ever told by a professional wrestling promotion."

You could say that it was his rivalry with Rhodes that allowed Flair to grow into his role as arguably the greatest heel of all-time, but bear in mind that even through the summer of 1985, Flair was still a very popular champion who just so happened to enjoy the finer things and a lavish lifestyle.

Things changed in September 1985, when Flair instigated an attack on Rhodes by his storyline cousins, Arn and Ole Anderson, that severely injured Dusty's leg. Six weeks later, a month away from *Starrcade '85*, The Dream would respond with possibly the single greatest babyface promo of all-time.

> I don't have to say a whole lot more about the way I feel about Ric Flair; no respect, no honor. There is no honor amongst thieves in the first place. He put hard times on Dusty Rhodes and his family. You don't know what hard times are daddy! Hard times are when the textile workers around this country are out of work, they got 4 or 5 kids and can't pay their wages, can't buy their food. Hard times are when the auto workers are out of work and they tell 'em to go home. And hard times are when a man has worked at a job for thirty years, thirty years, and they give him a watch, kick him in the butt and say 'hey a computer took your place, daddy,' that's hard times! That's hard times!

The match at *Starrcade '85*, then, culminated some of the most famous promos and one of the most famous assaults in wrestling lore, as well as the laying of the foundation for pro wrestling's preeminent stable, The Four Horsemen, and the start of a virtually unmatched five year run by Flair. When anyone talks about Flair being the greatest wrestler ever, the stretch between the second half of the Rhodes rivalry through the end of his saga with Terry Funk in 1989 is primarily the reason why. Context shapes reality and the reality is that, without context, a match like the Rhodes-Flair rematch at *Starrcade* is only about half as good.

Then consider how the match ended: the original "Dusty finish." Rhodes seemingly won the NWA Championship that night, pinning Flair in the middle of the ring, but the decision was later reversed when senior referee Tommy Young, who had been knocked out during a calamitous final few minutes, decided that Flair should retain on account of interference from the Andersons causing a disqualification. The booking strategy became infamous, but was innovative at the time and kept

Rhodes on the chase for that much longer; Jim Crockett Promotions made a lot of money off of that decision.

"Whether you like or not, you better learn to love it because it's gonna be here for a long, long time!" – Ric Flair

"The Four Horsemen...they need to ride on another planet because I reserved the stratosphere for me and you." – Dusty Rhodes

It was not until after *Starrcade '85* that The Four Horsemen officially came to be, so while the Rhodes-Flair rivalry kept blazing toward its summer conclusion, there was the added element of The Horsemen for The American Dream to contend with in a more official, factionalized capacity. So much history was encapsulated throughout one incredible story; the NWA even transitioned during that period to using the big gold belt synonymous to many with World Championship Wrestling in the 1990s and WWE's World Heavyweight Title in the 2000s.

Finally, on July 26, 1986, during the Great American Bash tour in a Steel Cage Match at the Greensboro Coliseum, Rhodes defeated Flair to definitively capture his third and final NWA World Championship, thus bringing the saga to an end.

The duality between "The Man" and the common man has often been imitated and at times to much greater critical acclaim in the ring and financial success. However, Ric Flair vs. Dusty Rhodes remains one of the most influential stories ever told.

#35
The Shield vs. The Wyatt Family
Elimination Chamber
February 23, 2014
Top 5 Match in 2014

In one of the greatest matches of all-time, this six-man faction clash pitted the arguable stable of the decade, The Shield (Roman Reigns, Dean Ambrose, and Seth Rollins), against The Wyatt Family (Bray Wyatt, Luke Harper, and Erick Rowan). Historically, the only match on its level for elevating that many new stars in one setting was the Triangle Ladder Match at *WrestleMania 2000*. Influentially, it represents the value of NXT's talent recruitment and development strategies. Critically, it is *The Dark Knight* of WWE stories, "a canvas for a broader scope of human emotion."

Through it we witnessed the rise to considerable prominence of the generation of stars that have formed the backbone of WWE in the second half of this decade. Reigns, Rollins, Ambrose, and Wyatt have become the most successful class of rookies to debut within the same physical year since the OVW Class of 2002. Highlighting their accolades as of 2018, Rollins was WWE Wrestler of the Year in 2014 and 2015, Reigns had main-evented four straight WrestleManias, Wyatt had feuded with a Who's Who of the WrestleMania Era, and Ambrose had become WWE's top utility wrestler, more durable and versatile than all of his peers.

Four of the six wrestlers involved had already had star-making moments previously, but The Shield vs. The Wyatts nevertheless felt like a coronation ceremony for the arrival of the next generation (and NXT's at least behind-the-scenes ascent). Interesting, is it not, that the February 25th-airing of NXT Arrival (the developmental brand's first major event) on the February 24th-launching WWE Network took place in the two days after the original crown jewels of NXT that would go onto lead WWE out of the Cena Era started assuming command of the wrestling world with this virtuoso match?

The NXT Call-Up Class of 2012/2013 came at a perfect time. Wrestling had grown up and so had a big portion of its core fanbase. Young fans will always be the lifeblood of WWE, but it has for going on 35 years been cultivating enthusiasts who, as they got older, came to think of wrestling as a pastime right alongside sports, comic books, video games, and movie franchises; couple long-term passion for pro wrestling with the accessibility to WWE provided by the internet and there is now a sizeable legion of followers who openly discuss daily a desire for the product to evolve with the times in order to maximize what it can be.

Earlier this decade, CM Punk and Daniel Bryan became the avatars for diehard enthusiasts who wanted WWE to shift into a new era. WWE does not always get the credit it deserves for its innovation and style throughout the WrestleMania Era, but it certainly took its time embracing Punk and Bryan types in the big picture until Triple H intervened on WWE's behalf as the new head of talent development, creating NXT to help mold the future of the company. The Game would probably appreciate Thomas Jefferson's quote, "In matters of principle, stand like a rock; in matters of style, swim with the current." Like Mike D'Antoni, Gregg Popovich, and Steve Kerr adopted international principles to modernize the NBA style of play, Triple H responded to the growing trend of more athletic wrestling and less-conventional stars being recognized on the independents as the best in the world on account of their skill level more than their looks by changing how WWE scouted and developed talent. The Shield waging war with The Wyatts overtly expressed that we were on the brink of a new era in WWE, one that simultaneously acknowledged historical preferences and embraced forward-thinking patterns.

The reaction to the soon-to-be regarded "iconic" six-man tag between The Wyatts and The Shield spoke volumes about how ready fans were to embrace contemporary stars deployed with the same kind of care that had been afforded previous generations. One month after Cena and Orton had received one of the most rebellious responses in WWE lore, the audience showered The Shield and The Wyatts with a thunderous "This is Awesome" chant before the bell even rang, which certainly had never happened before in WWE and has happened only rarely since, even more recently when "This is Awesome" gets chanted multiple times every week.

Watched on the same day alongside matches from numbers 65, 43, 33, 19, and 1 of this book's rankings, The Shield vs. The Wyatts was, according to one forty-year fan of professional wrestling, "Just as good as the best ever."

It really was a brilliant match. The term "perfect" is dangerously hyperbolic when discussing professional wrestling, but could you honestly imagine it having been any better? Bray Wyatt was at his apex as the deranged psychological puppeteer, setting the tone for the performance in his promos during the build-up by targeting the cracking unity of The Hounds of Justice and baiting them into a battle that they could not win without their bond mended. As the pre-match introductions were wrapping up, Wyatt specifically antagonized Ambrose, the loose cannon whose destiny for months had seemed to be the splinter that would permanently fracture The Shield. The Wyatts pushed The Lunatic to the fringe throughout the match itself and made him the first domino to fall, and then they dissected Rollins and Reigns piece by piece.

Wrestling as performance art has few better examples than The Hounds seeking justice against The Eater of Worlds and his disciples. One of the remarkable things about talents like The Shield and Bray Wyatt particularly is that, in an era of incredibly fast-paced, false finish-heavy in-ring work, they all strive to incorporate the more theatrical storytelling of WWE fame with the popular style of the independent scene. The Wyatts vs. The

Shield was a great example of how to blend athleticism and innovation with highly intelligent dramatic composition.

Take your pick for MVP of the match; Wyatt's aforementioned narrative-driving cerebral warfare, Luke Harper's evolutionary Bruiser Brody or Kane performance, Ambrose's character act of bordering on the insane, Reigns having a night when it appeared he was putting it all together as the heroic hard-charging bad ass, and Rollins looking like the next HBK; it was pretty amazing how they all (Rowan included) seized the day.

The Shield vs. The Wyatt Family is one of those matches that has not yet had the chance to fully pass the test of time, so it is very likely to climb the ranks. Give it a few more years and it could be Top 25 all-time. For its historical impact, its outstanding critical achievement, and its consuming rewatchability, maybe it already should be...

#34
The 2004 Royal Rumble Match
January 25, 2004

Top 5 All-Time Royal Rumble Match / Top 5 All-Time at Royal Rumble / Top 5 Match in 2004

The very first Royal Rumble Match actually took place on a house show as a test to see how the concept of a reverse battle royal would look ahead of its television debut on the USA Network in January 1988. Little did anyone know that the gimmick would eventually be second only to WrestleMania as the most profitable idea that WWE ever concocted. Such is why it should come as no surprise that several Royal Rumbles have already been featured.

Discussed among the Honorable Mentions and Top 100 have been or will be the blueprint for the Rumble Match as we know it, the best performance by one man in the Rumble Match, and the most shocking moment in Rumble Match lore. Yet, channeling the voice of Howard Finkel, "It is now time" to talk about the all-time *best* Royal Rumble Match.

There are plenty of reasons that the 2004 Royal Rumble Match must be dissected, not the least of which is that, if we do not take the time to do it here in the context that this book presents, it may become forever buried by WWE's understandable disassociation with its winner, Chris Benoit, and sadly one of the most amazing collective performances by a group of wrestlers that you could ever see would then become a distant memory.

Focusing first on why it is the best in its genre's history, the '04 Rumble left nothing to be desired. Everything that you could possibly want from a Royal Rumble Match was there. Offering a simple comparison to its most prominent peers, it presented a series of outstanding moments which combined to equal the impact of the ultimate surprise from 2008 and provided one of the betas to Ric Flair's alpha in Benoit's near 62-minute trek from first entrant to winner. However, as we get a little bit more detailed, it was the fluid action taking place during Benoit's journey and in between the wide-eyed, hands-to-head moments where the '04 Rumble shined brightest.

A common phrase among analysts of pro wrestling is "maximizing your minutes," stated in regards to the amount of time afforded to a talent to get across, either verbally or physically, that which makes him/her special. The Royal Rumble Match is widely considered a yearly main-event showcase for wrestlers who are nowhere near the main-event level and top stars alike, but in a ring chock full of bodies, space on a 20'X20' canvas is limited; generally, the less wrestlers involved at one time, the greater the chance exists to maximize minutes. The '04 Rumble, via swift eliminations that helped frequently maintain just four or five wrestlers in the ring at once, gave even entrants with sub-minute total time spent in the fray the opportunity to make impactful appearances. Some editions can get bogged down by too many people and have to rely too heavily on hard-resets via elimination sprees to free up the ring. 2004 had no such issues, its lone reset, post-entry #17, coming after nine superstars who had spent five-minutes or less in the match had already been ousted.

No more than seven wrestlers were in the ring at any given time until after the 28th entrant, saving the classic trope of the ring filling up for the climax featuring Goldberg, Chris Jericho, Rob Van Dam, John Cena, Big Show, Kurt Angle, and Chris Benoit – for those of you that have read *The WrestleMania Era*, 16% of the Top 45 stars of the last 30+ years – and capping off a supremely well-paced Royal Rumble Match with a highly engaging final ten-minutes.

The Rabid Wolverine went onto last eliminate Show, punching his ticket to the main-event of WrestleMania, the connection to which is one of the biggest draws of the Rumble. Of the many bonds that have been formed to create the fabric of WWE as we know it, the one between 'Mania and the Rumble is stronger than any other. The Rumble is, thus, at its best when the booking acknowledges that bond beyond just the winner getting the title shot on the grandest stage, as was the case in 2004 when the Rumble, in addition to providing near-unparalleled quality, also acted as a trailer for *WrestleMania XX*.

Teasing his return to The Deadman character that made him famous, Undertaker's iconic "gong" hitting before entry #13 surprised not just the fans, but Kane as well; Taker would make his official return to the dark side opposite his "brother" at 'Mania. Mick Foley "stole" the #21 spot in order take out Randy Orton, whose inspiring work as the second entrant was cut short; a brawl ensued that segued to the returning legend having his first match in four years at "The Show of Shows." When Goldberg came out at #30 and cleaned house, Brock Lesnar showed up to spoil his party in an electric interaction unfortunately sullied by their stinker of a clash seven weeks later. Also earning developments that would further fan the flames for 'Mania storylines were Cena being eliminated by his rival, The Big Show, and Christian and Y2J hinting at their deteriorating friendship. Of the seven most hyped matches at *WrestleMania XX*, six took minor-to-significant storyline steps during the '04 Rumble Match.

Of course, there is no getting around the fact that Chris Benoit, the most infamous wrestler to have ever lived, won the 2004 Royal Rumble, casting a shadow over the match that will forever threaten to usurp its greatness.

Some people have been able to draw a hard line of distinction between Benoit's final hours and the legendary career he forged in professional wrestling, particularly his odyssey that culminated in going coast-to-coast in the Rumble and winning the World Heavyweight Championship. For many fans, it is impossible to separate the greatest technical wrestler at least of his generation and perhaps of all-time with the man who pathologically murdered his wife and son and then committed suicide. For them, any mention of *Rumble '04* (or of

WrestleMania XX) immediately triggers pent-up emotions. Enthusiasts, rather like wrestlers themselves, have a tendency to develop a deep psychological attachment to wrestling; the experience of Eddie Guerrero's death stands as a prime example of how fans can *feel* things about wrestlers, on or off-camera, as if they had happened to someone close to them personally in their everyday lives. If Guerrero's unexpected passing was heart-wrenching, though, how should one describe his/her feelings about the acts Benoit committed?

It is a difficult subject, but it begs the question as to whether or not Benoit's legacy in pro wrestling should really be erased. Fans can make the choice that WWE cannot; and this book chooses not to ignore the incredible contributions of Benoit, the wrestler, simultaneously without ever ignoring the final hours of Benoit, the human-being.

The 2004 Royal Rumble Match was not just a one-man show; regardless of how you feel about Benoit, it was a tremendous collaborative achievement worthy of remembrance for being the perfect amalgamation of what makes the gimmick so great. Its primary story was very well told, its booking was intelligent and intricate, its run-time flies by like no other version before or since, and it characterized the association between WWE's two most profitable events. It was a masterpiece...and it should not be forgotten.

#33
Magnum TA vs. Tully Blanchard
Steel Cage "I Quit" Match
NWA United States Championship
Starrcade
November 28, 1985

Top 5 All-Time Cage Match / Top 5 All-Time at Starrcade / Match
of the Year in 1985

You know the expression among wrestling fans, "It's still real to
me, damn it"?

There is a fascinating dichotomy to be discovered when studying
the WrestleMania Era from its inception point (as specified in
this book) to present day. Kayfabe, the old carny term used for
so many generations to (among other things) describe the veil of
illusion that pro wrestling was more sport than entertainment,
was still very much in effect circa the mid-1980s. WWE's
industry takeover largely eliminated kayfabe before the new
millennium.

The NWA, particularly when it was still spearheaded by Jim
Crockett Promotions (until 1988), was primarily responsible for
maintaining the well-established traditions of professional
wrestling, including kayfabe, in the early 'Mania Era. Converse
with fans whose opinion of the business was shaped by the NWA
and you will likely find a vastly different attitude toward what
wrestling has become today than someone whose formative
fandom was largely influenced by WWE.

Performance is the name of the game under the modern guise of
sports entertainment. Compare a generally agreed upon 4-star
match today with a 4-star match from the NWA in 1985, though,
and perhaps the most appropriate word to describe the change
in the product across three-plus decades would be a loss of
"realism." Earlier in the book, it was mentioned that there might

not be a more realistic-looking match in the WrestleMania Era than Greg Valentine and Roddy Piper's Dog Collar Match; the reason for the qualifier was that, two years later at *Starrcade '85*, Magnum TA and Tully Blanchard wrestled the definitively most authentic-looking match since the advent of modern wrestling. If someone tried to replicate what Magnum and Tully did then on a WWE show now, the debate would rage for weeks as to whether or not it was a "shoot" - an honest-to-goodness fight.

Tommy Tomlinson from SportsonEarth.com wrote an insightful article on the match several years ago. In it he states, "It wasn't the sweaty ballet you normally see in a great wrestling match. There were no graceful moves or daring stunts. There was just the dark drama of two guys full of hate beating the hell out of each other. The match is great because it felt real."

Within a few minutes, Magnum was already bleeding from a cut on his forehead and, soon after, Blanchard's arm was lacerated; comparable amounts of blood have been spilt in other matches, but none so realistically. They rolled around the ring, punching and grabbing at each other and gouging at each other's eyes, their striking and selling an upgrade in believability over 99.9% of all other matches the vast majority of you reading this have ever seen. Their visceral screams, which began as reflections of their respective desires to seize the day, later became primal bursts of emotion born of pain and agony from open wounds and deep bruises. On the outside of the ring, Tully's "Perfect Ten" valet, Baby Doll, seemed legitimately concerned, covering her mouth with her hands as if almost nauseous from the combination of blood and sweat permeating from mere feet in front of her.

By the climax, they appeared as though they had been through hell and back. We had heard them each yell in other's face, "Say it," so many times that one could not help but wonder if anything could actually make one of them say, "I quit," but Baby Doll's insertion of an old wooden chair into the ring instantly shook away the doubts and simultaneously interjected a tone of inevitability. The ensuing use of the wooden spike created organically from an absolutely perfect shattering of the chair on the canvas by Blanchard was borderline uncomfortably violent. Tully shoving the spike with all his might toward Magnum's forehead evoked a similarly uneasy feeling to watching the scene in *Saving Private Ryan* when Ryan Goldberg's character dies in a knife fight. Magnum's escape and ultimate victory offered a brand of catharsis reserved for the utmost examples of cunning perseverance.

As gritty and raw as it was, it has basically become a relic from a by-gone era when professional wrestlers could tell stories to a mainstream audience that escalated to such a savage level. It seems ridiculous that a match in the twenty-teens can choreograph elaborately dangerous moves off of a ladder that increase the risk of injury to its performers ten-fold for the sake of entertainment, but a match cannot allow its wrestlers to become unwaveringly gory as a means of telling a tale of serious intensification of hatred between two gladiators hungry for championship gold. A cut on the arm is as visually affecting a storytelling device as a dive from sixteen feet high, but takes two weeks at a maximum from which to heal as compared to the shoulder separation, broken bone, or torn muscle made more likely by the dangerous stunt; it is also far more emotionally engaging, its "wow" factor rooted in getting lost in the physical hostility of a match instead of an appreciation of extreme visual artistry.

The preceding statement inherently asks an interesting question regarding violence in professional wrestling: just how violent does it need to be capable of being? If you sway more toward the argument that blood and a higher degree of violence should have a more prominent place in WWE today, then would it not be logical to ask where the line should be drawn to designate what is considered to be too much? And is not the uncomfortable levels reached by Magnum and Tully an ideal example of too much? Conversely, if you support the more PG rating of modern WWE and feel it unnecessary to allow greater violence, you cannot deny the effectiveness of permitting two men to beat each other bloody and senseless considering the notoriety earned by Blanchard vs. Magnum TA, the highest spot of which was a double ax handle smash from off the top rope.

And so we cycle back to kayfabe and its demise. There is something oddly endearing about an era in pro wrestling when heels were so legitimately hated that, as Tomlinson recounted from a fan's comments to Blanchard during a convention in 2013, "Twenty eight years ago, I wouldn't have spit on you if you were on fire." That Tully smiled delightfully in response speaks volumes about a period that emphasized realism over performance; it was his job to make that fan hate him that much and the fan's feelings toward him confirmed that he had done his job very well.

That the authentic-looking fight between Blanchard and Magnum TA ranks as highly as it does reflects its status as essentially an outstanding period-piece, but that so many performances rank ahead of it reflects the merits, critically and financially, of the paradigm shift across the years.

Let the debate rage on! The Steel Cage "I Quit" Match is one of the few matches from the WWE vs. NWA skirmish which preceded the Monday Night War that has maintained its sterling reputation historically. People never really stopped talking about it or asking its participants about it, and they never should.

#32
Edge vs. John Cena
WWE / World Heavyweight Championship
New Year's Revolution 2006 to Unforgiven 2006; 25th Anniversary of WrestleMania to Backlash 2009

Top 10 All-Time Ladder Match / Top 5 All-Time Last Man Standing Match / Match of the Year in 2006 / Top 5 Match in 2009

As John Cena has climbed the historical hierarchy and become a candidate for the WrestleMania Era's greatest overall superstar, the profiles of his top rivalries have all been elevated too, but the placement of his feud with Edge was challenging. It certainly seemed Top 50-worthy from the outset, if for no other reason than their 2006 Feud of the Year that culminated in the 2006 Match of the Year, though the Top 25 seemed a stretch. How do you properly rank one of the defining rivalries of an era that largely lived in the shadow of Attitude and that pre-dated Cena's peak?

Settling here was the result of how important it was to both their careers. Most of the time, when you see a wrestler make it to the main-event scene and enjoy a run or two at the top, he does much of the same things upon arrival that had been done previously to reach that level in the first place. Very short is the list of wrestlers that gets to the top and exhibits yet another gear, ultimately earning the reward of consistently being booked like a foundational building block of the product and being a threat to main-event the biggest shows each year. Cena is obviously on it, and Edge absolutely should be when you consider that he was the top villain of a WWE brand from 2006 to 2009 and wrestled for the World Heavyweight Championship at four straight WrestleManias.

What makes the Cena-Edge rivalry exceptional, then, is that we found out about both their next-level abilities when they were dominating Monday Night Raw in 2006, trading back and forth the WWE Championship with each other. The inaugural Money in the Bank cash-in was epic, but then Edge attacked his opportunity to hold the title for three weeks between *New Year's Revolution* and *Royal Rumble* with such ferocity. He had scratched and clawed and put his body through hell in the TLC Era to get to that spot and he performed in the "Live Sex Celebration" with Lita and the first singles TLC Match with Ric Flair on Raw like his life depended on making an impression that would ensure his long-term main-event relevancy. Modern domestic TV ratings for WWE shows have, since the Attitude Era, seen very few spikes as sharp and steady across one month as during The Rated R Superstar's initial three week run as WWE Champion; he was a hit.

Edge talked in his documentary about there being a lot of powerful voices behind the scenes that did not think he was capable of making it as a top star, but that his biggest supporter had been Vince McMahon himself. "I remember him saying to me, 'Prove me right and prove everyone else wrong,'" Edge shared. When he assumed the lead heel role after 'Mania that year, he just took off, never looking back until his injury-stimulated retirement five years later.

Cena had other motivations when his storyline with Edge took further shape. He had ridden his hip hop persona to the WWE Title at *WrestleMania 21*, the same night Edge won the pioneering Money in the Bank Ladder Match but, for someone so anti-establishment on the way up, he proved to be the perfect pick by the establishment to lead the company back to its family-friendlier roots once he reached the WWE zenith; and that is no back-handed compliment. Cena gear was enormously successful at the merchandise stand with kids, who flocked to him like nobody since Hogan; he was young, good-looking, very well-spoken, and charismatic. However, his original fans thought he was his generation's Stone Cold, not his generation's Hulkster.

2006 was the year that the pressure on Cena rose immensely as it became clearer who he was intended to be for WWE: the franchise / face of the company.

He had to show more than he had in 2005 and Edge was the guy – not JBL, Christian, Chris Jericho, Kurt Angle, or Triple H – who helped bring it out of him. "There are few people in this business that have elevated me to heights that I thought were unachievable and Edge is one of those guys that made me so much better than I ever thought I was capable of being," Cena said years later. Opposite Edge, Cena seemed for the first time to carry himself week-to-week like "The Man" who could be counted on to lead WWE through the second half of the decade and beyond.

It was mutually beneficial; they took big leaps in their careers together. After Austin and Rock transitioned to the next phase of their lives, WWE kept a steady stream of top Attitude Era holdovers involved in the main-event programs needed for drawing most. It was not until Edge vs. Cena that WWE entrusted a pair of fresh headliners with that kind of responsibility, raising the stakes that much higher for both of them.

Though the first chapter in their story may not have culminated in the best of pay-offs – it would be fair to call their *Rumble* bout a critical flop – without Edge's ratings grab, there may not have been new chapters written later in the year; and, when they did renew their rivalry post-'Mania, they were given the ball and were expected to score. Interestingly, the creative tactics were very reminiscent of Attitude's finest, particularly Edge coming to Cena's childhood home and slapping his father and Cena throwing Edge into the Long Island Sound. Edge also cost Cena the WWE Title to RVD at the second-annual *ECW One Night Stand*, and they headlined *Summerslam* near Cena's hometown with a showing that warranted its main-event positioning.

Tables, Ladders, and Chairs offered the setting for their final showdown – at least until they picked back up prominently to headline (along with Big Show) *The 25th Anniversary of WrestleMania* and delivered one of the Top 5 examples of the Last Man Standing Match at *Backlash '09*. "A match you've never had; a match *I've* never lost," Edge would memorably say in the lead-up. The reaction that The Rated R Superstar received from his hometown faithful in Toronto – the place that birthed the immense fandom that fueled his own wrestling career and in the building that, 25 months earlier, had poorly received him at *Summerslam '04* – was unbelievable. "It was tough not to [cry]. That was the one moment where my heeldom [vanished]...I lost it," Edge later said.

It was the first time that the TLC Match would be used in a pay-per-view main-event for the WWE Championship and it was the version of the gimmick that truly made the Ladder Match sub-genre such an integral part of the WWE calendar; Edge took TLC to the top with him. Typically creative as one might expect from a production featuring a Ladder Match maestro like Edge, Cena reaffirmed his toughness with the kind of performance that his supporters would go on to point out for many years whenever fans jaded by Cena would continue to press on about how he could not wrestle. It was a fantastic brawl.

Association with one of modern WWE lore's less heralded periods may influence a tendency to slip down the all-time hierarchy but, until that day, clearly history should smile on the John Cena vs. Edge rivalry.

#31
Stone Cold Steve Austin vs. Triple H Summerslam to No Mercy 1999; Survivor Series 2000 to No Way Out 2001
Top 5 Match in 2001

When Stone Cold Steve Austin came back from his late 1999 neck surgery, the WWF was in the midst of arguably the greatest overall year that it ever had, combining critical success with staunch box office drawing power on television and pay-per-view; and it did so without the man most synonymous with the era. Triple H was, along with The Rock, one of the two primary reasons why the WWF thrived in Austin's absence.

To that point in the WrestleMania Era, the WWF had never faced a situation in which the unquestioned top star went down for that long and then was able to come back. Wrestling years fall somewhere in between human years and dog years in terms of how quickly time flies, so Austin returned in 2000 to a vastly different landscape than the one he had left. Kurt Angle had come on strong, The Rock had taken firm command of the "face of the company" role, the general depth of talent was far greater, and Triple H was striding towards a contender for the greatest year-long run of excellence in modern pro wrestling lore. The Game had retired Mick Foley at the climax of an unbelievably awesome rivalry, segued straight into the renewal of an arguably even better rivalry against The Rock, in the middle of which he started his rivalry with Chris Jericho that hit its crescendo in the top Last Man Standing Match ever, and then followed with a pair of underrated feuds opposite Angle and Chris Benoit. So, not only was Austin trying to once again reach the zenith then-occupied by The Rock, but Triple H was also standing firmly in his path.

The WWF had a good problem on its hands, having to figure out how best to execute the details of Austin's comeback, the seeds for which had been planted by a hit-and-run storyline on the night of *Survivor Series '99*, but it was a unique problem. The Game certainly had no desire to relinquish his position to a returning Austin and, from the company's vantage point, you could imagine that it did not exactly see as much of a need to reinsert Stone Cold into the spot that he had left vacant as perhaps it had expected there would have been when a very Austin-dependent 1999 concluded with The Texas Rattlesnake going under the knife. However, Austin proved up to the challenge of rekindling the tremendous fire that his character had built for the last few years prior to the new millennium and, as such, saw no reason why he did not deserve to return to the WWF throne. Given Triple H and Austin's on-screen characters and real life-personalities, there emerged a fascinating rivalry between them.

It should be noted that thought was given to this ranking somehow perpetuating the critical belief that Triple H, despite being regarded as one of the most important figures of the WrestleMania Era, was perhaps not quite the caliber of superstar that he or his McMahon family thought that he was. The post-Attitude world became more apt to judge wrestling and wrestlers by their worst qualities rather than their best, magnifying traits about greats like The Game such as his lackluster performances in so many "Show of Shows" main-events and downplaying such footnotes of immense historical proportions like the utter fact that, regardless of Austin and Rock being more associated than him with the Attitude Era, neither one of them had as complete a year – from titles to ratings to classic matches to pay-per-view buyrates to awesome work as a character – during that incredibly competitive time period as Triple H.

The importance of the above note is made so by the recognition that placing a rivalry of this magnitude outside of the Top 25 makes a statement about the Attitude Era and how it is viewed in this context. In the breakdown between eras that shape the Top 25, the Reality Era and the post-Attitude Era have just as many entries as Attitude; the lack of inclusion for Triple H vs. Austin, therefore, sets the tone for the final quarter of this book not necessarily favoring Attitude as the be-all, end-all period for great matches, rivalries, and stories in the WrestleMania Era and instead viewing the Attitude Era as of course a wonderful and transcendent period, just one that does not deserve to overshadow everything else that ever happened from 1983 to present day.

Frankly, a fair overall assessment of Triple H vs. Stone Cold is that it was a very good feud between two wrestlers who truthfully did not have top end in-ring chemistry with one another; it exhibited creative flair in subtly turning The Game into a protagonist ahead of revealing him as the mastermind behind the hit-and-run, reinvigorating his top heel status, copying the formula used by The Rock one year prior; it climaxed in a phenomenal, era-specific fight, but the overall saga struggled to a noticeable enough extent at capturing the same magic that did Austin-Rock, Austin-McMahon, Triple H-Rock, or Triple H-Foley that it did not deserve to be placed on the same pedestal as its Attitude Era peers; it did not warrant a spot in the Top 25 that would have confirmed it as an exemplification of all that made the most celebrated period in wrestling history so great. Hence, here it sits.

What the Austin vs. Triple H rivalry really *did* exemplify was the strength of their characters and that, when you put two all-time-level stars together who are at varying points along their career personic peaks, you are bound to eventually get something amazing out of it. The WWF showed patience in allowing the dynamic between them to coalesce into what you might expect when you see on the marquee the biggest star of all-time versus, statistically, one of the Top 5 stars of the WrestleMania Era; and the payoff was *No Way Out 2001*, at which their famous Two-Out-Of-Three Falls Match took place.

"Three Stages of Hell" was the rivalry's enduring legacy. The exhaustive near-forty-minute affair was, at times, bowling shoe ugly but, seeing as how it perfectly put on display the relentlessness of the Stone Cold psyche and how it gave The Game the ideal platform to show the world what it would be missing by excluding him from the momentous *WrestleMania X-Seven* main-event at the Reliant Astrodome, it would be historically irresponsible not to acknowledge that, in spite of its imperfect aesthetics, it was quite possibly the most riveting brawl ever, a director's cut, of sorts, that took what worked so well for the likes of Funk vs. Flair and extended it out another ten-to-fifteen minutes. Sans for a stretch of the "standard" first fall portion, the vast majority of the overall presentation featured Austin and Triple H just beating the living hell out of each other. As Mario "Mazza" Rousetty of LOP Radio's *The Right Side of the Pond* has said of his favorite match of all-time, "You won't find many more bitter and brutal ways to end a feud."

#30
Mick Foley vs. Randy Orton
Hardcore Match
Intercontinental Championship
Backlash
April 18, 2004
Top 5 Match in 2004

Mick Foley's name has already been highlighted several times among the greatest matches, rivalries, and stories ranked thus far. Foley was a pro wrestling savant whose incredible performances, complete as they were with masterful character work and an unrivaled, all-time willingness to put his body on the line for the enhancement of the overall presentation, have an enduring quality to them; they will quite literally never be equaled.

Therefore, it matters, especially within the context of a list such as this, when a Hall of Famer of Foley's caliber labels one of his particular classics as "probably the greatest match I ever had in my life." That match is not *Mind Games* with HBK or the 'Mania show-stealer with Edge or the Hell in a Cell with Taker or the "I Quit" against The Rock or even the Street Fight with Triple H; Mick Foley believes that perhaps his pinnacle in-ring achievement was against Randy Orton at *Backlash 2004*.

For The Hardcore Legend, the match with The Legend Killer was a brilliant reminder of that which made Foley special. It was incredibly creative, it was perfectly paced, it was jam-packed with emotional high points, and it was, of course, delightfully hardcore; he lost, as he had always been prone to do in similar situations, but he went down in a blaze of glory and made Orton look like the industry's next great star in the process.

Nobody in wrestling history was quite as adept as Foley at putting someone else over. Like he had done for Triple H and

The Rock and like he would go onto do for Edge, Foley *made* Randy Orton a bonafide main-event star through not only his rightfully glorified ability to take an astounding beating and to dish out punishing offense using everything but the kitchen sink in return, but also his underrated, not as often contextualized ability to bring the best out in who he was working against; to maximize the benefit of working with Foley, his opponent had to rise to the occasion, bringing with him a readiness to go through a physical hell that, while not on the same level as Foley's, still had a defacto tendency to significantly raise his toughness-profile. Foley was simply incomparable.

Randy Orton's name has also been mentioned on numerous occasions throughout this countdown. Though not nearly as historically revered as Foley, the wrestler formerly known as The Legend Killer is, statistically, no less than a Top 15 superstar in the WrestleMania Era, his championship resume stout, his longevity at or near the top of the card already in the 99th percentile, and his natural grace in the ring unquestionable. His own best-of list is worthy of praise, as well, but that the Hardcore Match with Foley remains the greatest of his career presents a unique dichotomy between the way that the savage April 2004 brawl has served Orton's legacy, both in the short and long-term, versus the manner in which it has served Foley's.

For The Viper, the match with The Hardcore Legend has come to represent many things. First and foremost, it legitimized Orton as a stud performer that WWE could build part of its future around; a legitimate argument could be made that, without it, Orton would not have become the youngest World Heavyweight Champion in WWE lore four months later. It was Orton's potential realized, the match that for years people would look to as evidence of his considerable value whenever immaturity or a documented tendency to coast threatened to derail him. As the years have gone by, however, it has in some ways become a microcosm of the narrative that, as good as he has been, Orton has left a lot on the table, that he quite frankly could have and should have been even better.

273

It is an oddity, is it not, that with all the opportunities that he has had to top the Foley match, the general consensus is that he never has? Even Orton himself still refers to it as his personal favorite. Larry Bird used talk of his teammate, Kevin McHale, as someone so naturally gifted that he could have been one of the best ever if he just had worked as hard as Bird. Triple H speaks that way about Orton. Even on the documentary designed to celebrate Orton's contributions to modern WWE history, The Game was prominently featured in saying, "So many people have told Randy that 'You have it all and you can get all this, you just have to work for it' that he's afraid of failing; he's afraid that the more he gets, the more he has to lose." Orton vs. Foley, so much as it was The Viper's high-watermark on the 20'x20' canvas, simultaneously symbolizes the most he ever got and, consequently, the most that he ever had to lose.

Nevertheless, the match itself stands tall as one of the masterpieces of the 21st century. It can be watched head-to-head against anything ranked above it and not display much if any noticeable drop-off in quality, despite the fact that Orton was still very much in his formative stages and that Foley was well past his prime. It means now and it meant then so much to both of them, and that clearly translates when watched again today. "I put a lot of pressure on myself and we delivered," Foley said of the match. "He needed that moment to shine, but I needed the moment just as bad for myself; I needed to know that I had that one match left in me...and I ended up being better than I'd ever been." Just as irreverently, Orton has said, "Mick was gracious enough to go out there and have a match [with me] that I know I'll never forget. [On] that night, I grew up and I became a man, so to speak. What I put my body through, what I put Mick's body through, I think I got that respect."

Unfortunately, considering its marginal setting (can you imagine if it had taken place at *WrestleMania XX* instead?), the less fondly remembered period in which it took place, and The Viper's debatable historical reputation, Foley vs. Orton may never receive quite the upper-end appreciation that it undoubtedly should, but it was a tremendous rivalry capped off by a superbly brutal match that left both men bloodied and beaten. "You won't see a match that violent in WWE ever again," Foley has predicted. We probably will not see a match quite like it ever again, period.

#29
The British Bulldog vs. Bret Hart
Intercontinental Championship and WWF Championship
Summerslam 1992 and In Your House: Season's Beatings

Top 10 All-Time at Summerslam / Top 5 Match in 1992 / Top 5 Match in 1995

When WWE made the decision to move *Summerslam '92* from Washington, D.C. to London, England, Bret Hart went to Vince McMahon and told him that, while he was okay with the plan for him to drop the Intercontinental Championship to Shawn Michaels, "If me and [The British Bulldog] Davey Boy Smith wrestle in Wembley Stadium, it'll be the greatest match of all-time."

McMahon acquiesced to Bret's suggestion and, though it was not the greatest match of all-time, it proved to be a match unquestionably in the conversation all these years later for one of the Top 25 matches of the WrestleMania Era.

It was also an incredibly significant match for a variety of reasons. Five and a half years earlier, Randy Savage and Ricky Steamboat had set a standard for pure in-ring excellence in the WWF. The Intercontinental Title for which they wrestled that night in Pontiac, Michigan, accordingly became in the eyes of many the golden representation for the top worker in the company. The WWF's main-event style, for all its sizzle, rarely produced the quality of steak that did Steamboat-Savage and the other great IC Title battles that followed. Yet, it was the bold and loud personalities that continued to watermark the top of the WWF hierarchy. Hart and Smith, each former Tag Team Champions who had spent much of the first wrestling financial boom helping to make shows better on the undercard, were a pair who preferred to let their wrestling speak for them but, with personalities neither bold nor loud, were not afforded opportunities to main-event.

Atypical though they may have been for WWF headliners of that era, they were the pioneers who entered uncharted waters with their match for the Intercontinental Championship earning the show-closing spot at Summerslam.

The consequent pressure to deliver was immense. Only a match the caliber of Steamboat vs. Savage would likely have validated McMahon's decision to put Bret vs. Davey Boy on last instead of a WWF Championship match. Bulldog developed a reputation during his career, often pedaled by his outspoken brother-in-law, of being very much a follower, a talented but naive human-being. Surely Davey Boy understood the gravity of his opportunity, but as history would prove, Bret was one of those rare wrestlers who had ice water running through his veins when the lights were brightest. There was added pressure on Bret to absorb some of the intimidation off of Bulldog. Fortunately, The Hitman was teeming with self-confidence, accepting and embracing of the stakes.

You certainly could not fault Davey Boy for being nervous. He had been involved in big matches before, such as the main-event of the Chicago portion of *WrestleMania 2*, but he had always shared the responsibility with a trio of other pros in tag team wrestling. In his singles career, he had never come close to anything quite like Wembley Stadium. It had to have felt like a cross between exhilarating and overwhelming to stand among over 80,000 of your countrymen (what proved to be the fourth largest audience in WWE lore), especially when experiencing such a special atmosphere for the first time. With its distinctly English football-type crowd involvement, Summerslam in Wembley produced one of the five most unique environments in the history of WWE.

Take nothing away from Davey Boy because it takes two who can tango at an elite level to have one of the Top 30 matches ever, but the *Summerslam '92* main-event will always be regarded chiefly as a "Bret Hart match," and deservedly so. The primary reason why Hart vs. Smith did not crack the Top 25 was the handful of miscues from Bulldog that, while certainly not stripping any of the enjoyment from their momentous achievement, did make it much easier to push a few peers ahead of it in the rankings via head-to-head analysis.

The fact of the matter is that, in just about every way but whose name was listed as the victor, it was the coming out party for Bret Hart instead of Davey Boy Smith. Tasked with guiding Bulldog through the main-event at one of the most heavily attended WWE shows ever featuring one of the most incredible crowds ever with the owner of the company sitting at ringside for commentary, Bret painted a masterpiece on the 20'X20' canvas that in the years since WWE itself has named the greatest Summerslam match of all-time.

Typically, it would be superfluous to unequally divide the credit due a fantastic match, but the distinction proves pertinent in this case because of what the *Summerslam '92* main-event afforded its defeated half. While for his contributions, Davey Boy held the Intercontinental Title for less than three months (but was released from the company by 1992's end), for his pantheon performance, Bret became WWF Champion less than two months later.

Not only had an Intercontinental Championship match headlined a PPV, but a wrestler's wrestler without a gregarious persona became the World Champion. A perception had developed that someone like Hart could never achieve anything greater than the Intercontinental Title. Bret was a game-changer. He was the first wrestler of his type – great in the ring, limited charisma – to ever become the alpha male in Vincent Kennedy McMahon's sports entertainment empire. The Hitman did not fit what had become the traditional model of entertainment in the WWF, but utilized the sporting element of pro wrestling to create the entertainment.

With Bret's arrival at the foremost position in wrestling came the departure of the Hulkamania Era main-event style; the ensuing upgrade in performance acumen was like trading Arnold Schwarzenegger for Robert De Niro. There is a reason why the vast majority of WWE's contributions to the greatest matches of all-time came after Bret had become McMahon's #1 star and that reason is the emphasis he placed on having classic matches, on telling stories so well defined by their execution, psychology, and selling that even young kids could organically gravitate toward them over the simpler tales often told by those more bombastic characters who had once dominated the WWF's main-event level.

For Davey Boy Smith and England, for WWE itself, and for Bret Hart and others like him, The Hitman vs. The British Bulldog at *Summerslam '92* was a milestone. Davey Boy would main-event numerous PPVs in the 1990s and have a handful of other classics, but his career peaked that night in London. WWE was never quite the same; as much as Dragon vs. Macho Man had set the standard, Hitman vs. Bulldog embodied the old adage that "a rising tide lifts all ships" and prompted four-star matches to eventually become an expectation instead of a once-per-year (or so) phenomenon. Bret, meanwhile, used the chance that McMahon took on him and his brother-in-law as a springboard to one of the ten best careers of the WrestleMania Era. Despite all of his amazing matches, many of which are still yet to be discussed on these pages, during his Hall of Fame speech in 2006 he singled out the one with Bulldog at Wembley as the favorite match of his career.

Adding to the historical profile of Davey vs. Bret, their World Championship match three years later would have certainly been conspicuous by its absence on these pages. Missing from *In Your House 5* was the grandeur and raucous environment of *Summerslam '92*, but The British Bulldog was a much more polished performer by 1995 and, as such, he and The Hitman's sequel was technically better than the original. Hart getting busted open took this anticipated rematch to a different level, adding a crimson shade of violence to the family affair. It too was one of the decade's true gems.

#28
The Ultimate Warrior vs. Hulk Hogan
WWF Championship
WrestleMania VI
April 1, 1990

Top 20 All-Time at WrestleMania / Match of the Year in 1990

There can be no questioning the importance of *WrestleMania VI* to the careers of Hulk Hogan and The Ultimate Warrior. One of the biggest matches in sports entertainment lore, Warrior vs. Hogan captivated the fanbase of the early WrestleMania Era in a manner it had never before experienced, offering two iconic heroes from which the audience was asked to choose allegiance. In defeat, Hogan put forth the finest in-ring performance of his prime. In victory, Warrior not only became the inaugural superstar to simultaneously hold the World Heavyweight and Intercontinental Championships, but also the first man to cleanly pin The Hulkster.

Yet, as Warrior once alluded to, the legend of The Ultimate Challenge is less about the destination and much more about the journey, both to that amazing night at Sky Dome in 1990 and to the place it deserves to hold in WWE lore.

Hulkamania ran wild, not just figuratively in the sense of the catchphrase but also literally in terms of dollars and cents, for a long time. Hogan had already told stories of historic proportions with Piper, Orndorff, Andre, Million Dollar Man, and Savage from '85 to '89 – the greatest consecutive pro wrestling hit-list ever. All good things must come to an end and, by the turn of the decade, legitimate questions were beginning to be asked about whether or not Hulkamania had been given its last call.

At the end of the same year that Hogan famously vanquished Andre, Ultimate Warrior debuted. Within a year, he became the face of the Intercontinental Title division, initially mowing through the longest reigning IC Champ of all-time, The Honky Tonk Man, at *Summerslam '88*, and very clearly establishing his longer-term potential during his rivalry with "Ravishing" Rick Rude. By mid-1989, Warrior's popularity had exploded. "It [was] every ten year old kid's fantasy world come to life," Triple H said of Warrior. There was something more mythical about him than Hogan; The Hulkster was like a superhero, but Ultimate Warrior was like a god.

The two year peak of The Ultimate Warrior coincided with the two year transitional period between Hulkamania's apex and its rapid decline. No one had ever come close to overthrowing Hogan as the alpha of the pride before Warrior, who took advantage of incredible momentum and perfect timing to temporarily supplant Hulk as the industry's #1 star. "There was a tremendous rivalry [that developed between them] in terms of competitiveness," Vince McMahon noted in Warrior's WWE Network documentary. "You were competing for your spot," he added about their mindsets. "I'm trying to take something from you because I don't want you to get what I have."

On April 1, 1990, Hogan and Warrior collided in Toronto's Sky Dome. All the stars had to align for such a spectacle to take place between wrestling's equivalent of The Incredible Hulk fighting Thor, a fact that was transferred over to the performance between the ropes from two pros better known for their charisma and character than for their mastery of intricate in-ring storytelling. It was a marvelous match.

Here is the thing about greatness, though: destiny demands that the greatest will always be topped eventually by something greater. Such has been the case for the iconic battle at *WrestleMania VI*. To this day, it is one of the finest representations of the various characteristics that have come to define the main-event of "The Granddaddy of Them All," combining the grandeur of Hogan vs. Andre with an aesthetic appeal from bell-to-bell that no other 'Mania headliner equaled until Rock-Austin II in the new millennium. Through the first decade and a half of the WrestleMania Era, Warrior vs. Hogan was one of the most rewatchable performances, a sure-fire Top 10 all-time selection on account of its legacy, but time caught up with it and, head-to-head against its more modern peers, its reputation today can perhaps best be summed up by the sentiments of a near 30-year fan who said, after watching it for the first time since his youth, "That was not as good as I remember it."

It struggles to compare to today's best, many of which were quite honestly designed – by wrestlers who once watched The Ultimate Challenge as kids – to captivate an audience to an even greater extent in an even greater match.

Given the circumstances of the 2005 WWE Home Video production, *The Self Destruction of The Ultimate Warrior*, which just so happens to be one of the most blatant attempts you could ever witness in sports or entertainment of a corporation unabashedly slandering one of its biggest icons, it would seem fair to ask in how much higher esteem enthusiasts would hold Hogan vs. Warrior if the WWE hype machine had been behind it from 1990 onward instead of it spending a decade languishing in the stench of WWE's character assassination of Warrior. It was like if *Star Wars: Episode VII* had opened with Princess Leia drunkenly telling war stories and falling through a glass table. What the hell was that? Shame on WWE, seriously.

Edge, for a long time, was basically the inadvertent public caretaker of The Ultimate Challenge's memory, consistently citing it as the reason he got into the business, but it may not have been enough.

Young fans and new wrestlers should study it, frankly. It is a remarkably simple match on account of the audience's investment in their personas. They just did not have to do much; similar to Hogan-Andre, they let the atmosphere carry a big part of the presentation. Warrior and Hogan also worked their butts off, just within a format tailored to the inherent advantage of the utterly amped crowd. "The electricity was at a different level," Edge, who was famously in the crowd, has been quoted as saying numerous times. "I swear you could see it, like the bolts [were] going throughout that building. I'll never forget it." And the finish – Hogan "Hulks up" and hits the big boot, but Warrior rolls out of the way of the leg drop and quickly hits his signature running splash for the clean win – is one of the greatest ever.

Two days before his death, Ultimate Warrior got his long overdue induction into the WWE Hall of Fame. Mere hours before his death, he cut one final promo on Monday Night Raw: "Every man's heart one day beats its final beat, his lungs breathe their final breath; and if what that man did in his life makes the blood pulse through the body of others and makes them believe deeper in something larger than life, then his essence, his spirit will be immortalized." What both Warrior and Hogan did in The Ultimate Challenge deserves immortality, recognized as one of the greatest matches to have ever taken place.

#27

Chris Benoit vs. Triple H vs. Shawn Michaels
World Heavyweight Championship
WrestleMania XX and Backlash 2004

Top 20 All-Time at WrestleMania / Match of the Year in 2004

The main-event of *WrestleMania XX* was a triple threat in the truest sense of the phrase, each participant possessing his own unique story underneath the histrionics of WWE television. So, even though the reputation of the match will always suffer from the violent, unspeakable actions that ended the life of its victor, what this match meant to all three of their careers is, combined with its classic status as what is generally agreed upon to be the preeminent bout of its match-type, plenty reason enough for it to have reached its impressive ranking, looming in the shadows of the Top 25.

Take Shawn Michaels, capping off the year that made him realize that he could go back to wrestling far more than for just a brief comeback tour. The Heartbreak Kid had begun to regain his full confidence and had renewed his rivalry with Triple H at an ideal time when Monday Night Raw, as a brand, mightily needed something positive in its main-event scene to end a 2003 that had featured the likes of a washed up Scott Steiner, Kevin Nash, and Goldberg competing for the World Heavyweight Championship. With Lesnar on his way out and the trio of Cena, Orton, and Batista still a year away from being ready to headline 'Mania, Michaels was more than happy (and ready) to fill a need fit for an Icon.

The match itself is not often discussed in the pantheon of HBK performances, explainable to a degree because of persona non grata's involvement, but somewhat puzzling from a different perspective. Though he was absolutely the third wheel at Madison Square Garden that night considering that The Game was clearly the villain and that Chris Benoit was the crowd's pick to win, Michaels was still a huge part of the bout's overwhelming

285

success. The Triple Threat is no worse than his fifth best WrestleMania outing; and HBK's fifth best anything in professional wrestling is among the greatest. *'Mania XX* was The Showstopper's version of Michael Jordan's 1997 or 1998 series against the Utah Jazz in the NBA Finals, legendary to a level that few could ever hope to equal, despite a natural tendency for it to be regarded beneath his "of all-time"-level work. His off the top turnbuckle-to-floor moonsault onto both Benoit and Triple H, plus the wearing of one of his goriest crimson masks, stand out as two of the match's most memorable moments.

Next take Triple H, who more than ever before needed to deliver to the expectations of the position to which he had risen as WWE's most bankable top star. Austin was gone, Rock was Hollywood, Foley was a special attraction, and the Attitude Era was over; Triple H was still there and was expected to carry the company. Since September 2002, many an enthusiast's choice for the greatest professional wrestler ever, Ric Flair, had touted weekly on WWE airwaves that The Game was essentially his spiritual successor, "The Man" and the modern best in the sport. However, Hunter had mightily struggled to back up such praise. In between chapters in his saga with HBK, he had failed to have any classic matches, rivalries, or stories; granted, the majority of his opposition was yesterday's news, but he bore his fair share of the blame, especially from the burgeoning online-commentating community.

What *WrestleMania XX* was, then, for The Game was a night when he reminded the wrestling world why he had been entrusted to lead the charge on the flagship show, post-Attitude. He was supposed to be the measuring stick and, on March 14, 2004 at Madison Square Garden, he wrestled like it. Triple H had never previously come close to having the best match on the grandest stage, out-classed in every instance since becoming a 'Mania headliner in 2000, so it was validating for him to have the Match of the Year on a night that also featured Cena, Orton, and Batista's 'Mania debuts, The Rock and Brock's last matches for eight years, the return of The Undertaker's beloved Deadman character, and a wrestling purist's dream scenario in Angle vs. Guerrero for the WWE Championship. The Cerebral Assassin went onto have even better performances at "The Show of Shows," but he was never involved in a main-event anywhere near as good as the Triple Threat.

Put them with Chris Benoit, the highly respected veteran who had fought tooth and nail to reach the pinnacle of his profession. Following in the footsteps of a fellow technically-oriented Canadian grappler who had worked his way from perennial mid-carder to the main-event, The Rabid Wolverine's no-nonsense, workmanlike approach earned him the supreme appreciation of both the audience and his peers. Benoit was the other side of the Eddie Guerrero coin; if Latino Heat was like hitting a million dollar jackpot in the lottery, The Rabid Wolverine was like proving that you could make a million dollars if you work hard enough and for long enough, each a representative of anything being possible. Winning the Royal Rumble Match and then becoming World Heavyweight Champion in the main-event at *WrestleMania XX* was a reward for incredible consistency.

It was the ultimate achievement for Benoit, the peak of a seven month stint in the main-event scene the likes of which he would never equal again. The best match of his career might be a stretch given the quality of his all-time #1 at the Rumble-contending bout a year prior, but *WrestleMania XX* was unquestionably the greatest night of his career. If anything had been gained from The Game's dominant yet critically panned late 2002 through 2003, it was that it reinforced how much it meant when someone defeated him, so watching Benoit tap-out Triple H was an incredibly cathartic experience for an audience that so equally wanted Hunter to lose and Benoit to win. Benoit's post-match celebratory, tearful embrace with Guerrero remains one of the seminal moments of the WrestleMania Era in terms of its unique emotional tie to the diehard fanbase and the inspiration that it gave fellow wrestlers of a comparable stature and/or ethnicity.

The rematch a month later at *Backlash '04* was not nearly as historically weighty, but is certainly worth mentioning. Samuel 'Plan wrote in *101* that *"WrestleMania XX* will be Chris Benoit's most remembered, most celebrated hour, but [the rematch] was undoubtedly his finest, when must-see was made preface and the greatest ever match of its kind reduced simply to Chapter 1."

Of course, *WrestleMania XX* will continue to be the driving force behind the Triple Threat's place in any "all-time" debate, standing as it does as the foremost symbol of excellence in Chris Benoit's outstanding career and the best World Championship match at WrestleMania from the man who has had more World Championship matches at WrestleMania than any other superstar (Triple H), in addition to featuring a pantheon performance from Shawn Michaels.

#26
The Rock vs. Mankind
WWF Championship
Survivor Series 1998 to Monday Night Raw
February 15, 1999

Top 5 All-Time at Royal Rumble / Match of the Year in 1999

1998 was an integral year for the WWF's resurgence in the Monday Night War. The creative juices were flowing and overall popularity (as primarily measured by TV ratings and pay-per-view buys) was surging to levels not produced by the WWF since Hulkamania. Skyrocketing to the top of the superstar hierarchy was The Rock, who was living up to all of his self-given nicknames and, by year-end, had begun to push Stone Cold Steve Austin for the role of WWF's lead protagonist. Mankind, meanwhile, had reached a crossroads in his career and could see retirement looming quickly in the aftermath of Hell in a Cell. At *Survivor Series*, their fates would become intertwined and they would embark on the first truly great main-event rivalry of what we came to know as the Attitude Era.

The "Deadly Game" tournament to crown a new WWF Champion at the '98 November Classic proved quite eventful. In the semi-finals, Vince and Shane McMahon successfully executed the climax of a conspiracy to prevent Stone Cold from regaining the title he had vacated and, in the finals, Montreal-esque screwed Mankind, who had gone into the night as the McMahon-endorsed favorite. The Rock was the beneficiary, becoming the Corporate Champion in a shocking moment that brought to an abrupt (albeit temporary) halt the momentum he had been gaining as the potential next huge babyface star.

"[It was] a foregone conclusion that [Rock] was going to wrestle Stone Cold Steve Austin and it was going to be huge when the time was right," Mick Foley has said about what came next after *Survivor Series*. "And it was almost like, 'There's this period of time that needs to be filled really well' and [Rock] needed to be ready [for Austin]." Foley had been in WWF Championship matches before in challenger-of-the-month type scenarios and against already established top guys who needed someone to help make them look good, but never against a wrestler who needed his help to get to another level. "I looked it at as the ultimate honor," he said.

Mankind completed in the final month of 1998 the metamorphosis from the dark, wounded soul to a wonderfully endearing tragic figure whose sense of humor transcended the uglier parts of his inner-self. The Rock joining The Corporation simultaneously, then, triggered monster heat for The Great One and substantial resonance with and sympathy for Mankind.

It was a tremendous time to be a fan because so many characters were peaking, a microcosm for which was the January 4, 1999 episode of Raw. Mankind vs. The Rock for the WWF Championship was the main-event, The Corporation and D-Generation X were at ringside, and Stone Cold interfered leading into the finish that made the formerly deranged and now beloved third "Face of Foley" the new holder of the richest prize in the industry. That night was infamous for WCW's Tony Schiavone, handed the WWF taped results by Eric Bischoff to read on-air, spoiling Foley's title win and snidely commenting, "That'll put a lot of butts in seats." Designed to boost their own ratings, WCW's broadcasting decision completely backfired, as the better part of a million people immediately changed the channel to watch an ultimate underdog like Mankind become World Champion.

He had accomplished an impossible dream in becoming champion and, though his primary job to advance Rock had not changed, Foley was going to live every second of his dream sequence like it was his last as a wrestler. With an act freshly accented by the power of his uncanny ability to make people laugh (see Mr. Socko), Mankind charged toward a *Royal Rumble '99* WWF Title defense full of charisma and confidence.

However, the laughter was about to stop as Foley's Hardcore nature yet again took center stage. The Winter Classic was site of the 1999 Match of the Year, the "I Quit" Match revered by some and regretted by others.

"I wanted to give people a very physical match that would show an extra side, another dimension to The Rock, one of ruthlessness and viciousness," Foley explained in his WWE-produced documentary. "It showed a mean-streak that The Rock needed." Mission accomplished.

Much of the discussion of the match, historically, has focused on the sheer violence of it, with Rock sending Mankind crashing from ten feet high onto a massive electrical circuit board and Rock blasting Mankind with eleven consecutive unprotected chair shots to the head. "His desire to entertain an audience through great impact to his body was mind-boggling," Rock said in his own documentary. "The things that Mick would allow me to do to him were incredible." The image of a beaten and bloodied Mankind with his hands cuffed behind his back laying prone on the entrance way elicits a guttural reaction to this day. "We raised the bar and he raised the bar in terms of taking punishment and pain," Rock concluded. However, Foley has called it "the one match where afterward everyone agreed that maybe we went a little too far."

There is a sense of irony in Foley calling the "I Quit" the match that took it too far when just seven months prior he had volunteered to be thrown from 25 feet in the air through a small plank of wood and there is also some irony in the fact that the same match that, better than any other in his career, showcased The Rock as sadistic and tough as nails was also the match that provided him such a memorable platform with which to talk trash and exhibit the top 0.001% charisma that turned him into the most well-known personality ever to come from the world of wrestling. There he was, kicking the monkey crap out of Foley all over God's green earth, while at the same time continually being handed a microphone used to rattle off a few seconds of verbal gold. He never came even close to quitting and he had a sharp-tongued zinger ready for each time the mic was shoved in his face. For a match to be so exceptionally brutal, The Rock also made it wildly entertaining.

The "I Quit" Match has had a tendency to overshadow the staggering, first-time ever accomplishment of The Rock and Mankind wrestling for the WWF Championship on four consecutive pay-per-views, not to mention the two classic television matches that saw the title change hands on each occasion, the first already mentioned and the second (the "Empty Arena" Match) on the highly successful *Halftime Heat* special aired at the mid-way point of the Super Bowl. They also innovated the Last Man Standing gimmick in their final PPV encounter. Mankind vs. The Rock is a rivalry heralded mostly as the main-event coronation of The Great One, but never fail to take into consideration that it also confirmed Mick Foley as one of the foremost stars of the preeminent period in pro wrestling history.

#25
Stone Cold Steve Austin vs. Mr. McMahon
Monday Night Raw September 22, 1997 to
WrestleMania XV

It is quite appropriate that Austin vs. McMahon would defy the conventional criteria set forth to rank the greatest matches, rivalries, and stories of the WrestleMania Era. Considering that it bucked pro wrestling's bog standard tradition from the outset with its heavy emphasis on counter-cultural ideals, why would anything less be expected?

The WWF presented a very simple product from 1983 to the mid-1990s. The conflicts between heroes and villains were well-suited to a family audience. Perhaps no better feud reflected that period more than Hulk Hogan vs. Andre the Giant, sports entertainment's literal take on David vs. Goliath. Yet, by the time Stone Cold Steve Austin won the 1996 King of the Ring tournament, the world demanded that popular television shows like WWF Raw tackle more complicated issues, and the entertainment industry was forced to mature.

The real world is not as black and white as earning success through "saying your prayers, doing your training, and taking your vitamins." Not to discount the important role that those things can play in being successful, but the reality is that people work hard and fail all the time; or even worse, their efforts to advance their position are thwarted by repressive business (and moral) practices. On September 22, 1997, the WWF brought that to the forefront when corporate wisdom clashed prominently on Raw with an employee's rabid desire to reach the pinnacle of his profession. The boss, Vince McMahon, tried to keep Austin from pushing himself to and beyond his perceived limits; Stone Cold responded with a physical assault. For the first of many times, the employee cathartically one-upped his oppressive superior.

Austin vs. McMahon would continue on for years, peaking at *WrestleMania XV* and igniting popularity for pro wrestling that eclipsed even that of the original Hulkamania-driven boom. It was also the catalyst for adapting the theme of this book beyond matches and rivalries. When you think of a great match, you think about something like Bret Hart vs. British Bulldog; when you think of a great rivalry, you think about a series of great matches like Kurt Angle vs. Brock Lesnar. Austin vs. McMahon, whose most prominent one-on-one encounter took place at *St. Valentine's Day Massacre* in February 1999, was not a great match; their pay-per-view bout combined with their battles on Raw certainly did not in the traditional sense produce the caliber of matches necessary to be coined a great rivalry. Yet, Austin vs. McMahon still told a tremendous *story*.

Television has predominantly played a secondary role in pro wrestling history. At first, it was used as a promotional advertisement for live events. The advent of the super card created a formula in which television then became the primary hype machine for PPVs. During the Attitude Era, priorities shifted to placating the increasingly massive weekly viewership for Raw with stimulating content, a motivation that when combined with winning the TV ratings battle with WCW created a need for PPV to boost TV interest as much as TV was needed to boost interest in PPV. Suddenly, Raw was no longer a wrestling TV show – it was a TV show about wrestling. Featuring quite possibly the greatest ensemble cast in WWE history, Austin vs. McMahon was the primary narrative that drove the success of Raw.

A Who's Who of WWE lore were utilized as plot devices in the Austin-McMahon saga, including but not limited to Mick Foley, Undertaker, Kane, Big Bossman, Shane McMahon, Big Show, and The Rock. Everyone involved, down to the bit players like Hall of Famers Pat Patterson and Gerald Briscoe as Mr. McMahon's "Stooges," played their parts extremely well. Even legendary boxer/personality Mike Tyson knocked his role out of the park.

WWE's second financial boom period happened in large part because Raw was a captivating weekly episodic program that, like many great shows do, built a sizeable viewing audience. Wrestling has been called a "male soap opera"; never was that more accurate than from late 1997 to early 1999, when Austin vs. McMahon was the stimulus for weekly Nielsen ratings increasing from 2.4 on the 9/22/97 episode of Raw that saw the Texas Rattlesnake first give Vince the Stone Cold Stunner to 6.4 on the Raw before *WrestleMania XV*. To those of us that were WWF fans during the 2.4 days (or are still presently WWE fans who have watched ratings slip back to 2.4 and lower), it seemed like everyone watched wrestling during the height of Austin's career. With characters that engaging and story arcs written in such compelling fashion, it was hard to watch once and not become a repeat viewer.

At least half of all the greatest moments in Monday Night Raw history took place during the 18 month stretch that best featured Stone Cold vs. Mr. McMahon. The aforementioned original Stunner to Vince; the impeccably well played Austin and Tyson confrontation (with McMahon screaming at Austin during the conclusion "You ruined it, damn it!"); the pair of shows right after *WrestleMania XIV* when the corporate viewpoint was unquestionably emphasized and Stone Cold's rebellion kicked into a higher gear; the very first match between Austin and McMahon (which ended the near two year ratings dominance by WCW Nitro); Stone Cold driving a Coors Lite truck to ringside and giving Vince, Shane, and Rock a beer bath. The list goes on and on.

There was an untouchable four week Raw run in Autumn 1998. In response to being screwed out of the WWF Championship at *Breakdown: In Your House* on September 27th, Austin drove a Zamboni to the ring and attacked McMahon on September 28th. The storyline-injuries the Chairman suffered put him in the hospital for the October 5th episode, toward the end of which Austin showed up dressed as a doctor and classically continued his assault (this same episode also debuted Foley's "Mr. Socko").

On October 12th, Stone Cold filled Mr. McMahon's Corvette with so much cement that every window shattered. In retaliation for being fired at the end of *Judgment Day: In Your House* on October 18th, Austin kidnapped McMahon on October 19th, dragged him to the ring, and held up a toy gun to his head that yielded a small flag bearing the words "Bang 3:16" ("McMahon 3:16" proceeded to piss his pants). On October 26th, Shane McMahon became a featured part of the storyline when he showed a similar knack for the business as his father, turning on his dad to sign Austin to a new contract. Can you believe, in hindsight, that all of those classic episodes took place in the span of a month?

Atypical as it may have been when compared to its peers in this book, Austin vs. McMahon was and still is the creative benchmark for all future storylines to live up to. The bottom line is that there was no chance in hell of Stone Cold vs. Mr. McMahon being anything less than Top 25; no story in WWE lore catalyzed the same fervor among existing wrestling fans or was as responsible for creating new ones. It was the most financially impactful feud in pro wrestling history, stimulating impressive PPV buyrates but, more so, absolutely incredible television ratings charged by powerfully emotive moments that spawned indelible memories.

#24
CM Punk vs. Brock Lesnar
Summerslam
August 18, 2013

Top 10 All-Time at Summerslam / Top 5 Match in 2013

The simplest way to educate someone who knows nothing about sports entertainment to is describe it to them as a "performance art." At its core, it is a highly physical method of telling a story. Like on the big screen and on the theater stage, its greatest stories possess enough emotional depth to be interpreted in many ways.

Take, for instance, CM Punk vs. Brock Lesnar.

In life, one of the most destructive forces is the fear of failure and one of the most unfortunate things about the fear that most people build around failure is that it is based on someone else's definition of success.

Parents begin the trend with their habit of creating rules in the household that are often narrowly focused, even when a view through a wider lens might show a stricter attitude to be detrimental to their child's development and ultimate prosperity. The patterns established during youth typically carry over into adulthood, with fear continuing to be a driving force that dictates future direction. Fear of failure manifested through a punishment versus reward model for the marks earned on a scholastic report card frequently becomes manifested in a similar way later in life through a paycheck. If you make poor grades, then beware of grounding and/or less opportunity at a higher education; if you make too little money, then beware of poverty and/or a lesser place in society's hierarchy. Not to abide by the traditional requirements perceived to govern success sets you up for an unhappy life, or so it is said. Once instilled, fear can be activated by a wide variety of triggers; once patterned to live your life around fear, it can become a hard habit to break.

Fear itself, though, is not generally an empowering emotion. Napoleon Hill once studied the wealthiest people in the world to write a book on their common qualities and discovered that confidence driven by a positive attitude was among their mutually defining traits; they were not at all afraid to fail and were instead consumed by passion for what they did and a mindset centered on accomplishing their goals. It was not money that made them happy, but the satisfaction of having made life pay off on their own terms.

We tend to be inspired by the people who, rather than cower to fear, meet it head on in an attempt to conquer it. In WWE, CM Punk – like Austin before him – became symbolic with going against the grain to achieve incredible pro wrestling success. He had none of the traditional advantages, nothing was ever handed to him, and yet, through a rabid desire and an unwavering self-belief, he still became one of the Top 25 stars of the WrestleMania Era. He did it *his* way and, for that as much as anything else, people gravitated toward him.

Brock Lesnar, conversely, had every perceived advantage in WWE and, thanks to an unmatched legitimate wrestling and fighting background, he became pro wrestling's ultimate representation of fear. The Beast Incarnate may as well have been nicknamed "Doomsday" because not even Superman could escape his wrath. He was the last human-being in WWE's fictional universe that you would ever have wanted to be facing your favorite wrestler because, in all likelihood, Lesnar was going to destroy him.

For CM Punk, his battle with WWE's preeminent symbol of fear was triggered by the combination of loss and betrayal, both of which run parallel with real world influences that each of us could encounter in any given year. After 434 days of sustained success, Punk lost the WWE Championship to The Rock, failed to win it back in a rematch, was defeated by John Cena in his last chance to earn another shot, and then fell victim to Undertaker's vaunted WrestleMania Streak. As many are prone to do when the going gets tough, Punk focused inward to regain his touch. Paul Heyman, his long-time advocate, took exception to being amicably pushed aside and betrayed him, consequently becoming Punk's primary fear-monger. Also the spokesman for Lesnar, Heyman unleashed his Beast on The Second City Saint.

Winning and losing in the *Summerslam 2013* match between Punk and Lesnar was essentially about conquering fear and simultaneously dealing with that which had caused it to rear its ugly head in the first place. Defeating Lesnar would have ended Punk's run of losses to WWE's most historically elite superstars; it would have put Heyman to shame for egregiously throwing away their friendship; and it would have exorcised the fear that Punk would never truly be allowed to ascend to the heights in WWE that he and many of his supporters thought that he should.

Replaying it years later, you can still get swept up in their powerful, beautifully told story. The tag team of fear (Lesnar) and betrayal (Heyman) proved quite potent and at times looked unstoppable. However, Punk valiantly persisted in the face of overwhelming odds. In that respect, the match was a microcosm of Punk's career; he looked his greatest obstacles in the eyes and worked tirelessly to overcome them in very individually-authentic fashion.

That he did not win the match could easily be misconstrued as abject failure, but to view it that way would so narrowly define success. Indeed, fear got the best of him that day; we all have days like that. He stayed true to himself, though, and put up the fight of his life. The world is not so black and white that the only ways to win are to put fear to sleep for a decisive three count or to Anaconda Vice fear's arm into submission; to even face fear is in and of itself a victory; to work so hard that others aspire to equal your ethic is a victory; to earn the respect of your peers is a victory. The underlying lesson of Punk vs. Lesnar, therefore, was to remind us that genuine determination and passion pays off in various gratifying ways that do not always fit the bog standard model of success.

Of course, that is just one interpretation, but regardless of how you process the performance, that it is one of the greatest matches of all-time is indisputable.

As to why it ranked ahead of #25...

Because of its unique qualities, it is difficult to judge Austin vs. McMahon against these other rivalries. Not a single adversary that wrestled Austin on behalf of McMahon or within the conspiratorial web spun by McMahon to destroy Austin produced a match with Stone Cold worthy of inclusion in the Top 100, much less one that was in the same league as CM Punk vs. Brock Lesnar. Austin-McMahon is like watching a season of *Daredevil* on Netflix, while Punk-Lesnar is more like watching *The Dark Knight*; both are great in their own ways, but if you have to choose between the two, naturally you go with the one it takes a couple of hours to view instead of the one that takes you several weeks.

#23
John Cena vs. Daniel Bryan
WWE Championship
Summerslam
August 18, 2013

Top 10 All-Time at Summerslam / Match of the Year in 2013

Daniel Bryan is one of the most fascinating stories of the WrestleMania Era. He was a transcendent talent who, for about one year in total, rose to such incredibly popular heights that only names such as Cena, Austin, Rock, Hogan, and the like could equal his peak crowd reactions.

He kicked down the door that CM Punk cracked open for wrestlers who made it to WWE via the post-WCW independent scene and reached the very top of the mountain, only for an injury to derail his main-event career just as it was starting. Fans of pro basketball might relate him to Bill Walton or more recently Derrick Rose in that regard, but enthusiasts of any sport or entertainment avenue can relate to a star succeeding at the highest level possible, then shortly thereafter vanishing from the limelight, prompting a mere three years since his/her unfathomable rise to seem like double or triple the time had passed in his/her industry.

In April 2014, prognosticators spoke of Bryan in the same vein as Shawn Michaels; Bryan was just 32 years old at the time and the rest of the decade's biggest shows could have been his for the stealing. Two months later, he would be sidelined for the first of nine agonizing months and, after a brief but memorable three month comeback in 2015, he was almost done for good.

At the same age that Bryan spent his initial stretch on the disabled list, John Cena had just been featured in his fifth consecutive World Title bout at WrestleMania and was already climbing the historical WWE Superstar hierarchy in a hurry. He was WWE's Wolverine, developing a reputation for overcoming an assortment of major injuries faster than any athlete on the planet, giving him the longevity at the top that Bryan may never get the chance to achieve. Durable as could be, by the time he collided with what would become known as the "Yes! Movement," Cena was on his way to surpassing Hogan as WWE's longest-tenured #1 star ever. Nevertheless, in spite of all the accolades earned through rivalries previously and not yet discussed on these pages, to a core of diehard fans, Cena was not on Bryan's level as a *wrestler*.

In Bryan's autobiography, *Yes! My Improbable Journey to the Main Event of WrestleMania*, he took issue with WWE having become, in his mind, a parody of professional wrestling. Cena and his generation took a lot of heat from wrestlers like Bryan for making WWE so much more about performing, selling t-shirts, and being famous than putting together combat dramas realistically portraying fights over relatable issues. "I wanted something more," Bryan said of what he hoped to do with his opportunity to headline in WWE. "I didn't want to be a parody of wrestling anymore. And in my mind, being a wrestling parody was the worst possible thing that a wrestler could be."

Effectively, the main-event of *Summerslam '13* was rooted in a similar conflict as the one that had made Cena's rivalry with Punk so engaging. Call it the great 21st century battle between the mindset that a tremendous in-ring performance is the most important thing in pro wrestling and the sports entertainment-centric viewpoint that overt displays of larger than life personality are nine-tenths of the proverbial law; WWE was regularly proven right in the pay-per-view era – a decent match pitting two dynamic characters against each other made a much greater financial impact than a 5-star classic featuring two lords of the ring – with Bryan's responsibility for an underwhelming second biggest event of 2013 buyrate one of the last vestiges of evidence prior to the WWE Network's launch six months later.

Bryan vs. Cena was the best representative to date of modern wrestling's philosophical struggle; Bryan was the avatar for great wrestling being enough, and Cena was the avatar for the ethos of sports entertainment, parody as it may be to Bryan and his supporters, being superior. The debate has gotten progressively louder since all the way back in the 1980s. Today's society thinks more critically than ever – kids included – and, in that environment, an attitude has proliferated that wrestling matches should be of a very high quality. It is, therefore, conceivable that Bryan's ideology may dominate the future, as WWE Network conceptually favors the most ardent fans. Greatness is in demand, so it seems probable that the next huge WWE star will strike a balance between everyman wrestlers-who-can-entertain like Bryan and entertainers-who-can-wrestle like Cena.

Even without the intangible advantage of the underlying theme, Cena and Bryan unquestionably supplied greatness in a terrific match which ebbed and flowed so well for nearly a half hour and was of a class destined to pass any test that time could throw at it. For pure bell-to-bell quality, it was the best match of Bryan's WWE tenure, and arguably Cena's as well. They had such firm command of the crowd and provoked a rather rare-for-the-modern-age investment by the audience in their characters. Los Angeles has been known to produce rather lackluster crowds despite its Hollywood glamor making it a regular WWE host city, but fans in attendance that night were exceptionally invested in Bryan's cause, as well as vehemently against Cena's.

The climax saw everyone in attendance unforgettably stand in unison to chant "Yes!" as Bryan revved up to deliver his running knee finisher and pin Cena clean in the middle of the ring to win the WWE Championship, but the most memorable moment of the match might have been the sequence of events that preceded it. Bryan had this bit on the go-home Raw six nights prior where he told Cena about a Japanese tradition of the wrestlers slapping each other out of respect in order to motivate themselves, only he would not acquiesce to Cena's request that Bryan slap him because Cena was "not a wrestler" (instead a parody) and, therefore, did not deserve it. When Bryan reneged on that stance during the match and, after Cena had taken him to his limit, traded slaps with the all-time great, it was a tip of the cap between two outstanding and very different professional wrestlers (and perhaps subtly an acknowledgment of the possibilities when two opposing schools of thought can find common ground).

Not to be forgotten was, of course, what some diehard fans insist was the cruel intention by WWE to dangle the carrot of Bryan being given the chance to carry the company by beating their golden boy without shenanigans, only to deliver a hard and swift counter-punch that knocked out Bryan's prospects as "The Man" and reaffirmed sports entertainment's supremacy. Triple H, the special referee, infamously turned heel to assist a return to villainy of his former pupil, Randy Orton, who then cashed in his Money in the Bank contract. Ironically, The Authority went on to propel Bryan to even greater heights and then, just as ironically, Bryan got hurt and could never sustain his place.

In the end, Bryan described the match with Cena as one of his favorites. "It had a championship feel to it," he said, "And we went out and wrestled without it being a parody. I loved it." No matter what happened later, so did we...

#22
The 1992 Royal Rumble Match
WWF Championship
January 19, 1992

Top 5 Royal Rumble Match / Top 10 All-Time at Royal Rumble /
Match of the Year in 1992

In Ric Flair's autobiography, *To Be The Man*, Bobby "The Brain" Heenan said of the 1992 Royal Rumble, "It was the best match I ever announced, the only time I ever felt that a match I was calling was 100% real."

Any reflection back to the famous '92 Rumble, considered by most to be the greatest edition of WWE's most popular gimmick match, must begin and end with both Flair *and* Heenan. The Nature Boy's WWF Championship-winning display has rightly been heralded one of the greatest in Rumble lore and has justifiably earned him top billing, but at a close second was The Brain, whose unabashedly subjective commentary provided a brilliant audio soundtrack to Flair's physical performance.

Flair and Heenan were tied together from start-to-finish of Naitch's original WWF tenure, which began when the reigning NWA Heavyweight titleholder left WCW and came to the WWF with the big gold belt still around his waist, proclaiming himself to be "The Real World's Champion." WCW had nowhere near the scope in the early 1990s that did the WWF, so while it may seem unfathomable to a diehard wrestling fan in hindsight that not everybody who watched the WWF knew of Flair, there was some Nature Boy education that needed to be done when Naitch arrived in September 1991. Heenan was by Flair's side on his opening night and was largely responsible from then on for helping establish Naitch's credibility as a major star. While Flair set out to show a new audience the talent that made him the Wrestler of the 1980s in the NWA, Heenan went to work hyping Naitch at the announce table.

One could say that The Brain had a lot personally invested in Nature Boy's success, making it unsurprising to read that Heenan felt the '92 Rumble Match to be all too real. The emotion behind his commentary certainly seemed authentic to viewers. Every wrestling fan at some point in their lives watches the 30-Man Over-The-Top-Rope Battle Royal and vociferously cheers on *their* guy; if it was ever revealed that Flair was not one of The Brain's all-time favorite wrestlers, it would be shocking. Heenan, perhaps the most entertaining personality in WWE lore, was presented as the ultimate Nature Fanboy. His words during the '92 Rumble either incited further Flair's detractors or echoed the desires of Flair's supporters. There are not five more famous calls of a match in the WrestleMania Era.

Heenan's classic lines from the match read like the track listing on the back of an old CD cover; it features hits such as "This isn't fair to Flair," which Joey Styles once suggested would have been the theme for a best-selling T-shirt on WWESHOP.COM had the modern day marketing machine been running back then; "Hey you, stupid, get me something to drink"; "The room is starting to spin, I'm getting dizzy!"; after Flair eliminated Big Bossman with entry #15 just seconds from entering, "Flair wins it! He's the champion of the world!"; "Please let him win it – I'll never do or say anything bad again"; and maybe the greatest of them all, "Thank you, Roddy, it's a kilt, it's not a skirt...you no good creep, you skirt wearing freak – it's not a kilt, it's a skirt!" Of course, the prompts and retorts by Gorilla Monsoon that created the duets to all of the above cannot be undervalued either.

For Flair, providing the in-ring storytelling to accompany Heenan's audio coverage was easy. Known as the "60-Minute Man" in NWA/WCW for his marathon matches, being the central figure for an hour in the Royal Rumble was just another day at the office; and he was THE central figure. It was his storyline actions that led to the WWF Championship being on the line in the Rumble, as he had assisted in Undertaker defeating Hulk Hogan to win the title at *Survivor Series '91* and had been heavily involved in the controversy during the return match just days later at *This Tuesday in Texas*. The Rumble was the culmination of Flair's attempts to back up his braggadocios "Real World's Champion" claims; all eyes were on The Nature Boy and he delivered in the clutch.

The vast majority of the match watched like a Ric Flair highlight reel. The classic moves and mannerisms that made him already the greatest ever in the opinions of many may as well have been his statement to the WWF fanbase, locker room, and management: "That's right, ladies and gentlemen...*This* is what you've been missing!" All of the nicknames that he had earned throughout his career for his in-ring prowess were demonstrated. In addition to the aforementioned "60-Minute Man," he showed the world why he was called "The Dirtiest Player in the Game" and why the moniker "*The* Man" had been popularized by his run as the preeminent star of the NWA. By match's end, he was "*The* Man" in the WWF and "The Real World's Champion."

Samuel 'Plan, in *101 WWE Matches To See Before You Die*, identifies that 1992 "marked the year in which [The Royal Rumble] stopped being a novelty" and that "1992 was its coming of age story...the first year of the rest of its life." Thus, the significance of the match was shaped by more than just the artistic endeavors of Flair and Heenan. Before 1992, the Rumble was little more than an entertaining exhibition. It was important and important things happened during it, but it did not carry the sense of importance that has come to define its role on the Road to WrestleMania until something more tangible was on the line. The title being up for grabs by itself made the '92 Rumble a grander event.

The alteration of the presentation from exhibition to high stakes affair created a palpable shift in the tone of the action; winning the match had never before felt so crucial because it had never before been so crucial. The result was a sweeping narrative that began with a thoroughly engaging first 25-minutes dotted by the appearance of ten current or future Hall of Famers within the first fourteen entries and standout runs from Davey Boy Smith and Shawn Michaels (in addition to Flair); by the time Flair last eliminated Sid, the tensions had been expertly and steadily elevated through Roddy Piper's showdown with Naitch, Jake Roberts playing his cerebral game of chess before Macho Man exploded to the ring to destroy him, Hulk Hogan attempting to get payback on Flair and Undertaker, and the appearance of eleven more current or future Hall of Famers.

All discussions of the '92 Rumble, though, inevitably lead back to Flair and Heenan, who anchored the match from start-to-finish.

In a post-match interview with "Mean" Gene Okerlund, Flair gathered with Heenan and the third member of their highly entertaining triumvirate, Mr. Perfect. The Brain proudly exclaimed "I was never so impressed with anything I've seen in all my life." The Nature Boy proceeded to cut one of the best promos of all-time, beginning with the line, "I'm gonna tell you all, with a tear in my eye, this is the greatest moment in my life." It may also have been the greatest moment in the history of the Royal Rumble.

#21
Edge vs. The Undertaker
WrestleMania XXIV to Summerslam 2008

Top 20 All-Time at WrestleMania / Top 5 All-Time at Summerslam / Top 5 All-Time Hell in a Cell Match / Top 20 All-Time Ladder Match / Top 5 Match in 2008

Watching a former World Champion in wrestling attempt to follow his career year is like watching a pro football player motivate himself after he has already won his first Super Bowl; it is as if, in reaching the highest level he ever thought possible and admitting to himself, "OK, I have achieved greatness," he then wonders, "Alright, can I be all-time great?"

Unquestionably, The Rated R Superstar proved himself as a headlining attraction in 2006, but every main-event talent has his peak rivalry and his peak match and, in Edge's case, both peaks were with Undertaker in 2008. Edge accepted the personal challenge of topping his flagship-carrying feud with Cena, rendering what proved to be a storyline instrumental to a generation the second banana on his best-of list. Re-read the accolades at the top of the page again; much like when reading the C.V. on Edge's overall career, you may not fully appreciate Edge vs. Taker until you stop and take notice of its resume.

Theirs was a near-18 month saga that began at the conclusion of The Deadman's Cage Match title defense against Batista discussed many pages ago. Edge cashed in the Money in the Bank contract that he had masterfully manipulated from the clutches of original holder, Mr. Kennedy, becoming the new World Heavyweight Champion upon returning to Smackdown. At *Survivor Series* and also *Armageddon* later that year, Edge twice more cost Taker the title, regaining the championship in the latter instance.

Yet again, a woman played an all-important role for Edge. With Lita, he had been infamous as the linchpin heel on Raw in the aftermath of the Matt Hardy scandal, but when the notorious womanizer started an on-screen relationship with the beloved Eddie Guerrero's widow, Vickie...well, that was just a whole other level of deplorable. His emotional manipulation of this impressionable, vulnerable woman, who had recently been named General Manager of Smackdown, was so overt; they took the long-time negative perception of Triple H marrying into his cushy top guy role via Stephanie McMahon and amplified it using the equivalent of The Game wedding *Linda,* like watching your mother get duped into a relationship with a younger guy who clearly wanted her money. It was a brilliant power-play for Edge's character, and Vickie responded by doing everything a GM could do to keep him on top, becoming one of the most hated antagonists of the 21st century in her own right.

WWE managed to hold off on their first title bout for nearly a year, finally presenting it as the main-event of *WrestleMania XXIV.* Edge revealed his added incentive during an excellent backstage promo – brilliantly right after Ric Flair's swan-song – that not only reiterated his plan to take firm command of The Phenom's position in the WWE hierarchy, but that also brought to light his desire to pluck the innocence from the youth in the crowd who counted on Taker to stay undefeated at 'Mania the same way that his own innocence had been lost as a young Hulkamaniac in attendance at *WrestleMania VI,* when Hogan lost to Warrior.

As 'Mania show-closers go, it is firmly entrenched in the discussion for the Top 10's mid-range, featuring an especially fantastic second half that well-displayed Edge's penchant for looking at signature offensive sequences for individual superstars as chess pieces to be moved around in various combinations in order to achieve the ultimate victory of superb match quality, prompting Cena to herald him the "Einstein of professional wrestling" years later. To differentiate his match against Taker from The Deadman's previous best, "I would be the guy that countered everything that he did," Edge once stated in an interview with Christian. "And then we he tried again, I would re-counter. So, it was all about counters until finally he figured out my counters and countered [them]."

Edge, both during and after his career, was one of the superstars whose WrestleMania insight viscerally connected with WWE enthusiasts. He could articulate what set "The Show of Shows" apart from all other major events in a way that resonated with fans who *felt* that difference every year from January to April. Main-eventing 'Mania had become, in an era of more frequent World Title changes and multiple brands, wrestling's Holy Grail, its pinnacle triumph. When Edge reached his only 'Mania main-event, you got the sense that few in history understood the gravity of that accomplishment to quite the extent that he did. The next time you watch Edge vs. Taker at *WM24*, think of the way that Edge has described his entrance – "I'm walking down the aisle, I see The Undertaker standing in a corner, my arms are numb [because] I'm so amped up...I felt like I could've fought the world at that point" – and try to stop the goosebumps.

WrestleMania has traditionally played host to the end, or at least the beginning of the end, for major rivalries but, for Taker and Edge, it was the launching point for their saga to reach Top 25 all-time heights. In five months, they wrestled at five pay-per-views, including a terrific TLC Match at *One Night Stand* that too few talk about, culminating in the main-event of *Summerslam '08*.

Impressive as it is to own a Top 20 all-time WrestleMania match, it might be a little bit more impressive that they wrestled one of the Top 5 matches in Summerslam history. Doubling as one of the Top 5 greatest Hell in a Cell matches, the '08 Summer Classic main-event was absolutely fantastic. That it established the blueprint for how best to utilize the modernized, taller version of the Cell adds another accolade to a long list and that it so thoroughly concluded their rivalry – with Taker cycling back through all of The Rated R Superstar's transgressions from the prior 18 months – was long-term in-ring storytelling at its finest. Even in defeat, Edge never looked more like a mega-star than he did that night in Indianapolis; anyone who ever doubted how great Edge could be has to see *Summerslam '08* as evidence of how wrong they were.

Much of the focus here has been on what it meant for The Ultimate Opportunist, but Undertaker considerably benefited as well. Though his two greatest rivalries are still to-be-discussed, the feud with Edge was his chance to be a more traditional, emotionally-investing hero. As amazing as he was for twenty-five years, the only time that The Deadman ever got to be the top babyface overcoming the dastardly, maniacal plans of the top heel was on Smackdown in 2007-2008; in all other instances, Taker was an Andre-like special attraction. Between May 2007 and August 2008, The Phenom was Batman and Edge was The Joker.

Though it may not carry the same historical weight as some of its peers featuring bigger names, it was the magnum opus of one of WWE's most historically underrated all-time great stars. And, as if there were not enough honors already bestowed upon it, let us close the discussion on Edge vs. Undertaker with this weighty fact: as of 2017, they were the only one-on-one match to be featured in the WrestleMania main-event and the Summerslam main-event.

#20
John Cena vs. CM Punk
WWE Championship
Money in the Bank to Summerslam 2011;
Summerslam to Night of Champions 2012;
Monday Night Raw February 25, 2013

Match of the Year in 2011 / Top 10 Match in 2012 / Top 5 Match in 2013

The end of the 2000s was a tumultuous time for the professional wrestling business. TNA was beginning its downward spiral, Ring of Honor (ROH) was struggling to advance its cause, New Japan Pro Wrestling was just starting to overcome its dark times of the early 2000s; so many promotions across the globe, including in Europe and in Mexico, were faced with the reality that WWE would forever be the undisputed king from that point forward and that achieving any scenario comparable to what happened with WCW in the 1990s was virtually impossible.

Even the king was struggling to a degree. Sure, WWE was still making a lot of money as the worldwide leader in sports entertainment, but the creative moxy that largely built its empire had stalled. From after the Attitude Era ended through the beginning of the next decade, ratings steadily declined, pay-per-view prices skyrocketed to accommodate for a lot fewer buyers, and interest in the product just was not there like it used to be. John Cena and the OVW Class of '02 were unquestionably successful in the back half of the decade, as were a few others, but WWE's talent recruitment strategy had found way too many dull rocks and not enough gems, and the pool of truly elite talent was drying up (or so it seemed).

Paul Heyman had stumbled upon a diamond in the rough named CM Punk before getting fired in 2006; however, the so-named Straight Edge Superstar looked radically different than the prototypical "sports entertainer" and had, in ROH, made his name initially as one of the top guys to emerge from the post-WCW independent wrestling scene, which WWE made very clear during John Cena's era was not its priority. WWE basically said, "it's prototypical new star or bust," and it felt strongly about its developmental process being capable of creating stars on its own without needing any help from the wrestlers performing in bingo halls and armories; there was an apparent lack of respect by WWE higher-ups for the independents.

CM Punk quietly fought the system from his WWE hiring in 2005 through 2010, building his reputation as more than just "The King of the Indies," as he had jeeringly been nicknamed backstage, and becoming a key second-tier player for the company after the mass exodus of Hall of Fame talent to retirement or part-time status from April-to-April in 2010 and 2011. However, by June of 2011, he felt that there was nobody in the entire business that was a better pro wrestler than him and his pride could not tolerate being overlooked again.

Meanwhile, the fans that had grown up with WWE as one of their pastimes during the WrestleMania Era were still around, were still stimulating discussion about WWE across the internet, and were just waiting for WWE to accept that the industry had transitioned and that it was time to embrace what the post-Monday Night War top prospect had become; it had become CM Punk, a maverick and a creative savant who simply connected with *wrestling* fans even though he lacked the look or pedigree of a conventional WWE star. The diehard audience had grown impatient, desperate to be treated as a group to be cultivated by WWE instead of shunned in favor of the almighty casual viewer, and they accordingly felt under-served and underappreciated, just like CM Punk. Cliché as the following statement may be, it is undeniably true: these fans had a voice, but they felt voiceless...

Punk's contract was set to expire in July 2011 and he had every intention of leaving and not coming back. In an attempt to get him to re-sign, WWE booked him in a title match against Cena at *Money in the Bank*, which just so happened to take place in

Punk's hometown of Chicago, Illinois. To build the match, Punk was given a rare opportunity for a modern WWE star: to air his grievances to the world. "I hate this idea that you're the best," he began the closing segment of the June 27th edition of Raw, addressing Cena. "You're not the best, *I'm* the best; I'm the best in the world." By the time that WWE officials had cut his microphone following personal insults about the McMahon family, Punk had dropped the infamous "Pipe Bomb" and sparked the next phase of WWE's evolution. Not only did his words, like a flame for moths, resonate on a deep, visceral level with the increasingly jaded diehard fanbase, but every major news outlet, it seemed, was talking about CM Punk; even sports personalities who abhorred pro wrestling were bringing him up. The attention that he brought to WWE and the manner in which he went about bringing it was perception-altering for wrestlers like him.

The Second City Saint, over the next two-and-a-half years, would go onto shape so much of how the modern WWE product functions. He was his era's "Macho Man" Randy Savage, a trailblazer who left such an immense impression on the audience and on the business, and his rivalry with John Cena was always the perfect on-screen manifestation of his plight and his desire for change. Cena had come to represent everything that diehard fans wanted to change about WWE and it was almost as if their revolt against WWE's chosen, Cena-led direction for all of those years manifested itself as CM Punk. They wrestled epic matches together, did Cena and Punk, fitting of a mammoth clash of ideologies, both completely righteous to their respective causes; and it was so very emotionally engaging to watch, with *Money in the Bank 2011* perhaps the most immersive viewing experience in WWE lore for the roughly quarter-million people who watched it on pay-per-view and the 15,000 who saw it live in Chicago.

It was the most important feud of Punk's career and one of the most important feuds of Cena's career. Through it, Punk became an irreplaceable legend and, as The Voice of the Voiceless, infused WWE with so much energy and enthusiasm; and *that*, for more than any other reason, is why fans still chanted his name at WWE shows four years after he abruptly quit the company in January 2014. For Cena, only Edge and The Rock were as influential to his gigantic success as Punk, who pushed Cena in the ring harder than anyone else; it is generally regarded in critical circles that there is a pre-and-post Punk period to Cena's performance level between the ropes and that the post-Punk period helped round Cena into one of the inarguable greatest of all-time by any metric.

Be it at *Money in the Bank*, *Summerslam*, *Night of Champions*, or Monday Night Raw, their one-on-one matches caught lightning in a bottle that cannot be readily recaptured on replay, ever-increasingly removed from the emotional connection to them in the moment. The Punk vs. Cena legacy stems from what their matches best represented: the change that the diehard fans wanted and that WWE itself, as the industry leader, needed.

#19
The Rock vs. Hollywood Hulk Hogan
WrestleMania X-8
March 17, 2002

Top 15 All-Time at WrestleMania / Top 5 Match in 2002

The *WrestleMania X-8* introduction video, set to a brilliant composition by Steve Jablonsky called "Trailblazing," featured the various wrestlers on the card describing the aura of "The Show of Shows." The Rock's account might have stated it best as, "That x-factor, that intangible I can't explain; you just have to feel it." Take the magic associated with the World Cup or Game 7 of the NBA Finals or the Super Bowl, mix it with the exuberance that the Star Wars franchise brings with each new release and you get an adequate interpretation of the grandest stage x-factor. At its best, there is nothing like WrestleMania.

If there has been one match that captured the essence of what sets WrestleMania apart from every other sports entertainment event in history – one which packed that indescribable feeling that fans young and old alike get throughout the winter leading up to and through the day of "The Granddaddy Of Them All" - it was The Rock vs. Hulk Hogan.

"You talk about headlining, main-eventing, WrestleMania after WrestleMania after WrestleMania. Well, Hulk Hogan, The Rock says, 'How do you feel about headlining one more WrestleMania with The Rock!?'" It was one of those rare occasions that turned grown men into giddy little kids again, calling other grown men to tell them to drop whatever they were doing so that they could tune into the show and experience a characterization of electricity. From the second that The Great One's music hit on Monday Night Raw – interrupting Hogan four weeks prior to *WrestleMania X-8* to lay down the iconic challenge – through the match itself, the wrestling world stood in awe.

Theirs was the quintessential definition of a dream match because it was the least likely of any that have ever qualified for that extremely extraordinary category to actually happen. Hogan was thought to have spent his twilight years in WCW, sparking the second wrestling boom as part of the competition against Vince McMahon and Co. Given his participation in the steroid trial of his former boss and his role in helping Ted Turner put McMahon on the ropes, surely there was no way he would ever be allowed back into the WWE family. Yet, there he was, once again standing on the stage that he unquestionably built. The atmosphere produced by the Icon vs. Icon showdown at Sky Dome in Toronto was its own unique brand of amazing. 68,237 people responded with "Top 5 best crowds of all-time"-level enthusiasm.

Critics have often uttered the ridiculously annoying sentiment, "If you turn the sound off, then the match is terrible." Well, that is asinine. Why would you turn the sound off? That is like saying, "The match isn't very good if you cover half the screen." The audience participation was, indeed, a huge part of what made the match so successful, but you cannot watch wrestling in a bubble; the entire presentation has to be taken into account to properly appreciate it.

For the two of them personally, there was a lot of motivation to deliver a performance that nobody would ever forget. Hogan, 49 years old at the time, received a new lease on his career by returning to WWE. The WCW experience was both highly lucrative and tumultuous for him, and many felt that his reputation was tarnished by going down with the Titanic, so to speak; he wanted to validate the investment made in his comeback by McMahon with a match that lived up to nearly unprecedented hype. Just as importantly, he needed to prove to himself that he was up to the task of going toe-to-toe with the industry's top new star. For The Rock, meanwhile, the legendary encounter with Hogan was, for a goal-oriented person like him who had already done everything that there was to do in professional wrestling, a huge challenge creatively and a chance to do something that none of his historic peers in the conversation for the greatest of all-time had ever accomplished. Never before and perhaps only one time since had there ever been a match quite like it, and that it worked so well was testament to The Rock for seeing things that were possible in business that others (like Austin) could not see.

The success of the match was paramount to both men and what they achieved that night has become a substantial part of their respective legacies, as etched into WWE's core mythology as any other single performance.

Rock-Hogan produced many a great sequence of events within their 16-minute run-time, but the most memorable might well have been the first classic Hogan comeback on the WrestleMania stage in nine years, the release of pure, childlike joy that it evoked, and the astonishment of Rock's ensuing counter-comeback that stopped Hulkamania from running any wilder. Sentimentality was pumping through the life-force of not just every person who had ever called themselves a "Hulkamaniac," but of everyone who ever saw Hogan in the red and yellow standing up to all walks of evil. That "Hulk Up" and then the big boot and then the leg drop took all the material that had sewn the fabric of the pro wrestling industry as we had come to know it since 1984 – Hulkamania's birth, *WrestleMania 1*, Hogan slamming Andre, The Mega Powers Exploding, The Ultimate Challenge, the steroid trial, Hogan signing with WCW, the formation of The New World Order, the Monday Night War, and the Attitude Era – and combined it with historically unmatched nostalgic resonance to create a recipe for a giant, collective release of emotion...and then The Rock kicked out! It was one of the greatest false finishes of the WrestleMania Era. To this day, it is difficult not to get swept up in the whole thing when replaying it.

Given the incredible drama of the match itself, it can sometimes be lost in the shuffle that the post-match happenings were significantly affective in their own right. The mutual show of respect between them, Hall and Nash turning on Hogan, Rock making the save, and finally the Hulkster performing his three vintage bodybuilding poses while The Great One stood in the corner grinning from ear-to-ear, mirroring the expressions of so many fans watching around the world...they were the icing on an unforgettable cake.

WWE has arguably been chasing after similar magic ever since, to find the next, as Jim Ross called it as the two trailblazers approached one another before the opening bell and the flashbulbs made the background look like a dark sky full of fireflies, "WrestleMania Moment." Financially, there have been a few bigger drawing matches than Hogan vs. Rock turned out to be, but none ever *felt* bigger. Hogan vs. Andre was the only one that came close, yet even it was unable to facilitate quite the caliber of moment in which "time stood still," as JR also appropriately expressed. Quite frankly, there has never been another Rock vs. Hogan...and there probably never will be.

#18
Shawn Michaels vs. Triple H
Summerslam 2002 to Armageddon 2002;
Monday Night Raw December 29, 2003 to
Badd Blood 2004

Top 5 All-Time at Summerslam / Top 10 All-Time TV Match / Match of the Year in 2002 / Top 10 Match in 2003 / Match of the Year in 2004

In the WrestleMania Era, nobody's unexpected retirement to date felt more unfortunate at the time than that of Shawn Michaels. When HBK left immediately after dropping the WWF Championship to Stone Cold Steve Austin at *WrestleMania XIV*, one could have been forgiven for immediately queuing up memories of the 1995 kayfabe-retirement angle's "Tell Me A Lie" tribute produced for Michaels. "Say that you won't go" indeed; the professional wrestling world lost a superstar whose career had been peaking from '95 to '97 and who had already amassed a reputation as one of the greatest in-ring performers ever.

Taking nothing away from the surprise return in 2002 of Hogan and The N.W.O., whose own respective improbable comebacks were just as mind-blowing at the time – all were major reasons why nostalgia has become such a dominant strategy for selling wrestling fans on WWE's biggest events in the modern age – but HBK returning for a match at *Summerslam* connected on an entirely different emotional level, at least for the people who appreciated Michaels the most.

Much of the audience back then had gotten its education in sports entertainment in the 1980s when Vince McMahon unleashed Hulkamania on the world. There was a part of that audience who had stuck around after WWF's fall from grace to see Michaels emerge as one of the industry standard-bearers during The New Generation; when wrestling had ceased to be cool, the fans who never left created a new kind of diehard enthusiast, one whose love for the game was unaffected by wrestling's pop-culture status. To many of those fans, Michaels coming back was a bigger deal than Hogan or The N.W.O. showing up again. The last few months we had seen of Michaels could be best characterized by the Montreal Screwjob and its aftermath, which in many ways seemed like a cruel and sad but karmic series of events. To see him step back in the ring, with his life in order, facing Triple H? That was powerful.

Triple H had, of course, co-founded D-Generation X with Michaels just a few months prior to HBK's devastating back injury. As a leading pair flanked by Chyna and Rick Rude, they were as hot an act as Stone Cold. When Hunter was thrust into the solo spotlight the night after HBK's presumed retirement match, he thrived and, by the time Michaels got the itch to wrestle again four years later, HHH had become an all-time great in his own right during the most celebrated period in WWE lore. So, while not quite the battle of generational icons that was Hogan vs. The Rock, Michaels vs. Triple H was still one of the rare instances in history when top stars of different eras squared off on a huge stage.

Many of the fans watching in 2002 had never seen HBK perform at the highest level. Ratings for WWE were in the mid-2s and 3s and pay-per-view buys for even WrestleMania struggled to crack 300,000 during The Icon's zenith. Even when business was slumping post-Attitude, the general viewership was substantially larger, taking into account international growth, and the PPV buys for the top-tier events were double and triple what they had been in the mid-1990s. For fans who had seen The Showstopper earn his nicknames and for those just excited to see The Game fight "that guy who he started DX with" alike, everyone was in for a treat on August 25, 2002.

What an amazing match it turned out to be. With all due respect to Hogan vs. Rock, the story told during the Unsanctioned Street Fight between HBK and HHH was just in a league of its own. Especially marvelous was how well Michaels sold his injury history; from the moment that Hunter had kicked him in the gut during a teased reunion of the original DX, signifying that Michaels was going to wrestle one more time, HBK was hounded by two major questions that he would be forced to answer come bell time: 1- Could his back hold up? and 2- Would he be able to recreate his legendary big-match magic? The first question should have been easy to answer, but Michaels was so convincing that it was actually easier to get wrapped up in the fiction than assume that all of the hard-hitting action meant his health was very much intact. Right after the initial Triple H assault on HBK's back, Earl Hebner asked The Icon, "What do you say?" In other words, he wanted to know if Michaels was going to stop – if he was going to give up. In a gripping moment of character acting, HBK did not just say, "No." He stated, "No. *I can't!*"

Both questions were resoundingly answered by nearly a half-hour of breathtaking work. Kudos to Jim Ross and Jerry Lawler for their excellent commentary and kudos to The Game and The Showstopper for a match that holds up as one of the six or seven that will always come to mind when conversing about the most glorious moments of WWE's second biggest event (it ranked third on this book's list for Summerslam and it was the primary stimulus for HBK vs. HHH's Top 20 all-time ranking).

Triple H went on to dominate the product for three years, while Michaels began a new chapter in his career. HBK became The Game's top rival during that period in between Attitude and Cena's ascent, with the pair wrestling each other three other times in one-on-one PPV headliners – a Three Stages of Hell Match, a Last Man Standing Match, and the longest Hell in a Cell Match in history – as well as in the climax of the inaugural Elimination Chamber Match and the pair of Triple Threats (with Benoit) that main-evented both *WrestleMania XX* and *Backlash 2004*. Their chemistry was always undeniable, even if those other one-on-one PPV matches may not have been able to live up to the standard set by their Street Fight.

They did, however, wrestle a fantastic World Heavyweight Championship bout on the final Raw of 2003 that without question lived up to the reputation established at *Summerslam '02*. Michaels was coming off the match that more or less brought him all the way back to being The Showstopper (at *Survivor Series '03*) and his hometown title shot roughly a month later provided the platform for HBK to continue his momentum with arguably the greatest match in the history of WWE's flagship television show. Featuring sublimely fluid action not seen from them in their past, heavily-gimmicked one-on-one encounters, Michaels and Triple H put together a performance reminiscent of Ric Flair vs. Ricky Steamboat in 1989. Given The Game's modern take on The Nature Boy from 2002-2005, it would be fair to state that Hunter's match with HBK was easily his best Naitch impersonation, right on down to the Dusty Finish.

Had they brought out the best in each other in every outing, we would be talking about HHH vs. HBK as one of the Top 10 rivalries ever almost without question. That they achieved Top 20 status is testament to the fact that, when they did bring out the best in each other, few pairings were ever better.

#17
Triple H vs. The Rock
Intercontinental Championship and WWF Championship
Over the Edge to Summerslam 1998; WrestleMania 2000 to Summerslam 2000

Top 5 All-Time at Summerslam / Top 10 All-Time Ladder Match / Top 5 Match in 2000 / Match of the Year in 1998

"Your greatest competition comes from
guys that are trying to strive to be
the best at whatever they do"

There have been rivalries that produced better matches but, make no mistake, there arguably has never been a greater professional rivalry in sports entertainment history than Triple H vs. The Rock. Debuting in 1995 and 1996, respectively, they began to find themselves as characters in 1997 and, by the summer of 1998, were fast approaching Austin-levels of success as leaders of opposing factions integral to turning the tide against WCW in the Monday Night War. In 1999 and 2000, Stone Cold was their only peer in the business. They blossomed into all-time great superstars and took the industry to its combined critical and financial peak.

For The Rock and Triple H, opportunity was attacked in professional wrestling like a shark does blood in the water, and the first time that opportunity knocked loudly for them both was the night after *WrestleMania XIV*. That particular Monday Night Raw on March 30, 1998 was the coronation of the Austin Era, but it tripled as the night that The Rock, in the midst of one of the longest Intercontinental Championship runs of the last 25 years, became The Nation of Domination's alpha male and that Triple H, with D-Generation X's future in doubt, formed an "Army" with X-Pac, Chyna, and The New Age Outlaws and pushed DX to even greater levels of popularity than it had reached with HBK at the helm.

Culminating in an all-time classic Ladder Match at *Summerslam '98*, the feud between DX and The Nation helped define the late 1990s WWF comeback in the "War" with WCW. The factions exemplified the Attitude Era and its tremendous, edgy television that showcased stars driven to succeed like few that the business had or would ever see. For DX, in particular, the April to August stretch in 1998 produced over half of their most memorable moments, consisting largely of phenomenal segments such as their literal (and groundbreaking) invasion of WCW and their hilarious impersonation of The Nation.

By the time that "The Highway to Hell" had ended at Madison Square Garden on August 30th, The Rock was the best heel in the business not named Vince McMahon and could not get five steps beyond the curtain without getting rained down upon with "Rocky Sucks" chants; Triple H, meanwhile, had fully transitioned from sidekick to budding mega-star as the president of pro wrestling's favorite fraternity. The stage was set, the Intercontinental Championship was hung high above the ring, and the two young studs embraced the pressure that came with being on the marquee at the second biggest show of 1998 to deliver the Match of the Year. Their Ladder Match to this day stands out as unique to the rest of its genre. "We changed the perception of that match to be more of a brawl," Triple H aptly described the shift in presentation. It was a fantastic battle between two guys that wanted so badly to be the best.

Summerslam '98 brought them each to the brink of the main-event, but it was The Rock who, later that year, got to the top first, winning the WWF Championship at *Survivor Series*, having the awesome rivalry with Mick Foley, and main-eventing *WrestleMania XV*. On the same night that Rock battled Austin for the first of three meetings on the grandest stage, Triple H turned heel on DX in a move that disappointed and frustrated his fellow DX members and the fans, but that also catapulted him back to

Rock's level. "[DX] all came to me individually...like why are you doing this, man," Hunter recalled in his WWE documentary. "It's not the time to do this. Let's ride this wave [they said]. No [I replied], the time is now for me."

It has been said before that changing character allegiance (from good to bad or vice versa) ideally happens when the persona is already connecting really well with the audience. As The Rock's status as the primary antagonist was being questioned due to the overwhelming support he was starting to garner with the same crowds that had once hated him, Triple H saw an opportunity to take the lead heel role, did not waste the chance, and was challenging Rock and Austin for WWF supremacy by the turn of the century.

A July 1999 sit-down interview with Jim Ross proved pivotal to Triple H's main-event career and memorably segued into his first WWF Title win on the night after *Summerslam*, but it was his unlikely on-air association with Stephanie McMahon that truly sparked his quest to become "the most hated guy that there's ever been in the business." For television, that Hunter drugged Stephanie at her bachelorette party, secretly married her in Las Vegas, and revealed the scandal to the world during her wedding on Raw was one of the most reprehensible acts ever performed by a pro wrestling character. When life imitated art and they started the relationship that ultimately led to their real life nuptials, Triple H became a villain behind the scenes as well; to some, he would forever and always, like baseball players who use steroids, be condemned in sports entertainment as a pariah for supposedly marrying into success.

Triple H describes being a top guy in WWE like having a gun put to your head and giving all of your peers the bullets, and the fact of the matter was that, in 1999 and 2000...well, you know the two words that he had for anyone who thought that they could assassinate his professional or personal goals. As the pressure mounted from both his newly earned spot and his burgeoning romance with Stephanie, he charged forward with complete conviction.

Though The Rock had a breakout year in 2000 as a mainstream media darling and as the top babyface in a traditionally hero-driven enterprise, it was Triple H who ruled the WWF television product as the focal point of the biggest storylines of the year. It can be contended, then, that Triple H as the top heel was the #1 overall star, as reflected in Hunter's sterling record against Rock in pay-per-view matches for the WWF Championship, including his victory over Rock (in a Fatal Four-Way) to notably become the first heel to leave WrestleMania as World Champion.

It seems odd in hindsight that none of their stellar one-on-one encounters (like their *Judgment Day '00* Ironman Match) main-evented a Big Four PPV. Nevertheless, the magic conjured by their series of WWF Title bouts had a palpable effect on the entire company. Monday Night Raw ratings held steady without Austin, the PPV buyrate average in 2000 reset the 1999 record, and Smackdown was firmly established as a major success. Stone Cold is often given credit for professional wrestling's peak. However, Austin was not the guy who was on top when wrestling hit its apex in 2000; that honor belongs to The Rock, the media wunderkind who became the public face of the WWF, and Triple H, who had one of the greatest years ever recorded by a wrestler.

They continue to push each other to this day, with Rock having become one of the biggest movie stars in the world and Triple H (along with Stephanie) the heir to Vince McMahon's WWE empire.

#16
Kurt Angle vs. Shawn Michaels
WrestleMania 21 and Vengeance 2005

Top 10 All-Time at WrestleMania / Match of the Year in 2005

Shawn Michaels, in his physical prime, redefined the athleticism expected of the main-event level wrestler by taking what Ric Flair had done in the 1980s to the next highest degree. He is rightfully regarded as the most accomplished in-ring performer of the WrestleMania Era on account of both his combination of innovation, pace, and wrestling IQ and his unparalleled body of work. As such, HBK has well-earned his reputation as the performer that every wrestler for the foreseeable future will aspire to be like and eventually surpass.

What makes his 2005 rivalry – and particularly his match at *WrestleMania 21* – with Kurt Angle fascinating is that, at his peak, Our Olympic Hero legitimately had a shot at supplanting Michaels atop the pantheon of all-time great in-ring performers. Angle further redefined main-event level athleticism in the early 2000s, taking what HBK had done in the 1990s to an even higher degree, and it would be historically irresponsible not to point out that Angle was well on his way to producing a comparable body of work as The Showstopper when his body started to fail him.

Recall the build-up to his *WrestleMania XI* semi-main-event with Diesel, when Michaels said at a press conference, "I will give you a show like you have never seen before. Why? Because I can." That statement characterized his entire career, but especially his WrestleMania career. He played a constant game of "Try and outperform me if you dare" with his peers. Well, Angle dared, but when he was rounding into a form that could have realistically overtaken Michaels circa *WrestleMania XIX*, he infamously re-injured his neck.

Most wrestlers have about a two-three year prime in which they put it all together and reach their zenith as superstars, from the tip-top form of their characters to their corresponding opportunities to maximize their in-ring achievements on the grandest stages – think Savage '87-'89, Hart '92-'94, Austin '98-'99/'01, HHH '00-'02, Punk '11-'13, etc. Everything after that is, overall, just legacy building essentially. Angle, like Michaels did from '95-'97, was fortunate to hit his similar career crescendo from '01-'03, but instead of an additional eight years to enhance his historical reputation like Michaels got after his return in 2002 (including eight straight WrestleManias), Angle's final injury-plagued years created a cascade of events that ushered him out of WWE, the backlash of which blackballed any possible return until his career was basically over.

God bless Angle, he gutted through his nagging (friekin') neck problems for a few years and unrelentingly pursued becoming the industry standard-bearer, but he also had The Showstopper back in the fold arguably stealing the show from him in his first and only WrestleMania main-event, which the gold medalist wrestled risking paralysis, and also at the next year's 'Mania when Angle's purist fantasy come to life against Eddie Guerrero for the WWE Title was again hindered by his neck and overshadowed by the main-event featuring Michaels in the greatest Triple Threat Match ever.

By 2005, as Michaels was continuing his miraculous career renaissance, it had become fairly clear that Angle's neck had robbed him of the chance to reach his true ceiling and that he would never quite be the same again. However, an opportunity to wrestle Michaels in a dream match at WrestleMania offered Angle a platform to showcase that, even if but on a special occasion, he could still tap deep within himself and find just enough to remind the world of how good he was at his best.

Angle was the story of their match at *WrestleMania 21*, both throughout the hype and in the execution on the night of. Indeed, HBK coined the nickname "Mr. WrestleMania" in the lead up to the Staples Center-hosted "Granddaddy" and, indeed, he lived up to the moniker while delivering a trademark presentation of guile and guts in Los Angeles, complete with one of the most dramatic pre-tap out renditions ever seen in sports entertainment during the bout's climax. However, their rivalry was Angle's extended moment in the sun during what proved to be the twilight of his WWE tenure; the match that he had with Undertaker in February 2006 was his parting shot to the library of classics that he had amassed on the 20'x20' canvas of the world's preeminent pro wrestling empire, but his storytelling opposite HBK from *Survivor Series '04* – when Angle first hinted at their upcoming match – off-and-on until their *Raw Homecoming* rubber match a year later was the final example of the overall package that made him a prodigious future Hall of Famer.

Relishing the task at hand to pen the details of an emotional confrontation between legends, Angle was fully in his element. Nobody in WWE lore has been able to better master the combination of comedic timing and intensity, character acting skills that set him apart from each of his Top 15 all-time peers with the exception of one Dwayne "The Rock" Johnson. He offered a PhD level course on the subject in response to, as he would tell it early on in the build-up, the disrespect he had felt since back in 1996 when, to some, Angle's gold medal paled in comparison to HBK gliding down from the rafters, beating Bret in the Ironman Match, and fulfilling his boyhood dream. Angle plucked major plot points from HBK's career timeline and recreated them to show Michaels how there was nothing he ever did that Angle himself could not equal (and Michaels would never be able to replicate Angle's gold medal; Oh, It's True!) Among other things, Our Olympic Hero made a remix of Shawn's "Sexy Boy" theme song and even brought Sherri Martel back to sing it with him – the memorable "Sexy Kurt" segment that had us laughing out loud. He later had an intense TV match with Marty Jannetty that tore the house down.

Substitute a couple more of the standard, safer post-neck re-injury spots in place of Angle's highest risks in the match at *WrestleMania 21* and it would have been regarded as a classic regardless, but Angle held nothing back against Michaels and turned back the clock to his 2002 zenith, connecting with a top rope Angle Slam and executing his gorgeous moonsault to push their match to a level that kept elevating the drama ever further. Bobby Heenan told Michaels afterward, "That was the best match I've ever seen." As has been referenced in The Doctor's Orders on LOP for years, "I dreamed about how their match would look, and they went out and had that exact match."

Michaels was brilliant, harkening back to the glory days of his flamboyant persona that originally made him The Icon with his brash antagonism of Angle before settling into the "scrappy legend who wanted it more than everyone else" routine, reminiscent of Jordan's last-legs efforts with the Bulls, that he used so well until retirement.

What does it say that such a hit from the HBK collection played second fiddle to his opponent's performance? Angle was sublime. There was a relentless desperation to his portrayal that night, fueled as it may have been by a burning desire to be "the best in the business," a phrase he used to describe himself while going back up the entrance ramp after tapping Michaels out to end a 27-minute masterpiece. He had won an Olympic gold medal, the ultimate achievement in freestyle wrestling. When he joined the professional ranks, he set his sights on becoming the best ever, but injury and HBK stood in his way. On that night, though, he pushed all the way through his chronic ailments and bested Mr. WrestleMania at WrestleMania in every important way.

Angle and HBK went on to have a pair of acclaimed rematches, one at *Vengeance '05* that some have called even better than their WrestleMania classic and the other an Ironman Match in October '05 that Samuel 'Plan listed in a particularly noteworthy position in *101*. All three matches – like his match with Taker at

No Way Out '06 – highlighted the banged up but capable place that Angle had reached with his health, a form to which Michaels could relate and from which HBK learned to pick and choose his spots. It makes you wonder how Angle's career might look like if WWE's Wellness Policy (which better protects the talents from themselves) had been developed a few years earlier or if WWE had adopted its penchant for utilizing part-time stars (in legacy-building mode) at the year's biggest shows just a half decade sooner. Make no mistake about it, Angle was just as good as HBK. With more time to get healthier, just a couple of better breaks, and a lighter, top-heavy schedule, he likely would have been able to keep the "versus HBK and Taker" quality going for at least another few years; then, it would not have been so easy to put Michaels atop the performance pedestal.

#15
Kurt Angle vs. Chris Benoit
WrestleMania X-Seven to Monday Night Raw June 11, 2001; Unforgiven 2002 to Royal Rumble 2003

Top 10 All-Time Cage Match / Top 5 All-Time at Royal Rumble / Top 15 Match in 2001 / Top 10 Match in 2002 / Match of the Year in 2003

Technical wrestling, a combination of chain grappling and submission-based work, is a style that very few have mastered; when executed at its peak, it can be the catalyst for a brilliant athletic chess match. Chris Benoit is widely considered the greatest technical wrestler of the WrestleMania Era, with perhaps only Olympic Greco-Roman champion Kurt Angle in his league. It should not be surprising, then, that the greatest technical wrestling matches of all-time were produced during the incredible rivalry between Benoit and Angle.

Their series began at *WrestleMania X-Seven* with a very unique match. The chain wrestling done at the beginning was very different from even the best previous examples, with a heavy focus on the amateur style. Benoit had come from the famed Hart Dungeon and he was arguably the best wrestler to graduate, perhaps even better than Bret; Angle being a gold medalist, it was engaging to see someone able to keep up with him. The first half of the bout was dedicated to establishing how badly they wanted to submit each other for the win instead of earning a pinfall, whereas the second half integrated more of the traditional modern pro wrestling approach. "The *wrestling* that we did, [while keeping] the people captivated at the same time, [that's] very difficult," Benoit pointed out in his WWE-produced documentary.

It ended up being a proving ground for both of them, as Benoit continued to show that he could be a major player for WWE while Angle displayed further that he was rounding into rare form. The match has generally been celebrated for being such a perfect complimentary performance on a popular choice for greatest WrestleMania of all-time.

Backlash '01 offered an even more unique match between them. Angle said in a 2015 interview about Benoit, "The chemistry I had with him – because I could actually amateur wrestle and Chris was able to counter – I never had anybody match [me] except for Chris." In a scenario that they likely could have only pulled off together, they wrestled a 30-Man Ironman Match where the only way to earn falls was via tap out. Dubbed, "The Ultimate Submission Match," it featured a similar but better dynamic as the normal Ironman, the psychology much more logically demanding an acknowledgment early on that falls in situations that would not have typically involved falls was a given considering that submissions inherently suggest the strong possibility of injury and that the match was a half-hour long guaranteed; it later progressed around the mid-way point, using the first four falls which put Angle ahead 3-1, to set-up the themes for the last half of Angle desperately clinging to his lead and Benoit attempting to come from behind. Ending up tied at 3-3 when the clock ran out, forcing overtime, seemed a subtle nod to HBK-Bret in '96.

The saga continued into the following month when, at *Judgment Day*, they competed in a Three Stages of Hell Match. Out of all of their famous wrestling bouts, it was probably their weakest effort, but even an at times awkward performance with faulty match dynamics between Benoit and Angle is better than 90% of anything else you will see. The first fall could only be won by pin, the second only by submission, and the predictable third fall was a Ladder Match. Though the Ladder Match was an opportunity for them to showcase a different style against each other, it was not the right gimmick for their pairing. Three weeks later, however, they were involved in a Cage Match that main-evented the June 11, 2001 Monday Night Raw and proved a better platform for them to change up the format from the pure wrestling matches for which their rivalry became famous.

Because of three body-punishing moves that undoubtedly contributed to their future neck surgeries, a conversation about Angle vs. Benoit rarely gets too far along without someone bringing up the Cage Match. It has endured as one of the most memorable matches in Raw history and sits in the pantheon of the Cage Match genre as well. Just one of the big spots would have indelibly stood out and potentially kept the hard-hitting affair in the discussion among the greats, but to have performed three of the most awe-inspiring spots off of a steel cage ever – a German Suplex off the middle of the top rope, Angle's moonsault from the top of the cage, and Benoit's diving headbutt from the top of the cage – within the span of just eight minutes? That makes it incomparable.

Two of the stunts proved too much for Benoit's neck to handle and he was under the knife for a cervical fusion surgery within a month of the Cage Match. When he came back from injury in the summer of 2002, Angle had basically become the best wrestler in the world. In Benoit's absence, Angle went through the final phases of his development into the can't-miss, all-time great who was WWE's MVP from the summer of 2001 until he too went under the knife for neck surgery shortly after *WrestleMania XIX*. Our Olympic Hero re-engaged Benoit when The Rabid Wolverine was traded to Smackdown in July and a series of classic matches ensued that, with all due respect to their previous efforts, were simply on a different level in regards to timing and execution. At *Unforgiven '02*, they painted the first of their two masterpieces, a brilliant 14-minute mat clinic with an unforgettable climax featuring counters to the Ankle Lock and Crossface that just made you nod your head in appreciation and shake it moments later in veneration.

Angle was like an NBA player making his "third year leap" in 2002, taking the things that he had already shown he could do well enough to be near-universally praised as "very good" and finding a way to elevate himself to that rarefied air where only the best of the best in history can breathe. "The guy can get on the mat and go faster, harder, and better than just about anyone," Benoit once said. He was the perfect opponent with whom Benoit could remind the WWE brass how important he too could be to the promotion.

Benoit and Angle were the anchors of one of wrestling lore's most underappreciated periods – the Paul Heyman-led "Smackdown Six" era – so it was fitting that the WWE Championship was at stake in their all-time great match at *Royal Rumble '03*. In all of their previous one-on-one matches on PPV, a championship had never been on the line; and their near-unparalleled rivalry brought them all the way to the match to determine who would main-event *WrestleMania XIX*. Hailed immediately as a classic for the ages, Angle vs. Benoit was one of those rare moments in time when every wrestling fan in the world would have bet their house that the champion, Angle, would retain so he could go onto his long-rumored showdown with fellow amateur extraordinaire, Brock Lesnar, but damned if they did not have even the most experienced analysts jumping out of their seats thinking that the challenger was really going to win in a surprise reversal of fates. Regarding the match, Angle noted in the 2015 interview, "You're not going to get a match any better than that, even my match with Shawn."

Benoit famously received a standing ovation from the Boston crowd after tapping out. For what they achieved both on that night and in all of their other great matches, they both deserved one frankly. Oh it's true! It's *damn* true!

#14

Edge and Christian vs. The Dudley Boyz vs. The Hardy Boyz
The TLC Era
No Mercy 1999 through WrestleMania X-Seven

Three Top 5 All-Time Ladder Matches / Top 15 All-Time at WrestleMania / Top 5 All-Time at Summerslam / Top 5 Match in 1999 / Three Top 10 Matches in 2000 / Top 5 Match in 2001

Can you imagine the world without cell phones? In the early-to-mid-1990s, there were a few of them and they were unquestionably innovative, but it was not until the late 1990s and early 2000s that their use became so inherent to our everyday lives. Similarly, the Ladder Match has become intrinsic to the WWE product. It was innovated in the early 1990s and utilized sparingly thereafter, but on October 17, 1999 at *No Mercy*, Edge and Christian faced The Hardy Boyz (then as The New Brood) in the first Tag Team Ladder Match and, from that point forward, the Ladder Match became such a frequently utilized gimmick that one might struggle to imagine WWE without it.

In the initial phase of its history, the Ladder Match was more of a plot device for high profile feuds involving bonafide stars. The success of HBK vs. Razor and Rock vs. Triple H, in particular, proved the ingenuity in using a ladder to enhance a rivalry. Yet, the explosion in the Ladder Match's popularity came as a result of the approach that Edge, Christian, and the Hardys took to it: visually assaulting the senses.

"They were re-defining what a match could be," Mick Foley once said; therein lies the key to fully appreciating what those four young studs accomplished. Pro wrestling will always base most of its top storylines on more traditional in-ring storytelling and sometimes a ladder might even be involved, but the Tag Team

338

Ladder Match at *No Mercy '99* offered a new way to become a superstar. The point of it was not to tell a tremendous story, but to get noticed; and noticed E&C and the Hardys most certainly got. They came to the ring and got marginal reactions, woke up the crowd with their innovative content, had members of the audience bowing to them by the climax, and received a standing ovation after the match.

As a result, they sparked the most dangerous game of one-upmanship in wrestling history. Chris Jericho described them as "Four guys who put their lives on the line – literally." He was right, but neither Y2J nor the rest of us had seen anything yet.

By the end of the inaugural WWF Tables Match at *Royal Rumble 2000*, the offense utilized three months prior had been made to look basic. The Dudley Boyz added a more violent element to the formula developed by the Hardys, Edge, and Christian. In the Hardys, Bubba Ray and D-Von found kindred spirits in the hardcore grappling arts. As a result, the very first Tables Match remains the very best WWE Tables match ever; the intricacy of the spots and the commitment to the performance has never been greater in such an environment. It was also where the use of tables, ladders, and chairs were first combined.

Much has been said about the resultant TLC series spawned by the success of the Tag Team Ladder and Tables matches. The Triangle Ladder Match, the first official Tables, Ladders, and Chairs Match, and TLC 2 cast a long shadow that no combination of wrestlers may ever be able to step beyond. The enduring legacy of the TLC Six may well be that they set the bar impossibly high; you can take to the bank that one of those three matches will *always* be the greatest of its Ladder Match style. Cesaro put it best when he said, speaking about TLC 2, "I think it's almost unfair to compare other matches to it because it's just one of those matches done at the right time at the right point in the right place." You could say that about any of them.

Neither Edge, Christian, Bubba Ray, D-Von, Matt, nor Jeff could ever nor will ever escape the TLC shadow either. Edge brought TLC to WWE's main-event scene. Jeff's last WWE PPV until 2017, *Summerslam '09*, concluded with him losing a TLC Match; he returned in a Tag Team Ladder Match. Christian won the World Heavyweight Championship in a Ladder Match. All three became multi-time World Champions. All six are legends and all six will feel the effects of TLC for the rest of their lives; too many holes were punched in their bump cards. We are unlikely to ever see again such stunts as the Swanton off the 20 foot ladder, the head-first front flip through a table, or the crash so hard from 25 feet that it made double stacks of tables explode. And thank God. Man, were those incredible sights, though...

The size and scope of the Ladder Match since the second TLC at *WrestleMania X-Seven* is astounding. 2005 debuted the Money in the Bank spinoff; TLC and MITB have their own theme-based pay-per-views; you would struggle to name a top flight WWE Superstar that has not competed in some variation of the Ladder Match since 2001; so many careers have been enhanced or outright made thanks to Ladder matches of the stunt-brawl variety popularized by TLC.

In 2004, WWE's roster voted the Triangle Ladder Match the second greatest match in the history of WrestleMania. Seeing it for the first time is comparable to an initial viewing of Mick Foley being thrown off and then through the top of Hell in a Cell. The images of the "tables, ladders, and broken bodies along the way," as Jim Ross described them that night, get burned into your memory. One could say it is even more impactful than Foley's falls because there were so many of them. It was so chaotic, with spot after spot creating maximum carnage.

TLC 1 at *Summerslam 2000* was even crazier; it saw Edge, Christian, the Hardys, and Dudleys speed up the pace and condense more destruction into a smaller time frame. The respect earned from fans should go without saying, but the respect earned from their peers is not as often discussed. "They were curtain sell-outs," Jerry Lawler said of the TLC matches. "The other superstars were watching through the curtains or watching on a monitor in the back."

The TLC Six were the only wrestlers ever to face each other at WrestleMania and Summerslam, and then at the following year's WrestleMania as well. At arguably the greatest wrestling event ever, TLC 2 was one of the semi-main-events. The crowd investment during the entrances was palpable, in such stark contrast to the introductions at *No Mercy '99*. The consequent pressure was incredible. They all wrestled like it was their last match and delivered yet another classic. Sitting at ringside on commentary, Jim Ross noted afterward, "My God this was amazing! What do you think about these six? Couldn't raise the bar anymore? They did it!"

After TLC 2, they really could not raise the bar anymore. Tag Team wrestling has never been the same. Neither have Ladder matches. Those three duos were the perfect combination of guts and moxie, and it took a special blend of wrestlers to achieve what they did together, collectively reaching previously unreachable heights.

#13
The Rock vs. John Cena
WrestleMania XXVIII and WrestleMania XXIX

Top 15 All-Time at WrestleMania / Match of the Year in 2012

"It's not in the stars to hold our destiny but in ourselves."

The quote by William Shakespeare, displayed to begin the hype video package preceding the first Rock vs. John Cena match at *WrestleMania XXVIII*, means that it is what we choose do in life that dictates our futures, not fate. Some magical nights in pro wrestling history seem like they are driven forward largely by destiny but, while the stars may have indeed aligned so that Rock and Cena could face each other in an epic main-event, it was not just fate that brought them together, it was work ethics without rival in the WrestleMania Era.

Cena and Rock are both two of WWE's greatest success stories. The Rock, after having accomplished so much in WWE during the company's most celebrated period, set a goal for himself to become the biggest movie star that he could be without the aid of the WWE promotional machine. Meanwhile, during Rock's absence, Cena became "The Man" in WWE, famous for his tireless efforts to be a role model, to be the face of the brand, and to expand WWE's enterprise as much as he could. Chris Jericho called him, "The ultimate WWE Superstar; the perfect example of what you want in the top guy – in the face of the promotion – as far as look, attitude, work-rate, desire, passion, and commitment." By the time Cena was shaking hands with The Great One to confirm their match for April 1, 2012 in Miami, he had already become one of the biggest icons in WWE lore, a model of modern consistency at the top of the industry rivaled in WWE only by Hulk Hogan and owner of as many WrestleMania main-events and World Title reigns as The People's Champion.

Once Rock had prospered on his own in Hollywood, he saw in Cena a chance to come back to WWE for another dream opponent with loftier visions of grandeur than ever before. "The goal," Rock said later, "was to put on the biggest match of all-time and create the biggest WrestleMania of all-time."

That Rock and Cena accomplished their goal is one of the primary reasons why their feud ranks among the Top 15 greatest ever. For three consecutive WrestleManias, Rock and Cena were the focal point feud en route to the largest trio of pay-per-view buys in professional wrestling history. *WrestleMania* in Atlanta drew 1,124,000 buys, *WrestleMania* in Miami drew 1,219,000 buys, and *WrestleMania* in New York/New Jersey drew 1,104,000 buys; the fifth, first, and fourth highest total numbers of buys of the pay-per-view era. It was the only time in history that WWE topped the one million buy mark at WrestleMania three times in a row.

In addition to being the modern benchmark for a WWE box office attraction, Rock vs. Cena was also groundbreaking in terms of its creative scope. Cena had been doing quiet business on smaller news outlets like radio shows for years prior to their initial on-screen interaction, clearly irked by what many had called Rock's somewhat elitist attitude at the 2008 WWE Hall of Fame ceremony during which he humbly inducted his father and grandfather, but at times came across like "this wrestling thing is beneath me now." He felt no qualms about calling out Rock for what he perceived to be hollow claims regarding his love for WWE.

It was three months after *WrestleMania XXVII* that the term "Reality Era" caught on thanks to the "Pipe Bomb," but it was long before that when Cena took shots at Rock on real world public forums, hoping that it might lead somewhere down the line; and it was during the build-up to the 2011 "Show of Shows" that Rock returned and verbally tore down Cena in a manner that pulled hard on the narrative threads created by WWE's most ardent supporters for several years prior. The People's Champion gave the fans on the "Cena Sucks" side of the spectrum an on-screen voice, chastising him for his Hogan-esque white-meat babyface persona, colorful merchandise primarily aimed at a younger sect of the audience, and once-edgy-but-later-silly catchphrases. Nobody had verbally dressed down Cena in quite that way before, arguably because WWE did not have another star on Cena's level with whom they might have felt comfortable allowing to do so. Cena had been heavily protected as WWE's top commodity for years, but when "Finally, The Rock [came] back home," his star power seemingly gave him free reign to launch whatever verbal barb he wanted.

Announcing the match a year in advance was also novel. After costing Cena his WWE Championship match with The Miz in Atlanta, Rock made the choice the next night on Raw to wrestle his first one-on-one match in nine years some 362 days later against Cena. Throughout the year that followed, they also made original use of social media to further their conflict. Twitter was promoted by WWE as it and similar platforms were in the infancy of their eventual massive popularity; The Rock was considered instrumental in helping WWE discover the full extent of how such media could be used to help further angles on television, as well as in aiding WWE to become a very frequent "trending" topic; to the jaded fans leery of WWE's constant promotion of social media use back then, Rock was someone who helped legitimize the outlet. In regards to the Rock-Cena match, social media allowed them to taunt each other no matter where they were in the world with millions of wrestling fans following them.

Of course, being verbally engaged by one of pro wrestling's all-time greatest talkers, Cena was put in a sink-or-swim situation. It is one thing to be passed a torch or to receive your PhD in big match performing by legendary figures of sports entertainment, but quite another to be the top guy for the better part of a decade and compete in one of the three quintessential dream matches of the WrestleMania Era opposite someone widely considered by your critics to be your vast-superior. "There's a part of John Cena, I know for a fact, that has listened to critics for years say, 'John Cena is great, John Cena is a star attraction, John

Cena is the franchise, but if he'd been here in the Attitude Era, John Cena would have been hanging out in the mid-card somewhere,'" Triple H revealed in the documentary made for USA Network about the first Rock-Cena match. The pressure was immense for both of them; the pressure was a different kind of enormous than Cena had ever previously been exposed to. He rose to the challenge and confirmed that he was every bit the superstar as The Rock.

Hip Hop icon Sean "P. Diddy" Combs introduced Machine Gun Kelly and Skylar Grey to play Cena to the ring with the song "Invincible," and was followed by Flo-Rida returning serve for The Rock with his hit tunes, "Good Feeling" and "Wild Ones." There was a sense of occasion that mirrored the billing of the match as the biggest ever. All the while, the musical performances were a study in contrast, with MGK's lyrics painting Cena as the star looking to ascend to the highest level of greatness. The Cleveland-born rapper stated after his set, "Tonight is much more than a wrestling match; tonight, millions of people around the world are tuning in to see one of the biggest egos get beat by one of the biggest underdogs. An underdog is defined as a person who participates in a fight that is not expected to win...an underdog is John Cena; an underdog 'Rises Above Hate.'" Flo-Rida's more tonally fun-natured songs reflected that The Rock, wrestling his first singles match since *Backlash '03*, was already confirmed as "The Great One."

Few instances have ever equaled the atmosphere as Rock and Cena approached each other, ready to finally tell their in-ring tale. The roar of the crowd before their first lock-up was as loud as Hogan-Andre, Warrior-Hogan, Austin-Rock, or Rock-Hogan. Great announcing calls from the past echoed through the memories of fans watching at home, Gorilla Monsoon's classic "The irresistible force meeting the immoveable object" and J.R.'s iconic, "This is a WrestleMania moment."

What followed from bell-to-bell has rarely gotten enough credit in the years since for the thoroughness of its psychology and storytelling. Cena's approach was smart, going after The Rock's mid-section, logically assuming that his opponent would gas himself from the anticipation after not having been in that situation for so long. For a thirty-plus-minute match, they picked a perfect time to transition from the early attack of Rock's ribs into teases of their respective full comeback routines, but counters at opportune moments allowed space for them to hit their finishers and it seem possible for the match to end at what proved to be shortly after its mid-point.

Later, when Cena sunset-flipped into the ring and shifted right from his pinfall position on Rock into the STF, it was believable that The Great One would tap out; Cena had put down Triple H, Shawn Michaels, and Batista with the same move on the grandest stage. Rock nearly passing out in the hold was a prime example of the match's propensity to replace the increased move-sets of the era with an old school focus on small details; that they were able to elicit such a response to Cena nearly knocking Rock unconscious was an achievement in and of itself. The People's Elbow after the STF sequence was just as strong an example of smart booking to ensure a believable near fall for Rock leading into what proved to be a shocking climax.

During the closing moments, The Rock took his incredible return performance to a level not thought likely when he came off of the top turnbuckle with a flying cross body block, but Cena spoiled the impressive feat not seen from The Great One since the Maivia days of his youth by rolling through it and countering into the Attitude Adjustment that pretty much everyone assumed would earn the three count. Cena's proceeding moment of arrogance proved his downfall, as his mocking attempt of The People's Elbow was countered into the deciding Rock Bottom. The image of Cena sitting on the ramp with the clear Miami night sky and the very bright-colored WrestleMania entrance set in the background – a defeated man coming to the realization that he had lost the one match in his career that he had said repeatedly prior to that he could not lose – offered a final bit of storytelling for an overall magnificent main-event presentation.

"Once in a Lifetime" was a tag-line that diehard enthusiasts of WWE scoffed at when Rock and Cena squared off in the main-event again in 2013, but the expression perfectly fit the first match. Similar elements may one day create a comparable encounter, but nothing will ever duplicate those exact circumstances.

About Rock-Cena II, there was unquestionably a bit of "Cena Wins, LOL," as a sign in one of the first few rows of the audience aptly stated, but the rematch was actually a very good example of a sequel to an epic performance, one of the hardest things to do in wrestling. They wrestled the match like they had studied their initial encounter intently and deserve praise for it.

The legacy of The Rock vs. John Cena rivalry is vast, mostly centering on the achievements of the *WrestleMania XXVIII* main-event. "How do announce a match a year away and make it special," Cena once asked rhetorically. You create unprecedented hype and then you deliver a match that, as Cena stated in answering his own question, "Was better than you could ever imagine." Like with Hogan-Andre, its economic impact was staggering, but also like with HBK-Angle, it told a story that holds up against matches of far greater critical acclaim; the end result is an overall greatness nearly unparalleled in the WrestleMania Era.

#12
"Macho Man" Randy Savage vs. Ricky "The Dragon" Steamboat
Intercontinental Championship
WrestleMania III
March 29, 1987

Top 10 All-Time at WrestleMania / Match of the Year in 1987

WrestleMania III was such a landmark event, a record-setting night that really signaled the start of the WrestleMania Era as we know it. The conversation about it rightfully begins with Hogan vs. Andre, forever to be known as one of the biggest matches ever, but then discussion quickly turns to the performance that became the standard-bearer for every match in WWE lore that ever followed it: Ricky "The Dragon" Steamboat vs. "Macho Man" Randy Savage for the Intercontinental Championship.

Steamboat, who owns the distinction as the only wrestler in the WrestleMania Era to have had the Match of the Decade in both of the two most popular professional wrestling organizations, was so good at being a good guy that everyone loved him, plus he was arguably the best in-ring performer in the world not named Ric Flair. Macho Man was just as superlative in his own way, a star of incredible proportions comparable but not equal to Hogan, the lone member of the all-time Top 10 who will absolutely never be replicated; Savage's perfectionism may have rattled the cages of his co-workers, but nobody who watched him could deny his brilliance in providing more incredible matches and memories than anyone else during the first third of the WrestleMania Era. In 1987, they were both in their absolute primes.

From laying the foundation for the development of the WWE style utilized for thirty years and counting to practically inventing the concept of "stealing the show," The Dragon vs. The Macho Man holds a special place in history; and, insomuch as it is famous for its twenty-plus two counts and its transcendent pace-to-content ratio, it is also revered for the story it told between two icons at their respective peaks. Its historical significance is deep-rooted.

If you ever find the time, go back and watch the preeminent bouts from prior to Savage-Steamboat. One thing you will notice is that they all look different than what you now know, specifically in regards to the manner in which they flow through their run-times. Then watch Dragon vs. Macho again, and keep replaying the library of outstanding bouts beyond *WrestleMania III*, noticing how they all start to look more familiar. Samuel 'Plan, in *101 WWE Matches To See Before You Die*, astutely identifies their in-ring work as "a fourteen minute walk-through of everything any WWE fan recognizes as commonplace today." The details have changed, particularly the degree of risk taken in high spots and the abundance of flashier signature offense, but the formatting has remained largely the same ever since. Steamboat vs. Savage developed the modus operandi for bell-to-bell performance in WWE, what 'Plan calls WWE's "in-ring language."

Macho Man was a perfectionist who bucked the traditional method of calling every part of a match but the finish on the fly, wanting more control over the step-by-step process of sharing his physical artwork on the 20'x20' canvas. He had an awareness of such things as the Pontiac Silverdome being set to host the largest audience for which he would ever perform, and it drove him to want his match with Steamboat to be perfect. Though no one has ever gone to the extreme of planning out (and sometimes practicing) all of the minutiae of a performance like Savage was prone to do, the resounding success of his match-design philosophy, with Savage-Steamboat the shining example, led to the vast majority of his peers over these past three decades following his lead. Today, WWE stars heavily organize at least the major spots in their matches ahead of time.

For many wrestlers and wrestling fans, its most overt distinction is, of course, that it stole the show from Hogan and Andre, imbuing from that point forward a greater sense of anticipation by the audience for matches that were not the primary selling points of super-cards and psychologically stimulating within the minds of the wrestlers from just beneath the main-event all the way down to the undercard the knowledge that they can be the most memorable part of the show. That has been an incredible positive for WWE, both in terms of the healthy competition it further instigated among the performers throughout the hierarchy and in terms of the impact that it has had on the overall quality of special events.

In stealing the show at arguably the most significant event in professional wrestling lore, it established the benchmark for what a great wrestling match in WWE looked like and shifted the industry standard away from needing to wrestle for up to an hour in order to maximize in-ring achievement (as Ric Flair made famous in the NWA) by packing thirty-minutes' worth of storytelling into half the time. Savage and Steamboat formed the consummate combination to take the squared circle performance in a faster, more exciting direction. It was as if they sat down and identified that the goal of every wrestling match may have been to get from narrative A to narrative B, but that if they could get there faster without sacrificing any of the story, then they might be able to accomplish something magnificent; and they certainly did just that, prompting as many wrestlers from Chris Jericho's generation to get into the business as any other match or individual superstar and serving as the motivation for Bret Hart's generation to ascend to even greater critical heights in the ring.

Though it has so often been contextualized as having put the concept of show-stealing on the map, one must always remember that many of the venerable show-stealers throughout history were very much expected to rise to a higher level on the occasion than anyone else, making the pressure that much greater and making their achievement that much more impressive. Ahead of the pre-match video package on the night of, Gorilla Monsoon referred to it as "one of the biggest confrontations of all-time." Hart, in the past, has described it as "sold out for the wrestlers in the back" and that "every single wrestler in the dressing room watched it." Before the bell even rang, their peers knew it was going to be special. The audible buzz in the Silverdome suggested that the fans knew it too. Macho Man, if his backstage promo before making his entrance said anything about how he felt, surely knew it. "I am the lord and master of the ring and you're gonna find that out...right now," Savage loudly and proudly bellowed in his ever-distinctive tone of speech. "History beckons the Macho Man! Yeah!" Indeed it did.

Wrestlers in the years since have spent countless hours studying its mastery – how Macho Man and The Dragon built layer upon layer of story from at first a revenge-fueled grudge match to the climax featuring pure desire to win the Intercontinental Championship – to better inform their own performances; fans of all ages call it one of the preeminent bouts in WWE lore. From past to present, Savage and Steamboat have earned the undying respect of fans and peers alike; its place in history is untouchable.

#11
Shawn Michaels vs. Razor Ramon
Ladder Match
Intercontinental Championship
WrestleMania X
March 20, 1994

#1 All-Time Ladder Match / Top 10 All-Time at WrestleMania /
Match of the Year in 1994

So, what can top the creativity and exhilaration of twenty-two near falls?

How about the aesthetic of watching two elite athletes falling or jumping off of a ladder?

Shawn Michaels and Razor Ramon took a great storyline concept of a returning Intercontinental Champion, who had vacated his title due to injury, disputing the validity of the reigning, official Intercontinental titleholder and added a unique, highly intriguing stipulation not previously seen on a larger WWF stage. It may be difficult to do this, but try to remember what it was like not to know how a Ladder Match functioned; do you remember the first time that you saw one, as was the case for so many in 1994, and how mesmerizing it was? How unbelievable it seemed when someone climbed to the top of the ladder only to launch themselves off from so high in the air? How emotionally gripping it was to see the competitors battling from either side of the ladder, inching closer to taking possession of the title off of its hanging hook? That was HBK and Razor's gift to wrestling history; and it was utterly spectacular.

Without question, it was partially the volume of intangible qualities born of extreme innovation that has allowed the match to endure against historical competition featuring more fleshed out characters – both Michaels and Ramon were key mid-card players, but still very much up-and-comers in 1994. However, it is the combination of the story within the story told that night at Madison Square Garden and the importance of the match to the careers of each participant, especially Michaels, that creates separation between HBK-Razor and contemporaries such as Steamboat-Savage as well as its peers from the Ladder Match library featuring far more eye-popping risks.

The Heartbreak Kid and The Bad Guy had a difficult task on their hands at *WrestleMania X*, unlike anything that Savage had ever tackled. Macho Man stole many a "Show of Shows," each time from a main-event featuring Hulk Hogan, an engaging character but one married to a formula from which he rarely deviated. Savage utilized nuance in his matches to incredible success, but even he was not on the level of Bret Hart when it came to piecing together cerebral in-ring masterpieces, aided as they were by The Hitman's silky-smooth, technically-perfect style; and it was Hart from whom HBK and Razor had to steal the show.

WrestleMania X hosted the first 4-star-plus level competition for the night's best match in the annual extravaganza's history. Bret's one-night story to both end a family feud with his brother, Owen, and recapture the WWF Championship from Yokozuna set the bar extraordinarily high, mainly on account of the amazing Bret vs. Owen match that jerked the curtain, but also due to the show-closing moment that saw the babyface locker-room come to the ring to triumphantly hoist the WWF Title-clutching Hitman onto their shoulders. Hart's glory on any other night would have been virtually impossible to usurp in WWE lore, but it was HBK and Razor that earned the majority of the 5-star praise for a match that has in many ways overshadowed what arguably was the greatest night of Hart's career. Hall of Famer, Gorilla Monsoon, pulled Michaels aside afterward and told him that it was the best match he had ever seen (and it would not be the last time that an iconic WWE personality with a wealth of experience would offer that compliment to HBK).

The tale that they told in the ring was awesome and the driving force behind the match being so infinitely rewatchable all these years later, but the legacy of the match is tied to Razor and HBK as hungry young men channeling constant struggles with their demons and their vices into an insatiable thirst for success as pro wrestlers, as dream-chasers who found a source of stability in climbing figurative ladders to grab proverbial brass rings who manifested their visions into climbing an actual ladder to snatch top spots in the WWF from would-be contenders, stealing the show from The Best There Is, The Best There Was, and The Best There Ever Will be in the process.

Technically (and, certainly, somewhat ironically), the concept of the Ladder Match had originated in the 1970s from the Hart family's Stampede Wrestling promotion in Canada, leading to Bret's suggestion of the gimmick to Vince McMahon and the first WWF version taking place in 1992 between Hart and Michaels at a house show. But this was not a house show; this was *WrestleMania X*. Since Steamboat-Savage and the rest of Macho Man's reputation-building exploits, WrestleMania had become the anticipated stage for each year's greatest matches and had accordingly developed a mystique that set it apart. "It's not just another event," Chris Jericho has described. "You can have the best match in the world at a live event and that's great, but the next day it's like it never existed. You can have a great match on Raw and tear the house down; it lasts a little bit longer. But WrestleMania is the night where classic matches are made."

Nobody more overtly came to be synonymous with WrestleMania's classic matches than Michaels; and that esteemed association began at *WrestleMania X*. Though HBK was known as an innovator and a great wrestler before March 1994, the Ladder Match catapulted him to a different level. The next WrestleMania Season, he won the Royal Rumble Match as the first entrant and challenged for the WWF Championship at *WrestleMania XI*, and then became "The Man" the following year when he won another Royal Rumble Match and beat Hart to win the title at *WrestleMania XII*; and just as the TLC Era popularized the Ladder Match after HBK vs. Razor practically invented the gimmick, Michaels would go on to popularize stealing the show at WrestleMania after Macho Man had practically invented the concept. All of The Showstopper's immense success and all of his classic show-stealers really stemmed from *WrestleMania X*.

Underemphasize Razor Ramon's contributions to or resultant titanic career from the Ladder Match at your own peril, as history has seemed prone to do, but be clear that it is not hyperbole to suggest that Michaels could not have worked that match to the same level of success with anyone else and that Scott Hall showing up on WCW Nitro in 1996 to fire the shot that turned the tide of the Monday Night War in Ted Turner's favor would not have been nearly as big of a deal without his performance at *WrestleMania X*. Razor was one of the most important figures of the 1990s, underratedly so, and he was a thoroughbred in the ring, Clydesdale-sized but race-horse quick with a sharp mind for the business and the ability to work against any wrestler of any style. It has always been far, far more surprising that he never won a World Title than it was that he was involved in one of the greatest matches ever.

The Ladder Match was the launching pad for two all-time great careers and a leap forward in pro wrestling innovation. The only thing preventing Top 10 status was the lack of a truly memorable rivalry, but it will likely be decades before it is overtaken in the Top 15.

#10
Ric Flair vs. Ricky "The Dragon" Steamboat
NWA World Heavyweight Championship
Chi-Town Rumble 1989 to WrestleWar 1989

Three Straight 5-Star Matches in 1989 / Match of the Year in 1989

Ric Flair's greatest rivalry and Ricky Steamboat's greatest triumph begins the final phase of our journey to #1, a phase in which each entry ranked from here on could conceivably, by some criteria, be considered for the top overall spot.

The Nature Boy and The Dragon's unbelievable three match series through the first several months of 1989 over the NWA World Heavyweight Championship built its case on timeless wrestling ability and nearly unmatched in-ring chemistry. That it was the preeminent series of matches ever produced by Flair, a popular choice for the greatest wrestler of all-time, does not hurt its cause either. Insomuch as Flair-Steamboat is the prettiest feather in the cap of The Nature Boy's career, it also stops you in your tracks when you consider what The Dragon accomplished by adding his win over Flair to become the NWA World Champion and the two glorious rematches to a resume from the 1980s that also included the recently-discussed WWF Match of the Decade from *WrestleMania III*.

Steamboat was an icon whose legend would only grow as the reputation of his clash with Randy Savage became so important to the ethos of WWE as we came to know it. When he came back to the NWA and challenged Flair for the title, it was a very big deal. Remember, Ted Turner had only just purchased Jim Crockett's territory and had only just begun the rebranding to World Championship Wrestling, and he picked Steamboat to come back and take the title off of Flair instead of homegrown talents like Sting and Lex Luger. Lesser men would have folded under the pressure; Steamboat's response was a trio of five-star matches still discussed to this day as the best matches in the overall history of the WrestleMania Era. The Dragon's 2009 WWE Hall of Fame induction was many years overdue; that man was out-of-this-world amazing in the ring.

For Flair, it might be the most enduring thing that he ever did inside the squared-circle. When the likes of Shawn Michaels and Triple H claim him to be the greatest wrestler of all-time, capable of putting on a great show for an hour with a broomstick, fans who never saw him wrestle in his prime need substantial proof that Flair was as good as advertised; and the Steamboat series has transcended eras just like his promos and character have. The three matches were intricate for their time, lightning quick, stunningly executed, and highly dramatic; truly astounding achievements to be clear. WWE bouts from the last fifteen or so years should only hope to be held in that high a regard someday.

Their dynamic was comparable to Flair vs. Rhodes, with Steamboat the family man instead of the common man and Naitch emphasizing his extravagant relationships with the fairer sex instead of his wealth; their chemistry as characters was only surpassed by their chemistry in the ring.

The first in the series emanated from the Windy City at the *Chi-Town Rumble*. Steamboat won his only World Championship that night, but believe it or not that is Flair's favorite of the trio, not The Dragon's. What The Nature Boy has, in fact, called the greatest match of his career has frequently gone over as the preference of the modern fan due to its WWE main-event-like run-time of less than 25-minutes. Truthfully, it is the only match of the series for which an appreciation for the Flair-inspired late-1980s NWA style is not required for the maximum viewing experience; one need only an enjoyment of faster-paced, characterful, smart wrestling to know from the first watch on why people hailed it such a masterpiece.

Steamboat's favorite of the three was the vaunted Two-out-of-Three Falls Match at *Clash of the Champions VI* at the Super Dome in New Orleans. Tremendous as *Chi-Town Rumble* was, the return match switching the role of champion and challenger rightfully enjoys, to present day, the hypothetical trophy for the superlative bout of the trio, for the simple reason that it was the best showcase of what made Ric Flair who he was, what made Ricky Steamboat who he was, and what made the NWA World Heavyweight Championship what it was.

Naitch was known as "The Sixty-Minute Man" on account of his ability to wrestle for an hour, sometimes twice in one day, and make each match fantastic on account of his cardiovascular conditioning and style. The 55-minute second match with Steamboat was one of the very few televised examples of that nickname that the majority of the fans ever got to see, making it the most overt display of athletic ability in his career. Hall of Famer Michael "PS" Hayes once talked about how "the stamina alone is amazing, to go at that rate, at that speed, for that long." Indeed.

Steamer was known primarily for his ability to so convincingly portray the good guy, especially the manner in which he would sell physical agony. "He made people in the crowd feel his pain," master wrestling psychologist, Jake "The Snake" Roberts spoke of The Dragon. "When you're able to do that, you're super-charging the fans because they *believe* it and they desperately want to quit hurting; they're waiting for that comeback." What better opportunity could he get to showcase his top trait as a wrestler than to battle his arch-nemesis for nearly an hour, with struggle and strife inherent in the task.

The NWA World Heavyweight Title was, in contrast to the WWF Title during the glitzy and glamorous Hulkamania Era, the *pro wrestler's* top prize. It embodied a more mature approach to the art form, and Steamboat vs. Flair offered the most mature World Championship bout ever in their Two-out-of-Three Falls Match. Jim Cornette said it best on The Dragon's documentary: "[It was] the peak of an entertaining sport vs. sports entertainment; there was enough entertainment that the people were on the edge of their seats, but there was enough sport that you could actually believe that they were really wrestling for something that they were vying to win."

Marvel at the pace the next time you watch it and recognize that they essentially had three *Chi-Town Rumble* matches in one night at *The Clash of Champions*. That said, the third match at *WrestleWar '89* in Nashville was the perfect blend of the previous two and unquestionably another all-time classic in its own right. Pro wrestling never utilized better the entertainment of sport, with NWA icons Terry Funk, Lou Thesz, and Pat O'Connor scoring each 15-minute period at ringside in case the amazing finale went the full hour time-limit without a decisive victor. They book-ended the series with inside cradles for pinfalls, the first going to Steamboat and the last going to Flair; inside cradles are old school gentlemanly tips of the cap from one wrestler to another that both are the best in the game and that there is no need to accordingly have one go over so conclusively.

The Nature Boy vs. The Dragon well represents the National Wrestling Alliance in the 1980s and NWA/WCW overall during the WrestleMania Era as the best example ever of what made WWE/F's greatest historical competition unique.

#9
Triple H vs. Mick Foley
King of the Ring 1997 to Monday Night Raw September 22, 1997; Royal Rumble 2000 to WrestleMania 2000

#1 All-Time at Royal Rumble / Top 5 All-Time Hell in a Cell Match / Top 10 Match in 1997 / Match of the Year in 2000

A classic rivalry seemingly only improving with the passage of time is Mick Foley putting his various "faces" against then-emergent Triple H. Foley has become the Attitude Era's Randy Savage, its one wrestler that will never be duplicated; and, of all his feuds, none can quite equal the memory created by the one with The Game. Triple H's own reputation may have seen its highs and lows over the past two decades, but at this point can anyone really deny that he is a bonafide Top 10 (arguably Top 5) star in the WrestleMania Era whose matches with Foley in 2000 kick-started one of WWE lore's most iconic years ever?

Foley vs. HHH has it all, from any historical perspective. It was a hit at the box office; their performances combined for what remains the most complete presentation of feud and pay-off in the history of The Royal Rumble; it appeals to aficionados who most appreciate exceptional characters, with Hunter well on his way to confirming himself as the most hated man in sports entertainment when he and Stephanie created the McMahon-Helmsley faction in late 1999, seized control of the company, and fired Foley, whose triumphant return brought with it the first appearance of Cactus Jack in a couple of years and built such quick momentum leading up to the Winter Classic that the Street Fight at Madison Square Garden turned into one of the biggest WWF Championship matches of the era (despite Hunter having just won back the title from Big Show the first week of January); plus, lest we forget, their personas held a lot of animosity toward one another for that which took place between them years prior.

Indeed, though it is tempting to concentrate the bulk of our Foley-HHH attention on early 2000, we cannot forget about Chapter 1 of their saga. Hunter Hearst Helmsley was decidedly a mid-card act until he rubbed elbows throughout the summer of 1997 with Mankind, beginning most prominently with a victory over him in the King of the Ring Final. Foley was, at that time, going through his transformation from a deranged psychopath to the beloved sympathetic figure with whom he is most associated historically, specifically through the sit-down interviews that he did with Jim Ross explaining his origins (famously establishing his connection to Madison Square Garden, "the hitchhiking story") and introducing both the Cactus Jack and Dude Love characters. Helmsley provided a foil to the increasingly popular Foley developments; with Chyna, his bodyguard who was fast becoming a star in her own right, by his side, the perception of his short and long-term potential drastically shifted.

Their feud had set the tone for each to take the next step in his career. By the time it concluded in a Falls Count Anywhere Match during one of the most famous Raw episodes ever (the one where Austin first hit the Stunner on McMahon at MSG), Hunter had formed DX with HBK; and people cared that Michaels was aligned with Hunter because of the Helmsley-Foley rivalry. Foley, meanwhile, had been alternating between his various character incarnations to raucous praise. The most overt display of his intermingling personas came just before the blow-off at Madison Square Garden. Dude Love appeared on the 'Tron with Mankind in a pre-taped segment where two of the "Three Faces of Foley" discussed how such a hardcore match was more befitting of...Cactus Jack! A smartened up New York City crowd ate up Jack's appearance with the proverbial spoon; and what ensued was roughly ten minutes of the most uniquely styled wrestling ever before seen in a WWF ring. Cactus and Helmsley battled all around the arena, hit each other with everything but the kitchen sink, and finished with a Foley piledriver of Hunter through a table on the stage!

The benefits of Hardcore realized, Foley's value for the streaking WWF better understood, and Hunter's growth into a legitimate top-level prospect apparent, their rivalry paused while they each went onto enormous heights during WWF's comeback in the Monday Night War, but Triple H later won his first World Championship from Mankind on the night after *Summerslam '99* and, by the turn of the century, it was yet again time for them to prominently clash.

In addition to their respective character arcs seeming destined to intersect, the other historically noteworthy aspect of their early 2000s rivalry renewal was the point that both had reached behind-the-scenes. Foley was too beat-up to continue, his career comparable to an NFL running back with a physically-punishing style with a short but glorious prime; he was ready to hang up his boots and the matches with Triple H were to be his last hurrah. The Game was freshly anointed a headlining singles star and WWF Champion a few months before the millennium; he simply had not proven himself yet at the main-event level, but he well understood the value in being the other half of Mick Foley's presumed parting shots to the wrestling business. Just as would be the case six years later with Edge, Foley's motivation meshed perfectly with Hunter's and the result was a pair of all-time classics.

The Street Fight at MSG was the most brutal World Title match to that point in history, chock as it was full of crimson masks, barbed wire, and thumbtacks but, unlike in past high profile matches involving Foley, Cactus Jack was not the only one enduring ungodly physical punishment; Triple H took more than his fair share of violent licks and exhibited the resiliency necessary to overcome the odds and beat Foley at his own game.

On the go-home Raw, Hunter had said: "I'm going to let you in on a secret. As sadistic as you can be, at *The Rumble*, I will reach down to a place that I have never been in my life and be that much more sadistic, that much more twisted, be *that much more* evil than you could ever imagine that you could be in your life."

When he backed it up, pinning Jack clean in the middle of the ring with a Pedigree onto thousands of thumbtacks, a new kind of heel was born, an antagonist that talked extremely tough and that proved his bravado was not all talk with definitive actions and results. For a historically babyface-driven company, Triple H's dominant brand of villainy stood in stark contrast to its modus operandi, a statement aggressively driven home by The Game's defeat of Cactus Jack for a second time at *No Way Out 2000*, with Mick Foley's career on the line inside Hell in a Cell. Heroes just did not lose matches in which retirement was at stake; in doing so, however, Foley put over Triple H as strong as anyone has ever put over anybody.

Theirs was a rivalry that, on multiple occasions, enhanced their respective professional lives and our respective wrestling fandoms immeasurably. Foley legitimized Triple H, first as a burgeoning break-out star and later as a wrestler to be taken seriously when he started egotistically referring to himself as "The Game," as in better than the best (Rock and Austin); Triple H gave Foley arguably his greatest rival and unquestionably one of the greatest sendoffs into retirement from full-time wrestling that any superstar could have asked for, in addition to being the catalyst for Foley's lone WrestleMania main-event; they collectively gave us a body of work rightfully in the discussion among the Top 10 feuds in WWE lore.

#8
Daniel Bryan vs. The Authority
WWE World Heavyweight Championship
WrestleMania XXX
April 6, 2014

Top 20 All-Time at WrestleMania / Match of the Year in 2014

Fourteen years later, Triple H was still the best villain in the game. He had a lengthy, reasonably successful babyface run and had settled very well into playing the legendary special attraction, but when Daniel Bryan emerged in 2013 as the most organically popular protagonist since Eddie Guerrero and John Cena each caught lightning in a bottle a decade earlier, The King of Kings, alongside his wicked queen, Stephanie McMahon, found his way back to his evil throne; the creation of a digital age version of Vince vs. Stone Cold ensued, as the #YesMovement ran into the agonizingly oppressive Authority.

The overwhelming support that Bryan built after getting shafted in the pathetic 18-second farce of a World Heavyweight Championship match at *WrestleMania XXVIII* was, for many fans, like reliving the glory days of the Austin vs. The Corporation saga at ages when they thought that they would never get quite that swept up in a wrestling storyline again. In hindsight, it was very gratifying to be along for such a thrilling ride. As enthusiasts age, their perspective on life changes, so imagine being a fan since childhood who saw Hulkamania and later the Attitude Era unfold, then watching the business evolve to where someone like Bryan could generate the kind of momentum that *maybe* five other stars in the WrestleMania Era had equaled; it was magical to witness it. His WWE Title victory over John Cena at *Summerslam '13* felt like a changing of the guard...for less than five-minutes and until Triple H turned heel and handed Randy Orton, who also turned heel, the championship via easy Money in the Bank cash-in.

Though he was already shifting to more of a corporate role at the dawn of the philosophical shift to former independently promoted talents reshaping the WWE roster, Triple H was the perfect fit to lead the charge against the likes of Bryan as the diabolical, on-air boss. Perhaps no wrestler in the early digital age (the early-to-mid-2000s) garnered a more negative reputation among some fan circles than Hunter. That perception has softened thanks to NXT, which The Game has taken from pet project developmental system to the 2nd most popular American wrestling promotion, but the notions that he was only out for himself and his pals for the bulk of his career and that he earned his position of influence by "marrying the boss's daughter" were certainly not distant memories in 2013. Stephanie took center stage, as well, and still very much in vogue was the perception of her having carried over to the modern era some of the same (real or perceived) institutionally restraining philosophies of her father. WWE brilliantly combined Triple H's notorious repute with that of his wife's and molded them into the most hated villains of the decade.

The Authority was a foundational TV storyline-building block for the product to revolve around, but they needed Bryan to make it work; villains are only as engaging as their opposing heroes after all. WWE had developed this giant fanbase of people for whom wrestling had been a childhood pastime; these people just wanted whatever got over with the audience to be the driving force for advancing careers, like it had always been. When Triple H and Stephanie continually expressed, on-camera, what so many fans had taken as gospel on the internet about WWE's narrow view on what a star should look like, it was as if they poured lighter fluid on a fire that had already been growing inside the minds of diehard enthusiasts around the world for years.

There was already such angst regarding Bryan, who had come into WWE with the quiet reputation of being the best technical wrestler in the world and who had then surprised many with how well he took to the character side of bigger business, which was the catalyst for how he was able to capture the imagination of the wider fanbase. When he did not get the same opportunities that someone as over as he was deserved, it got the people fervently riled up; adding Triple H and Stephanie to that mix with The Game's well-groomed pupils, Orton and eventually Batista, made the entire situation combustible. Wrestlers and long-time fans alike looked at the situation and saw *WrestleMania XXX* written all over the story from post-*Summerslam '13* onward, with Bryan the obvious Royal Rumble winner and Triple H somehow getting involved in the ring with him to boot. Batista made his comeback and won the Rumble instead, with Bryan not even entering the Rumble at all. Grown men in the digital age have never responded to anything with the same degree of keyboard-vitriol as they did with the Rumble result in 2014; Mick Foley actually became the voice of fan disgruntlement.

January turned to February, February turned to March, *WrestleMania XXX* was fast-approaching, and the presumed main-event for the biggest show of the year was the hated Orton vs. "Boo-tista," as The Animal was dubbed in response to his unwelcomed push to the top. On the March 3rd Monday Night Raw in Chicago, the door opened for Bryan to wrestle Triple H at "The Show of Shows," but it could not erase the feeling that WWE was going to miss a big opportunity not to culminate Bryan's revolt against The Authority with a World Heavyweight Championship victory in the biggest match of the year. Trips and Steph, with every scathing remark - "That's a good little spot for you, Daniel" / "You're a B-plus player" / "Without my family, you would have nothing" / "We *made* you" / "Everything in this arena right now, including [the fans] and you, belong to us" - made the desire stronger to see Bryan not only beat Triple H on the grandest stage, but somehow take the title as well. As it turned out, their latest stinging verbal barrage was merely setting the stage for the March 10th Monday Night Raw in Memphis.

Playing on the social media #OccupyWallStreet movement (and others like it) protesting corporate and political corruption, Bryan led a sizeable portion of fans in Memphis on a #OccupyRaw crusade. "You are not listening to any of us," he strongly proclaimed, and then proceeded to occupy the ring and the ringside area along with a passionate group of supporters, never budging despite a variety of different Authority-directed attempts to quell the protest. Frankly, watching Stephanie and Hunter lose their cool was arguably the most cathartic part of the entire Daniel Bryan experience. They could each be so infuriatingly smug, so to see them finally cave to Bryan's request for a match with Triple H at WrestleMania still sends shivers up the spine to this day.

When Bryan smiled brightly in response to his challenge being accepted and rubbed salt in The Authority's wound by stating, "That's not exactly all that I want," it was for many fans like Bryan won the World Heavyweight Title in the WrestleMania main-event right then and there. The pent-up frustration burst through the seams with the collective zealous intensity of a rocket blasting through the atmosphere as the dream scenario of diehard members of the #YesMovement from Australia to India to the UK to the USA and Canada and everywhere in between came to fruition before our very eyes.

Bryan defeated Triple H in a great contemporary technical wrestling match with top notch psychology and a wonderfully emotive built-in story to open the in-ring action at "The Showcase of the Immortals" a few weeks later, and then Bryan tapped out Batista to capture the WWE World Heavyweight Championship from Orton in a highly underrated main-event (featuring an incredible Batista Bomb-RKO connection to Bryan through the announce table) after which 75,000 people in the New Orleans Superdome came unglued and "yessed" to their hearts content. Perhaps because there was a sense of knowing in advance that Bryan would spearhead in assured victory a pair of Match of the Year-contending, legacy-enhancing performances from all involved at 'Mania, the most emotional triumph for

Bryan's supporters was found in him merely getting the opportunity to do it, and him actually doing it was the icing on the cake.

No matter that he was the rare modern protagonist who was as close to universally loved by all sects of the audience as anyone had been since Austin or that his "Yes!" catchphrase had caught on in the mainstream media or that he was the best technical wrestler since Benoit, nothing could change the fact that Bryan's appearance was not larger-than-life. Nevertheless, Bryan was part underdog story and part revolutionary tale of the people speaking their minds, unabashedly stating their desire to see WWE change their creative direction; the people chose Daniel Bryan and their support made him larger-than-life, he got to be the focal point of *WrestleMania XXX* because of it, and we were all rewarded with an unforgettable story.

#7
Triple H vs. The Undertaker
WrestleMania X-Seven; WrestleMania XXVII to WrestleMania XXVIII

Top 5 All-Time Hell in a Cell Match / Top 10 All-Time at WrestleMania / Top 15 All-Time at WrestleMania / Top 40 All-Time at WrestleMania / Top 15 Match in 2001 / Top 5 Match in 2011 / Top 5 Match in 2012

Let it be known that their April '01 era-specific brawl on the grandest of stages, climaxing with a dynamite pair of Last Ride Powerbomb sequences – one countered by Triple H's use of a sledgehammer in mid-hoist and one iconically landed from out of the corner where Hunter had briefly paused a ten punch-assault for a taunt – was The Streak's finest outing through 14-0 and would have flirted with Top 100 inclusion on its own. However, the primary reason for the over-arching rivalry's Top 10 status is the pair of WrestleMania matches that came a decade later.

In 1972, Francis Ford Coppola brought a Mario Puzo novel to the big screen and introduced to moviegoers a different perspective on the mafia. *The Godfather* was groundbreaking for what film critic David Sterritt once praised as the "acute psychological depth and meticulous attention to detail" with which Coppola portrayed mafiosos from the viewpoint of the Corleone family. It was, thus, a movie that changed the way that people viewed the mob.

Undertaker vs. Triple H at *WrestleMania XXVII* was pro wrestling's equivalent to *The Godfather*.

Every match, rivalry, and story detailed in this book that was produced by WWE has generally taken place within the confines of a certain narrative style. Whether sped up to a fast-forward pace like Mysterio vs. Angle, set up to favor one wrestler's dominance ala Brock Lesnar's "Beast Mode," or even designed through a gimmick's creative freedom to aesthetically astound, each performance thus far discussed (and to be discussed) has by and large followed the formats created by the superlative work in Randy Savage's career; each performance, that is, with the exception of The Game vs. The Deadman.

Triple H vs. Undertaker offered wrestling fans the most psychologically deep story ever told in a wrestling ring and, as Samuel 'Plan aptly put it in *101*, "tore up the rule book fans assumed was necessary." It consequently created a fascinating way to wrestle a match, one that has, like *The Godfather*, carved out a niche for itself that sets it apart from its historical peers.

It escalated almost immediately to places that 99% of all great matches in WWE history progress toward. Mankind and Taker's Hell in a Cell went straight to fifth gear too (sixth really), but what separated HHH-Taker was that it never downshifted. In the first five minutes, we bore witness to Taker's over-the-top rope dive and a spinebuster through the announce table. Midway through the 30-minute affair, they had already exhausted their full arsenals. Absent the standard match sequencing, the bout quite well lived up to its billing as "The War of Wars." They gave each other no quarter from the moment the opening bell rang to the uncomfortable moment when Triple H tapped out after a lengthy struggle locked in The Deadman's desperation Hell's Gate submission.

For fans that just wanted to see two of the Top 10 stars of the WrestleMania Era beat the you-know-what out of each other, the match was an overwhelming success. However, it is not the physical annihilation that made Taker vs. Triple H at *'Mania 27* so brilliant; it was the psychological nuance shown by the characters throughout the run-time. Undoubtedly appreciate the level of brutality shown with the plethora of Tombstone Piledrivers, Pedigrees, and chair shots, but do not miss the body language, the dialogue, and the facial expressions.

Two particularly striking examples stood out from the rest.

The first occurred after Triple H had weathered the storm of the classic Undertaker comeback routine, but was struggling to put away The Deadman using his own signature offense. He ravaged The Phenom with several chair shots and implored him to "stay down," a subtle verbal jab referencing exactly what Taker had told Hunter's best friend, Shawn Michaels, in the closing moments of the prior year's 'Mania main-event.

Exceptional was the look on The Game's face when Taker goozled him soon after; the tried and true sign that the tide had turned in The Deadman's favor was met with a look that emphatically stated, "No way. Not this time." In fact, he completely no sold it, shaking his head as he gazed down at him like his 'Mania-undefeated opponent's hand was grasping at straws rather than grasping his throat. Hunter easily escaped, mocked him using Taker's own throat-slashing gesture, proceeded to deliver a Tombstone Piledriver accompanied by a primal scream of "It's over," and covered him just like The Deadman would with his tongue extended to his chin. When Undertaker kicked out, Triple H exhibited a riveting emotional response which mirrored how all of us felt; that right then, it had seemed as though The Streak was over.

The second instance occurred as Triple H sat in the corner besieged with anxiety. Taker had just kicked out of the Tombstone. The internal monologue read something like, "Do I have anything left to throw at him? Oh yes, there is one weapon remaining: the sledgehammer. But do I have to go that route? Of course I do; I'm out of alternatives."

That is just one interpretation of The Game's inner conflict, but he was so demonstrative with his body language that neither he nor the commentators needed to verbalize what he was thinking; it was written all over his face. He did, indeed, go for the sledgehammer. His resistance to utilizing it combined with his methodical walk toward The Deadman and his momentary pause before striking the death blow allowed Taker just enough time to create an opportunity. The Phenom caught Triple H off-guard and pulled him into Hell's Gate. The mixed-martial-arts submission was locked in for longer than any preceding occasion. The Game got hold of the hammer, but his body was incapable of executing the actions that his brain was instructing; he dropped the hammer and finally had to tap out.

The story did not end when the bell rang. Undertaker's music played for several minutes as his Streak extending to an epic 19-0 was celebrated with pyrotechnics, yet he did not stand and he could barely move. Triple H, meanwhile, recovered, stood, and watched Taker attempt to walk out under his own power and fail; he even lunged to help break Taker's fall before backing away and leaving the scene. There was no celebration by The Phenom, no spotlighted pose acknowledging his gratefulness to the "Creatures of the Night." Only silence. Taker was carted off not to be seen again for another year.

Samuel 'Plan calls it, "WWE's psychological odyssey, its creation of an entirely different style of professional wrestling." The moments referenced above were synergistic with the classic Raw segment on February 21, 2011, in which the two legends engaged each other without ever saying a single word. Such complete mastery of their characters is what has come to define the genius of their match at *WrestleMania XXVII.*

Recapturing such an incredibly high level of artistry is almost impossible. *The Godfather: Part II* proved it could be done in film; it has been preserved in the National Film Registry at the Library of Congress for being "culturally, historically, and aesthetically significant." As with the sequel to *The Godfather,* the Triple H vs. Undertaker rematch at *WrestleMania XXVIII* arguably topped its prequel.

While maintaining theatrical thematic elements from the first match, there were four key changes that made the rematch more popular with the majority of critics and fans alike. The first was the utilization of the more traditional in-ring format, a steady escalation toward the emotional high points and a progression through the gears rather than an immediate and permanent shift to fifth gear. The second was the expected role reversal of who played the aggressor. The year before, Triple H sought out a match with Taker and had a clearly defined purpose: "become the 1 in 18-1." Taker had displayed uncharacteristic hubris before and during the match in Atlanta. However, the way that the encounter ended humbled The Deadman and sent him into exile from which he emerged the instigator of the second match. In Miami, Taker aggressively sought retribution, while it was The Game exuding the haughtiness.

The third major difference was the presence of Shawn Michaels as the special referee. Like Coppola had decided that a greater emphasis on past history would catalyze for *The Godfather: Part II* a reputation that could stand apart from its predecessor, the HBK ingredient assisted in distinguishing HHH-Taker II from the first match. HBK's history with both men was, of course, extensive. During a succinct, top notch backstage interview right before match time, he noted that something was coming to an end that night; either The Game or The Streak. During the match, he had every self-righteous reason to want to see The Streak live on, meaning that his best friend could not do what he himself could not do; on the other hand, Undertaker ended his career. All the while, he had the utmost respect for both.

Drawing from that history, he put on a clinic of how a third personality can add to a match without stealing the thunder from the primary combatants. Triple H and Taker both tried to influence him, either through verbal manipulation or physical coercion. His wide range of affective responses (anger, compassion, remorse, disbelief) coupled with his physical involvement (taking away the sledgehammer, Sweet Chin Music in retaliation for Hell's Gate) were a big part of the match's tremendous success.

Finally, the fourth variation was the enhanced usage of dialogue. When Triple H emerged with the upper hand following The

Phenom's early onslaught and proceeded to decimate Undertaker with a steel chair, he told Michaels impertinently, "End it! Or I will!" Given what had happened the prior year, HBK seriously contemplated calling the match, but Taker would not allow it. *"Don't* stop it," he urged. The Game's relentless use of the chair and his signature sledgehammer only amplified HBK's consideration of agreeing to his best friend's request. Knowing that Michaels was on the verge of acquiescing, Taker locked him in Hell's Gate. It was a riveting moment. Later, when The Deadman had overcome all odds to completely regain the advantage, he turned the table on Triple H and yelled at him to "Stay down!"

Triple H's powerful choice of words at *WrestleMania XXVII* was an engaging component to making their story so dramatic, but strip what was billed as an "End of an Era Hell in a Cell Match" of the verbal communication between the three characters at *WrestleMania XXVIII* and it is a much lesser performance, entertaining surely, but nowhere near as poignant. Again, it goes back to character mastery. A marque phrase like "End of an Era" and a gimmick like "Hell in a Cell" certainly provided all that fans needed to get invested, but HBK, HHH, and Taker went the extra mile with their storytelling and the final result was a captivating masterpiece.

At the end of the rematch, Jim Ross stated on commentary that he had "Never, ever witnessed anything like what we've just seen." Such a statement perfectly describes both matches. It is quite possible that we may never, ever see anything like the Triple H vs. Undertaker series again. So, here is an offer you cannot refuse: you go find the time to watch these matches and you will be happy, capisce?

#6
Chris Jericho vs. Shawn Michaels
WrestleMania XIX; Judgment Day 2008 to No Mercy 2008

Top 20 All-Time at WrestleMania / Top 10 All-Time Ladder
Match / Top 5 Match in 2003 / Match of the Year in 2008

Shawn Michaels and Chris Jericho are two of the greatest superstars of all-time. Their rivalry was legendary, initially starting out in 2003 as the tale of a young lion rising up to challenge the pride of WrestleMania history and later, in 2008, blossoming into perhaps the best post-Attitude Era representative of sustained creative excellence, a period that pushed Michaels to his most complete character performances and that Jericho has called the superlative of his career.

It began with a simple statement of superiority. Jericho interrupted Michaels the night after HBK had lost the very World Heavyweight Championship that had punctuated his unlikely comeback in 2002 and boldly proclaimed his skills to have surpassed The Icon's. Y2J was in a rather enviable position, looking to exploit The Showstopper's forthcoming return to "The Show of Shows." What could Jericho do to follow defending the Undisputed Title, which he had become the first man ever to hold, at *WrestleMania X-8*? How about combine with the man who in many ways paved the way for his peak success to create a show-stealing match that would go on to be remembered as the finest in his personal WrestleMania library and one of the top matches in the history of WWE's signature event?

The set-up for their *WrestleMania XIX* encounter was 2003's best, in terms of quality storylines. Michaels responded to Jericho's December 2002 comments with a baritone rendition of Sweet Chin Music. In classic fashion, they further-established their saga through the Royal Rumble Match and consistently stayed in each other's business for weeks on end ahead of a memorable go-home Raw before 'Mania, during which Y2J explained that he had once wanted to be like Michaels and had patterned his career after HBK's. They had indeed followed similar paths, with Jericho rising the ranks through the Cruiserweight division in WCW just as Michaels had climbed the WWE hierarchy via the tag team scene. By the end of their respective fourth years in mainstream pro wrestling, they had held the WWE Intercontinental Championship en route to becoming World Champion shortly thereafter and, by their mid-thirties, were already legends of the WrestleMania Era.

However, Jericho was not quite on the HBK-level. Michaels had revolutionized the concept of stealing the show at WrestleMania and had already delivered on the grandest stage the Ladder Match and the Ironman Match, but you could see it in his body language when he hit the stage at Safeco Field that his comeback was never going to be complete without a show-stopping performance on par with his past achievements. Nobody lived for WrestleMania quite like HBK and, though it clearly meant the world to him just being there, he renewed his demolition license before coming to Seattle, fully prepared to tear the house down.

For Y2J, there was never going to be another chance quite like the one to work with Michaels on HBK's return to "The Showcase of the Immortals" for the first time since his forced-retirement match in 1998; there was never going to a better opportunity for Jericho to leave the kind of legacy at WrestleMania that Steamboat and Savage had left, prompting a generation of young men like him to want to get into the business. As Jim Ross, on commentary, alluded to when listing some of the characteristics that separated WrestleMania from every other major event, Y2J battled Michaels at *Mania XIX* intent on enhancing his reputation on a stage where "memories lasted forever."

They wrestled a marvelous match, so smooth in its execution that it has aged like a fine wine. If we define greatness as something above the pure elements of in-ring storytelling, then HBK vs. Y2J is not one of the greatest WrestleMania matches ever, but Michaels vs. Jericho absolutely fits the definition of

WrestleMania's *best*. The manner in which they weaved layer after layer into the fiction was just beautiful to witness and only seems to improve with each passing rewatch. Through it Jericho created his ever-lasting WrestleMania memory and Michaels announced figuratively to the rest of the sports entertainment world that, from there on out, his peers would once again have to concern themselves with following his act.

After the match, a despondent Jericho hugged Michaels as he struggled to gain a grip on the reality of his loss, but a kick to the groin reiterated his position as one of HBK's foils and, though it took five years, their rivalry was eventually renewed in 2008.

Jericho was at a much different place in his career after *WrestleMania XXIV*. He had said during his feud with Michaels years earlier that he had grown out of wanting to be what many were calling him - "the next Shawn Michaels" - and had desired instead to become the first Chris Jericho, but he had in many ways become HBK-Lite after all; a show-enhancer more than a show-stealer; great, Top 30 caliber all-time, but not all-time Top 10 great. Two years away had done little to change that; when he came back from his own hiatus, Y2J struggled to get his bearings. Opportunity again presented itself, however, in the form of a familiar foe and, just as he had in 2003, he took full advantage of it.

Y2J was the guest referee for a match between Michaels and Batista in April 2008, won by HBK after the cunning veteran had feigned a knee injury to gain the edge. Jericho reacted like a disappointed friend; mocking his old rival in jest, he awarded him a faux-Oscar for his acting skills. HBK, like a man with a stubborn and righteous streak, doubled down and insisted that his injury was legitimate. Then, the week before a scheduled match between the two, Michaels let up and confessed to Jericho that he really had been working everyone and apologized...without further explanation.

It was an interesting arc to lay the foundation for the second chapter in their story. History tells us that most professional wrestling sagas are built on simple concepts like jealousy or prestige or plainly "who's the best?" By comparison, righteousness is a deeper and more emotional plot device that tears down traditional narrative lines. Jericho essentially took the position of it being hypocritical of the professed good guy to adopt an attitude of "win at all costs." Michaels drew a line in the sand also, but with rather flippant conviction. So, who would be the antagonist? Many would naturally point to Jericho, but would you not be inclined to agree with Y2J in principle? You see, it was not so simple; it was a thinking man's wrestling angle.

At *Judgment Day*, they wrestled what could be analogized to a pick-up basketball game that starts off reasonably friendly and then quickly devolves into a heated competition. There were no obvious stakes in the match, so it came across like an exhibition, but the escalatory tone of the contest from game of cordial one-upmanship to cutthroat game of physical chess hinted at something more. Jericho, seemingly confused and frustrated by HBK's actions before bell time, ended the bout borderline incensed after losing via nifty counter to his Walls submission. He kept his cool, offering Michaels a handshake that HBK reluctantly accepted, with each teasing a sneaky assault in a nice riff on the post-match happenings at *WMXIX*. They had reached a stalemate rather than a resolution, organically insisting that the conflict continue and grow.

The evolution of Jericho took its next step when he snapped and slammed HBK's face into the screen of the TV on his Highlight Reel set. He stated his outright disgust at Michaels lying to everyone yet still getting cheered, climbing atop the proverbial high-horse and thumbing his nose at the audience for maintaining their support of HBK. In reply, The Showstopper cost Jericho the Intercontinental Championship and, braggadocios in a way that we had sparingly seen since he came back from the career-threatening back injury, remarked that

Jericho's real issue was not with Michaels lying, insinuating instead that Y2J was jealous of his place in history. HBK claimed that, if he retired right then and there, he would be remembered more than Y2J no matter what Jericho did from that point forward; how truly cocky it was of him to say. Again, this was far more indie-flick kind of dialogue than WWE's typically Michael Bay-esque material. Those two performers and the creative staff helping them were diving into the shades of gray in our world.

Adding another emotional wrinkle to the on-going saga was the eye injury that Michaels suffered from the face-to-TV incident. In their rematch at *The Great American Bash* in July, Jericho ended a dual-portrayal of emotionally gripping character by bloodying Michaels above his injured eye. The referee was forced to stop the match after Y2J repeatedly pummeled HBK to where he had lost so much blood - in one of the greatest and most narrative-enhancing blade jobs ever - that he could not continue. Oddly enough, for specific types of Jericho fans, they could be forgiven for feeling vindicated by Y2J's decimation of HBK in such a manner after the arrogant comments Michaels had made about their favorite.

The dynamic between them shifted again when Jericho spent the weeks leading up to Summerslam wearing a suit and proselytizing about the virtues of his actions, ditching much of the Y2J persona that had initially made him a renowned star for a Javier Bardem in *No Country For Old Men*-inspired act who spoke condescendingly toward everyone and threw his verbal weight around. The transition has proven famous for Jericho, as the development helped make him WWE's MVP in 2008 and 2009.

More linear stories in WWE would have culminated at the following month's *Summerslam*, but they instead used the second biggest show of the year to further enhance the heat on their rivalry and build to even bigger matches in the fall. Michaels, in the weeks leading up to the event, suggested he might heed doctor's orders and retire from the ring because of his eye. At *Summerslam*, he even went so far as to walk out with his teary-eyed wife and appear to say goodbye before Y2J interrupted and insisted that HBK admit to everyone, including his family, that the reason for his retirement was actually Chris Jericho. HBK agreed, on the condition that Jericho, in turn, admit to his family that he would "never, ever be Shawn Michaels." As The Icon turned to leave, Jericho spun him around for one final blow, but HBK ducked and Jericho struck Rebecca Michaels right in the mouth, legitimately bloodying her lip. It was a powerful segment - one of the finest ever really - that continued the feud-long trend of producing material far more psychologically-dense than sports entertainment is known for; such a wide range of emotions were encompassed within its run-time.

His wife assaulted, any plans to retire were immediately thrown out the window, as Michaels sought revenge. Both men signed hold-harmless agreements in a contract for a Non-Sanctioned Match at Unforgiven. It was perhaps even more physically brutal than the match two months prior that had seen HBK leave quarts of blood in the Nassau Coliseum. Jericho was dissected by Michaels, who was relentless in his assault to the point where the same referee who had stopped the match on HBK's behalf at *The Great American Bash* was forced to do the same for Jericho.

About their matches at *The Bash* and *Unforgiven*, they were arguably the pioneers for the more complex storytelling that became the standard in WWE subsequent to HBK's *WrestleMania 25* match with Undertaker. High-definition came to WWE in January 2008 and brought with it a clearer motion picture of facial and physical expression, perhaps necessitating that wrestlers emote during matches to a greater extent than ever before. Michaels accepted the challenge and found a new gear with his emotional selling capabilities against Jericho, whose own work consequently rose to new heights.

No Mercy '08 was the site of their final showdown, a tremendous crescendo named Match of the Year by many. Having already tackled themes of righteousness, jealousy, and revenge, the prestige of the World Heavyweight Championship was added to the mix in quite possibly the best story-driven Ladder Match ever. Jericho had wormed his way into a Scramble Match to win the title less than 90-minutes after HBK had beaten him to a ref-stoppage at *Unforgiven*. For the man who would soon justifiably claim himself on a regular basis to be "The Best in the World," it was the first time he had held World Championship gold in 6 ½ years, validating his stellar transformation through the spring and summer into one of the most celebrated character arcs of the 21st century. Naturally, Michaels would want to take that symbol away from him, but the hubris in selecting a gimmick match that he had popularized failed to take into account both Jericho's own penchant for Ladder Match success and the emblematic nature of a climbing device in a story partially built on Y2J's desire to join HBK on wrestling's hierarchical pedestal.

In the end, both chapters of the Y2J vs. HBK saga were about a lot of things, but most of all their tale was about Jericho maximizing his potential and working his way into the discussion to be among the ten all-time greatest of the WrestleMania Era. Ironically, HBK was eventually proven to have been right all along. He retired in 2010, while Y2J went on to continue building his resume but, no matter what Jericho achieved, he never became Shawn Michaels. Y2J is WWE's Kobe Bryant, HBK its Michael Jordan, linked by their similarities as well as the gap between them historically. So, Michaels is arguably the greatest of all-time, but Jericho is unquestionably an all-time great; and the same can be said of their rivalry - perhaps not the greatest but, without a doubt, Top 10 all-time great.

#5
Bret Hart vs. Owen Hart
WrestleMania X to Summerslam 1994

#1 All-Time at Summerslam / Top 20 All-Time at WrestleMania
/ #1 All-Time Pay-Per-View Opening Match / Top 5 All-Time
Cage Match / Match of the Year in 1994

Bret Hart vs. Owen Hart may not have been the most glamorous feud with the most high profile matches and it may not have taken place in the most lucrative era but, like in boxing when a fighter is called the best "pound for pound" in the world, their brotherly duels made up the best "match for match" series of the 1990s, including the greatest opening match on pay-per-view ever and the blueprint for how to work a deeply affecting, wildly entertaining technically-styled match (at *WrestleMania X*), and the smartest Cage Match in history that doubles as the all-time best overall match at Summerslam, having gone head-to-head with the other 5-star caliber bouts in August Classic lore to earn that distinction.

The simplicity of it, from the start, was the source of its brilliance. Owen was a sparingly used wrestler who had been around for a while, but who had never caught his big break. His older brother, Bret, meanwhile, was the first Grand Slam Champion (holder of all the major titles at some point in time) and the leader of The New Generation. Theirs was a story of intense jealousy and, though we had seen that before between larger-than-life personas, the manner in which the Bret vs. Owen story was told embraced the understated demeanor and workmanlike approach of The Hitman that tonally defined the period between 1994 and 1997 and was, as such, made to feel like it could be happening to you or someone close to you; perhaps no prior rivalry in the WrestleMania Era had ever been so relatable.

At *Survivor Series '93*, the Hart brothers (Bruce and Keith included) teamed up for a traditional Elimination Match.

Unquestionably, it was the biggest thing that Owen had ever been given the opportunity to do in the WWF but, though he looked like a million bucks in that match – every bit the horribly underutilized wrestler that he was – he was the lone Hart to be eliminated, thanks to an inadvertent collision with Bret.

The story that they would go onto tell over the next year has become timeless; and that it can be interpreted differently now than it was told then is one of its greatest strengths in such an "all-time"-centered discussion. What WWF presented in 1993/1994 was Bret, the wise older brother and very much the protagonist in the story, trying as hard as he could to save his family after his little brother's envy came close to tearing it apart, but who was eventually driven to fight after Owen had taken things too far; and the presentation was so marvelously acted by both that it stands the test of time as it was presented. Interpretation of something so genuinely relatable, however, allows for the Owen-Bret situation to be reframed in a different context: with Owen as the protagonist.

How easy is it to connect with Owen's arc too? Even if you had no sibling to rival, you could still relate with a best friend horsing around and causing you to roll your ankle before the big game, consequently keeping you on the sidelines while your team achieved a great victory; or a best friend with an amazing career costing you a job that you really wanted; or any number of similar instances of someone with everything you desire knowingly or unknowingly making you feel held down in some way. Can you imagine then being able to play in the big game to redeem yourself for missing the previous, being wide open for the win, and your best friend fumbling your chance away like Bret did to Owen at *Royal Rumble '94*? Though Bret had managed to talk him down over the holidays in 1993 and make amends by getting them a Tag Team Championship shot at *The Rumble*, Owen again came away feeling like his big brother had tried to hog the spotlight in what The Rocket had outright stated in a pre-match backstage interview was "the biggest match of his life." Bret hurt his knee and, rather than tag in Owen, he tried a last ditch attempt at The Sharpshooter before his leg pain became intolerable and the referee stopped the match to protect him.

In today's world, Owen would likely have been embraced by an audience sympathetic to his cause but, back then, Owen was so good at being such a jerk about what had happened (i.e. verbal tirades galore and kicking Bret's "leg right out of [his] leg") that he emerged as the top heel character of 1994. Framed in whichever context resonates with you most on any given viewing, particularly of their first match, it is hard to argue that the Bret-Owen family drama is quite possibly the most rewatchable saga in WWE history.

WrestleMania X was a legendary night for the brothers Hart. Bret, in his autobiography, expertly described the fine line that they so seamlessly walked in order to ensure that Owen's eye-popping skills did not turn the crowd in his favor. "He played the nasty little brother, cheating viciously at every turn, and I kept outsmarting him, but never in a way that made me look overconfident or cocky," he said. Owen was insufferable throughout the match, his impressive mastery of the envious younger sibling surely due in part to honest emotions that he tapped into and up to which he turned the detestable volume to ten. Bret, aided by his arguable-best-of-all-time grasp of how much more raw emotion pro wrestling is capable of drawing out of people when theatrics are deemphasized, put in one of his many performances worthy of a Best Actor nomination; there was not a single moment of the match in which he did anything to threaten his status as the protagonist. Also, to further emphasize a common theme from that era, Vince McMahon and Jerry Lawler were excellent in their roles on commentary, King never wavering in his affection for Owen born of his hatred for Bret and McMahon gloriously cheesy in his steadfast defense of Bret's virtues.

It was a masterpiece in storytelling, a benchmark for elevating a lower card talent, a perfect example of what made The Hitman one of the Top 10 stars of the WrestleMania Era, and the definitive case for why Owen deserves the Hall of Fame nod...and yet it still was not quite as good as their Cage Match for the WWF Championship at *Summerslam*.

WWE set-up *WrestleMania X* perfectly. Owen was showcased as Bret's equal in the opening contest and, being craftier than the master of craftiness, cleanly pinned The Hitman with a counter to a Victory Roll. Bret, of course, went onto defeat Yokozuna to regain the WWF Title in the main-event. The Rocket had a legitimate claim to a title shot. To further enhance Owen's resume, he won the King of the Ring tournament in June, outsmarting Tatanka, submitting 123 Kid, and getting by another of the era's top stars in Razor Ramon with a little bit of help from his brother-in-law – and most notably Bret's long-time tag team partner – Jim "The Anvil" Neidhart, who earlier in the night had helped The Excellence of Execution retain the WWF Title. The Anvil had colluded with Owen to both ensure The Rocket's King of the Ring coronation and guarantee that Bret would remain champion long enough for Owen to get a chance to take the title from him. The Anvil's decision to side with The King of Harts added another dynamic to the family's on-going turmoil as *Summerslam* approached.

More and more members of the Hart clan were highlighted, leading to the vast majority of the family (including the returning Davey Boy Smith) sitting at ringside for the WWF Championship bout at *Summerslam*. The Cage Match stipulation became necessary for the purpose of keeping the likes of Neidhart, who played a central role between *King of the Ring* and *Summerslam* as the figure who had initially planted the seeds of jealousy in Owen, and other Harts out of the fray. The Cage raised the stakes; and there is just something to this day about that old blue-barred cage that enhances the look and feel of the gimmick.

Unostentatious as The Hitman himself, the Cage Match between Owen and Bret stands out as the most unique version in the stipulation's long and storied history, a performance that asks its audience to be patient and to pay attention to detail and then rewards everyone willing to go along for the ride with continually elevating emotional peaks and valleys. The underlying theme of the match-type so often, as demonstrated so well by the earlier-mentioned Blanchard-Magnum TA "I Quit," was imprisonment in order to facilitate violence. A bloody war Bret vs. Owen was not; the battle between the Hart brothers was simply about winning...because winning means you are the best, holding the WWF Championship means you are the best, and beating your brother means you are the best. In this case, the only means to victory were escaping over the cage or through the door, and so for over thirty-minutes they scratched and clawed toward escape.

The animosity between them did not so much spark a desire to hurt each other physically, then, as it lit within each of them a burning passion to emerge the best wrestler from a family whose very existence had revolved around wrestling for fifty years. Though the match threatens to watch as far too tame for its genre due to the typical standard, it actually ends up being riveting due to the constant sense that it could be over at any moment; Owen vs. Bret is like methodical sex peaking with the perfect climax. Much like the Ladder Match at *WrestleMania X*, Owen and Bret's Cage Match is so smooth and authoritative in its intent that it compares favorably even to sub-genres that are far more aesthetically-engaging; using another analogy, it is like jazz, whereas Hell in a Cell or more violent editions from the Cage Match library are like hard rock. Bret vs. Owen, it should be noted, was certainly not without its fair share of crescendos, citing specifically their roughly-dozen falls from the top rope and steel bars, chief among them Bret's Superplex of Owen from near the top of the cage.

Bret Hart denies that it was the greatest Cage Match of all-time, admitting only that "it was surely the best one without blood," but in respectful disagreement with The Best There Is, The Best There Was, and The Best There Ever Will Be, no other Cage

Match can claim to be quite so idiosyncratic, so special that nothing else watches quite like it.

It remains to be seen if the rest of the Top 10 greatest matches, rivalries, and stories will be able to endure quite like Owen Hart vs. Bret Hart has for the last twenty-five years. Confidently, if these rankings had been made fifteen years ago, Owen-Bret would have been in the Top 5, it remains in the Top 5 presently, and when these rankings are revised fifteen years from now, it will assuredly still be in the Top 10. It is an eternal all-time Top 10 member.

#4
The Ultimate Warrior vs. "Macho King" Randy Savage
Career-Ending Match
WrestleMania VII
March 24, 1991
Top 5 All-Time at WrestleMania / Match of the Year in 1991

WWE officials adamantly avoid the use of the term "professional wrestling," having spent the last forty years trying to distance the company from any previous association with the stigma that professional wrestling carries by re-educating the public to the virtues of their preferred performance art label, "sports entertainment." Their strategy has had a tendency to annoy analysts and former wrestlers, aka sports entertainers, who feel that Vince McMahon and Co. have taken the business too far away from the good things, like simpler storytelling, about its pro wrestling roots. Regardless of vernacular, though, there is indeed a clear difference between most professional wrestling matches produced by non-WWE entities, most notably NWA/WCW historically and more recently the independent scene and New Japan Pro Wrestling, and the stories conducted on WWE's sports entertainment stage.

The #1 reason why this particular match sits within the Top 5 is, therefore, very simple: it is the definitive example of sports entertainment, the most "WWE match" of all WWE matches.

Judge Ultimate Warrior vs. Randy Savage as a traditional pro wrestling contest and you will miss that which makes it brilliant, but analyze it as the sports entertainment masterpiece that it is and discover how it was the match that unlocked the full potential of the WWE philosophy.

First, there was the stipulation. After months of attacks, the most famous of which cost him the WWF Championship at The

Royal Rumble, Ultimate Warrior finally agreed to face The Macho King, but the animosity had grown to such a level that they each put their career on the line at *WrestleMania VII*. With the stakes so high in what was predominantly still a kayfabe world in 1991, WrestleMania for the first time had a featured match that was not for the WWF Title that could have just as easily been that year's main-event. There was a palpable aura surrounding the Career-Ending Match fueled by the nature of such insinuated finality and both superstars rose to the occasion to sell it through their facial expressions, body language, and combative actions.

The entrances were muted versions of the more grandiose productions that would follow in the years to come, but were still quite grandiose for their day. Warrior bucked a tradition that he followed for the rest of his WWF career and walked deliberately to the ring, psychologically in-tune with the energy that he would expend if he had run his standard sprint. Even his choice of attire, for fans who look at the smallest details in WWE's presentation, raised the stakes, featuring as it did a picture of the WWF Title on the back of his trunks surrounded by the words "Means Much More Than This." Macho King and his "Sensational" Queen Sherri, meanwhile, were carried on a platform-throne by their subjects in a manner that a deeper thinker might suggest was symbolic of his intentions to remain at the top of the mountain.

In regards to Sherri Martel, the role that she played was incredibly versatile. She had been a central figure in the build-up, trying to mentally break the Warrior's resolve in order to get her King a title shot and simultaneously serve her own interests. During the match, she was part equalizer for Savage, a constantly distracting presence given that the Warrior character's hatred for her ran so deep, and antagonist for Savage to be able to lose as a villain but, in the immediate aftermath, reunite with Miss Elizabeth to send him "into retirement" with a hero's reception. Sherri delivered the performance of her Hall of Fame career in a truly tremendous reminder of the value that managers can bring.

Warrior and Savage both had more famous matches – Warrior had the Hogan match from the year prior and Savage, of course, had the Steamboat match at *WrestleMania III* and his own battle with Hogan at *WrestleMania V* – yet neither man was ever better than he was in the Career-Ending Match.

Sports Entertainment as a concept is epitomized by character-acting, a total commitment on the part of the performer to what his character would do in any given situation. The level of engagement that both superstars showed in this instance puts the match in an extremely rare class; it is virtually dripping with character. The Warrior was so defiant of the King and Queen from the very beginning of their feud. During the match, from his slap across Macho Man's face to his refusal to treat Sherri as a "fair lady" to kicking out after five of Savage's patented Flying Elbow Drops, his ability to physically emote that defiance was arguably the most memorable part of the bell-to-bell run-time because it stands in such contrast to the majority of his overall body of work. Then, after Macho miraculously kicked out of the Ultimate Gorilla-Press, Running Splash combo, the conversation that Warrior carried on with whatever mythical being from which he always drew his power was perfectly-executed drama. Without a doubt, it was the match of Warrior's life.

Savage was renowned by that point for what would eventually become known as "stealing the show," but it did not stop him from delivering his career best too. Macho Man accomplished more in about forty minutes that night than most wrestlers accomplish in thirty years. He always wrestled like the manic human-being he truly was; the prospect of his career being ended sent his character into an internally-relatable zone, seemingly the one of the two involved who was feeling the immense pressure of the stipulation the most. With your livelihood threatened, you would expect to have trouble controlling your emotions, both constructive and destructive; Savage was able to find that conflict within himself and express it to all of us while cheating like crazy to the point where he could still get booed. His incredulous looks when Warrior slapped him or when he lost all the early momentum or when Warrior kicked out of his Elbow Drop spree made it possible for facial expressions to stand out as one of the indelible memories of a match. The timing of his reactions to Elizabeth being in the ring and their ensuing embrace was just poetic; if your heart is beating, surely that still sends a tingle up your spine when you relive that moment.

Warrior-Savage was essentially the birth of the modern day WWE main-event. The use of what has become a standard trope of kicking out of each other's finishing moves to add a plot twist to the composition was novel back then. In 1991, a finishing move from one combatant which failed to finish a match was not uncommon, but *trading* finisher kick-outs was as awe-inspiring as an initial viewing of a Ladder or Hell in a Cell Match, a visually-stunning and eye-popping occurrence that made you stand up out of your seat; rare has a top-billed match since then not utilized the exchange of finishers. The ensuing exhaustion displayed to such a heightened extent by Savage in particular should also look quite familiar on replay. Many of its peers in the greatest of all-time discussion have borrowed from its playbook.

On commentary, Gorilla Monsoon and Bobby "The Brain" Heenan were just magnificently complimentary to the story being told in the ring. Warrior vs. Savage would have been 75% of the match that it was in 1991 had it taken place with modern commentary. Monsoon and Heenan never failed to point out the important nuance central to the emotional lines being cast by the in-ring performers, combining to hook the televised audience and reel them further and further into the fiction as the match progressed. Commentary is an art, a lost art in today's WWE in the minds of many, reliant on the team being as invested in what is happening in the ring as we are, while also cognizant of what the wrestlers are attempting to physically communicate. "Appropriately histrionic" would be a suitable phrase to describe Heenan and Monsoon's commentary for the Career-Ending

Match; a certain amount of verbal theatricality was needed to fit the situation, especially for the reunification of Macho and Miss Elizabeth, perhaps the most dramatic moment of its kind in WWE lore. It cannot be understated just how excellent a duo that Monsoon and Heenan were; if they made compilations of awesome commentary, the Heenan and Monsoon call of Warrior-Savage would surely make the list.

WWE is inherently a melodrama as much as it is an exhibition of elite athleticism, hence the sports entertainment label. From top to bottom, from the establishment of the modern main-event plot device of spectacularly engaging finisher kick-outs to the commentary to an unforgettable "WrestleMania Moment" to character-acting of the highest order that wrestling has to offer to elaborate pre-match routines, Warrior vs. Savage was a microcosm of sports entertainment as a philosophy and taught us everything that WWE matches could be.

#3
Stone Cold Steve Austin vs. The Rock
WrestleMania Trilogy (XV, X-Seven, XIX)
Top 5 All-Time at WrestleMania / Top 10 Match in 1999 / Match of the Year in 2001 / Top 5 Match in 2003

The Monday Night War that inspired the WWF Attitude Era was the most competitive period in pro wrestling history. Not only was there a weekly ratings battle between two companies at the peak of their all-time popularity, but there was an internal struggle in each locker room to see who could grab the proverbial brass ring and capitalize on wrestling history's greatest financial boom. With elite talent from the undercard to the main-event scratching and clawing to get to or stay at the top, the products produced by WCW and the WWF never felt more must-see. All but five of the Top 30 stars of the entire WrestleMania Era played roles in wrestling's 1997-2001 peak.

Emerging as the two dominant personalities who stood heads above their peers during that stretch were Stone Cold Steve Austin and The Rock. If Austin vs. Mr. McMahon was the greatest story told during wrestling's most famous era, then Austin vs. The Rock was unquestionably the greatest rivalry. At three of the biggest WrestleManias ever, Rock and Stone Cold clashed in headlining matches with much at stake both personally and professionally, their desire to be the absolute best elevating each other and everyone around them to new heights.

WrestleMania XV in Philadelphia was the site of their first epic battle. "At that time, the company was trendsetting and groundbreaking and we were ushering in this incredible era, so it was important to me that I was the one leading the pack; I didn't want to be second when I knew first was available and Steve Austin sure as hell didn't want to be second," The Rock stated in his WWE documentary released in 2012. Ask Austin and he would have told you that first was never available while he was running at his hottest in 1998 and 1999.

The Stone Cold truth was that Austin was king. The Rock may have become WWF Champion at *Survivor Series '98* the previous fall and may have subsequently felt that he was "The Man," but the primary story being told on WWF television was Austin's quest for redemption against McMahon and his Corporation. WWE has, for the bulk of its history, been a babyface's world, built around telling stories that end with the hero standing tall. As the "Corporate Champion," Rock was set-up to be Austin's final hurdle en route to regaining the WWF Championship. Carrying the title into WrestleMania is one of the industry's highest honors, trumped only by leaving WrestleMania as titleholder; in 1999, Rock got the second highest honor and Austin the highest.

Nevertheless, The Great One had spent the entirety of 1998 breathing down Stone Cold's neck in an attempt to put himself in position to take the #1 spot. What made the *'Mania XV* match so special was that Rock managed to get red hot. Hindsight will show that, when compared fairly, Austin was white hot and at the peak of his character's powers while Rock was still ascending; however, the sheer entertainment of Rock's trash talking and the creative verve of his rivalries with Triple H and Mankind put him on near-equal footing with the Texas Rattlesnake. One of the best compliments that can be paid to Rock vs. Austin I was that it felt like the biggest match in WrestleMania lore to many of the then-record 800,000 people who ordered on pay-per-view to watch it; that does not happen without the unprecedented occurrence of two monumental stars rising in unison during quite possibly the most enthralling year of television WWE has ever produced.

WrestleMania X-Seven in Houston offered a completely different context for Rock-Austin II. In the fall of 1999, Stone Cold underwent cervical fusion surgery, leaving the #1 spot up for grabs. Triple H, who did his best to turn WWE into a heel-driven enterprise during his peak, once said that "What made Steve successful and what made all of us successful is we're all a bunch of sharks; and Steve's injury was like chum in the water." As much as Trips tried to change the game, Rock was the one who assumed Austin's previous spot as the lead protagonist. With that role comes the branding as "face of the company" and all of its corresponding media responsibilities, to which The People's Champion took like a duck to water.

Therein lies one of the fascinating aspects of the dichotomy between Austin and Rock. Stone Cold had the charisma to be able to do mainstream appearances and carry himself well, but he perfectly represented the classic "pro wrestler" side of the sports entertainment vs. pro wrestling argument. He was a blue collar guy from Victoria, Texas who just wanted to be the top guy in the wrestling business. Rock was the consummate sports entertainer – the embodiment of what that term was designed to describe. He was the third-generation star with National Championship pedigree identified from day one of his career by Jim Ross as the one who would "be the man"; and it was no surprise when he eventually became a movie star because he always looked Hollywood. The Most Electrifying Man in Sports Entertainment, given a broader scope to showcase his personality, took the media by storm.

Some worried that the WWF might be in trouble when Austin went under the knife. The Rock did not; and that is where their rivalry took a turn.

"Who could have ever thought – as huge as Stone Cold was – that there could ever be anybody who could rival him and in fact eclipse him when it came to mainstream attention," Mick Foley noted in Rock's documentary. "[Rock] was able to capture a larger share of the mainstream audience." Ratings did not go down; PPV business held steady; Rock slam-dunked his hosting gig on *Saturday Night Live,* spoke at the Republican National Convention, and landed a cameo role in the 7th highest-grossing film of 2001, *The Mummy Returns,* which launched his movie career. As he aptly put it, Rock "took the brass ring where it's never been taken."

When Rock first became a star in 1998, he was living in Austin's world. When Austin came back from his injury in 2000, it was no longer his world; it was Rock's. History has proven that, once a wrestler tastes the success of being #1, their competitive internal fire will burn a hole in them if they do not do everything that they can to take another sip. Stone Cold's feud with Triple H, as hot by that point as any heel ever had been in the WWF, went a long way toward rebuilding his momentum. By winning a very memorable Royal Rumble Match in January 2001, Austin seemed poised to tell another redemption story at *WrestleMania X-Seven*; by main-event's end at *No Way Out '01* in February, it became clear that standing in his way once again as WWF Champion would be The Rock. This time, there would be no face-heel dynamic to identify an obvious favorite.

The mere announcement of the match and a brilliant interview with Jim Ross were all that were needed to sell out the Reliant Astrodome with 67,925 fans and to re-set the PPV buy record with 1,040,000 (970,000 of which came from the United States, a domestic record that stands to this day). Their lines from the sit-down with JR set the stage for an iconic encounter. "I will give you every drop of sweat, every drop of blood, every ounce of energy I have...you are going to get the absolute best of The Rock at WrestleMania." Stone Cold responded, "I *need* to beat you, Rock; I need it more than anything that you could ever imagine."

The presentation on the night of brought the anticipation to an incredible level. Paul Heyman, on commentary, called it "a match that both men *have* to win and that neither man can afford to lose." Then, WWF production aired Limp Bizkit's "My Way" blended with noteworthy quotes and brawls between the combatants in the best pre-match hype video package ever created. One of the greatest matches of all-time ensued, a superlative encounter that brought to life a sound bite from Jim Ross that expertly contextualized the occasion: "It's all about heart, it's about personal issues, pride, and about who's gonna be the top man in this business."

Ironically, Austin would win the match by turning heel. He could do no wrong in front of the partisan crowd in Houston; he looked every bit the star in that match as he had in 1999 and it was arguably the best performance of his career. However, The Rock had proven why he had become "The Man" and Austin did not feel like he had reestablished himself to his previous peak, so Stone Cold and Mr. McMahon did the unthinkable and joined forces.

Debate the creative decision at the climax if you wish, but the application of the phrase "all-time classic" to Rock-Austin II cannot be debated.

WrestleMania XIX in Seattle hosted the final battle in the Austin vs. Rock trilogy. The rivalry as we had known it was over by then. They helped set the Safeco Field attendance mark, but no more ratings or PPV records would be set. Two years is a long time in the wrestling industry. By 2003, the Attitude Era was over, Rock was a part-time wrestler transitioning to a full-time Hollywood career, and Stone Cold was breaking down physically to the point that his last match with The Great One would be his last match period.

The letters "OMR" adorned Austin's black vest for Rock vs. Stone Cold III; "One More Round" it was indeed, with much of the Rattlesnake's work during the feud and the match watching like a tribute to that which he had already accomplished in his career. Two years prior, he left WrestleMania as WWF Champion and went on to have his last great year in the business, but had been a shell of himself since. Contrast him to The Rock, who left the post-WrestleMania Raw in 2001 to start filming *The Scorpion King*, becoming the highest paid actor for his first starring role in Hollywood history. Even without the WWF Championship, he remained the bigger star and would continue to pull away from Austin in 2002 and 2003. The Rock's magnificent run as the Hollywood heel leading up to

WrestleMania XIX was a bold statement that he was the absolute best that the industry had ever seen.

For as engaging and enjoyable as the first Rock-Austin WrestleMania match was, it was also the culmination of Austin's feud with McMahon; Rock deserved the best supporting actor award for his role in WWE's greatest story ever told, but Vince was truly the company's top heel back then. For their second WrestleMania match, they were near character equals; arguments could be made for either of them being the best. For their final match at WrestleMania, it was crystal clear that Rock was on a different plane.

Nevertheless, history remembers Austin-Rock III for many things. In addition to Rock's staggering zeal as an entertainer, the combination of Stone Cold's courageous real life effort to gut his way through the match despite having been admitted to the hospital on the night before and the fact that it was effectively Austin's retirement match have made the semi-main-event of *WrestleMania XIX* one of the most historic, entertaining, and emotional bouts ever. Jim Ross, who rivaled his Top 5 all-time best call of Austin-Rock II with his efforts that night in Seattle for the third installment, poignantly stated after the match, "You are looking, ladies and gentlemen, at two of the greatest that this business will have ever offered you. They gave you everything they had in a night that I know in my heart I will never forget as long as I live."

The Rock and Stone Cold Steve Austin are the only pairing in WWE history to main-event two WrestleManias and co-headline a third. Their rivalry continues to be discussed to this day, their extraordinarily rewatchable WrestleMania Trilogy an avatar that fuels the debate of who really was the greatest.

#2
Bret Hart vs. Stone Cold Steve Austin
Survivor Series 1996 to WrestleMania 13
#1A All-Time at WrestleMania / Top 5 All-Time at Survivor Series / Top 5 Match in 1996 / Match of the Year in 1997

Many things can be disputed when arguing one side or the other in the Rock vs. Austin debate, but one thing that remains indisputable is that Stone Cold was the catalyst for the rise and immense popularity of the Attitude Era, not Dwayne Johnson; Austin was the trailblazer in the mid-to-late-1990s. Many things can be disputed when arguing, as well, about the positioning of their rivalry in the all-time greatest debate – Austin vs. Rock characterized the extremely competitive atmosphere that set the Attitude Era apart from all others and, thus, could be said to have best represented what made the most celebrated period in pro wrestling lore so special – but what fifteen years of hindsight have made clear is that even their finest efforts could not equal the over-arching achievement of Stone Cold's rivalry with Bret "The Hitman" Hart.

Very little separates 5-star feuds featuring 5-star caliber matches, so while Austin vs. Hart checks all the boxes that any wrestling fan could ever want in a rivalry like several of its peers, it does so with a little something extra. They produced matches so incredible that you could readily show them to someone who knew nothing of wrestling and expect him or her to enjoy them (in other words, you would not be embarrassed to show anyone that *this* is what you love); their characters exhibited a wide range of relatable emotions toward one another – contempt, respect, and rage to name a few – as they progressed their story from one phase to the next; they had that rare sort of chemistry that made every aspect of their character clashes click, from the physical and the verbal on down to their goals and motivations behind-the-scenes; their work together was timeless, watching every bit as well to the novice just finding his/her bearings as a wrestling fan as it does to the person reliving it for the fiftieth time; and it made a huge impact on the industry as the rivalry that essentially segued the WWF into Attitude.

When you think of all that Austin would go on to do after his rivalry with The Hitman concluded in 1997, particularly from the standpoint of catalyzing pay-per-view buyrate, merchandise, and ratings records, it would be understandable to historically under-appreciate a feud that peaked on The November Classic with the third worst buyrate of the 1990s and on the least purchased WrestleMania in history, but because Austin vs. Hart was near-perfect in pretty much every other way, it has never gotten left out of the conversation about the all-time greatest matches and rivalries and it likely never will. In terms of in-ring achievement, it was the best thing that either Austin or Hart ever did, but it also meant so much more to each man's career than the artistic hole-in-one of a double-turn (face to heel for one, heel to face for the other) or the label of "greatest match ever."

Stone Cold mythology reminds us that the "Austin 3:16" coronation speech at *King of the Ring '96* was his break-out moment, but his true origin story was in the build-up to *Survivor Series*. Austin's words were greater than his actions before his first marquee match against Bret at Madison Square Garden that November, and every powerful word that he said in dressing down the returning legend ("Put the letter 'S' in front of "Hitman" and you have my exact opinion of Bret Hart") made his margin for failure when the bell rang smaller. There was tremendous anticipation for the match, so Austin had to have the match of his life; it was going to be career-defining either way, it just depended on whether or not it would be for positive or negative reasons.

Austin delivered in spades and there remains no better example of how good he was as a technical wrestler before his neck injury at *Summerslam '97* altered the long-term course of his career. He was what you would see if pro wrestling was more like mixed-martial-arts (unscripted) and a kid from a rough neighborhood who saw that you could make millions wrestling professionally (think Conor McGregor, only from Victoria, Texas) decided that he was not satisfied with being tough enough to stomp a mud-hole in your ass and walk it dry, so he developed the elite ability to out-wrestle opponents and make them submit too.

Nobody has ever come close to replicating Austin's blend of hardened bad-ass and technical wrestling acumen; add in his perfect-for-the-period persona and ability to communicate his rhetoric to the people and he was like a pro wrestling unicorn. Unorthodox and rough around the edges as it watched, his style was nevertheless a beautiful thing to witness. After his neck injury, he never regained that peak level of athleticism again, so the *Survivor Series* match was the only chance we got to see him at quite that capacity as a performer at that advanced a level on the card and, for that reason, it should be held in the highest esteem, certainly not on the level of the Submission Match four months later, but too fantastic not to get its due historically.

Before taking Bret to the limit only to have one of his submission holds countered into a sleek pinning combination, Austin gave us a glimpse of what the future looked like and, even though nobody was really ready yet for a future that featured a foul-mouthed bully as the #1 star in the industry, he gave the wrestling world no choice but to adapt and get on board. He was demonstrative and destructive, and it was fascinating; and the bottom line was that, if Austin 3:16, conceptually, was a glass of water roughly half full before *Survivor Series '96*, the success of his performance against Bret ensured that Vince McMahon and WWF creative would pour more water into the glass.

For The Hitman, in contrast, the Austin saga shoved the heroic, genuinely likeable persona that he had used to become the cornerstone star of The New Generation violently into the counter-cultural movement that had defined much of the 1990s while the WWF continually tried to replicate the virtuous formula that had worked so well the decade prior. Vince

McMahon could be called an idealist, a boy at heart who just wants his on-screen world to be as simple as a youthful game of cops and robbers. Bret was the every-man hero in a simpler time, down-to-earth and not the slightest bit over-the-top, with an aw-shucks charm that made him an idealist's role model, so it was a twist of fate when Stone Cold thrust the WWF into the more complicated throes of real life.

Go back and watch again their pre-*Survivor Series* match backstage promos with Todd Pettengil; Austin's was in your face, full of attitude, and a virtual preview of what would become a babyface promo in the Attitude Era, while Bret's more wholesome approach, praising the venue and talking about his fans around the world, was a relic of what would soon become a by-gone era. Both interviews were genuine reflections of the men giving them, but the problem that Bret slammed into was that he rather quickly began to represent an old guard in need of being swept aside to make room for the force of nature that was Austin and everything that The Texas Rattlesnake stood for.

To Bret's undying credit, he adapted extraordinarily well to the changing times, turning into the whiny antagonist obsessed with the way things were (or "should be") and becoming a fantastic villain whose many gripes made him genuinely dislikeable. The downside was that it seemed like the man got lost in the character's transition. When all he really wanted to be was the respected champion of the World Wrestling Federation, admired by fans and peers alike, Bret instead was re-cast as a stick in the mud standing in the way of a revolution. It felt wrong back then, watching him devolve from the revered "wrestler's wrestler" into the "get off my lawn!" old man, of sorts. He left a piece of his soul in 1997, as much because he abandoned the best part of his authentic self to become a critically acclaimed top heel as because of the events with Shawn Michaels leading up to Montreal. Thanks to Stone Cold, he had to abandon his highly successful comfort zone.

He was never the same after the Austin feud, which he ironically asked for in the first place leading up to *Survivor Series '96*. Their match at MSG mirrored the reality that Bret saw something in the former WCW mid-carder that few others did, offering him a platform to showcase his considerable talents while simultaneously adding to his own growing legend. None of Bret's classic matches are as underrated as his first match with Stone Cold at the Garden. Forming an awesome technical-brawling hybrid, they married grappling with kicking ass like perhaps no other opponents ever have. They so perfectly complimented each other and at the same time forced each other to prove that one's strength was not the other's weakness; Austin got down on the mat and wrestled Bret's game, then Bret came back with fists flying and had a school-yard scrap with Austin.

The Hitman picked up the cunning victory, but it proved a mutually beneficial endeavor thanks to Bret's ability to adapt his in-ring game and his willingness to give so much to a relative newcomer on the rise. That it was also the final time in such a high quality situation that we saw Bret play the protagonistic role that made him famous is both iconic and sad, but that was the ultimate achievement of their pairing as opponents – there was not an emotion that professional wrestling is capable of eliciting that Austin and Hart did not bring out of the fans across their nearly year-long storyline.

As the decreasingly valiant former WWF Champion scratched and clawed toward taking back the title that he so famously dropped to Michaels at *WrestleMania XII*, Stone Cold screwed The Hitman over repeatedly. Austin cost Bret the 1997 Royal Rumble Match, when Hart eliminated Stone Cold while all the referees were tending to a ringside melee, allowing Austin to sneak back in and eliminate Bret; he even cost Hart the title the night after The Hitman had finally won it back at *In Your House: Final Four*. The Submission Match at *WrestleMania 13* was the culmination of Hart's frustrations boiling over, prompting him to absolutely lose it on the go-home episode of Monday Night Raw and head into the Chicago-hosted "Granddaddy of Them All" with his temper flaring beyond the point of rational response.

Some people respond to seemingly never-ending setbacks by heavily drinking, others by getting extremely depressed and others still, like Bret Hart, by becoming extraordinarily angry; each way is an exhibition in the human condition, particularly of the worst sides of ourselves. Relatable to most everyone as his actions may have been, nobody really wanted to see someone like The Hitman, who had shown us glimpses through his character of the best sides of ourselves, falling into the abyss of negative emotions that so often wreak havoc on our own lives. Such is what set the tone for Hart and Austin to simultaneously switch allegiances in Chicago.

"We've watched as our heroes stepped down from their pedestals," the voice of the WWF's pre-pay-per-view video packages told us at the beginning of *WrestleMania 13*, referencing Hart. What an appropriate and powerful choice of words, and ultimately one of the biggest slights that could possibly have been levied at the leading star of The New Generation. And Austin just kept coming, building more momentum with each passing month despite acts that even six months prior would have been considered dastardly, especially if aimed at The Hitman. Any conventional thinker who insisted that the next time Hart was "screwed" by Austin, it would finally be the point when the crowd would stop increasingly cheering Stone Cold and decreasingly booing Bret was proven wrong time and again. The anti-hero was born.

Jim Ross prophetically mentioned on commentary ahead of the *'Series* classic, "I think it could come down to a Submission Match." At *WrestleMania 13*, the actual Submission Match became one of the two greatest matches ever, interchangeable with a match from twelve years later depending on your stylistic preference.

No match in professional wrestling history has ever been quite so captivating from start to finish, as it added layer upon layer of story, particularly for those who either lived the era that produced Bret and then Stone Cold as the industry's top stars or can deeply appreciate it in hindsight.

It was thrilling for anyone who swore undying allegiance to one wrestler or the other; those who revered Austin for the method by which he climbed the hierarchical ladder to immense success in the WWF, bucking tradition at every turn and flipping off anyone who stood in his way – or even for just how damn good he was – got to see Austin open up a can of whoop-ass in the uncrowned main-event of *WrestleMania 13* (Sid vs. Taker was second-page stuff by comparison) and exhibit the greatest exemplification of the phrase "a picture is worth a thousand words" in pro wrestling lore; those who venerated The Hitman saw him batter and bloody Stone Cold and make him pass out due to blood loss and pain while locked in the Sharpshooter and have another 5-star classic to add to the list of in-ring reasons why they loved him.

For anyone on the fence about either wrestler, it was the ultimate emotional roller-coaster. Going into the match, those who admired and respected The Hitman for being an idyllic figure in their lives held on with a firm grasp that he might exorcise his Austin demons and gracefully move on with his honor intact, apologetic perhaps that he had let himself go so far but, as the match wore on, their grasp loosened until Hart, the idol, fell, replaced with a bitter, scornful shell of the man he used to be; it was disappointing to watch. Those, meanwhile, who initially felt disdain for Austin when he first started targeting Bret were, by the climax of the Submission Match, deeply respectful of his intestinal fortitude at least and capable of being won over by his commitment and his toughness at most; his will to win and to keep on fighting, with blood pouring down his face as he struggled to escape the Sharpshooter, was downright inspiring.

As the most readily identifiable genesis point for the Attitude Era, as one of the two greatest matches ever, as the platform for the career defining moment of the most popular wrestler in WWE history, and as the spark for the most characterful year on Bret Hart's Hall of Fame resume, the Submission Match bleeds with intangible qualities that vault it to the top of the all-time discussion. Plus, as everyone has that movie that they can watch over and over again and never get bored, Hart vs. Austin at *WrestleMania 13* is the most rewatchable professional wrestling match ever for a great many wrestling fans. Its legacy will endure through the generations.

So, indeed, many things can be disputed when arguing about the top 0.001% of the matches and rivalries in pro wrestling lore and there are good points to be made for several already discussed entries on this particular list, but it is indisputable that Bret Hart vs. Stone Cold Steve Austin was a feud between two of the top ten WWE superstars ever that produced critical masterpieces of epic, historical proportions which featured two of the finest big match climaxes ever on huge stages during one of the most important periods in wrestling history. Do an honest, thorough evaluation of greatness as defined on these pages and say that you did not come up with Austin vs. Hart as #1 or #2...good luck with that. It might very well be the best there is, was, or ever will be, not because Stone Cold said so, but because the bottom line is that, by any analytical standard, only one other rivalry actually rivals it.

#1
Shawn Michaels vs. The Undertaker
In Your House: Ground Zero to Royal Rumble
'98; 25th Anniversary of WrestleMania to
WrestleMania XXVI

#1 All-Time at WrestleMania / Top 20 All-Time at WrestleMania / #1 All-Time Hell in a Cell Match / Top 5 Match in 1997 / Match of the Year in 2009 / Match of the Year in 2010

WrestleMania has an uncanny appeal. It has an incredible magnetism that draws people in like no other professional wrestling event. The wrestlers share the sentiment, placing "The Show of Shows" on a pedestal and recognizing it as the definitive supercard on which to make their mark. Heightened audience enthusiasm and performer recognition of the occasion creates an electric emotional combination.

Many WWE Superstars have excelled on wrestling's Super Bowl stage, but perhaps no two ever more so than Shawn Michaels and Undertaker. It is where they built the foundations for their legacies. Ric Flair once called Michaels "the man who is synonymous with WrestleMania." Indeed, HBK earned the "Mr. WrestleMania" moniker by consistently out-performing his peers when the lights were on brightest; this book has paid tribute to each classic match he offered us at "The Granddaddy Of 'Em All." Simultaneously, for a different set of reasons, Undertaker is synonymous with WrestleMania too. As has also been highlighted in this book, The Phenom's twenty-one WrestleManias without defeat are as legendary a collective accomplishment as has ever been achieved in pro wrestling. Champions will be crowned and unbelievable matches will take place at future WrestleManias, but "The Streak" will never be duplicated.

By the *25th Anniversary of WrestleMania*, both "The Streak" and "Mr. WrestleMania" were well-established as two primary selling points for the biggest event of the year as "The Showcase of the Immortals" enjoyed its rise to unprecedented success. Undertaker's sparkling 16-0 Streak included defeats of Hall of Famers Jimmy Snuka, Jake Roberts, Diesel, Big Bossman, Flair, and Edge; he held victories over WrestleMania main-eventers King Kong Bundy, Big Show, Triple H, Randy Orton, and Batista and his fabled storyline-brother, Kane, as well. Edge argued that Taker's Streak was more important at its peak than the World Championship...and it would be hard to argue against him. Meanwhile, HBK's WrestleMania curriculum vitae featured one Match of the Year candidate after another, beginning with the Ladder Match and the Ironman Match before his first retirement. Upon his return, he took his WrestleMania reputation to new heights in matches against Chris Jericho, Triple H/Chris Benoit, Kurt Angle, John Cena, and Flair.

Steve Austin vs. The Rock had pitted against each other the two biggest stars of a single era. Hulk Hogan vs. The Rock had literally been a dream come true. Never, though, had we witnessed a clash between two wrestlers who been able to build such substantial WrestleMania legacies without ever having crossed paths on WWE's grandest stage. It was wrestling's equivalent of Michael Jordan (the NBA's greatest clutch performer) somehow taking his Bulls to the NBA Finals to battle with Bill Russell (the NBA's greatest winner) and his Celtics. Two massively influential bodies of work constructed over multi-decade long careers; "Mr. WrestleMania vs. The Streak."

Michaels and Taker had a captivating history together, of course.

Believe it or not, there was a match in 1997 that some would say was almost as good as Austin vs. Bret at *'Mania 13* – Michaels vs. Taker in the inaugural Hell in a Cell Match at *In Your House: Badd Blood*. In the same year that The Phenom won the WWF Championship in his first WrestleMania main-event, HBK was in the midst of an envelope-pushing personic transformation that nearly as well characterized "Attitude" as Stone Cold. His sophomoric antics, on which D-Generation X was built, found an intriguing target in Undertaker, who had never really had his straight-forward, silent warrior buttons pressed by an antagonist quite like Michaels.

Their exploits at WrestleMania, both separate from and against each other, tend to combine with the down-period reputation of the WWF, pre-'Mania XIV, to overshadow the outstanding work that both men offered in their 1997 feud but, by itself (separated from the overall rivalry), their Hell in a Cell is a Top 25 all-time contender, a five-star outing that put to full use the willingness of HBK to put his body on the line, highlighted by a bloodied and beaten Michaels crashing from off of the side of the Cell through the announce table in a moment in time overshadowed in its own right by both Austin's iconic blood-soaked primal scream in the Sharpshooter and Mick Foley's June 1998 "that killed him" fall from off the top of the Cell.

Michaels, thanks to his tremendous matches with the likes of Diesel, Sid, and Vader, had developed a well-known knack for working either as a heroic or villainous David opposite Goliath, but Taker was regarded already as on a level or two above in the big man category. To see the Goliath of the 1990s against the giant-slayer of the 1990s was enthralling, then the addition of a massive cage with a roof on it took it into the stratosphere for potential all-time greatness. By the time HBK imploded the announce desk, he had already endured a glorious beating, tossed around like a lawn-dart for the better part of a quarter-hour; Kane's debut to cost his "brother" the match capped the original Cell as the night that HBK came as close as he ever could to replicating his idol Ric Flair's mastery of getting his ass kicked only to sneak out with a victory by the skin of his teeth. It may not be the complete package in hindsight, but when a match of its caliber serves as the enhancement part of your rivalry's resume, clearly something has been done very right.

Months later, the back injury occurred during their Casket Match at *Royal Rumble '98* that caused HBK's first retirement. When Michaels came back, it took until the brilliant climax of the 2007

Royal Rumble Match for them to have any meaningful interaction, but it was worth the wait; it acted like a teaser-trailer for their renewed rivalry to come. Then they were #1 and #2 in the 2008 Royal Rumble Match, fanning the speculative flames that they would soon be meeting at 'Mania. WWE was smart to wait.

WWE, along with HBK and Taker, also deserve credit for not resting on their laurels when it finally came time to execute the long-awaited showdown. The greatest matches, rivalries, and stories should be able to transcend any era; and Undertaker vs. Michaels is a timeless story. Twenty years from now, fans may not be able to fully comprehend the context of simply "Mr. WrestleMania vs. The Streak"; part of the allure of the match in 2009 was that many of us were around to see the progression of both careers. However, any future fan should be able to appreciate "Heaven vs. Hell."

At *Royal Rumble '09*, Taker approached HBK backstage and delivered the ominous message, "Sometimes, it's hell trying to get to Heaven." Michaels would later respond with a unique brand of mind games, drawing from his real life faith in an attempt to fill The Deadman character's dark world with light. They accentuated the duality in their pre-match entrances, with HBK (dressed in white) descending from a raised platform with near-blinding light behind him, plus a Church-like chorus, and Taker (dressed in black) ascending from beneath the stage to his typical funeral march. Even today, it never fails to set the tone for rewatching the encounter.

Think, for a moment, of the pressure on HBK and Taker to deliver. The expectation was "greatest match of all-time." Anything less than a strong contender would have been considered a disappointment, not just from fans and critics, mind you, but from their peers; they may well be the two most revered wrestlers in WWE lore backstage. Michaels had spent all of 2008 convincing the wrestling world that he was still on top of his game. Undertaker was in the shape of his life and was coming off the two most critically acclaimed years of his career. The anticipation for their match at *WrestleMania 25* was off the charts, a fact reflected in one of the most frenzied live crowd reactions in WWE lore.

The first half of the match played out in accordance with the TV hype. Michaels, drawing confidence bordering on cockiness from his unblemished past record against Taker, continued getting in The Deadman's head, slapping him and feigning injury to gain any possible advantage. The Phenom seemingly ended HBK's upset bid by locking him in the aptly-named Hell's Gate submission and shortly thereafter swatting him out of the air like a pesky fly during an attempted moonsault off the top turnbuckle to the outside. However, Taker's ensuing ill-fated dive over the ropes changed the tone of the match.

Taker's head-first collision with the floor intensified the drama beyond what diving into a cameraman could have accomplished; the supernatural facade was broken and Taker rendered a mere mortal. If the first 16-minutes, then, were more about "Heaven vs. Hell" and less about "Mr. WrestleMania vs. The Streak," then the second 16-minutes switched the dichotomy. The way that Michaels sold the dive and the subsequent potential of winning by count out was a break from the calm self-assurance that had marked his persona throughout the hype and the match to that point. From then on, it was about beating that Streak by any means necessary. No near count out has ever been emoted so strikingly.

The reason why so many of their peers, such as Y2J, refer to Michaels vs. Taker 1 as "the best match of all-time...by far" is because of the epically emotional roller-coaster ride that began with the dive. Undertaker side-stepping the super kick into one of the best chokeslams ever delivered, only for HBK to kick out of the pin attempt; Michaels connecting with Sweet Chin Music out of nowhere, only for Taker to kick out; the gorgeous, all-time great Last Ride sequence, ending with another HBK kick out; Michaels skinning the cat as he had done so many times before right into an awaiting Undertaker Tombstone Piledriver, only for HBK to yet again kick out (and Taker to very mortally sell disbelief as well as he ever had); the second Tombstone attempt which Michaels countered into a DDT to start his tried-and-true comeback routine, culminating in a big-time, tuned-up rendition of Sweet Chin Music despite which Undertaker again avoided defeat; the physical and mental exhaustion that they both sold so well during the final ten-minutes; and, finally, Michaels performing a moonsault but being caught in mid-air by Undertaker for a decisive Tombstone, HBK's desperate dig into his old bag of tricks leading to his undoing.

What a beautiful, beautiful performance...

Yet, certainly, the obvious question in the context of this book's theme is, "Why does it deserve to be #1 over what was basically just referred to as the 'perfect match'?"

Oddly, the answer is "it does not."

If wrestling were only about what took place in the ring, then honestly Hart vs. Austin would have been #1. To the purist, it may not sit well that other factors are considered, but it does not change the fact that all relevant criteria must be accounted for to conduct a thorough historical analysis. Ranked head-to-head, HBK vs. Taker at 'Mania 25 and Bret vs. Stone Cold at 'Mania 13 actually rate equally. Comparing the most basic qualities – selling, psychology, execution, and climax – Hart vs. Austin is the better match; HBK vs. Taker draws a much more vocally emotional response from the audience, though, thanks in no small part to the strength of its false finishes and its long, storied pre-match history and hype; it also dominates at the box office, edging it to a photo finish at the end of the race.

So, truthfully, despite all the elements identified in an attempt to make a definitive comparative declaration, the most heralded matches in the top two rivalries of the WrestleMania Era actually tied. Taker-HBK and Austin-Hart are the greatest matches ever; #1 and #1A.

The Heartbreak Kid vs. The Deadman sits at #1, instead, because, in addition to the merits of the first-ever Hell in a Cell, there was also a clear victor when their second match at WrestleMania was compared to the other of the classics in the Hitman vs. Stone Cold series at *Survivor Series '96*. Though one of the best technical wrestling matches of the 1990s, Hart and Austin's initial encounter is, overall, humbled by HBK's final performance.

Shawn Michaels and Undertaker stamped themselves as arguably the two greatest in-ring storytellers wrestling has ever seen in their second match. In the rematch, it was more personal. As it was not as theatrical as the first match and carried a more serious tone, there are some who favor HBK-Taker II as the superior effort.

The story was indeed riveting. Michaels grew desperate to end "The Streak," but Undertaker would not grant him another shot at breaking it, leaving all of us to ponder his reasoning. At that time, Undertaker was World Heavyweight Champion. During the 2010 Royal Rumble Match, HBK was eliminated while literally scratching and clawing to hold onto the top rope; his quest to earn another match at 'Mania with The Phenom thwarted, he essentially wrote the "how to sell disappointment" chapter for the Pro Wrestling 101 textbook. He proceeded to cost Taker the title and, in response, The Deadman not only granted the rematch but also raised the stakes.

How do you even try to top the (1A) greatest match ever? At *WrestleMania XXVI*, it was "Streak vs. Career." That was how...

To reiterate a point made throughout the book, one of the most impressive things you will see on the 20'X20' canvas is the manner in which wrestlers create nuance in consecutive matches against each other.

HBK vs. Taker II was presented in such stark contrast to the original. Jim Ross called the first match a battle between "defiance and destruction." That was actually a more fitting theme for the rematch. Michaels had no special entrance, which accented what was at stake for him and that he was entirely focused on winning, but Taker came up from below the same as before; there was a much faster pace throughout, the run-time having been reduced by ten-minutes to create a sense of frenzy; it was the more psychologically sound match, exemplified by Taker injuring his knee while performing Old School and Michaels making it a focal point for the rest of the match, even targeting it during a courageous moonsault from the top turnbuckle to the announce table; HBK perfectly sold the desperation of the moment and Taker did a wonderful job fluctuating between anger, frustration, disbelief, pity, and pain; the little touches differentiating the big moments from the previous match were remarkable; and then the incredible storytelling that punctuated the climax, with Taker momentarily hesitating on his death blow and HBK's last act of defiance – a Taker-mocking throat-slashing gesture and a hard slap across the face leading to an emphatic (jumping) final Tombstone.

Another beautiful performance...

When you assess the totality of a wrestling rivalry, a certain theme emerges that defines its repute. What makes Undertaker vs. Michaels extraordinary cannot be simplified into a single theme. It is not just the barn-burner, the show-stealer, or the dream match; it is not merely about cutthroat competition, the dawn or end of an era, or proving oneself. If specifying the traits of greatness is akin to putting together a jigsaw puzzle, then Shawn Michaels vs. Undertaker is what the finished product looks like. HBK vs. Taker is WWE at its finest, the very best representative of integrating every theme discussed in this book.

Someday, a match, rivalry, or story will come along that takes away the all-time greatest title from them, but you must wonder if similar elements will ever blend together to create such a perfect storm as HBK vs. Taker again. Without question, we will enjoy the journey of finding out.

Rankings Reference Guide

The ranking process began with the performance of the best match in a rivalry or story (with one exception, Austin vs. McMahon) against its peers from the same year. Borrowing from the classic star ratings scale used to evaluate matches, 1-to-5 scores were given for the following specific categories to build an initial framework that could then be used to provide numerical data grouping the truly elite together at the top of the initial hierarchy: the quality of the build-up, climax, execution, false finishes, generated crowd response, plot twists, and psychology, as well as its historic nature, intangibles, time allotment, Match of the Year awards (from myself, the incomparable Dave Meltzer, and *Pro Wrestling Illustrated*), and a combination of its pay-per-view buy number/rate (or TV rating) and attendance. For example, Ricky Steamboat vs. Ric Flair's highest score among the three all-timers was 50.0 in 1989 compared to 51.5 for the Triple H vs. Mick Foley Street Fight at MSG in 2000. The process was repeated for both the best of each major event and stipulation match, the data for which was then blended with the year-to-year scores for greater clarity on the initial rankings.

Once the initial phase was completed, head-to-head competition allowed matches that were not in the raw-scored Top 100 to move in and occasionally climb high. The Top 100 you have just read was finalized by watching the greatest of all-time head-to-head, factoring in the overall resumes (see Edge-Taker), and applying a touch of simple logic.

For those of you who appreciate the nerdy fun I had creating this system, here is a breakdown of the rankings:

-Hart vs. Piper (40.0 in 1992) falls to Mysterio-Angle (40.5 in 2002) on account of year-to-year score, the latter also boosted by its intangible of being among the five greatest openers in WWE PPV lore

-Rollins vs. Reigns (46.0 in 2016) has a great raw score, but logically fell back so that it can win more critics over and pass the test of time. The 2011 Smackdown Elimination Chamber (43.5 in 2011) deserved a spot, but did not perform well head-to-head, which was the strength of the WWF period piece otherwise known as Orndorff vs. Hogan (39.0 in 1987).

-Batista vs. Cena (41.0 in 2010) got an assist from being a clash of an era's titans, but could not outshine the shock (and standing among Rumbles) of Cena's '08 January Classic (42.5 in 2008)

-Lesnar vs. Guerrero (39.5 in 2004) did well head-to-head against the aforementioned; it was not good enough, however, to avoid being overwhelmed by the considerable raw score for Race vs. Ric Flair (48.0 in 1983); the same issue was not to be found in the more aesthetically palatable Jericho vs. Punk (44.5 in 2012)

-Bret Hart's one night treble at King of the Ring '93, the best effort from which – a 37.5 in 1993 for Perfect vs. Bret in the Semis – is just flat better than Punk-Jericho, but Kane vs. Taker, especially when considered as a story, was so distinct that its raw score advantage (41.5 in 1998) was enough to usurp it.

-Slaughter vs. Sheik (49.0 in 1984) so dominated its limited peers in the early '80s that it earned a "this must make the cut as long as it does not suck head-to-head" (it did not) response, but it does not pass the test in a no rules environment against Edge vs. Foley (43.0 in 2006); Rollins vs. Triple H (still under review) was just such a great blend of new and old school that confidence remains in the face of great potential scrutiny that it will justify its position, in time.

-Midnight Express vs. Road Warriors (45.0 in 1986) benefited from being like nothing the two major promotions ever produced and a Starrcade gem (which mattered), but Triple H vs. Jericho (41.5 in 2000 / #1 Last Man Standing Match) was so good head-to-head; just not quite as good head-to-head as Edge and Mysterio vs. Benoit and Angle (43.0 in 2002), which was not quite as good head-to-head as Vader vs. Sting (40.0 in 1992) or Rock vs. Jericho (41.0 in 2002).

-Sting vs. Ric Flair (46.0 in 1988) offered excellent proof of the long-term viability of Flair's finest outings but, at its finest, Rock vs. Kurt Angle (despite 41.0 in 2001) is among history's most underrated; the same can be said for Bret vs. Diesel (42.5 in 1995), which despite being soundly defeated by Taker vs. Angle (40.5 in 2006) head-to-head can similarly be labeled as "held back" by its lack of crowd heat.

-Piper vs. Valentine (45.5 in 1983), like other innovators from the NWA in the 1980s, scored well enough across the process to land the top spot in the first quarter of the Top 100; its uniqueness failed to elevate it over such a prime example of what 'Mania has become, Triple H vs. Cena (44.5 in 2006), its own uniqueness failing to boost it ahead of the totality that was The Women's Revolution (46.5 in 2015 for Banks vs. Bayley, 45.5 in 2016 for Banks vs. Charlotte).

-Rock 'n Roll Express vs. The Andersons (48.0 in 1986) not only has the "you won't see anything else like this" thing going for it, but it also has one of those gargantuan raw scores that jump off the page from the original, year-to-year rankings; it just cannot compare to the gargantuan story of Hogan vs. Savage (45.5 in 1989), which cannot compare aesthetically to Mysterio vs. Jericho (despite 41.0 in 2009).

-Matt Hardy vs. Edge (just a 37.0 in 2005) blew away the field for about three straight months of head-to-head battles against everything discussed before it before running into a rivalry in Punk vs. Jeff Hardy (42.0 in 2009) that had similar qualities but a stouter resume; the same could be said for the rivalry that edged it out, Jericho vs. Benoit (40.0 in 2001).

-Team Austin vs. Team Bischoff (40.5 in 2003) was just such a tremendous viewing experience, but Michaels vs. Flair (47.0 in

2008), as a viewing experience, has few peers in its own right; the chemistry and overall feud quality of Orton vs. Christian (41.0 in 2011) elevated it considerably.

-The reputation that the Flair vs. Funk "I Quit" Match (40.5 in 1989) has maintained over the years kept it from dropping, but Angle vs. Shane (41.5 in 2001) was like Hardy-Edge in how it climbed so high via head-to-head competition before another of those comparable performances with a grander resume emerged to halt its upward trajectory, Cena vs. Umaga (45.0 in 2007), itself limited from moving up any further by the unusual but statistically stout Taker vs. Lesnar rivalry (40.5 in 2002).

-Hogan vs. Flair (42.0 in 1994) was validated by the head-to-head competition; WCW really did it justice at Bash at the Beach. Ambrose vs. Rollins (41.5 in 2014 / 40.0 in 2015) is an evolving modern achievement that should end up in the Top 30 someday frankly, but for now it has to work past a formidable Triple H vs. Batista saga (41.0 in 2005), which was slightly lesser overall than the generational Cena vs. Orton rivalry (43.5 in 2009).

-Hogan vs. Andre (45.0 in 1987) was an historic titan, the logical weight of its gaudy financial records carrying it all the way to right beneath Bret Hart vs. Mr. Perfect (45.5 in 1991), which much like Steamboat vs. Savage at WrestleMania III was just a timeless masterpiece, a distinction that Luger vs. Flair (47.0 in 1988) has rarely earned but that still remains one of the quintessential Nature Boy classics.

-Rock vs. Brock (43.0 in 2002) was basically Rock-Hogan Lite, in terms of it being a brilliant spectacle that holds up so very well against its event-specific peers, but Guerrero vs. JBL (43.5 in 2004) dominates everything up until the Top 50 head-to-head thanks to Latino Heat's career-defining, pantheon performances.

-WWE has developed a tendency to run good things into the ground; nevertheless, when it was peaking, Brock Lesnar: The Conqueror was an absolutely captivating story (44.0 in 2015 for

Lesnar-Rollins-Cena, 46.0 in 2015 for Lesnar-Reigns) that should hold up when the dust settles, maybe even overtake Bret Hart vs. The USA (43.0 in 1997), which for now remains the superior tale. Neither story, however, can compete with the inaugural Money in the Bank Ladder Match (46.5 in 2005).

-Batista vs. Taker (47.5 in 2007) provoked a lot of thought in the early Top 50 discussion, its spot here both advanced by its 'Mania ties and halted here due to the logic induced by not wanting to over-value its 'Mania ties; Taker vs. Mankind (44.0 in 1998) demanded a spot higher because the Hell in a Cell is so historic, which was also the driving force thanks to the star power on display (and economic figures) in Hogan vs. Michaels (42.5 in 2005). Punk vs. Taker (46.0 in 2013) was simply better head-to-head.

-Savage vs. Flair (47.0 in 1992), when dissected, just has an enduring quality to it for a plethora of reasons that make its year-to-year and 'Mania-specific scores unsurprisingly impressive, but War Games '92 (47.5 in 1992) falls into that "there is nothing else like this" category, which often helped the NWA/WCW entries on the countdown. Team Cena vs. The Authority (45.5 in 2014), though, is a modern masterpiece, another of those performances that raised its profile in head-to-head competition to a degree unexpected when the process ramped up.

-In addition to its juggernaut scores across the initial rankings phases, Cena vs. Michaels (50.5 in 2007) held up well head-to-head against stiff competition; only logic dictated that it not be even higher here. Logic favored, instead, rivalries like Lesnar vs. Angle (45.0 in 2003), which was subdued by Cena vs. Styles (Top 10 Rumble / Top 10 Summerslam), whose resume even without passing the test of time was just too impressive to ignore.

-Guerrero vs. Misterio (46.0 in 1997) forever will remain in the heat of battle in the Top 50 because of how well it held up against Taker-HBK HIAC and Hart-Austin in 1997, but Michaels vs. Bret Hart (50.5 in 1996), in spite of its flaws, was too tough head-to-head for a match primarily in its place here due to innovation to advance beyond. The singular qualities of Flair vs. Rhodes (46.0 in 1985), on the other hand, kept the NWA gem ahead of the iconic New Gen feud. Much like its fellow 2014 multi-man classic, The Shield vs. The Wyatts (despite a 42.0 in 2014) destroyed most everything in its wake when watched back-to-back.

-The '04 Rumble (47.0 in 2004) was the total package in the rankings, awesome against tough competition in its year, gimmick, and event. Magnum TA vs. Tully Blanchard (47.5 in 1985), though, overpowered contemporary matches, rivalries, and stories with its NWA charm and realism. Head-to-head in a tight race, Edge vs. Cena (48.5 in 2006) outlasted the Steel Cage "I Quit."

-Austin vs. Triple H (45.5 in 2001) cashed in on the merits of their Three Stages of Hell Match to nearly crack the Top 25, but perhaps no other match benefited more from the combination of all the various comparisons than Foley vs. Orton (47.5 in 2004). Bulldog vs. Bret Hart (45.0 in 1992) benefited more so from the perspective born of time; it is amazing how well their matches hold up all of these years later despite neither high profile encounter being remotely perfect. Warrior vs. Hogan (52.5 in 1990) was arguably perfect for what it was intended to be, and for that it was one of the few matches of the Hulkamania Era to verify its gaudy scores head-to-head against modern peers.

-Benoit vs. HHH vs. HBK (51.5 in 2004) was one of those matches that threatened to climb even higher, but anything Benoit related logically failed to get the benefit of the doubt that Rock vs. Mankind (47.0 in 1999) and others like it were afforded from having come from the most celebrated era in pro wrestling lore, which was taken to its creative heights in large part due to Steve Austin vs. Vince McMahon; though it may not have compared well due to this book's primary focus on the best match in a rivalry or story to shape rankings, it obviously could never have been any lower than the Top 25.

-Punk vs. Lesnar (46.0 in 2013) exemplified the upper limits of what a pro wrestling match could be; it was a fascinating piece of performance art with solid statistics in the toughest individual ranking competition (against its 2013 peers) throughout the entire process. Bryan vs. Cena (46.5 in 2013) was more the type of experience that brings legions of wrestling fans together emotionally in the traditional sense. Neither match's incredible qualities were enough to overcome the transcendence of the '92 Rumble and its stout resume (49.5 in 1992); and no match, rivalry, or story's total resume is truthfully as impressive as Edge vs. Taker (46.5 in 2008).

-Cena vs. CM Punk (47.5 in 2011), to be honest, may struggle for its preeminent match (at MITB) to remain highly rewatchable, but the experience for anyone who lived it continues to generate reverence like few matches ever have. Maybe it falls down in the rankings in five years; maybe it winds up closer to the Top 10. Rock vs. Hollywood Hogan (48.0 in 2002) maintains a similar, visceral aura for different reasons, its 'Mania ties aiding its cause. Michaels vs. Triple H (48.5 in 2002) sneaks in somewhat under the radar, sharing comparable qualities as Hogan-Rock. Head-to-head, there is little separating the three, so the raw scores came very much in handy.

-Rock vs. Triple H (48.0 in 1998 / 46.0 in 2000) advanced ahead of the prior group on account of its comprehensive resume, its best individual match coming from the Intercontinental chapter of the rivalry while still maintaining an iconic main-event presence in historical discussions. Angle vs. Michaels (54.0 in 2005), a pantheon performance from both, was removed from the Top 10 in the head-to-head phase, but its 'Mania classic gave it the nod over Rock-Trips; Our Olympic Hero's top individual performance, opposite Benoit (51.0 in 2003), simply won head-to-head over HBK-Angle, but the amazing resume of TLC (52.5 in 2000) nudged it ahead of Angle-Benoit.

-Rock vs. Cena (52.5 in 2012) statistically dominated and lived up to the hype of a dream match scenario in an almost impossible situation considering its critical demands, but it still is not yet Savage vs. Steamboat (50.0 in 1987) or Michaels vs. Razor (57.0 in 1994) in terms of their ever-lasting impact, which will be hard to historically duplicate.

-Logic played an important role in the Top 10 particularly, with some climbing where others fell simply because it made lots of sense. Flair vs. Steamboat (50.0 in 1989) remains famous in the critical community because of those three 5-star matches; Meltzer may have pioneered that thought process, but it has been repeatedly verified and, while it may not be science, there is damn sure consensus for that opinion. Foley vs. Triple H (51.5 in 2000) was the total package of statistical superiority and rewatchability in the most competitive and economically fruitful period in pro wrestling history. Daniel Bryan vs. The Authority (53.5 in 2014 for Bryan vs. Triple H) was Steve Austin vs. Vince McMahon, minus the legendary era defining, but still with era defining qualities all its own plus the added bonus of classic wrestling matches. Triple H vs. Undertaker (52.0 in 2012) presented two powerhouse matches unique to anything else in WWE lore at back-to-back WrestleManias. These decisions just seemed to make too much sense, supported by the numbers but not completely defined by them.

-The ranking for HBK vs. Y2J (48.0 in 2008) was the amalgamation of the two chapters of their rivalry; in combination, they gave you everything that you could ever want to see between opponents. Bret Hart vs. Owen Hart (49.5 in 1994) did the same, only a little bit better.

-Warrior vs. Savage (52.0 in 1991) sits almost on a different level, but that it was the birth of the modern day WWE main-event, that it was sports entertainment characterized in one performance, and that it was the single most head-to-head juggernaut this side of Austin vs. Bret at 'Mania 13 just make it virtually unparalleled.

-The Rock vs. Stone Cold Steve Austin (51.5 in 2001) is the greatest rivalry, which in combination with what it meant to wrestling lore's most time-honored period was enough to push it ahead of Savage-Warrior; if the book had limited its scope just to rivalries, it would have been #1.

-Bret Hart vs. Steve Austin (52.5 in 1997) in the Submission Match at WrestleMania 13 has no peer in terms of its rewatchability. In the ranking process, it was viewed approximately fifteen times across three years and it never got old, but between HBK and Taker's pair of rivalries in 1997/98 (47.5) and 2009 (58.0)/10 (52.0), they produced some absolutely epic work of their own.

<u>Acknowledgements</u>

There are so many people who were influential in this book being written, so please forgive me if your name does not get mentioned. I, first and foremost, want to thank my wife and my kids for putting up with the amount of time that it took these past five years to research and write another pro wrestling historical epic. I also want to thank all of the professional wrestlers who have touched my life since the late 1980s, particularly personal favorites such as Ric Flair, Ultimate Warrior, Bret Hart, Shawn Michaels, The Rock, Edge, Randy Orton, and most recently Seth Rollins; I admire all of you who ever laced up a pair of boots.

I especially want to thank my LOP family, from the Pain Lord himself to all of the columnists with whom I have shared the LOP main page to my fellow LOP Radio podcasters and, of course, to every single person from six different continents who has taken the time to read or listen to my opinions since 2004; special thanks to Davey Boy, whose columns inspired me to write about wrestling, as well as Mattberg, Sac, Gary "The Stinger" Smith, Brody "The Snowman," Eric "Q of Banditz," Joe Martel, Sean Taylor, Shane "The LOP Mystic," Neil "Maverick" Pollock, Mazza Roussety, Steven Bell, Samuel 'Plan, Rich Latta, and Dave Fenichel for the many good conversations that stimulated in my mind different ways to think about sports entertainment in the past and present.

Bibliography

Biographies or autobiographies from Bret Hart, Brock Lesnar, Chris Jericho, Daniel Bryan, Edge, Ric Flair, and Shawn Michaels

Other books include *50 Greatest Professional Wrestlers of All Time: the Definitive Shoot* (Larry Matysik), *101 WWE Matches to See Before You Die* (Samuel 'Plan), *Napoleon Hill's Keys to Success: the 17 Principles of Personal Achievement*, and *The WrestleMania Era: The Book of Sports Entertainment*

Podcasts including E&C Pod of Awesomeness, Talk is Jericho, The Doc Says, The Right Side of the Pond, WCW: The Legacy Series, and The Steve Austin Show

Special thanks also to David Sterritt, Jim Cornette, Pro Wrestling Illustrated, Roger Ebert, and Tommy Tomlinson

Websites including 24Wrestling, 2xzone, Bleacher Report, Cage Match, ESPN, Indeed Wrestling, Lords of Pain, ProWrestlingHistory, PWTorch, The Wrestling Observer, WWE, and Wrestling, Inc.

WWE Home Video best-of compilations for and/or documentaries on Batista, Bret Hart, CM Punk, Chris Benoit, Chris Jericho, Edge, Greatest Stars of the 1980s, Mick Foley, Mr. Perfect, Randy Savage, Ricky Steamboat, Shawn Michaels vs. Bret Hart, Starrcade, Sting, Stone Cold Steve Austin, The Road Warriors, The Rock, Triple H, Undertaker, and WrestleMania

WWE Network specials on The Shield, Ultimate Warrior, and including Hall of Fame Induction ceremonies, Legends w/ JBL, Live w/ Chris Jericho, The Rock vs. John Cena, WWE 24, and WWE Rivalries

YouTube videos produced by Elbow Productions, Jim Cornette, WrestleTalk, and WWE

33639093R00234

Printed in Great Britain
by Amazon